Strategic Assessment 1996

Strategic
Assessment 1996
Instruments of U.S. Power

NATIONAL DEFENSE UNIVERSITY

INSTITUTE FOR NATIONAL STRATEGIC STUDIES

NATIONAL DEFENSE UNIVERSITY
President: Lieutenant General Ervin J. Rokke, USAF
Vice President: Ambassador William G. Walker

INSTITUTE FOR NATIONAL STRATEGIC STUDIES
Director and Editor-in-Chief: Dr. Hans A. Binnendijk
Director of Strategy and Policy Analysis: Dr. Stuart E. Johnson
Editor for this publication: Dr. Patrick Clawson

National Defense University Press
Director: Dr. Frederick T. Kiley

Fort Lesley J. McNair, Washington, DC 20319–6000
Phone: (202) 287–9210 Fax: (202) 287–9475

Digital images used on pages ii and iii are courtesy of NASA/Goddard Space Flight Center, Earth Sciences Directorate.

The photographs on pages 14, 31, 86, and 169 are copyrighted and used with the permission of Wide World Photos, New York.

Library of Congress Cataloging-in-Publication Data

Strategic assessment 1996 : instruments of U.S. power/ National
   Defense University, Institute for National Strategic Studies.
      p.   cm.
   Editor-in-chief, Hans Binnendijk, editor, Patrick Clawson.
   Companion volume to Strategic assessment 1995.
   ISBN 0–16–048463–4
   1. United States—Defenses. 2. Military art and science—United States.
3. United States—Foreign relations. 4. National security—United
States. I. Binnendijk, Hans A. II. Clawson, Patrick, 1951–   .
III. National Defense University.   Institute for National Strategic Studies.
UA23.S82732   1996
355'.033073—dc20   96–2667
                                       CIP

Printed in the United States of America

For sale by the U.S. Government Printing Office
Superintendent of Documents, Mail Stop: SSOP,
Washington, DC 20402–9328
GPO Stock Number 008–020–01387–1
ISBN 0–16–048463–4

Preface

By LIEUTENANT GENERAL ERVIN J. ROKKE, USAF

President, National Defense University

Unpredictable change is what our nation's future national security dilemma is all about. Appreciation for this uncertainty is the beginning of wisdom in the post-Cold War era. Not only is international politics in flux, but, furthermore, technological breakthroughs relevant to national security are occurring with greater frequency and with more substantial impact than ever in history.

In this world full of instability and rapid change, the U.S. government needs to muster the full range of options at its command if it is to achieve its goals at a price consistent with the resources its citizens are prepared to devote to international affairs. Rather than simply deploring the constrained resources made available for some of the traditional foreign policy and national security institutions, we need to explore how to make use of the opportunities offered by change.

This report represents an effort by the National Defense University to examine what in this new world environment are the strengths and weaknesses of the various instruments available for influencing the behavior of foreign governments. We hope that it will prove to be of interest not only to policymakers, but also to all readers with an interest in security policy.

The *Strategic Assessment* applies the research expertise of the National Defense University, under the leadership of its interdisciplinary research arm, the Institute for National Strategic Studies, with the generous assistance of analysts from elsewhere in the U.S. government. Offering such analyses, in both general and more specialized areas of interest to the national security community, is one part of NDU's educational mission. That mission, as defined by the Joint Chiefs of Staff, is to educate senior military and government officials on issues related to national strategy, security policy, resources management, and warfare in the information age. It is our hope that this report is both authoritative and informative, and that its influence will extend beyond the narrowly defined national security establishment.

We wish to thank all those who contributed to the success of this project, particularly the many analysts both inside and outside the military who wrote or reviewed chapters of the *Assessment*. We hope that this report will stimulate further thinking, discussion, and research on the issues treated in its pages among both policymakers and policy analysts.

Strategic Assessment 1996 was written in mid-1995 and revised to include developments through November 30, 1995.

Foreword

By H A N S B I N N E N D I J K, Editor-in-Chief

I n 1995, INSS inaugurated its annual *Strategic Assessment* with a survey of the world strategic environment from the perspective of U.S. interests. This year, we continue the series with a look at the instruments by which the U.S. government can influence the behavior of other governments. Our current thinking is that the 1997 volume will examine flashpoints, i.e., the zones in which conflict and disorder may erupt in the next decade, and the 1998 volume will return to the 1995 format, that is, to update our 1995 survey of the key policy issues facing the U.S. government.

Structure

We begin this volume by setting the scene, with a chapter about how the world is changing from the perspective of U.S. security interests. Then we discuss the instruments of U.S. power, starting with those that use persuasion rather than force and proceeding to those that require progressively more use of force—that is why our first chapter is about diplomacy and our last chapter is about weapons of mass destruction. Using this principle, we divide the instruments of U.S. power into three groups:

- *Non-military instruments*
- *Political-military instruments*
- *Warfighting instruments*

The final chapter is an executive summary that also draws some general conclusions about how the instruments of U.S. power could be made more effective.

Our focus is on traditional foreign policy and defense issues. Some may argue that environmental security or economic security is, over the long run, a more vital issue than military concerns. While that may be the case, we feel that what we National Defense University analysts can do best is to concentrate on the areas we know best. In so far as we are able to, we try to touch on nontraditional areas of what might be called national security in its broadest sense, but we do not pretend to do justice to these topics.

Our aim is to analyze the means available to the U.S. government in the current period to affect the behavior of other governments. We want to stress several points about that aim. Our focus is on the instruments, not on the purposes to which they may be put. We concentrate on what has changed since the end of the Cold War and on what will continue to be the case for the next few years, not on the long sweep of history, not what may come to pass in several decades, nor what will be the burning issues over the next few months. Our net has been cast widely: we include in our set of instruments a variety of institutions and capabilities that perhaps are not policy instruments strictly speaking.

The *Strategic Assessment* is aimed at policymakers, analysts, and informed members of the public who want a serious summary statement of the tools available to the U.S. government for accomplishing its aims vis-a-vis other governments. It does not provide novel interpretations or detailed specialized research. Specialists in one subject are unlikely to find much new material on that issue here, although we hope they will find a succinct statement of the applicability of that instrument of national power, as well as some insight into the relationship among various instruments.

Although *Strategic Assessment 1996* strives to assess what factors are likely to limit or to enhance the power of each instrument, its primary intent is not to advocate particular policies or approaches to policy. It is neither a statement nor a critique of U.S. government policy. The views expressed in this document are those of the editors and do not necessarily reflect the offical policy or position of the National Defense University, the Department of Defense, or the U.S. Government.

Acknowledgements

The responsibility for any errors in this document rests wholly with me as Editor-in-Chief and Patrick Clawson as Editor, who worked under the guidance of Stuart Johnson, the INSS Director of Strategy and Policy Analysis. The credit for any insights belongs to the able team, primarily from NDU, that wrote the contributing papers.

The principal authors of those papers were:

Context Hans Binnendijk and Patrick Clawson, INSS
Diplomacy Edward Marks, INSS
Public diplomacy Robert Nevitt, National War College (NWC)
International organizations William Lewis, INSS
Economics Patrick Clawson, INSS
Intelligence Marvin Ott, NWC and colleagues
Productive and technological base Gerald Abbott, Industrial College of the Armed Forces (ICAF), and Robert Neilson, Information Resources Management College (IRMC)
Arms controls Thomas Graham and Doug Shaw, Arms Control and Disarmament Agency (ACDA)
Defense engagement in peacetime John Cope, INSS
Security relationships and overseas presence Patrick Cronin, INSS
Peace operations and humanitarian support Robert Oakley, INSS
Unconventional military instruments the staff of the Office of the Secretary of Defense—Special Operations and Low Intensity Conflict (OSD/SOLIC)
Limited military intervention INSS staff
Classical military instruments Stuart Johnson, INSS, and CAPT Michael Martus, USN, INSS
Emerging military instruments Martin Libicki, INSS
Countering weapons of mass destruction John Reichart, INSS Counterproliferation Center
Summary Hans Binnendijk and Patrick Clawson, INSS

We are grateful for the input we received from Lt General Ervin Rokke and Ambassador William Walker, the President and Vice-President of National Defense University respectively, and from: Sarah Botsai, NWC; Scott Cohen, Washington, D.C.; Theodore Curran, Washington, D.C.; Alan Goodman, Georgetown University School of Foreign Service; Christopher Kreugler, Harvard Forest; Andrew Natsios,[1] World Vision Inc.; Mackubin Owens, Naval War College; Jeffrey Record, Georgia Institute of Technology; Bruce Stokes, Council on Foreign Relations; and Michael Wheeler, SAIC.

Many of our colleagues at INSS also helped, including: Col Nancy Anderson, USMC; LTC Charles Barry, USA; LTC David Bentley, USA; Col Michael Dzeidzic, USAF; James Ford; Richard Hull; Michael Leonard; Ronald Montaperto; Vernon Penner; Jeffrey Simon; Brian Sullivan; and Judith Yaphe.

We would also like to express our thanks to the many military officers, civilian government officials, and outside analysts who gave us thoughtful comments on papers prepared as contributions to this report. A special thanks goes to Roger Donway, who headed the group editing the writing, to James Smith and John Waldron, who managed the graphics, and to the team at the Government Printing Office. Without their help, this document could not have been produced so quickly.

---

[1] Mr. Natsios' paper drew upon his article, "NGOs and the UN System in Complex Humanitarian Emergencies," in *Third World Quarterly*, Fall 1995. We are grateful for being able to use that material here.

Contents

Instruments of U.S. Power

List of Maps, Tables and Charts

List of Inserts

CHAPTER ONE

Context

This volume analyzes how the utility of various instruments of U.S. power has changed in recent years, primarily owing to the end of the Cold War. For that reason, we need to set forth our view of the changing international context within which the instruments are applied. Our perspective on the emerging new world order was set forth in the first chapter of Strategic Assessment 1995, which we summarize here with some changes in nuance to reflect developments during 1995 and with some additional material to extend the analysis beyond the realm of geostrategy.

The essential characteristics of the present strategic environment are uncertainty and change. The world is going through several types of dramatic changes. For heuristic purposes, those changes can be grouped into three broad categories—geostrategic, information, and, less clearly defined than the others, character of government.

Geostrategic Developments

The world geostrategic scene cannot be described as simply as during the Cold War, when the Western-Soviet confrontation was the prism through which all events had to be viewed. At least three perspectives are needed now to analyze the emerging international system: seen from the top down, the major powers have changed; seen cross-sectionally, states are arraying themselves into three categories depending upon their success at establishing democracy and free-market prosperity; and seen from the bottom up, transnational problems have become a more important part of the world scene.

Major Powers. In the past, the defining characteristic of a major shift from one world order to another was the transition in relations among the major powers (indeed, among the European powers). A shift in worlds was indicated by dramatic change in the answers to three questions: who were the major players, what they could do to one another, and what did they wish to do to one another. Perhaps the classic example is the French Revolution with its new player (democratic France), its new capability (the citizen army), and its new intentions (spreading liberty, equality, and fraternity). Similar transitions occurred with the Congress of Vienna in 1815, the unification of Germany in 1870, the Treaty of Versailles in 1919, and the developments following World War II, as well as with the end of the Cold War.

While the new world geostrategic environment is more complex than great power politics, one of the new order's basic defining characteristics remains the relationship among the major powers. Those powers are the U.S., Western Europe, Russia, China, and Japan, though India may join the group within a decade or so. At the end of the Cold War, some thought that the new world would be unipolar, that is, the U.S. would dominate the world scene. In fact, the American people have not been interested in that job. Instead of being unipolar, the world consists of asymmetric poles, in which one (the U.S.) is much the strongest but the others are nonetheless important independent actors.

In the first blush of enthusiasm at the end of the Cold War, the great powers were all cooperating. Now, relations among some are cooler, and differences of perspective are more pronounced: U.S.-China relations are characterized by suspicions and disagreements on many issues, the hopes for a new strategic relationship between the U.S. and Russia have faded away, the tone in trade disputes between the U.S. and Japan has become sharper, and the U.S. and Western Europe have disagreed about how to handle the Bosnian crisis. But peace prevails, and that is a powerful force for stability in the world. None of the great powers is currently preparing for conflict with another. That might change over time. If the powers were to consolidate around themselves political and economic blocs that were exclusive rather than open, tensions could emerge at the edges of the blocs, such as between Russia and Western Europe or between China and

the U.S. A **clash among great powers**, directly or through proxies, would be the greatest international threat the U.S. could face, though it is a remote possibility in the near term.

Factors shaping the behavior of the foreign great powers include the following:

● Russia is suffering from something similar to the Versailles Syndrome that hit Germany after World War I. It feels isolated, and it is bitter about the contrast between its post-Cold War situation and its past superpower status. Moscow thinks it is the victim, with others taking advantage of its temporary difficulties. It resents being treated as a loser in the Cold War when it feels that, rather than losing, it evolved in a way advantageous to all. Its military is in decline if not disarray. And, as important as any other factor, its economy has shrunk by half over the last decade, while the rest of the world has grown stronger. Yet Russia remains a nuclear power that can threaten the survival of the U.S. as a nation.

● China is feeling more powerful in world affairs because of its spectacular economic growth over the last fifteen years. By some estimates, China already has the world's third-largest output, after the U.S. and Japan. In contrast to the vibrant economy, the political system in China has been stagnant. The elite clings to a discredited ideology that even they do not practice. As the country hangs on the edge of a transition from one leadership generation to another, decision making seems paralyzed. The leaders seem to be afraid above all of anarchy, into which category they put democratization. In international affairs, China acts with ambiguity: sometimes like a normal player and sometimes like the stereotype of the Middle Kingdom —not well informed about what others are doing and how others behave, sure that its ways should prevail despite the objections of others, and assuming that it has a natural right to get what it wants.

● Japan is experiencing political turbulence about whether the old system of governance and economy is still the best. Five years of economic stagnation, with essentially no growth in 1990–95, has shaken national confidence. Meanwhile, the trade surplus with the rest of the world contin-

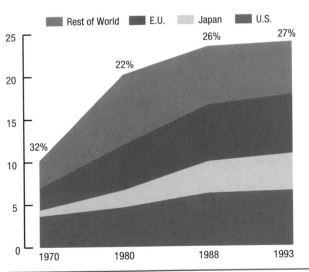

World Output, 1970–93
(\$ trillions)

SOURCE: INSS estimates based on World Bank data.
NOTE: Percent figure is U.S. share of world total.

U.S. Air Force F–16s flying with a German Mig–29 in Sardinia.

- The *market democracies* of free and prosperous—or at least rapidly developing—nations, were once found only in North America, Japan, and much of Europe. Large parts of Latin America, the newly industrialized nations of East Asia, and Central Europe are now joining this group.

- The *transitional states* of ex-communist lands, as well as countries such as India and South Africa, are progressing from a low economic baseline, which run the risk of becoming frozen short of freedom and prosperity with authoritarian politics, heavily politicized economies, and relatively low levels of economic development.

- The *troubled states*, primarily in Africa, the Middle East, and parts of Asia, are falling behind the rest of the globe economically, politically, and ecologically, often plagued with rampant ethnic and religious extremism.

These categories are not firm; some very important countries, like China, combine characteristics of two or even three groups.

Some of the troubled or transitional states may be tempted to divert attention from domestic problems by means of external aggression aimed at establishing regional hegemony. It should be no surprise were some such efforts by a rogue state, such as Iraq or North Korea, to lead to a **major regional conflict**. The proliferation of weapons of mass destruction, particularly nuclear weapons, could increase the propensity of aggressive states to threaten their neighbors and increase the risks for the U.S.

Conflict within troubled states is likely to be a common occurrence, and in some cases, the state will fail—the government will cease to function effectively, and civil society will degenerate into near chaos. In the 1990s, state failure occurred to one degree or another in such places as Bosnia, Rwanda, Somalia, Liberia, and Haiti. Most such internal conflicts will not pose a sharp threat to U.S. interests, though they may trouble U.S. humanitarian values. The great powers are often willing to provide **humanitarian and peace operations** for failed states. They are increasingly reluctant to intervene militarily in civil wars, however,

ues at levels that cause tensions in relations with the U.S., and to some extent with the European Union (EU) and tensions are increasing over the U.S. bases, especially those in Okinawa.

- Western Europe remains uncertain how it will structure itself in the future, especially in the area of security and the military. Whether agreement is reached upon a coherent system for making decisions will determine if Western Europe has the same weight in international affairs as it does in the world's economy.

Three Categories of States. Another geostrategic perspective is the cross-sectional view, in which the world can be seen as divided among three categories of states. At the height of the Cold War, there were also three worlds: a generally industrialized and free First World, a communist Second World, and an underdeveloped, largely unaligned Third World. By the late 1980s, these divisions had eroded, as some communist lands developed freer institutions and some underdeveloped nations evolved into industrial democracies.

In the new world order, the three categories of states are characterized by how successful they are at achieving the almost universally proclaimed goals of democracy and market-based prosperity:

unless a particular crisis takes place in their backyard, threatens to escalate to engulf other states, create a humanitarian disaster, or otherwise affect great power interests. The U.S. will have neither the means nor the will to intervene in every such case around the world, but it will intervene in areas of its historic and strategic interest as well as in situations of horrendous suffering that offend U.S. sensibilities.

Transnational Issues. A third geostrategic perspective looks from the bottom up at transnational problems, that is, those which do not stem from the actions of governments. Some of the major problems are:

● The internationalization of crime, especially drug cartels that operate on such a large scale as to threaten governments.

● Terrorists take advantage of more open societies to mount increasingly brazen attacks, such as the 1993 bombing of New York's World Trade Center. The March 1995 Tokyo subway attack by the Aum Shinrikyo cult, which caused twelve deaths and five thousand injuries, "demonstrates the threat a well financed, sophisticated and international terrorist group poses [in what could be the United States's] greatest national security concern in the years ahead," to quote Senator Sam Nunn (D., Georgia).

● Ethnic hatreds that erupt into genocide or ethnic cleansing, as in Rwanda or the former Yugoslavia. A related phenomenon has been the collapse of organized government under the pressure of warlords and clan rivalries.

● Sudden mass migrations becoming more common, partly in response to state failure and ethnic violence. These waves of people, who may or may not fit the traditional definition of refugee, can overwhelm poor neighbors. As illustrated by the experience with Haitians and Cubans, migrants can pose an unacceptable burden on industrial nations like the U.S. that are concerned that the refugees may become permanent residents.

● Environmental problems spilling over from one nation to another as the planet's resources are used more intensively. Dangers to the global commons multiply: all nations are affected by depletion of the ozone layer and global warming.

Coast Guard vessel picking up Haitian migrants.

Some of these threats seem to call for military forces to back up police forces that are outmaneuvered, overwhelmed, or outgunned. **Constabulary operations,** such as picking up illegal immigrants, intercepting narcotics shipments, and protecting delivery of relief supplies in failed states, do not require the specialized equipment and training needed for combat, but they can tie up multibillion dollar aircraft carriers and high-readiness troops unless a more cost effective rapid response force is developed.

Information Technology

The pulse of the planet has quickened. Computers, faxes, fiber optic cables, and satellites speed the flow of information across frontiers, as illustrated by the explosive growth of the Internet. Faster and larger information flows reinforce the political trend towards increasingly open societies. Ideas, people, and goods are moving across borders at an unprecedented rate.

Technology progress is not a new phenomenon. Historically, longbows, stirrups, gunpowder, steam engines, airplanes, and a host of other technological advances dramatically changed the nature of warfare. What makes the information explosion so revolutionary is not that technology is advancing but the pace at which it improves. While societies have often been confronted with profound social changes owing to advancing technologies, never before have societies been forced to adapt to a technology which for decades has been improving by an order of magnitude every three or four years. The speed at which computers function—the rate at which information can be transmitted over long distances—looks set to continue increasing at the rate of tenfold every three to four years, which translates into up to 1,000-fold per decade.

No one can foretell all the ways in which information technologies will enhance (or mitigate) traditional venues of national power, but some themes are beginning to emerge.

One is that access to information is being recognized as a *sine qua non* of economic growth. Mastery of information technology is surpassing mastery of heavy industry as the primary source of national power, whether exercised through commercial or military channels. A useful concept in this regard is "waves" of technology, popularized by Alan and Heidi Toffler. The new wave of computers and communications will be the key to future economic growth, but the older waves of agriculture and industry will remain indispensable elements of national economic life. Because the United States possesses the richest information flux, other countries have become increasingly interested in tapping into these flows. Linkages to sources of expertise (e.g., Silicon Valley), sources of finance (e.g., Wall Street), or sources of knowledge (e.g., universities, think tanks, and selected government agencies) are considered desirable and one more reason for nations to cultivate good relations with the United States.

Another trend is that the ubiquity of global communications is creating new avenues for the interests, culture, and values of the United States to percolate overseas (and *vice versa*). For the most part, this influence exists independent of national policy; in some cases, however, the existence of these channels makes it easier for the United States government to go over the heads of other governments and communicate directly to their citizens.

On the other end of the spectrum, the ability of the Defense Department (DOD) to generate and distribute vast quantities of intelligence permits the United States to influence the outcomes of conflicts in which it chooses not to intervene directly. At little direct risk, the United States can provide an "information umbrella" to its friends by providing imagery and weather data, software and other systems integration services, and, within the next few years, simulation and other training tools.

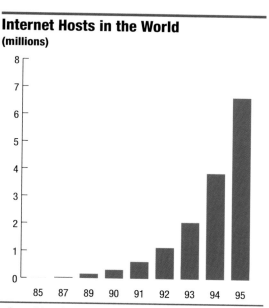

Internet Hosts in the World
(millions)

Source: International Data Corporation.

USS *Roosevelt* and carrier group

All these methods, taken collectively, intensify the ability of the United States to exercise what Assistant Secretary of Defense for International Security Affairs Joseph Nye calls "soft power."

The extension of the rapid communication and computer technological advances to the battlefield suggests that information-based warfare will become more widespread within a decade or two. Defense requirements will demand more investment in information systems and less in industrial-era configurations of tanks, planes, and ships. Information may come to rival explosive force as a factor in warfare. The development of an integrated approach—a system of systems—that combines sensors, communications, and processors with weapons delivery will allow further advances in the precision with which U.S. forces can strike. Improvements in precision are not new—on average, a target that took one bomb to destroy during Desert Storm required 170 bombs during the Vietnam War and 9,000 bombs during World War II—but the cumulative effect is becoming revolutionary. With more precise information about where to strike, weapons delivery systems can shrink in size, facilitating the trend towards striking from a long distance, possibly directly from the continental U.S. to the battlefield.

The nature and conduct of information warfare is becoming a subject of intense interest to defense analysts. Information looks set to be a new dimension in which warfare can be conducted, requiring defense against enemy actions that cause vital computer nets to malfunction and providing new opportunities for immobilizing an enemy.

The Changing Character of Government

After decades of increasing state involvement in area after area of society in country after country, central governments have been on the retreat since the late days of the Cold War. Publics in many countries seem to have changed their views about national priorities and the role of the government in achieving those national goals.

The Devolution of Power. The most obvious characteristic of the retreat of the state has been the end of the totalitarian systems in the Warsaw Pact, in which the state dominated all aspects of life, stifling the institutions of civil society. But in many other countries as well, a dramatic change has taken place in what citizens expect from their governments. After decades in which the power of central governments grew steadily, those central governments are now reinventing themselves, and power is diffusing from the center. Two changes stand out in particular.

First, central governments are ceding more power to regional and local governments. For instance, not only did the Soviet Union break up into its constituent republics, but Moscow has had to permit regions more free reign. In post-Mao China, the provinces acquired a large measure of economic independence that they used to deny resources to the central government, which finds that its budget is growing only modestly while the national economy races ahead. In the EU, after years of defining detailed unionwide directives, the new principle is "subsidiarity," under which responsibility for each problem is to be assigned to as local a level of government as possible—preferably local rather than national, and then national rather than EU-wide. In the U.S., the

1994 House Republicans' Contract with America exemplifies the strong interest in devolving to the states responsibility for programs that the federal government previously controlled.

Secondly, central governments are shedding functions, partly to reduce expenditures and thereby contain budget deficits. The most important reduction in the role of the state has been a wave of privatization that swept Western Europe, the ex-Soviet bloc, and Latin America, and created ripples elsewhere. In 1994, governments privatized about $80 billion in assets. The general mood is that states are poor managers of factories, and that selling off such enterprises is a way to raise growth rates. The change in attitudes in Latin America has been particularly sharp, from a general assumption that the state must organize economic development to enthusiasm for the rule of the markets.

A related phenomenon has been a greater attention to the domestic side of national power, especially the economic foundations of power, relative to the projection of national power abroad. A focus on domestic issues, especially economic problems, characterizes Moscow, Beijing, Tokyo, and Brussels (that is, the EU) as much as Washington. To some extent, that

is a reflection of the less threatening international environment. But there is also dissatisfaction about growth rates, which in the U.S. and the rest of the industrialized world have been much lower in the two decades since the oil shock of 1973 than in the preceding postwar decades. It seems likely that the highest priority in U.S. politics in the next few years will be long-term economic growth in a manner consistent with providing appropriate safety nets for the unfortunate, and addressing social problems, such as race relations. Concern about international and military affairs will be seen in large part through this optic. In addition, the U.S. body politic is of many minds about what issues are worth risking blood and treasure for: which values are so fundamental that they must be defended irrespective of the importance of the geostrategic interests at stake, which areas of the world are the most vital to the U.S., and which geostrategic interests are the most important.

As a result of the refocus on domestic issues, the U.S. public and publics in many other countries have less of an internationalist outlook and are less willing to spend money on foreign affairs. Calls are being heard to restructure the foreign-policy and national-security establishments to reflect the decreasing interest in international issues compared to domestic ones.

A Perspective on Isolationism and Unilateralism. The debate over the U.S. approach towards national security could be thought of as a compass, with two pairs of polar opposites. If the north pole is engagement, then the south pole is isolation, while the east is unilateralism and the west is multilateralism.

The strength of this analogy is that there are distinct and powerful groups pointing in each of the four directions. For instance, there are those (generally on the left) who believe that no matter whether the U.S. intervenes regularly or seldom, it should always do so through international institutions. Meanwhile there are those (generally on the right) who believe that the most important issue is that the U.S. always act in defense of its own interests and under its own direction, irrespective

National Defense and International Affairs in the FY 1995 Budget
($ billions)

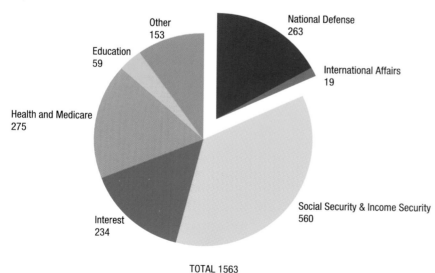

Other 153
Education 59
Health and Medicare 275
Interest 234
National Defense 263
International Affairs 19
Social Security & Income Security 560
TOTAL 1563

SOURCE: 1996 Budget.

of how often the U.S. decides to intervene abroad. That is, to the extent that the U.S. engages internationally, they want it done unilaterally, but they are not sure how much the U.S. should engage abroad.

Another phenomenon illustrated by the compass analogy is that a policy like isolationism can be approached from either right or left. The Right tends to believe that the triumph of democratic and free market ideals removes the rationale for active intervention abroad (building upon the thesis of the "end of history"). The Left is sympathetic to the argument that military and foreign expenditures are a drain on resources that could be better used at home (the theory of "imperial overstretch" as a cause for national decline). As one pundit described isolationists, those on the right do not want to inflict the world on America while those on the left do not want to inflict America on the world.

The compass analogy can be extended to include the groups at the intermediate points, e.g., those on the southeast who want the U.S. generally to remain aloof from foreign problems but to act on its own (or with its close allies in a subordinate position) when it does move.

On the whole, the mood in American politics in the immediate aftermath of the Cold War seems to have put the compass arrow towards north, or engagement. In the early days of the Clinton administration, the arrow swung so strongly towards multilateralism that it was in danger of going right on through towards isolation—that is, the popular reaction to the failures of multilateral institutions caused many to think that the U.S. should dramatically reduce its involvement in world affairs. Since then, the arrow has swung again. In 1995, the new Republican majority in Congress seemed to move the arrow to the right, towards unilateralism (e.g., the votes to lift the arms embargo on Bosnia irrespective of the U.N. sanctions). Given these wild swings, it is by no means clear where the compass will end up over the five to seven year time-frame of this report.

Reorienting U.S. Priorities

From the perspective of U.S. national security, an assessment of major trends in the unfolding world order includes grounds for both optimism and pessimism.

On the optimistic side:

+The major powers are still cooperating despite increasing tensions among them.

+Democracy and the market system are models to which nearly all nations aspire, tempering the potential for ideologically driven conflict.

+The U.S. is a world leader in the information technologies that are increasingly the source of national power, both economic and military.

+The U.S. economy has improved its performance relative to that of all the major powers other than China. Unemployment is less than half the rate in Western Europe; the growth rate since 1990 has exceeded that in Japan; and, of course, the U.S. economy is doing incomparably better than the Russian economy.

+The U.S. is the dominant military power in the world. Not only does the U.S. have the largest inventory of advanced equipment, and personnel as well trained as any in the world, but in addition, no other country can match the U.S. in strategic assets like transport logistics, intelligence and communications.

On the pessimistic side:

−Multiethnic states are fragmenting violently, in some cases falling into chaos, and massive humanitarian disasters offend values Americans hold dear.

−Traditional U.S. alliances are under stress, with differences about how to respond to failing states and how to incorporate the ex-communist states into new security structures.

−Transnational threats, from international organized crime to international terrorism, are increasingly being felt in U.S. cities.

−Nuclear proliferation may increasingly create instability in volatile regions and may require the U.S. to act to neutralize the threat.

−The U.S. focus on domestic issues and the pressure to reduce expenditures complicate the ability to respond to international threats.

There is still much that the U.S. can do to affect the character of the new international system emerging from the end of the Cold War system. But history suggests that shaping the character of the new international system will become more and more difficult as time goes by. International systems typically have a life cycle in which the relations among the major powers start out flexible and become more rigid. One of the more extreme examples was the early years of the Cold War. Right after World War II, the West and the Soviet Union had differences (for instance, over the Marshall Plan or elections in Poland), but it was not apparent to many that those differences would escalate into all-out political con-

frontation. In 1945–48, several European countries were attracted to both the U.S. and Soviet systems (Czechoslovakia, Italy, and France all had large communist parties but also large anti-communist groups), and it was by no means clear that states would become aligned with one camp to the exclusion of the other. But within six years, the lines were drawn, to remain largely unchanged for another thirty-five years.

In other international systems, the clarification came more slowly. For instance, Napoleon and Bismarck were able to start with opportunistic alliances that picked off their targets one at a time. But eventually the other countries realized that their salvation lay in alliance despite differences, and so the world order became structured around alliances with and against France and Germany, respectively. In other cases, the great powers agreed to maintain a balance of power in which no one state dominated the others, but over time they were unable to maintain the commitment, so the world order moved toward a system of alliances. (This is what happened to the post-Napoleonic "Concert of Europe," which fell apart when the price of that commitment became clear in the Crimean War; and also to the post-1919 League of Nations, which proved powerless when challenged by a resurgent Germany.)

If these historic analogies hold, then there is some urgency to resolving the domestic debates about what the U.S. wants from the new international system, because the international system may be more malleable in the mid 1990s now than it will be in a few years.

On the other hand, it would seem that one of the main differences between this international system and that of the Cold War will be greater ambiguity and more ad hocism. With regard to the U.S.'s friends, the new order is likely to see the U.S. increasingly acting with pick-up coalitions and outside of long-standing alliances. Greater reliance on coalitions, as distinct from alliances, poses problems such as coalition cohesiveness, interoperability with forces of other nations, and decision making at the top level (e.g., rules of engagement, strategic goals, and decisions to initiate and to terminate conflict). With regard to the enemy, the most likely conflicts

National Security Budget Authority, in percent of GDP

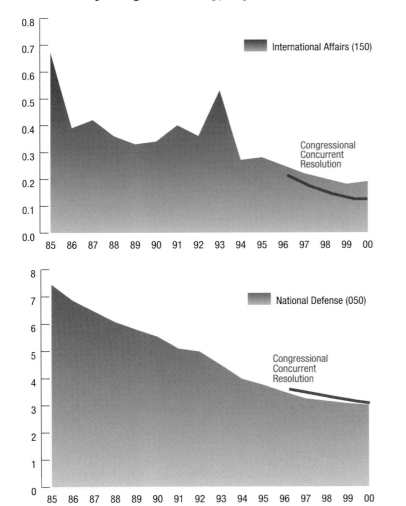

SOURCES: Budget of the U.S. 1996 and Congressional Concurrent Resolution.
NOTE: The 1993 increase in international affairs funding was due to an IMF quota increas.

An 82nd Airborne mortar drill

in the new international system will be those with poorly defined enemies who may switch back and forth from being dubiously neutral to actively opposed. In a high intensity conflict with a clearly defined enemy, such as a major regional contingency in the Persian Gulf, there may be significant ambiguity about whether the enemy has or will use chemical, biological, or nuclear weapons.

The challenge for the U.S. military is to balance the demands of preparing for the several types of conflict possible in the new system, while staying within the envelope of the resources that will be made available in this era of limited government. As we explained in *Strategic Assessment 1995*, in our view, the tasks for which the military must prepare are, in order of priority:

● *Hedging against the emergence of a peer competitor* equipped with the new information technologies. This requires investing in the future, through research and development and procurement. The percentage of the defense budget dedicated to this investment fell from 45 percent in FY 1986 to 30 percent in FY 1996. Reversing this trend will not be cheap.

● *Preparing for major regional conflict* (MRC). The *Bottom-Up Review* concluded that the U.S. must be ready for two nearly simultaneous conflicts of this scale. Current force structure allows for only a small margin of error in executing the two MRC

strategy. A high degree of readiness, force enhancements, strong overseas presence (both to provide confidence and to serve as forward staging areas), and increased preparation for coalition warfare would serve to increase that margin.

● *Countering proliferation.* Despite positive developments (the North Korea agreement, inspections in Iraq, elimination of nuclear arsenals in ex-Soviet states other than Russia, elimination of South Africa's programs, termination of Argentina and Brazil's efforts, and extension of the Treaty on the Non-Proliferation of Nuclear Weapons), at least twenty countries—many hostile to the U.S.—are still seeking to produce nuclear, biological, or chemical weapons and the means to deliver them.

● *Developing cost-effective responses to transnational threats*, that is, undertaking constabulary operations that back up local police forces, and addressing environmental problems without diverting military assets from their primary missions.

● *Engaging selectively in peace operations* for failed states. The selectivity should be both geographic and topical. Geographically, the U.S. will engage more readily in areas of vital national interest or of historic commitment. Topically, the U.S. will concentrate on humanitarian relief and conflict containment, rather than nation building or seeking to end age-old ethnic tensions.

These tasks for the U.S. military reflect the geostrategic developments, the information revolution, and the changing character of government in the post-Cold War era. In order to make its will felt most effectively in this new environment, the U.S. government is changing the way it uses its instruments of power. The rest of this volume examines in turn the non-military, political military, and war-fighting instruments.

CHAPTER TWO

Diplomacy

Introduction

Diplomacy arises out of the fundamental character of the nation-state system, with its basic assumption that nation-states are sovereign but divergent in their interests and unequal in their power. Diplomacy is about the process of interstate relations, while foreign policy concerns the objectives of those relations.

Following World War II, Washington's diplomacy adapted all of its foreign-policy instruments to the policy goals of the Cold War. In the diplomatic sphere, the United States adopted the activism of a superpower, leading a broad, military-political alliance. The U.S. relied heavily on bilateral relations to build a nexus of durable political and military coalitions as major diplomatic tools. These included anti-Soviet coalitions (such as NATO, CENTO, and SEATO) and institutions for the promotion of global economic and political development (such as the Marshall Plan and GATT). To implement this more ambitious foreign policy, the traditional departments were expanded in staff and resources, and a new family of government agencies was created with responsibility for a new range of activities, including covert intelligence collection and special operations, propaganda, and economic and military assistance.

With the end of the East-West rivalry as an organizing principle, governments and peoples are turning inward, focusing their attention on specific local interests. At the same time, a growing number of transnational issues bedevil countries large and small. Furthermore, a number of actors have recently assumed greater roles on the international scene: resurgent ethnic and regional nationalism; international organizations, such as the United Nations and the World Trade Organization; multinational corporations; and private voluntary organizations (PVOs).

The multiplicity of these interests and actors who, in the absence of a single organizing theme such as competition with the USSR, clamor for priority attention presents new diplomatic challenges implying the need for a more multifaceted and nimble diplomacy. For instance, while U.S. bilateral relations with Japan during the Cold War concentrated primarily on security considerations, trade and investment questions are now of increased importance, and the process of influencing Japanese behavior requires paying attention to a more diverse number of Japanese interest groups and power centers—the Ministry of International

Trade and Industry as well as the Defense Agency; the Japanese car industry as well as the Ministry of Foreign Affairs. At the same time, the U.S. finds its ability to pursue aggressive, bilateral diplomatic activity limited by expanding multilateral obligations arising from its leadership role (e.g., in NATO and the U.N.) and by the American public's growing insistence on a domestic focus.

Instruments

Retrenchment and reduction appear to be the dominant trend with respect to the American diplomatic organs. The best measure of the funding for diplomacy is the data on government spending by functional category. One of the categories is international affairs (the 150 account). The funding for the 150 account fell 46 percent in real terms from FY 1985 to FY 1995. Furthermore, both the FY 1996 budget proposed by President Bill Clinton and the congressional concurrent resolution on the FY 1996 budget project steep reductions in the 150 account

Until World War II, the building now known as the Old Executive Office Building housed the Department of State, Navy, and War.

between FY 1995 and FY 2000: their respective projections are for a 23 percent and a 43 percent decline in real terms.

Between FY 1985 and FY 1995, the reduction in the 150 account was primarily in international security assistance, i.e., military aid. The funding for the conduct of foreign affairs, other than peacekeeping assessments, is perhaps the category most related to diplomacy. That category rose by only 8 percent in real terms from FY 1985 to FY 1995. The Clinton administration forecast that it will decline by 19 percent between FY 1995 and FY 2000 (Congress

did not break down the 150 account forecast into the component elements).

Most of the existing official foreign-policy community—the National Security Council, the Department of Defense, the specialized agencies, and the foreign-affairs components of main-line departments—was created to augment the Department of State in the conduct of American diplomacy during the Cold War. Calls for budget-cutting in general are jostling for attention with proposals for reorganization. For instance, Senator Jesse Helms (R-North Carolina) proposed in 1995 the abolition of the U.S. Agency for International Development (USAID), the U.S. Information Agency (USIA), and the Arms Control and Disarmament Agency (ACDA) as independent organizations, with the transfer of their functions to the State Department.

Reorganized or not, the existing government organizations will continue to be charged with implementing American diplomacy in pursuit of U.S. interests utilizing a variety of instruments that can be mixed and matched to specific ends. These range from prodding North Korea into compliance with international norms on nuclear questions to protecting access to government contracts for American aircraft producers. The form in which they are used also can vary, from quiet bilateral contacts by resident embassies through "shuttle diplomacy" by senior officials to highly publicized summits of chiefs of state. The United States has also developed a program of regularly published official reports on specific subjects, such as human rights, narcotics traffic, and terrorism, that combine public diplomacy with public pressure on other governments.

Modern diplomacy is like an iceberg that lies largely underwater; most of the business of influencing other governments takes the form of myriad daily contacts outside the notice of the media and the public eye. In general, the stronger the overall bilateral relationship, the easier to settle specific issues, such as police treatment of an American citizen or access to the local market for a U.S. product. Conversely, the weaker the relationship, the more difficult effectively to use diplomatic tools to obtain changes in behavior, as seen in U.S.-Iran relations.

Treaties and International Agreements Concluded Annual Average, 1946–1994

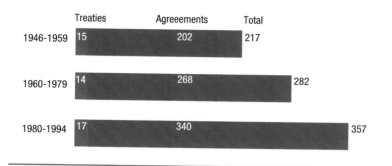

	Treaties	Agreeements	Total
1946-1959	15	202	217
1960-1979	14	268	282
1980-1994	17	340	357

SOURCE: State Department

The National Security Council

Established by law in 1947 as a body of cabinet-level officials, the National Security Council (NSC) advises the President on national-security policy. Its role was expanded during the Eisenhower administration, when a relatively small NSC staff organization was created to serve as a secretariat coordinating foreign policy.

The National Security Advisor (NSA) and his staff have since moved far beyond the Eisenhower-era concept of interdepartmental coordination. The position of National Security Advisor now has cabinet-level status, and is often seen as *primus inter pares* on the NSC. In the Kennedy administration, the National Security Advisor began to play a direct role in policy formulation, a role expanded by Henry Kissinger, who essentially assumed the power and role of chief diplomat as well as principal foreign-policy advisor in the Nixon administration. Although the trend of increasing power in the hands of the National Security Advisor slowed somewhat during the Reagan years, a new twist was introduced when the NSC temporarily assumed an active role in covert operations. Under President George Bush, Brent Scowcroft reintroduced the concept of the NSA as an "honest broker" who coordinated U.S. foreign policy. This approach, when combined with an engaged President and an effective Secretary of State (James Baker) in an atmosphere of collegiality among senior officials, produced a notably coherent, nimble, and well-integrated U.S. foreign policy, even in the hectic days of the Soviet Union's collapse.

The Clinton administration also aimed for a collegial relationship among its foreign-policy and diplomatic principals, and the current National Security Advisor appears to be operating more as an inside coordinator than external diplomatic operator. Correspondingly, the principal roles of the NSA and his staff appear to be prioritizing issues, seeking consistency, and coordinating instruments within the U.S. foreign-policy establishment, as well as adjudicating the underlying competition for resources among agencies and departments.

The NSC is challenged to keep up with the growing foreign-policy portfolio. Because the President's role in formulating U.S. foreign policy and directing diplomacy will remain central—despite an increasingly assertive Congress—the importance of the NSC's integrating role can only increase. At the same time, the roles of the National Security Advisor as a spokesman and negotiator cannot be completely curtailed, though they can be held in reserve for rare occasions when U.S. wishes to demonstrate the depth of its interest.

The Department of State

The State Department is the core diplomatic institution for the U.S. government. It employs all of the diplomatic instruments, from public spokesman to secret negotiator.

Trends in U.S. Government Overseas Presence 1984–94

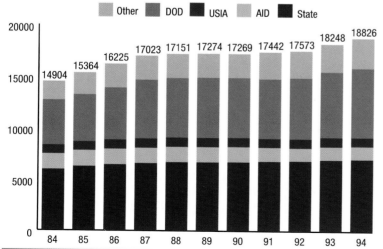

Legend: Other, DOD, USIA, AID, State

Year	Total
84	14904
85	15364
86	16225
87	17023
88	17151
89	17274
90	17269
91	17442
92	17573
93	18248
94	18826

SOURCE: State Department

NOTE: Includes military personnel only if assigned to embassies and missions. Excludes contract employees and military personnel assigned to regional CINCs.

President Clinton meets with family members at the memorial service for three U.S. diplomats killed near Sarajevo in 1995.

Arranging agreements—formal and informal, written and oral—is a basic function of the department. More than fourteen thousand treaties and other international agreements were concluded by the U.S. government between 1946 and 1994.

As the senior foreign-policy advisor to the President and chief of the core diplomatic organization, the Secretary of State can claim primary responsibility for the overall integration of these various special interests into a coherent foreign policy, subject to the wishes and governing style of the President. State's role as foreign-policy and diplomatic coordinator is performed at various levels: in the NSC itself, in the formal interagency process, and in the daily conduct of business between agencies in Washington and in embassies, not to mention informal arrangements, such as a weekly lunch among three or four principal cabinet officials. Coordination is a major responsibility of the department's component units, with the geographic bureaus focusing on bilateral relations with other governments (the warp), while the functional bureaus increasingly deal with the substance of specific issues (the woof).

The State Department has primary responsibility for communication with other governments. It manages this role through multiple channels: foreign embassies resident in Washington; the U.S. embassy network resident in other countries' capitals; participation in international organizations; official delegations; and (as discussed in the chapter on public diplomacy) formal public statements by senior officials or through the daily State Department press briefing. The bulk of communication with other governments, on subjects as far apart as the welfare of an American citizen in a Chinese prison to the alleged export of Chinese missiles to Pakistan, is conducted through these regular established channels. Increasingly, however, the end of the Cold War has seen these regular, established channels supplemented by more informal and ad hoc arrangements, none of them entirely new.

For instance, there is a growing tendency to use special envoys and representatives in crisis situations, ranging from Bosnia to Somalia. They are intended to reflect high-level interest in a subject, and often allow for a quick end-run around bureaucratic boundaries. President Carter's mission to Haiti, Deputy Secretary of State Strobe Talbott's trips to Russia, Ambassador Robert Galluci's voyages to Korea, and numerous envoys to Bosnia are all excellent examples of special envoys. They were attempts, successful in President Carter's case, to convince a government to take certain actions before the United States implemented more forceful measures. Successes by special envoys, however, must be weighed against the breathless character they sometimes give American diplomacy. Further, the short-term successes of a special envoy's mission sometimes confuse the difference between first-aid and major surgery, and blur the long-term responsibilities of the regular bureaucracy.

A number of other techniques have been prominently employed recently and appear likely to continue to be of regular use. Modern transportation makes formal state visits easier to accomplish, and mod-

International Security Affairs Budget Authority
(FY 96 $ billion)

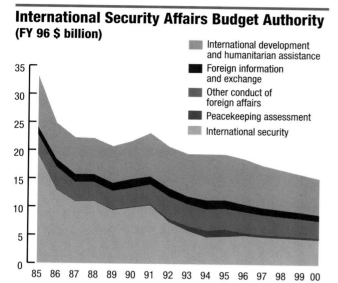

- International development and humanitarian assistance
- Foreign information and exchange
- Other conduct of foreign affairs
- Peacekeeping assessment
- International security

SOURCE: FY 1996 Budget.

NOTE: Excludes international financial programs, which are often negative because of debt repayments and spiked in FY 1993 due to IMF quota increase.

All data refer to fiscal years. After FY 1995, data refer to Administration proposal in FY 1996 budget.

ern communications make them both more useful and more dangerous. Thus, in dealing with local crises, the world's governments have energetically employed secret talks, as in the Middle East; proximity talks, as in Bosnia; contact groups, also as in Bosnia; and shuttle diplomacy all over the place, but notably in the Middle East and Bosnia. In many of these diplomatic developments, the United States has acted as a broker rather than as a principal party.

The State Department traditionally has not been an agency that designs and manages operational programs, but has worked in cooperation with and provided policy guidance to other departments and agencies that conduct programs overseas (such as USAID, USIA, Overseas Private Investment Corporation, the Export-Import Bank, and the Departments of Defense and Agriculture). During the Cold War, the State Department's responsibilities expanded enormously in response to the new global leadership role, then later to increasing economic and technological globalization and the emergence of so-called transnational or global issues. Some of these new responsibilities led to the creation of State Department operational programs with special congressionally authorized budgets to deal with international narcotics, terrorism, and refugees.

The basic professional skills of the Foreign Service consist of multidisciplinary and multicultural expertise, language skills, and operational diplomatic skills, such as negotiating, investigating, reporting, and analysis. To the traditional and still valid category of skills must be added specialized knowledge in rapidly developing areas, such as sustainable develop-

ment, narcotics, investment, and communications. These skills, combined with a personnel system that provides rank-in-person organization (similar to the armed forces) and worldwide availability, constitute the value-added qualities of a professional foreign service. The professional core of the Foreign Service is its approximately 3,000 commissioned officers, a number not significantly changed in almost forty years despite increased demands. Its continued usefulness depends upon aggressive recruitment and training, imaginative utilization, and adequate administrative support.

The growth of responsibilities and subjects in international relations, which began in a dramatic way after World War II, has required that the Foreign Service core be supplemented by large numbers of specialists employed partly by the State Department but mostly by other agencies. One way to note changes in the operating environment for American government employees deployed outside the United States is to check the rapidly expanding list graven in marble in the diplomatic entrance of the State Department of such employees who died in exceptional circumstances. It currently shows 171 names: 72 for the almost two-hundred-year period from the Revolution to 1960, and 99 in the period 1961–1994. The latter figure represents both State Department employees and those of other agencies—from Marines to DEA agents—who were serving at U.S. embassies or other posts.

Despite its prominence, the State Department is the second-smallest department of the U.S. government, with an annual budget of approximately $5.5 billion and a worldwide staff of approximately 25,000, of whom approximately 10,000 are foreign nationals performing mostly support functions. Within the context of a decline in overall spending on international affairs, the State Department's budget rose 24 percent in real terms between FY 1985 and FY 1995, but that was in large part a result of accounting procedures. A more relevant measure is the spending on diplomacy is the budget category called the conduct of foreign affairs, other than peacekeeping assessments. That measure rose only 8 percent between FY 1985 and FY 1995, despite a dramatic expansion in responsibilities as more countries became independent (e.g., with the breakup of the USSR) and world problems became more complex. Furthermore, as also noted above, the budget for the conduct of for-

eign affairs is projected to fall steeply between FY 1995 and FY 2000.

A variety of initiatives have been taken or are under discussion to reorient the activities of the State Department. To increase the priority given to functional, as distinct from regional, issues, and to clarify the chain of command, the Clinton administration reorganized the State Department into five areas, each headed by an undersecretary of state: political affairs (including all the geographic bureaus); economic, business, and agricultural affairs; arms control and international security affairs; global affairs; and management.

In late 1994 and early 1995, other and more dramatic proposals for significant reorganization of the foreign-affairs and diplomatic establishments were floated, from both administration and outside sources. Many of these proposals call for devoting fewer resources to diplomacy by cutting personnel, programs, budgets, and overseas diplomatic posts. As a result of this post-Cold War debate, reduction of the Department of State is under consideration—first as part of the overall reduction in the federal budget, and secondly as part of a reorganization effort by State Department management. The reorganization appears to focus on headquarters' needs rather than the field structure and on administration rather than substance. It will be difficult to implement the reduction while sustaining the capabilities to handle an increasingly complex package of U.S. national interests.

The Department of Defense

As described by General George Marshall, the only man ever to serve as both Secretary of State and Secretary of Defense, military force without diplomacy is pointless, and diplomacy not backed by military force is mere posturing. The traditional synergistic relationship between diplomacy and war has deepened to the point where these two instruments are deeply intertwined in daily activities.

In pursuing its responsibilities, DOD employs a large range of diplomatic instruments, but within a more restricted range of subjects than the Department of State: for example, base rights, training assistance, and equipment interoperability pro-

---

Tools of Diplomacy in Bosnia

The multiple efforts by the international community to end the conflict in Bosnia-Herzegovina during 1994–95 gave rise to the expanded use of several diplomatic tools that were either innovative or seldomly used in normal circumstances:

• The contact group is the most prominent example. It was designed to meet an old problem: how to separate out the principal players and engage them to reach agreement before getting the rest of the participants to join in the solution. The creation of the contact group evolved from a background of ill-fated attempts by the international community to hammer out a peace plan acceptable both to all parties at war and to all parties in the community responsible for implementing the plan. First, there was the Vance-Owen proposal stemming from the September 1992 International Conference on Yugoslavia (ICFY). Vance-Owen gave way to the Owen-Stoltenberg (or Invincible) package in 1993, but with no success.

• A special envoy for Bosnia, an exceptional diplomatic technique, was used by the U.S. in 1994. The envoy worked hard to achieve a Bosnia-Croat federation. At the same time, as proposed by the ICFY cochairmen, the principal powers reached a comprehensive accord among themselves and then undertook to sell it to the warring factions. Out of the envoy's and the contact group's efforts came the "51%–49% Map" to divide Bosnia's territory between the federation and the Bosnian Serbs, as well as a further series of notional principles to end the war.

• A special military advisor to the Secretary of State was appointed in March 1994, as part of the U.S. approach to bring together the Bosnian Croats and Bosnian Muslims. The advisor was given the mandate to achieve a better working relationship between the military commands of Bosnian Croats and Muslims, which only weeks earlier had been slugging it out. The advisor (first retired General John Galvin, and later retired General John Sewall) faced an uphill battle not only in Bosnia but in convincing the other members of the contact group that their advice was strategic and not tactical.

• Shuttle diplomacy, another time-tested by infrequently employed technique, was begun after renewed fighting in the spring and summer of 1995. After the U.S. NSA tested the waters with a series of exploratory meetings in Europe, Assistant Secretary Richard Holbrooke undertook a frenetic schedule of discussions with principal players and protagonists. He succeeding in bringing the right set of representatives to the conference table and got them to reach an accord on a cease-fire and then a peace agreement. While due in part to battlefield victories by the Croat and Muslim side, along with battlefield fatigue, Holbrooke's sucess was also due to skillful diplomacy, backed up with some classic diplomatic persuaders: lifting trade sanctions, providing economic aid, denying of diplomatic recognition, and enforcing of an arms embargo.

• Talks held in Dayton, Ohio, in November 1995 were the key to achieving a peace settlement. Unlike similar mediated efforts, such as the Camp David negotiations, these talks included many parties, (e.g., representatives of the contact group countries) brought together under the chairmanship of Holbrooke and the chief European negotiator, Carl Bildt.

Present at the creation of post-World War II U.S. foreign policy: Secretary of State Dean Atcheson (right) and Secretary of Defense (earlier Secretary of State) George Marshall.

grams among NATO partners; and human-rights obligations of armed forces, but not among the population in general.

While the military services long exercised a role in diplomacy through the military attaché, the Cold War saw the development in the Department of Defense of a so-called Little State Department. The Undersecretary of Defense for Policy has three senior assistants whose responsibilities specifically include relations and interactions with foreign governments and institutions, largely but not exclusively military (such as nongovernmental organizations involved in humanitarian assistance). These are the assistant secretaries for international security affairs, international security policy, and strategy and requirements.

On the military side, the principal player in diplomacy are the Joint Staff's Director for Strategic Plans and Policy (J–5) and the regional unified military commands, headed by regional commanders-in-chief (CINCs), who exercise active command of military forces deployed outside the United States and who are therefore in regular contact with foreign governments and forces on matters ranging from coalition formation to the provision of military technical assistance and the coordination of

contingency war-fighting plans. The role of the military in the employment of the panoply of diplomatic instruments has been strengthened by the Goldwater-Nichols Act of 1986, a congressionally mandated organizational and management reform that provides for greater integration and coordination. In particular, the enhanced role of the Chairman of the Joint Chiefs of Staff provides for greater focus on these areas for DOD as a whole; however, this enhanced role is a matter for current discussion, with some commentators arguing that integration of the various elements of DOD has gone too far.

In the heyday of the Cold War, there was criticism that DOD's role was too ambitious, preempting broader national goals in favor of security interests strictly defined. The current international environment calls for a more complicated and diverse role for DOD, fully integrated with overall foreign policy and under the State Department's diplomatic leadership—in order to avoid having one diplomatic organ pursuing activities that compromise or conflict with the work of another. For instance, the State Department is traditionally oriented toward individual countries, while the military is organized around regional commands, which cross country lines. Consequently, the military is more focused on security problems that cross country lines, while the State Department brings a bilateral approach to the interrelationship among problems.

Single-Issue Foreign-Affairs Agencies

During the Cold War, the United States created a series of essentially single-subject foreign-affairs agencies, such as USIA, USAID, ACDA, U.S. Trade Representative (USTR), and the Peace Corps. These organizations deal directly with foreign governments and international organizations through resident representatives and delegations, and employ the full range of diplomatic instruments, from public statements through negotiations to involvement in multilateral organizations. Each is the lead agency for policy formulation, and often implementation, in its area of responsibility, although all are subject to the policy guidance of the Secretary of State and the operational control of the President's representative on the spot—that is, the ambassador.

Each of these agencies provides important channels for communications with other governments. Except possibly for the Peace Corps, they have the advantage of specialized expertise and contacts, as well as a single-minded concentration in their area of responsibility. Some of these agencies can bring potential concrete benefits to the diplomatic table: USTR can offer or deny market access to the U.S., while USAID offers development assistance. Others, such as USIA, have more ambiguous relations with governments. Given the present organization of the U.S. government, single-issue agencies are the obvious instruments for seeking specific objectives in their areas of competence. For example, the Treasury Department would be the natural choice to handle negotiations on the codification of international norms for foreign investment, and USTR to handle bilateral trade negotiations.

However, single-issue agencies' institutional resistance to balancing benefits in their area of competence against costs in other areas can create tension, if not conflict, between specific and broad national interests. Thus, their activities require consistent and coherent central management to ensure that the agencies pursue their objectives within the context of overall U.S. policy and in coordination with other agencies.

The independent status of these agencies and the relative importance of their subjects are part of the overall debate on the reorganization of the State Department and the whole foreign-affairs establishment. The argument is that merging USIA, USAID, and ACDA into the State Department will provide savings by eliminating duplication of personnel and programs, and allow for better coordination of U.S. foreign policy. Defenders of the agencies counter that such a merger will result in the subordination of specific objectives to the general concern for good diplomatic relations. Thus, the question facing the reorganizers is whether these instruments would be better deployed in the post-Cold War era by a community of relatively specialized agencies under some sort of overall direction (coordination by guidance) or by a single diplomatic organization responsible for the whole range of foreign-policy concerns (coordination by organization).

Diplomacy by Domestically Oriented Government Agencies

Traditionally, diplomacy was a matter only for diplomats and foreign offices. But the increasing globalization of economics, as well as of politics and social developments, has led to expanding roles for other government departments once considered to be purely domestic in orientation. As they enter into foreign affairs, these departments are employing diplomatic instruments in their areas of expertise: enunciating U.S. policy, negotiating agreements, and maintaining regular relations with foreign governments in an ongoing process of suasion.

For example, the Department of Agriculture operates the Foreign Agricultural Service as an integral part of U.S. embassies, and manages a number of subsidy,

Recognition Policy as an Instrument of Diplomacy

The end of the Cold War witnessed both the collapse of several multiethnic states and the decline of ideology as a factor in international affairs. These events forced the United States to make a series of decisions concerning the diplomatic recognition of new states and new governments. The act of recognizing a country itself became a more prominent instrument of national power.

The success of the new recognition policies varied widely. On the one hand, recognition of the new countries formed from the former Soviet Union reinforced their independence, and in the case of the Baltic States contributed to their security. On the other hand, international recognition of a non-viable state like Bosnia contributed to the tensions that led to bloody conflict. Even the issuance of a visa to Taiwanese President Lee Teng-hui was read in Beijing as a step towards eventual recognition of Taiwan, and the Beijing government responded accordingly.

In the case of Vietnam and North Korea, both former Cold War adversaries, steps toward normalization and eventual recognition became an effective instrument by which to pursue U.S. policies on POWs/MIAs and nuclear non-proliferation respectively. Recognition policy has proven to be a powerful instrument that has received inadequate attention.

Warren Christopher on the USIA Worldnet.

grant, and sales programs, as well as programs to eradicate plant and animal disease. The Department of Commerce manages the Foreign Commercial Service, which also functions out of U.S. embassies. The Department of Labor, in conjunction with State, trains and employs Foreign Service labor officers and formulates U.S. policy toward labor unions outside the United States. The Department of Health and Human Services (HHS) is the lead agency for U.S. government participation in multilateral health organizations, such as the World Health Organization; HHS units such as the National Institutes of Health and the Centers for Disease Control are major international institutions. The Department of Treasury is the lead agency for policy toward international financial issues in general, as well as for U.S. government participation in multilateral financial organizations and groups, such as the World Bank, regional development banks, and the Group of Seven. The Justice Department maintains liaison with foreign police authorities, and is becoming a more active partner in the foreign-policy process and in diplomatic activity, as a result of U.S. government concern over narcotics, terrorism, and immigration.

These departments and agencies participate in diplomacy in three ways:

- Formulating policy.
- Providing specialized staff who may practice diplomacy as members of U.S. missions and delegations.
- Managing cooperative programs with other governments.

Like single-issue agencies, these departments possess specialized expertise and contacts in foreign countries, and can be used to pursue U.S. interests outside of their nominal area of responsibility. For instance, the Agriculture Department's food-export program is vital to humanitarian-assistance operations, and often plays a significant role in economic-assistance programs.

Embassies

Governments communicate in ways ranging from direct contact between home-based officials to public statements carried over CNN, but the bulk of business takes place through resident diplomatic missions. The United States maintains a diplomatic network of 263 embassies, consulates, and missions. Even with improvements in communication and transport technology, the explosion of intergovernmental business has increased the demands on embassies. The traditional tasks of representation, analysis, and negotiation must now be pursued across a wider range of issues: economic, social, environmental, and so on. Embassies now often include human-rights and environmental experts as well as political officers, military attachés, and vice-consuls. In a sense, embassies are the retail outlets for U.S. foreign policy, employing a toolbox full of diplomatic instruments on a daily basis in direct, regular contact with foreign governments and, in the process, conducting the bulk of everyday diplomatic business. They:

- Ensure that U.S. positions are known and understood in other countries by lobbying, explaining, and maintaining a regular dialogue with the local leadership.
- Learn the other country's interests, attitudes, policies, and plans at the source—especially as they relate to the country's leadership.
- Provide early warning of developing crises, as well as a readily available crisis manager on the ground.
- Oversee and manage foreign assistance, narcotics interdiction, and other programs.
- Provide consular services to U.S. citizens and foreign nationals, including the processing of visas.
- Support multilateral diplomacy by providing the direct link to national governments.

Yitzhak Rabin and Yasser Arafat sign the 1995 Peace Accord in Washington, as President Clinton and Egyptian President Hosni Mubarak look on.

The embassies are not, as some have suggested, obsolete institutions that have been superseded by summit meetings or other direct, high-level contacts. Rather, they are the support base and implementing tool for those two instruments. The capacity to communicate instantaneously affects and changes the role of resident embassies but does not eliminate their usefulness.

Traditionally, State attempted to provide overall coordination and management of all U.S. activities in a given country through the authority of the ambassador. While this situation still exists in theory, the growth in non-State personnel stationed in U.S. missions overseas (they now constitute almost two-thirds of overseas staff) and the range and complexity of programs have strained if not overwhelmed the department's management role. Various innovations have been made in an attempt to deal with this management problem. The Country Team concept, chaired by the ambassador and including all the agencies present in a country (except military elements serving under the command of a CINC), was introduced in the Eisenhower era.

During the course of the Cold War, as the influence and role of other departments expanded, and the resources of the State Department and the ambassador did not, the ambassador's ability to fulfill his role as manager of all U.S. programs in his country became increasingly strained. While an understandably satisfactory development from the perspective of the majority of agencies and departments involved, many saw in this trend conflicting agendas, duplicative functions and organizations, and lack of proper focus and concentration on the more important issues.

The size, cost, and mission of embassies and consulates is under review in the context of the wider review of the State Department and other foreign-affairs agencies. The expansion of the U.S. overseas diplomatic establishment following the Cold War—over twenty new posts—was not accompanied by commensurate increases in budgets or staff (except for specialized staff in administration and security, and in programs like counter-narcotics). Budget pressures led to a 1995 decision to cut in the next five years the number of overseas posts by nineteen and the number of personnel by up to 25 percent at some major embassies. These conflicting demands and pressures have been partially met by hollowing out the substantive core of U.S. missions—the professional political and economic staff. By reducing opportunities for representation and intelligence, the trend could have negative implications for the effectiveness of U.S. diplomacy, if only for the obvious reason that even the best diplomatic instruments require effective implementation by skilled and experienced officials.

Unofficial Diplomacy

Official diplomacy is practiced by the executive branch of the U.S. government, but various forms of congressional, quasi-official, and informal diplomacy—sometimes called Track II diplomacy—are practiced by Congress, ex-Presidents, and other former government officials, as well as by government-financed research institutions, lobbyists, and nongovernmental organizations.

Congress has long promulgated the basic limits and parameters of U.S. foreign policy, and congressional action itself can be a powerful instrument of U.S. policy. One need only remember the Marshall Plan. In the two decades after the end of World War II, however, a tradition of bipartisanship in foreign affairs was generally respected by legislators on Capitol Hill. Members of Congress and their staffs travelled extensively around the world on investigative missions, but tended to abstain—at least publicly—from negotiating or representing positions different from those articulated by the executive branch.

The erosion of the bipartisan congressional tradition in foreign affairs began during the Vietnam War and was subsequently exacerbated by the decline in party discipline, the exponential increase in professional staff in Congress, and the lack of policy consensus in the post-Cold War world. Congressional figures—both elected members and staff—now regularly engage in public communication and even in negotiations with foreign governments, international organizations, and other international entities. A similar development is now seen among ex-Presidents and other former senior executive-branch officials; President Jimmy Carter has institutional-

ized his interest in influencing foreign policy through the Carter Center. From this base, he has played a significant role as a mediator or intermediary in a number of political situations, e.g., the 1994 agreement with North Korea about nuclear proliferation and the 1994 voluntary departure from Haiti of the military rulers. Such figures appear inclined to take up active, personal diplomatic roles—although generally with at least the informal blessing of the White House.

Congressional delegations are a peculiarly American diplomatic instrument, which arise from the division of powers in the U.S. federal system. Members of Congress are senior government officials but are not part of the executive branch, which gives them a unique admixture of authority and freedom of action. Congressional members and staff use their trips and contacts with foreign representatives to promote their personal agendas and legislative responsibilities, sometimes on their own and sometimes in coordination with the administration. Congressman Bill Richardson (D-New Mexico), for instance, has made numerous successful foreign trips to pursue specific diplomatic issues, such as obtaining the release of U.S. citizens imprisoned in Iraq and the return of the body of a helicopter pilot lost in North Korea, inquiring about servicemen missing in action in Vietnam, and investigating the situation of Burma's leading democratic politician. When congressional figures are willing to coordinate their activities with the executive—which they often are —such activity provides additional communications channels for the executive branch.

Use of these eminent persons has its benefits and its problems from the perspective of officialdom. They offer opportunities for innovative interaction with other governments, and they provide a means to sound out the other side without committing the U.S. officially. That must be balanced against the dangers of blurring U.S. foreign policy with a multitude of voices. After all, Congress members and ex-officials are motivated by their own agendas, which may to varying degrees differ from those of the U.S. government.

Rep. Bill Richardson (D-New Mexico) meeting with Burmese Nobel prizewinner Aung San Suukyi.

More clearly unofficial diplomatic agents are advocacy groups, PVOs, and research institutes who often practice what has been called Track II Diplomacy. Advocacy groups for better relations with particular countries—such as the American Israel Public Affairs Committee—lend themselves to use as channels of communication and negotiation for the United States as well as for their clients. PVOs have become increasingly active and effective in the expanding interstices between national governments (see the chapter on International Organizations). Research institutes include those that are branches of the U.S. government (such as the Institute for National Strategic Studies), government-funded institutions (such as the Asia Foundation, U.S. Institute for Peace, and the National Endowment for Democracy), and private policy institutions that receive government contracts for specific projects, such as the University of California's government-funded series of conferences on alternatives for multilateral security in Northeast Asia. In the pursuit of their professional interests, these institutions closely follow international developments and can therefore be sources of intelligence and analysis. Their networks of international contacts, often at quite senior and influential levels, offer another conduit for proposing and exploring ideas and proposals unofficially. Current proposals to cut or eliminate federal government financial support for many of the quasi-government institutions will have an obvious effect on their usefulness as diplomatic instruments.

Conclusions

In the more fluid situation of the mid and late 1990s, the emphasis in diplomatic techniques is shifting from the large, formal, semi-permanent negotiating delegations between formal coalitions that occupied the center ring of American diplomacy during the Cold War, towards greater use of a wider ranger of instruments. An increasingly complex world, with each state less bound to a static coalition, and the more global character of the international environment call for more ad hoc arrangements involving special envoys, contact groups, and shuttle diplomacy. Furthermore, the non-executive branch players, ranging from Congress to PVOs, are playing an increasing role, influencing the behavior of governments.

The role and relationships between the various elements of the U.S. foreign-affairs establishment do not necessarily reflect the priorities of the new international situation. The role of the State Department as the core repository of expertise on regional and global issues, the integrating authority among an expanding number of specialized departments, such as DEA and the immigration service, and the overall manager of official diplomacy would benefit from review, and probably strengthening. In this perspective, a fundamental review of the U.S. government foreign-policy establishment, in light of the conflicting pressures of the current international situation and domestic budget-cutting imperatives, appears overdue.

U.S. diplomatic institutions are being asked to do more with less, in more countries and on a greater range of issues. Therefore, the programmed cuts in resources for these institutions and activities will pose a challenge for the U.S. ability effectively to pursue its national interest through the practice of effective diplomacy, especially preventive diplomacy.

CHAPTER THREE

Public Diplomacy

Introduction

The post-Cold War world is made more complex by rapid and pervasive information flows and expanding experiments in democratization. Foreign decision-making evolves less and less from tiny ruling elites and is increasingly influenced by public opinion when considering whether national interests coincide with those of the United States. Even in limited democracies, decisions by governments incorporate the input of academics, interest groups, political parties, and world public opinion. New technologies quickly convey masses of undifferentiated information reflecting global images heretofore only imagined, unimpeded by anything other than individual willingness to pay attention to it. In this atmosphere, in which fast exchanges of data drive decision making, the requirement for the United States to speak clearly, coherently, quickly, and persuasively to key foreign publics and leaders has never been greater.

The United States cannot assume that the opinions of these foreign audiences are based on a clear understanding of U.S. interests, actions, and intentions just because they have access to satellite dishes and on-line newsletters. Nor can the United States assure that its policies will be understood just by issuing a statement and hoping for good news play. The media may carry the President's speech or a report on a U.S. military action, but they may not explain the underlying history, culture, viewpoints, values, and intentions that enhance understanding and acceptance. Media reports may be laden with commentary that is inaccurate or distorted. Even upon hearing unbiased reports, different foreign audiences may require different explanations of U.S. policies and actions. For example, a proposition such as "supporting democracy" can mean different things in London, Singapore, Beijing, and Mexico City; the words used to describe the concept to U.S. audiences may not have the same meaning or connotations for other audiences. Lastly, beyond programmers' loosely defined standards of newsworthiness, no formula governs what will be covered by the media.

If the interpretation of U.S. policies is left to such reports, it may remain incomplete, distorted, misunderstood, and hardly persuasive. And when foreign audiences misinterpret U.S. policy, political costs escalate. Beijing may not find U.S. emphasis on human rights more palatable for understanding U.S. traditional values, but it might at least understand that criticism of China is not arbitrarily hostile.

The U.S. government will be more effective at influencing events abroad to the extent that foreign audiences understand U.S. actions and policy. That requires not only information about stated policy but also comprehension of such basics as the U.S. constitutional framework, the character of U.S. society, and contemporary U.S. politics. Creating that comprehension is the job of public diplomacy. This chapter examines the instruments for conducting public diplomacy and the implications of its practice in a world where political and economic centers of power are multiplying, where information is available as never before, and where publics are developing viewpoints that guide their nations' choices.

Instruments

Public Statements

Public statements from anywhere within the U.S. federal bureaucracy can affect global audiences. Some departments—such as Treasury and Commerce—are obvious objects of the world's attention, but even statements from such departments as Education or Housing and Urban Development can have international ramifications. A panoply of topics, such as population control, pollution, or food supplies, blur the lines between what is a domestic issue and what is international. However, most for-

eign attention is naturally fixed on the White House, the Department of State, and the Department of Defense.

Every day, the major parts of the executive branch consult with one another to ensure uniformity in understanding of policies and how they will be represented to the public. Ideally, policymakers will weigh public acceptance when the particular issue is discussed. During Desert Shield and Desert Storm, an interagency committee on public diplomacy fed advice into the decision process with respect to shaping decisions that would have maximum acceptance by coalition supporters and would be properly understood by Baghdad and its supporters. But in noncrisis situations, perceptions may not be considered until after policy formulation. In the worst of all worlds, discussion of damage control is the first time public reactions are considered.

By midday, spokesmen appear at podia in Washington to address a range of issues encompassing anything that might attract media attention. The world watches, but the process is not primarily designed for international audiences. Rather, the executive branch directs its explanations first at the U.S. public, Congress, and domestic special-interest groups. It is always possible that some statement or policy will arouse reactions abroad, which may lead to a protest at a U.S. embassy or even a phone call to the President or to a Secretary from a foreign counterpart. But foreign opinion is usually felt indirectly and has a weight different from domestic opinion. In certain cases—as when a head of state visits or when a message is intended to affect international negotiations—a statement may be specifically designed for a foreign audience, but even those statements are measured for their impact in the United States as well. That is as it should be. The U.S. audience gets first consideration, but it should not get the only consideration.

Of course, the media briefings at the White House, State, or Defense are not the only window into the policy world. Administration figures appear on talk shows; give exclusive interviews, sometimes to the foreign press; and speak at events. Their voices and the ideas they represent are, most importantly for global understand-

DefenseLINK

DefenseLINK is the Department of Defense's official World Wide Web information service. It is provided through the cooperative efforts of the Office of the Secretary of Defense–Public Affairs, the Defense Technical Information Center, and the Military Services. DefenseLINK is accessible via Web browsers, 24 hours a day, 7 days a week, at:

http://www.dtic.dla.mil/defenselink/

The Department of Defense Web Page.
http://www.dtic.dla.mil/defenselink/

The Assistant to the Secretary of Defense for Public Affairs Kenneth H. Bacon conducted his first press briefing on October 27, 1994.

Countering Disinformation and Misinformation

Although the Soviet Union has passed into history, its campaign of misinformation, disinformation, and other efforts to discredit the West in general and the United States in particular survives. AIDS as a deliberate American attempt to depopulate the developing world, the Jonestown (Guyana) suicides as a CIA plot, and assorted assassination conspiracies are just a few of the stories that have proven more durable than the regime that concocted them. Other groups hostile to the United States, such as terrorist groups and rogue states, continue to use the same techniques. The best weapons against such campaigns are early identification and emphatic refutation—part of the work of public diplomacy.

No misinformation campaign has been so persistent or damaging as the so-called "baby parts" story—the story that the rich West has children in underdeveloped countries killed to provide organs for transplants. Entirely without foundation, this myth has been perpetuated by major media first in hostile nations and then around the world, and has been accepted by gullible publics conditioned to think the worst about the United States. The myth accelerated in 1987, after Honduran official referring to the rumor was misquoted in a way that made it seem he was endorsing it. Cuban media and *Pravda* both published accounts citing the Honduran official as authority, leaving out his immediate retractions and the other authoritative voices dismissing the assertions. Subsequently, other anti-U.S. groups and media knowing a sensational story when they saw it kept it alive.

The USIA report to the United Nations of December 1994 provides the most thorough analysis of the baby parts story. It details the unusual willingness, in some quarters, of even sophisticated people to accept wild assertions as fact. The report further illustrates how the body of documentation for this myth is built on misrepresentations and cross-citations among unreliable sources. This report to the United Nations is used repeatedly by U.S. public-affairs officers abroad to counter further attempts to perpetuate this misrepresentation. Unfortunately, the very outrageousness of such stories plays on the public's interest in the sensational and makes countering these myths a permanent item on the public diplomat's list of duties.

Exterminio en el Golfo
Por Monsi

USIS Mexico dealt with many different perceptions of U.S. actions and motivation in the Gulf crisis. This cartoon—"Extermination in the Gulf" by Monsi—appeared in the Mexico City daily El Universal. The balloon caption says, "The Iraqis will do what the Border Patrol could not." The cover of the booklet reads, "76,000 U.S. soldiers in the Persian Gulf are of Mexican origin."

ing, amplified and explained officially through U.S. public-diplomacy mechanisms. From roots in the wartime agencies of World Wars I and II, the U.S. Information Agency (USIA) and its overseas arm, the U.S. Information Service (USIS), has been charged with carrying out America's public diplomacy. Reflecting, as public affairs must, the policies of the government it represents, USIA and USIS have been caught up in the Cold War tensions, from presenting to the world the U.S. case on the shooting down of Korean Air Lines Flight 007 to countering Soviet disinformation. But the unique role of USIA/USIS has been in its commitment to developing deep understanding abroad of U.S. society and culture as well as the policies and attitudes that flow from these.

Embassies and Field Personnel

While departments and agencies are agreeing on what can be said publicly at their U.S. briefings, 263 U.S. embassies, consulates, and missions around the world are striving to explain U.S. policies and actions in the nations where they are stationed in a way that advances U.S. interests. Clearly, Washington cannot be

contradicted. But at some point, Washington's vetting of the policy must end, and the U.S. spokesman abroad must make a statement. He must decide how to present the U.S. line to foreign audiences as positively as possible while still conforming to Washington's guidance. How best to do this must come from USIS professionals who speak the local language and understand the local public as well as the details of U.S. policy, so as to convey the U.S. position in clear, persuasive terms.

After a U.S. policy is announced to a foreign audience, the local media report, pundits ponder, analysts interpret, government bureaus and private companies inquire, and scholars are called on to explain, "What did the Ambassador (or President or Congressman) mean when he said . . . ?" All of these commentaries and inquires are examined as well as answered and subsequently reported as representing foreign public opinion—which may affect how the original policy is altered, or at least how it is presented in the next cycle of information exchange. Such authoritative and timely feedback provides Washington with a critical perspective on the consequences of its policies. These daily reports are supplemented by polling and surveys that measure attitudes more broadly and over the longer term.

Every embassy has assets for maintaining communications with the public, but USIS staff are required to get the most out of these assets. A trade specialist, the military attaché, or a Drug Enforcement Administration representative at the U.S. embassy can give background briefings to key media, academics, or others in anticipation of rising issues. The public appearances of the ambassador and his deputy can be orchestrated to give added weight to explanations in speeches, statements, and interviews. Cultural exchanges can help close the communications gap in a less direct way. A local official whose passion is music can become more approachable through an introduction to the conductor of a visiting American orchestra. Fulbright exchanges can fill scholarly gaps, and useful relationships can develop between people sitting on joint Fulbright boards. U.S. professional, political, and academic groups can be put together with counterparts who influence policy direction in the host country. In addition, outside authorities, academics, visiting administration representatives, artists, and experts can be called on to exemplify U.S. society and explain the country's policies.

The U.S. government could, of course, simply trust foreign audiences to soak up news from CNN and other worldwide news services, and then make their own best guesses about U.S. motivations and intentions based on available analyses. But the U.S. government is more likely to get its viewpoint across if it makes specific and tailored efforts to promote public understanding of U.S. government positions. Resources are being cut: USIA lost 600 positions in FY 1994–95 and is likely to lose a similar number in FY 1996, as well as the closing of five missions and eleven branch posts. The challenge will be to use new means to accomplish this task more efficiently.

Broadcasting and Electronic Media

Instant news coverage is not a substitute for a calculated presentation of U.S. positions, although it lends urgency to this task. The combination of an increasingly pervasive electronic media and an audience that has grown in size and become more important to decision makers presents a particular challenge to electronic public diplomacy.

CNN and rival news services strive to provide nearly instant coverage of events around the world. There is no question that CNN, particularly as an American enterprise, provides an important dimension to communication exchanges. But CNN broadcasts almost entirely in English. And it only tenuously reaches places such as Chechnya, Rwanda, Iraq, Iran, North Korea, and China.

Neither CNN nor any of its rivals is an official voice of the U.S. government, and the sound bite approach leaves out context. As news organizations, they pay attention to U.S. official positions, so if these positions are articulated well and presented at the right moment in unfolding events, there is an even chance that the public will get the outlines of official views by commercial means. But the chances decrease somewhat with a news network of another country, which will feel more compunction to give time to voices in its country of origin and whose commentators may have viewpoints less well informed in terms of American motives. And this is less apt to occur in a story that is not a major or continuing one. CNN may want a camera permanently at the Pentagon briefing room during a military crisis or even at USTR during major trade negotiations. But they will not have covered so thoroughly the lower-profile processes leading to other initiatives, and their output tends to be generalized for a global audience.

To complement commercial electronic media, the U.S. government employs its own broadcasting. Western research has shown that 90–100 million listeners tune in the Voice of America (VOA), the radio-broadcasting arm of USIA, each week. The Open Media Research Institute commissioned a series of studies of elites in the

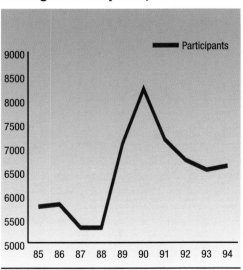

Fulbright Participants, 1985–94

Participants

9000
8500
8000
7500
7000
6500
6000
5500
5000

85 86 87 88 89 90 91 92 93 94

SOURCE: USIA

Nighttime Coverage to Balkans from Medium Wave VOA Facilities

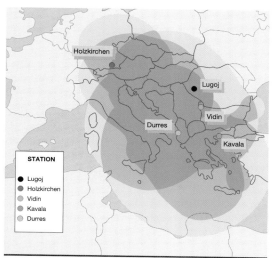

SOURCE: USIA

former USSR in the fall of 1994. Seventy percent of the leaders in Russia, Ukraine, Belarus, Poland, the Czech Republic, Hungary, and Slovakia use the Voice of America as a news source. As audiences in some countries turn away from shortwave, the Voice of America is utilizing new channels for its material. In January 1994, VOA became the pioneer international broadcaster to use the Internet. In late 1995, between 80,000 and 90,000 files are sent from VOA each week to computer users in sixty-eight countries. VOA broadcasts are sent to listeners throughout the world over thirteen wholly owned relay stations and fifteen shared facilities. The system is complemented by 1,250 AM and FM affiliated networks and stations, making VOA "local" in key places like the former Yugoslavia.

Public Diplomacy in the Former Communist World

The Voice of America has affiliation agreements with both private and state-owned broadcasters in Russia, Ukraine, Kazakhstan, Kyrgystan, Armenia, and the Baltic Republics. Near Volgograd, stations that jammed VOA in the past have switched to broadcasting its signals. In a national poll conducted by the Sociology Center of the National Academy of Sciences in Armenia, VOA was rated the most trusted news source by 35.2 percent of respondents. Russian radio/TV received 32.5 percent, Radio Liberty 22.1 percent, and the BBC 18.3 percent. Forty-two U.S. Fulbright scholars are studying in Eastern Europe this year, and Fulbright commissions exist in Romania, Bulgaria, Hungary, Slovakia, and the Czech Republic. More than forty Vietnamese Fulbright graduate students attend U.S. universities in the mid-1990s, mostly studying economics. One-man USIS operations have opened in Laos, Cambodia, and Mongolia in 1994–95. In Eastern Europe and the former Soviet Union, in 1989, USIA had branches in fifteen cities in eight countries; in mid-1995, there are posts in twenty-seven cities in twenty-six countries. The parliamentary deputies and ministerial staffs in Riga routinely use the American Library on-line services for real-time information on U.S. congressional actions. USIS Budapest, working with the International Media Fund and the University of Maryland, has established the American Journalism Center as part of the prestigious ELTE Lorans University. Cooperative programs have been undertaken with Albanian TV on private business development, with Romanian TV on service industries, with Russian and Latvian TV on tourism, and with Hungarian TV on the U.S. banking and financial systems.

Radio Free Europe/Radio Liberty (RFE/RL) have a long history as surrogate voices in the countries of Eastern Europe, where government radio prevented people from getting complete and accurate information. Radio and TV Marti have fulfilled the same role for Cuba. Whether such efforts are still required is arguable, but they continue, and there is a proposal for a Radio Free Asia. These are funded by the U.S. government but differ from VOA insofar as they present news of the target countries exclusively. By late 1995, RFE/RL was down from 1,700 employees in Prague to 300, broadcasting mostly to the former Soviet Union. Radio Marti broadcasts almost twenty-four hours a day, reaching an audience that can only be estimated (because of the inability to poll audiences) at about 16 percent.

For more than ten years, USIA has developed "Worldnet," a twenty-four-hour direct television service from Washington reaching three hundred embassies and USIS information centers around the world via satellite to its own receiving equipment, as well as to interested foreign parties. Worldnet's "Newsfile" is seen by viewers in eighty countries and is produced in English, Spanish, Arabic, French, Russian, and Serbian. In 1994, Worldnet produced 550 of the new "Dialogue" show, which gives listeners overseas a chance to hear the views and ask on-line questions of American leaders. Vice President Al Gore, Secretary of State Warren Christopher, and Trade Representative Mickey Kantor have been guests.

The same interactive technique is used for nonbroadcast-quality (and cheaper) programs, such as a series of U.S. history classes for Russian university students, with a professor in Washington leading a class of students in Moscow. As Worldnet and technology have developed together, it has become a valued and unique direct satellite broadcast service to broadcasters and other audiences, where local receiving technology and laws allow.

Modern on-line technologies are an invaluable aid for conveying U.S. positions to a foreign audience. For example, during the NAFTA debate, President Carlos Salinas of Mexico contacted USIS daily for statements by congressional leaders and the resulting commentary. Potential foreign

Foreign Students in the U.S.: Totals by Region

North America
23.394
0.5%

Europe
64.811
3.2%

China
39,400
11.2%

Japan
42,280
3.4%

Middle East
30.246
2.5%

Taiwan
36,410
3.4%

Africa
20.724
0.8%

Asia
140,699
1.2%

Latin America
47.239
4.4%

Oceania
4.327
12.2%

	1994/95	% CHANGE
World Total	452,635	0.6%

SOURCE: Open Doors
NOTE: Percent change in 1994–95 compared to 1993–94.

USIS World Wide Web Home Page.
http://WWW.USIA.GOV

users are, on the whole, less plugged-in than Americans, and those who are share the problem of a bewildering number of information nodes available.

There are over 1,000 U.S. government sites on the World Wide Web, among 30,000 as of the end of 1995. Cultivating a reputation as a reliable source of information on any subject increases the chances that U.S. government sources will be consulted when questions arise on important issues. Even though certain items of information might be used against U.S. interests in specific instances, overall, U.S. diplomats find more advantage in being a source than in allowing someone else to be.

Where the information highway intersects with educational and cultural activities stands the traditional USIS library. Although books and journals are not denigrated, rooms of books have become too expensive to maintain and are being down-sized or eliminated in favor of information or reference centers, except in particularly information poor countries or where they are important symbolically, as in the reading room in Soweto in South Africa.

Educational and Cultural Exchanges and Events

Educational and cultural exchanges, while only indirectly related to immediate foreign-policy initiatives, can advance national interests in several ways. Understanding by key persons of why the U.S. government is doing this or saying that, is either adamant or flexible on a certain issue, may be promoted by a U.S. history course taken with a Fulbright scholar, a USIS-sponsored speech on free trade, a delegation of U.S. visitors meeting with their professional counterparts, or personal contacts with U.S. opinion molders during a USIA exchange program. A recognition of the role played by such experience in developing personal predispositions drives the modest U.S. investment in educational and cultural exchanges to reach a future generation of overseas opinion molders, agenda setters, and decision makers.

The United States has much to gain from validating its image as a place where ideas flourish. Officially extending an invitation to foreign scholars through prestigious USIA-managed programs, such as the Fulbright Scholarship Program and Humphrey Fellowship Program, confirms U.S. higher education as a seed bed of ideas. That reputation has led to extraordinary demand by private foreign students, an export that the Department of Commerce has calculated as worth $6.8 billion dollars a year. USIS acts as expediter for student exchanges through counseling services, and even more specifically as agent for exchanges among legislators, think tanks, youth groups, professionals, and similar groups reaching out for contact and helping to promote formal American Studies programs in foreign universities.

According to the Institute for International Education, 76,302 American students studied abroad for academic credit in the year 1993–94 (the latest year for which figures are available), which is only one-half of one percent of all American students in higher education. Of this group, only 16 percent spent an academic year or more overseas. In the early 1990s, 1,200 Americans were studying in Japan—more than 40,000 Japanese were studying in the United States. In 1992–93, almost 20 percent of the foreign students in the U.S. were from mainland China and Taiwan.

U.S. cultural, artistic, and sporting events staged overseas are increasingly common, organized on a commercial basis. The challenge for the U.S. government is to cooperate with business to make these events a celebration of the broad range of U.S. accomplishments, as well as to organize direct exchanges in areas that offer little commercial rationale. Under special circumstances, cultural exchanges can even become the principal medium for diplomatic relations. This was given a special name when developing relations with China were dubbed "Ping-Pong Diplomacy" because exchanges of table-tennis teams paved the way for further relationships.

The most targeted of the exchanges are short-term visits to the United States for rising leaders, such as those sent under the U.S. government's International Visitors Program. These can provide a better understanding of U.S. society and correct inaccurate views held even by foreign elites. In most cases, alumni of U.S. government-sponsored exchanges are predisposed to give the United States a fair hearing and the benefit of the doubt, sometimes with direct

or indirect ramifications for national security. For example, even in the midst of one of the United States's nettling trade rows with Japan, then Prime Minister Yasuhiro Nakasone was moved to tears during a speech in which he recalled his daughter's experience as an exchange student in the United States. This hardly made him a less vigorous proponent of Japan's national self-interest. But it did indicate his belief that the ongoing U.S.-Japanese relationship was too important to let it founder over a single transient issue.

High-Level Visits

All of this framework for public diplomacy serves a special purpose when the President, Vice President, departmental secretaries, and certain other high-level government spokesmen travel. Nothing will focus an issue more quickly and sharply than to have this level of government take it as part of the agenda for a foreign trip. USIS public diplomats play critical roles in making the most of these special occasions. Management of even the most basic public appearances by such principals in a foreign setting, taking into consideration local sensitivities and practices, ensuring that traveling press can get their story out, and providing local reference points for comments and statements is considered critical to maximizing the public impact of such visits. In addition to well-run press conferences and media interviews, public diplomats can make possible special, meaningful appearances, such as President Ronald Reagan's at the tombs at Xian in China; Vice President Dan Quayle's shooting hoops with Japanese school boys; and President Bill Clinton's itinerary in Russia. These are the events that provide the lingering visual images important to public appreciation of the United States, and they require the expertise that is the province of the public diplomat.

Democracy Promotion

During the Cold War, the United States discovered that its traditional democratic beliefs offered an effective counter to the spread of the communist ideology. With the collapse of communism, the U.S. continues to promotes democracy because experience has shown that democratic states are less likely to threaten U.S. interests and more likely to cooperate with the

---

The International Visitors Program

Margaret Thatcher wrote in her biography, *The Path to Power:*

I had made my first visit to the USA in 1967 on one of the 'Leadership' programs run by the American Government to bring rising young leaders from politics and business over to the U.S. For six weeks, I travelled the length and breadth of the United States. The excitement which I felt has never really subsided. At each stop-over I was met and accommodated by friendly, open, generous people who took me into their homes and lives and showed me their cities and townships with evident pride. The high point was my visit to the NASA Space Center at Houston. I saw the astronaut training program which would just two years later help put a man on the moon. As a living example of the 'brain drain' from which over-regulated, high-taxed Britain was suffering, I met someone from my constituency of Finchley who had gone to NASA to make full use of his talents. I saw nothing wrong with that, and indeed was glad that a British scientist was making such an important contribution. But there was no way Britain could hope to compete even in more modest areas of technology if we did not learn the lessons of an enterprise economy.

U.S. on security and trade issues. In most instances, democratic states resolve their conflicts in ways that allow continued co-operation afterward. Also, a larger pool of states committed to democratic ideals increases the potential to form coalitions for political, economic, and security interests.

Promoting democracy broadens the range of national power instruments that can be used to influence relations with the transitioning state. For example, when Eastern European states were ruled by communist governments, the instruments of national power available to the United States to influence those countries were limited to coercive (or at best non-cooperative) instruments such as economic sanctions and demonstrations of military readiness. Now that these states have more democratic systems of governance, the U.S. is more able to employ instruments such as military-to-military interaction, trade, foreign economic assistance, and heightened public diplomacy.

Presidents Clinton and Yeltsin greet USIA exchange program students during Yeltsin's state visit to the U.S.

The National Endowment for Democracy is a non-profit, bipartisan, grantmaking organization created during President Reagan's first term as a way of helping democratically-minded groups in foreign countries build more effective organizations and carry out programs in democratic education, human rights, and respect for the rule of law. Although it is a private agency, its funding is part of the USIA Budget and is used to provide grants to other private organizations. NED channels about 70% of its available grant money through four member institutes: the National Democratic Institute for International Affairs, the International Republican Institute, the Free Trade Union Institute of the AFL-CIO, and the Center for International Private Enterprise of the U.S. Chamber of Commerce. Those groups in turn decide which foreign groups will receive grants. The remaining 30 percent of the NED's available grant money is distributed directly to programs and groups. Although

modestly funded (the budget request for FY 1996 was $34 million), NED's ability to react quickly to support emerging democratic movements is one of its major strengths. Some of NED's most notable and recent success stories include support for human rights and labor groups in China, support for independent media in the former Yugoslavia, political party training in South Africa, assistance to election monitors in Mexico, support for human rights activists and the circulation of newsletters in Cuba, and training of pollwatchers in Ukraine.

A variety of programs discussed under Public Diplomacy and in other chapters of this volume support democracy abroad. The U.S. Agency for International Development (USAID) is the largest spender on country-specific programs to support broadening of political participation, improving accountability of government officials and enhancing government legitimacy, as well as conducting elections. USIA estimates that as much as twenty percent of its $1.4 billion dollar budget is spent on democratization initiatives in educational exchange, speaker programs, university support, radio and TV operations and general information exchanges.

The Department of Defense has used the International Military Education and Training (IMET) program to teach foreign militaries about the role of a military in a democratic society and the Expanded IMET (E–IMET) program to educate foreign civilians in some defense-related subjects thus enhancing civilian control of the military. The role of the military in a democratic society is the central focus of the Marshall Center, a separate DOD program aimed at helping the militaries of central and eastern Europe and the former Soviet Union transition to democratic systems.

The U.S. government also works with, and in some cases supports financially, the myriad of private voluntary organizations (PVOs) supporting democratization. Former President Jimmy Carter and the Carter Center in Atlanta have been instrumental in many initiatives to promote peace and democracy, including election-monitoring efforts and persuading Haitian military dictators to surrender power to democratically elected leaders. PVOs such as the International Foundation for Electoral Systems (IFES)) have been leaders in providing election assistance to countries in transition, and in monitoring elections to help ensure fairness. IFES maintains a resource center in Washington, D.C. which is a tremendous storehouse of information on technical election issues, political problems, and election failures.

Important as it is, democratization is not panacea for all social problems. In countries with strong ethical, racial, or religious tensions, long-smoldering tensions, previously held in check by superpower confrontation or authoritarian governments, can burst into flame if democratization occurs without the proper foundation and preparation. Conflicts in Burundi, Rwanda, and the former Yugoslavia were stimulated in some degree by poorly planned democratization without adequate protection for minority interests. Elections sometimes heighten expectations among the populace that western-style elections will result in western-style economic prosperity. The resulting disappointment when the elected government is not able to fulfill economic expectations complicates the democratization process, and sometimes results in calls for a return to the old way. While elections are critical to a functioning democracy, haphazardly rushing to hold elections without adequate foundations can exacerbate existing problems and slow, rather than speed, the transition to democracy.

Camera crews were already on the beaches when U.S. Marines landed in Somalia.

To provide international financial and technical assistance to achieve one free and fair election, and then to expect a nascent democracy to replicate the result on its own the next time is unrealistic. Continued engagement by the U.S., both unilaterally and multilaterally, makes more likely success at an enduring and far-reaching democratization. At the same time, the U.S. may lack the resources and the will to become involved in every situation. U.S. involvement is most likely, and most likely to succeed, where U.S. interests weigh greatly in the he balance and where democratization may take root with enough assistance.

Wartime Media Relations

Media-military relationships were at a high point during World War II, when correspondents like Ernie Pyle thought of themselves first and foremost as patriots. Vietnam, by contrast, represents the dark days, when the media were characterized as actively undercutting the war effort. Throughout the 1970s and 1980s, many in the military had a low opinion of the media. However, in the early 1980s, a system was instituted to promote better cooperation; under it a pool of reporters would be able to cover military operations in the field. The first use during actual combat was the 1983 Grenada invasion, when the press pool was denied access to communication facilities and to frontline troops for forty-eight hours. Cuba reported to its people the details of the operation before the U.S. public heard them. That precipitated serious, policy-level efforts to develop a modus operandi for the military and the media. Under advice from a panel of news and public-affairs people chaired by General Winant Sidle, Defense Secretary Caspar Weinberger announced a policy of access and positive accommodation in return for respect for the demands of combat. The 1989 test of the system, the U.S. invasion of Panama, was a flop. The conclusion afterwards by the military and the media was that the system had to work, because the military and the media needed each other.

In Desert Shield and Desert Storm, the pool system was not the principal form of coverage because thousands of journalists flocked to cover the story. The media had unprecedented access, but there still were problems. There are journalists who will never be satisfied with their access to either the action or a means of getting the story out. And there are military officers whose negative attitudes toward the press will overpower commitment to policy. But the relationship has developed into a less adversarial one than during the post-Vietnam days. Indeed, journalists have demonstrated a willingness to sit on stories when the security need is evident, as seen at the start of Desert Storm, when the planes taking off from Saudi bases were evident hours before they reached their targets.

A continuing challenge is the information revolution, because it means instantaneous coverage by large groups of reporters who flock to the most obscure parts of the globe in the event of a crisis. Television lights on a landing zone and satellite phone uplinks pose obvious problems for the military. So too does the problem of security for journalists, who want to be free to move at will but expect U.S. forces will rescue them if they get into trouble. On the other hand, the information revolution can be a powerful force multiplier for the military, with the media carrying to hostile forces the message about U.S. might and determination.

Conclusions

Two fundamental changes have taken place that alter dramatically the environment in which the United States conducts its public diplomacy. First, the message of individual freedom, democracy, and free market economy that the United States worked to spread during the cold War has borne fruit. Most former communist nations, military dictatorships, and other totalitarian societies have been opened up, due in no small measure to the success of our public diplomacy. Second, private news organizations, taking advantage of rapid advances in telecommunications technologies, are providing prompt, extensive coverage of global affairs and distributing it to all corners of the globe.

The challenge for the U.S. government and its public diplomacy has changed accordingly. It no longer need be concerned about the battle of the ideologies. U.S. public diplomacy can now concentrate on the twin tasks of promoting understanding of U.S. society and encouraging support for the positions of the U.S. government on more immediate issues.

Moreover, the role of the USIA and other U.S. government agencies is shifting: they are less sources of information and more organizers of information. That is, they are changing from generating the news to organizing and providing an appropriate context for news. CNN and other news organizations now move rapidly and efficiently togather and disseminate news and that news is available for the most part throughout the globe. There is much less

need for the United States to take unilateral action to ensure that news and information penetrate a closed totalitarian society. It is not necessary nor is it appropriate for the U.S. to compete head to head with private news organizations even if the U.S. government could do so effectively.

The role for USIA is evolving into ensuring that the U.S. position on a current issue or, when appropriate, the broader U.S. policy toward a region is presented fairly and well understood. As news organizations develop stories on issues in which the U.S. has a stake, it is important that the U.S. government be aware of the information that is reaching the publics. As required, USIA can provide the appropriate context, background, and information, to convey a clear understanding of U.S. policy.

The information revolution also demands competence and involvement in more media. in the last two decades, television has passed radio and the printed media as the primary source of news that reaches the global public. Increasingly, the elites of advanced nations are getting their information via electronic media, including via the Internet. As this and other media become more heavily utilized, it is important to provide the same ability to organize and provide appropriate context to the news.

Other aspects public diplomacy have changed as well. Resources have declined for government sponsored tours, student and cultural exchanges with foreign nations. On the other hand, there has been a rapid growth and expanded opportunity for travel and exchanges in the private sector. This provides an opportunity for USIA to work with private groups in ensuring a constructive opportunity for a greater understanding of the U.S. government and society on the part of participants.

What has not changed is that the communication of U.S. policy works best when a conscious effort is made at all levels of planning to co-ordinate U.S. public diplomacy. The continued investment of resources and close attention to public diplomacy will pay important dividends in a consistent and credible voice that communicates clearly the positions policies of the U.S. government to the publics throughout the globe.

CHAPTER FOUR

International Organizations

Introduction

At the conclusion of World War II, and in the years immediately following, the United States played a key role in creating, financially supporting, and otherwise enhancing the capabilities of the United Nations, specialized U.N. agencies, and regional organizations concerned with security matters. While the Cold War prevented these organizations from functioning as originally envisaged, they did at times serve U.S. interests by providing vehicles to ameliorate the plight of refugees, dismantle colonial empires, improve prospects for economic development among emerging nation-states, and manage some international conflicts that were not caught up in the U.S.-Soviet competition.

At the end of the Cold War, there was a burst of enthusiasm about the potential for international organizations. The major powers seemed to share a common vision about world problems, and it seemed that international organizations could provide the institutional framework for arriving at a consensus on what to do about each problem. The U.N. seemed to provide the best venue for addressing the principal post-Cold War security problem, that is, in-ternal ethnic and religious conflicts, separatist movements, and the so-called "failed state" syndrome. And it seemed that no one state could, on its own, resolve the many post-Cold War security issues that are transnational in nature—for example, narcoterrorism, refugees and mass immigration, and the criminal diversion of weapons of mass destruction (WMD) or WMD material.

But these hopes were soon tempered by the realization that international organizations, especially the United Nations, was unable to carry out fully the new responsibilities with their old structures and approaches. Furthermore, the United States, as well as some other major powers, were reluctant to provide international institutions with the resources and the clout needed to implement the mandates being assigned them. And differences among the major powers widened, making consensus more difficult. In the United States, the U.N. began to appear less attractive as a vehicle for addressing security concerns, while alliances, coalitions, and unilateral measures appeared more attractive.

In the wake of these developments, international organizations and agencies find themselves overburdened and in need of

U.N. System Staff and Headquarters, Early 1990s

Organization	Headquarters	Country	Staff
United Nations	New York	United States	13,900
U.N. Development Program	New York	United States	6,600
Food and Agriculture Organization	Rome	Italy	6,400
World Health Organization	Geneva	Switzerland	5,400
UNICEF	New York	United States	3,800
International Labor Organization	Geneva	Switzerland	3,100
U.N. Educational, Scientific and Cultural Organization	Paris	France	2,800
U.N. High Commission for Refugees	New York	United States	2,100
United Nations Industrial Development Organization	Vienna	Austria	1,800
International Atomic Energy Agency	Vienna	Austria	1,800
International Civil Aviation Organization	Montreal	Canada	1,100
International Telecommunication Union	Geneva	Switzerland	900
Other			2,000
Subtotal			51,700
IMF	Washington	United States	2,000
World Bank Group	Washington	United States	6,200

SOURCE: Erskine Childers and Brian Urquhart, *Renewing the United Nations System*, and INSS estimate.

revitalization. Many of these institutions overlap in terms of their field operations, since they cover similar problem areas. At present, Washington concentrates much of its efforts on the following:

● U.N. organs charged with conflict management (particularly the Office of the Secretary-General, the Secretariat, and the Security Council).

● U.N. specialized agencies that address transnational policy questions of direct concern to the United States.

● Regional groupings that have the capacity to support the United Nations in its conflict-resolution role.

● Private voluntary organizations (PVOs) that provide effective emergency assistance to populations facing humanitarian crises, such as natural disasters, civil conflicts, and other forms of upheaval.

● International financial institutions that have the potential to ameliorate the economic-development problems of less-developed countries. (These are discussed in the chapter on economics.)

Instruments

The United Nations

During the Cold War, the United Nations had only a limited capacity to contain or manage conflicts. Between 1945 and 1988, only two out of every five U.N. attempts to mediate disputes could be deemed successful. Of the international disputes during 1945–1988 in which there was some military engagement, the United Nations helped resolve only 25 percent of those referred to it for intervention. Nevertheless, the U.N. was an important forum in which to resolve Third World disputes not directly involving the U.S. and USSR, as well as to prepare the way for arms-control treaties, such as the Treaty on the Non-Proliferation of Nuclear Weapons (NPT).

With the end of the Cold War, the United Nations became the principal international institution through which a series of international problems were addressed. The result was several less than successful operations that have earned the U.N. much criticism in the United States. Unsatisfactory performances in Bosnia, Somalia, and Rwanda have called into question the organization's ability to serve as an effective vehicle for conflict-resolution and multilateral burden-sharing. (U.N. military deficiencies are discussed in the chapter on humanitarian and peace operations; questions dealing with organization and management are addressed in this chapter.) There are three problems. First, the anticipated unity of view among the Security Council's five permanent members (the United States, Russia, China, France, and the United Kingdom) was not sustained. Secondly, the U.N. leadership, specialized U.N. agencies, and major regional organizations have not proven adept in adjusting to the transnational challenges confronting the international community. Thirdly, several major members have not been willing to provide the requisite resources.

Among the reasons for the shortcomings in U.N. operations has been the United States's own uncertainty about its role in the post-Cold War world and its unwillingness to pay the unexpectedly high costs associated with U.N. operations. Congressional members expressed these feelings in mid-1995, with various bills reflecting a desire to shed many international burdens and to define U.S. concerns abroad in terms of narrow—predominantly economic—self-interest. For example, H.R. 2126 would require the president to consult with appropriate congressional authorities at least fifteen days before committing U.S. forces to any new peacekeeping, peace enforcement, humanitarian, or international disaster-relief mission. This requirement could be waived in emergency situations, in which case the President would be required to consult Congress within forty-eight hours after deployment began.

Another factor weakening the U.N. is a fear that it may grow too strong and could tread on the national sovereignty of its members. Within the United Nations, the majority of members—including the United States—are ambivalent about the U.N.'s post-Cold War interventions in civil conflicts. Not only are such interventions in apparent violation of the principle of national sovereignty, but the U.N.'s accomplishments have not always merited the resources committed. Worries exist in some quarters that enhancing U.N. capabilities in peacekeeping, human rights, and humanitarian assistance would create a slippery slope that could lead to an erosion of national sovereignty and the passing of decision-making authority to the Secretary-General and the secretariat.

A third factor is the fear that a strong U.N. would demand of its members greatly increased contributions of money and manpower, resources that are notoriously difficult for the U.N. to secure. Indeed, in August 1995, the Secretary-General announced that the organization was "bankrupt." Cash resources could not meet either current operating needs or existing obligations. As of the end of September 1995, member states owed two billion dollars in assessments not paid. The U.S.—the largest debtor—owed the U.N. $400 million under the regular operating budget, and $800 million under the peacekeeping budget. While acknowledging that the U.S. share of the annual operating budget and special assessments for unanticipated contingencies represents an excessive burden, President Bill Clinton has been unable to secure agreement for a reduction downward with offsetting increases by other member states. Excluding contributions in kind (such as the costs of U.S. forces borne by the U.S.), annual costs for U.N. peace operations were approximately $3.5 billion in the mid-1990s, an order of magnitude larger than the early 1980s. U.S. costs, including contributions to the U.N. and supplemental costs for U.S. forces working with these operations (but not costs the U.S. forces would incur anyway, such as salaries), averaged $3.5 billion during 1993–1995.

In short, there is a lack of consensus within the U.S. government—and elsewhere—about the U.N.'s future roles and responsibilities. Some suggest the U.N. should be equipped to undertake an effective and intrusive role. This would include creating a standing force of brigade size for rapid intervention in crisis situations, pre-stocking military equipment in various geographic areas, developing common peace operations training programs, and altering traditional peacekeeping rules of engagement to permit forceful interventions in conflict situations.

Contributing to the external forces weakening the United Nations has been serious internal management problems. In 1992, despite stubborn resistance to reform in some U.N. circles, the Secretary-General, supported by the General Assembly, reorganized the U.N. political and emergency management apparatus into three new departments. The Department of Political Affairs was formed to lend some coherence to a wide variety of long-standing small political units. The Department of Humanitarian Affairs was created, partly with staff from a dissolved badly run agency, to coordinate the functions of the U.N.'s large and largely

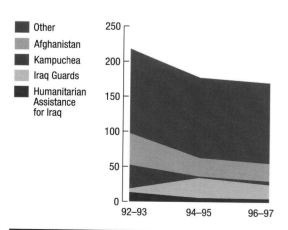

U.N. Department of Humanitarian Affairs Budget
($ millions)

Other
Afghanistan
Kampuchea
Iraq Guards
Humanitarian Assistance for Iraq

Source: U.N.

U.N. Assessments, 1995
($ millions)

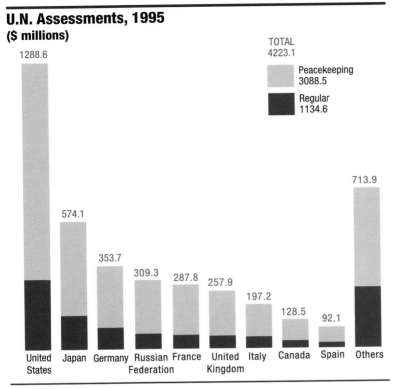

TOTAL
4223.1

■ Peacekeeping
3088.5

■ Regular
1134.6

SOURCE: U.N.

Arrears to the UN, June 1995
($ millions)

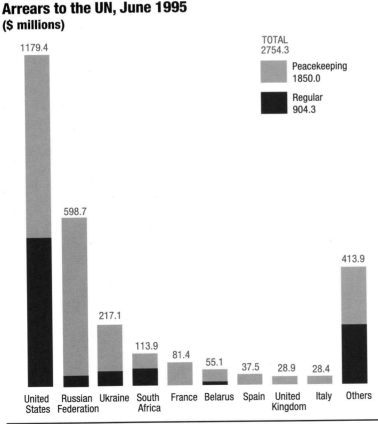

TOTAL
2754.3

■ Peacekeeping
1850.0

■ Regular
904.3

SOURCE: U.N.

independent humanitarian agencies. It did not perform well in 1993–94. The Department of Peacekeeping Operations (DPKO) came from greatly expanding what had been a small office in the Secretary-General's staff. As of mid-1995, DPKO's 420 staff members (including 118 military personnel), headed by an under secretary-general, included the military advisor (a major general), the 27-person situation center (which includes the 24-hour Duty Room and the U.N.'s only intelligence unit), the operations office, and the planning and support office. Under the DPKO, communications with forces in the field and crisis C^3, which were almost non-existent in 1990, have been dramatically improved.

A significant reform issue yet to be fully addressed is the role of the Secretary-General, who has gone from chief administrative officer to being also chief peacekeeping officer, international mediator, adviser to the Security Council, chief fundraiser and public-relations officer. These added duties have raised concern in some quarters about vesting too much authority in the Secretary-General. Furthermore, some in the United States are concerned that the Secretary-General at times takes action at variance with U.S. interests. For example, in 1993, the Secretary-General wished to have all Somali factions fully disarmed prior to the handoff of field operations in Somalia to the United Nations. Washington refused. On the other hand, the phased U.S.–U.N. intervention in Haiti in 1994–95 was a model of mutual accommodation.

Lastly, the United States is seeking to end excessive financial dependence on a single member state, to wit, the U.S. An equitable distribution of the burden among members in a position to pay would enhance the organization's capacity to meet crises. However, the organization's deteriorating financial position is in part a reflection of the low priority that member states accord the organization, and not just a dispute about burden-sharing. In 1995, the U.S. Congress mandated that the United States limit its payments for peacekeeping to 25 percent of the total cost, compared to the 31.7 percent required by the U.N. formula.

The U.N. Specialized Agencies

During the Cold War, the specialized agencies performed the useful role of codifying U.S. policy initiatives in several areas, notably arms control, respect for human rights, and the handling of refugee issues. Important agencies—such as the International Atomic Energy Agency (IAEA)—were established, and guidelines mandated by the General Assembly governing war crimes, genocide, and the rights of the individual became accepted standards. The role of the International Court of Justice was enhanced. During this period, the U.N. also became an effective forum in which to discuss and evaluate plans to end European colonial dominion in the Middle East, Africa, and Asia.

However, some of the agencies, such as the U.N. Educational, Scientific, and Cultural Organization, suffered from incompetent leadership, bloated budgets, and recourse to anti-Western propaganda and publications. The U.S. has had limited success in encouraging reorganization and structural reform, including consolidation of specialized agency operations, that is, elimination of some agencies and relocation of others.

As of the mid-1990s, several specialized agencies within the U.N. system have become important vehicles for advancing U.S. interests. Three stand out: the IAEA, the United Nations High Commissioner for Refugees (UNHCR), and the International Court of Justice (ICJ).

International Atomic Energy Agency. Washington views the IAEA, established in 1957, as one of the most important international organizations. Nonproliferation is a high priority of the U.S. national security agenda, and Washington is dedicated to enhancing IAEA capabilities to monitor and, when necessary, confront problem states, such as Iraq, North Korea, Iran, and Libya.

Within the terms of its mandate, IAEA has two basic responsibilities. First, in the words of its statute, is to ensure "so far as it is able" that nuclear programs under its purview are not used to further any military purpose. Under the terms of the 1970 NPT, all member states not possessing nuclear weapons are required to conclude a comprehensive safeguard agreement with the IAEA. Secondly, Article II of the IAEA's statues states that "the Agency shall seek to accelerate and enlarge the contribution of atomic energy for peace, health, and prosperity throughout the world." In an effort to extend the benefits of peaceful nuclear technology, the IAEA maintains substantial technical cooperation programs in such areas as nuclear power, nuclear medicine, and nuclear safety. This role of the IAEA at times appears to be in conflict with its NPT responsibilities.

After the 1991 Gulf war, the IAEA discovered for the first time a violation of a safeguard agreement. As a result of knowledge gained from its long-term monitoring activities in Iraq, the agency has significantly bolstered its safeguards system. This new approach also played a major role in detecting violations of the NPT safeguards agreement by North Korea in 1994–95. With the support of the U.S. and a few other key members, the IAEA was able to identify the nature of North Korean violations and to report them to the U.N. Security Council, validating the existence of significant undeclared nuclear activities in the country. Through continued persistence, the IAEA successfully negotiated access to key facilities and began to implement effective control and accounting of the irradiated nuclear fuel. The U.S. was thereby afforded an opportunity to launch bilateral diplomatic efforts with North Korea to defuse the looming crisis.

U.N. Peacekeeping Operations and Good Office Missions, 1974–1994

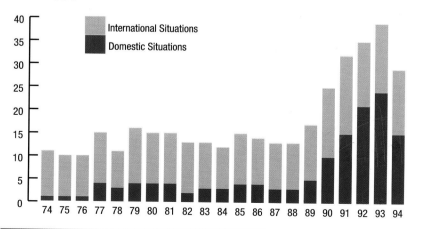

SOURCE: Barry Blechman, "The Intervention Dilemma," *The Washington Quarterly*, Summer 1995.

The U.S. has promoted efforts to strengthen IAEA safeguards and monitoring capabilities, particularly in safeguards inspections and materials control and accounting. As a result, in March 1995, the IAEA's Board of Governors adopted Program 93+2 which provides for, among other things, more intrusive inspections by the IAEA. As a result of the indefinite extension of the NPT in April 1995, reliance upon the the IAEA and its safeguards program as a deterrent to nuclear proliferation will increase.

A limitation on the use of the IAEA as a instrument of U.S. power is that, as an international organization, the IAEA represents the interests of all its member states, while meeting its obligation to implement international safeguards. Anytime the U.S. turns to the IAEA for help on an issue, it runs the risk of finding itself with an IAEA decision which it did not anticipate and may be contrary to its policy goals. For example, in 1995, Iraqi leaders lobbied the U.N. heavily for the lifting of sanctions against them, claiming they had met all the conditions placed upon them. The U.S. believed strongly that Iraq was still withholding information regarding its weapons programs and has been adamantly opposed to lifting the sanctions. The outcome depended in part on the continued vigilance of the IAEA inspectors of the Iraqi facilities. Had the Agency prematurely given

Iraq a "no discrepancies noted" report, it could have put its finding at odds with the stated U.S. policy of preserving the sanctions. The possibility of just such a dilemma has prompted the U.S. government to cooperate very closely with the IAEA and to share information and expertise as appropriate.

United Nations High Commissioner for Refugees. Prior to 1989, the U.S. government strongly supported UNHCR efforts to ameliorate the plight of refugees, for example, those who fled conflicts in Sudan, Cambodia, Ethiopia, Mozambique, and Angola. With the passage of time, however, the U.S. became concerned about inadequacies of UNHCR rapid-response capabilities, the capabilities of its field-operations personnel, and the high administrative costs of its operations. In addition, disputes arose over the legal status of refugees versus displaced persons; the U.S. has taken the position that the UNHCR definition of what constitutes "refugee" status has been unduly restrictive.

Despite these concerns, the role of UNHCR has grown in the post-Cold War world. A spate of intrastate conflicts has resulted in massive numbers of displaced peoples and threats to the stability in neighboring countries. In Bosnia, Rwanda, and northern Iraq, the UNHCR has played a major role in helping the victims of internal conflict. The issues surrounding massive flows of immigrants, refugees, and displaced person are of mounting concern within the United States and other Western states.

UNHCR data suggest an increasing demand for assistance to refugees and displaced populations. In the early 1970s, applicants for asylum in West European countries numbered about 1,000 per year; in 1991, there were 545,000 asylum seekers. By 1993, European governments, overwhelmed by the rising tide of applicants for asylum, began to introduce restrictive legislation. With respect to worldwide refugee populations, the trend is even more disturbing. In 1951, when UNHCR was founded, there were 1.5 million legally classified refugees worldwide; in 1995, there are some 20 million. In addition, an estimated 24 million people are displaced within their own countries, vic-

7th U.N. inspection team in Iraq, October 1991: destruction of dies for missile components by electric torch.

tims of civil wars, failed governments, and natural disasters. One in approximately 125 humans is uprooted as of the mid-1990s, with fresh waves of refugees and displaced persons expected during the remainder of this decade.

Restricting Iraqi Weaponry

At the end of the Gulf War, the United States, in conjunction with its coalition allies and members of the U.N. Security Council, passed several resolutions giving international organizations—the U.N. and the IAEA—responsibility for dismantling Iraq's weapons of mass destruction (WMD) and monitoring compliance with U.N. resolutions. U.N. Resolution 687, passed in April 1991, authorized the Secretary-General to establish a special commission to supervise the inspection and destruction of Iraq's facilities for WMD, including chemical, biological, missile, and nuclear capabilities, in cooperation with the IAEA. Resolution 715, passed six months later, reaffirmed and extended those powers. Terms of the resolutions included:

• Iraq's "unconditional acceptance of the destruction, removal, or rendering harmless, under international supervision" of all chemical and biological weapons, all stocks of agents, related subsystems, and components, and all research, development, support, and manufacturing facilities; and all ballistic missiles with a range greater than 150 kilometers, with related major parts and repair and production facilities.

• The commission's conduct of immediate on-site inspection of Iraq's WMD facilities based on Iraq's declarations and the designation of any additional locations by the commission itself. The Special Commission was also to supervise Iraq's "destruction, removal or rendering harmless" of all items the commission specified.

• Prohibiting Iraq from using, developing, constructing, or acquiring any of the above items and calling on the Secretary-General and the Special Commission to develop a plan for the future monitoring and verification of Iraq's compliance.

• Baghdad's unconditional agreement not to acquire, research, or develop nuclear weapons, subsystems, or components; declaration of all locations, amounts, and types of materials; and placement of all materials under the exclusive control of the IAEA for custody and destruction. Baghdad also had to agree to on-site inspection and monitoring of its future compliance with the resolution.

Other resolutions called for U.N. monitoring of Iraq's oil sales if Baghdad accepted an oil-for-humanitarian-aid offer outlined in subsequent U.N. resolutions. These examples mark one of the few occasions the United States turned to an international organization to implement a major arms-reduction program. Despite the continuing Iraqi foot-dragging, evasion, and occasional open defiance, remarkable progress was made during 1991–95 in detecting and destroying Iraq's weapons of mass destruction programs. The U.N. Special Commission (UNSCOM) charged with this task, led by Rolf Ekeus of Sweden, found numerous installations and weapons systems that had not been known to the West or had not been damaged during the war. For instance, UNSCOM destroyed 36 Iraqi mobile SCUD missile launchers, while U.S. air strikes during Desert Storm destroyed no such launchers despite 2,000 sorties (and despite intelligence assessments during the war that indicated that many launchers had been put out of commission).

Still, much remained to be done in late 1995 to establish with confidence that Iraq was in full compliance with Resolutions 687 and 715, much less the other U.N. Security Council resolutions. The U.S. has been careful to offer evidence and orchestrate opposition when other Security Council members have tried to ease sanctions on Iraq by suggesting, contrary to fact, that Baghdad was in compliance.

The International Court of Justice. While the ICJ was created by the U.N. Charter in 1945 as the principal judicial organ of the U.N., it is essentially a continuation of the Permanent Court of International Justice established after World War I. It is composed of fifteen judges, elected every nine years, with one-third of the judges coming up for re-election every three years.

Both during the Cold War and afterwards, the ICJ has been fairly effective in resolving maritime problems but not other issues. At the core of the debate over the effectiveness of the ICJ as a useful instrument lie two issues: jurisdiction and enforceability of judgments.

Jurisdiction is the authority by which the ICJ can hear cases, and it consists of two types: advisory jurisdiction and contentious jurisdiction. Only U.N. organs and specialized agencies may invoke the advisory jurisdiction, and advisory opinions are nonbinding. Of more interest is contentious jurisdiction. As its name implies, contentious jurisdiction is used to settle disputes, but only between those states that have accepted the ICJ's jurisdiction. Of the approximately 160 states eligible to accept the ICJ's contentious jurisdiction, fewer than one-third have done so.

When the ICJ agreed to exercise jurisdiction in a case filed by Nicaragua against the United States in 1984 in response to U.S. support of the Contras, the U.S. withdrew from jurisdiction of the ICJ in 1986. Withdrawal of the United States from the ICJ jurisdiction places the latter largely outside of the sphere of instruments available to the U.S.

Even in situations where a judgment is obtained from the ICJ, enforceability of those judgments remains problematic. Although the U.N. Charter requires any state that is a party to a case before the ICJ to comply with the court's judgment, no action has ever been taken by the Security Council to enforce compliance. Indeed, the veto power of the permanent Security Council members virtually eliminates any possibility of enforcing a judgment against their core interests.

The future utility of the ICJ as an instrument of national power is uncertain. States are still unwilling to accept binding third-party dispute resolution, particularly

General Shalikashvili with representatives to the 1995 Inter-American Defense College Summit.

where their national security interests are at state. However, in an era of increasing economic competition, the ICJ can still be useful in resolving the inevitable disputes that arise, but only when the parties themselves desire such third-party resolution.

While the International Court of Justice does not have any criminal jurisdiction, the U.N. Security Council, acting under its emergency powers to resolve conflicts, recently established two special War Tribunals to punish individual perpetrators of atrocities in the former Yugoslavia and in Rwanda. These tribunals do not abolish the jurisdiction of the local courts to punish such crimes under their national laws, but they are given primary jurisdiction over the offenses listed as international crimes by the Security Council. With respect to Rwanda, the Security Council establishes the precedent that certain offenses, previously only recognized as international crimes when committed during an international conflict, may also be treated as such when committed during a purely internal conflict. These recent atrocities also provided renewed impetus for completion by the International Law Commission of a draft treaty for a permanent international criminal court. Many international jurists believe that such a court would be preferable to a succession of ad hoc tribunals, because it would be applying uniformly laws which were well defined in advance of the trials.

Regional Organizations

A whole array of multilateral organizations include members of one region or type. Some of these define an area of interest that excludes the U.S., such as the Arab League or the Organization of African Unity. Some are concerned with a specific set of issues, such as the Organization for Economic Cooperation and Development (OECD), the organization of twenty-five industrial democracies, including the United States, Japan, and Western Europe. From a security perspective, the three principal regional organizations to which the U.S. belongs are those that group the states of the North Atlantic, Asia Pacific, and the Western Hemisphere.

North Atlantic. During the Cold War, the Conference on Security and Cooperation in Europe (CSCE) was part of the efforts to achieve political détente that evolved from the 1975 Helsinki Final Act. Its membership included the U.S. and Canada, as well as essentially all European states (some smaller states joined only in the 1990s). Some hoped the CSCE would produce a European peace treaty; others saw it as a means to promote Western values and engage in a substantive dialogue on security and human rights. Indeed, the leaders of the Soviet Union had committed themselves to the democratic ideals expressed in the Helsinki Final Act, which proved important to the development of the dissident movement in the USSR and Eastern Europe. CSCE provided the framework for the negotiation and implementation of arms-control agreements, such as the Stockholm Document of 1986, the two Vienna documents on confidence- and security-building measures (CSBMs), and the 1990 Conventional Armed Forces in Europe (CFE) Treaty. At the same time, the CSCE was only a process; it had no organizational structure, no institutions, and no permanent base of operations. Instead, the CSCE functioned on the basis of periodic follow-up meetings—which were designed to take place every three to four years to review adherence to the obligations included in the 1975 Helsinki Final Act—and, when appropriate, to reach new agreements.

The CSCE process played an important role in the fall of communism in Europe in 1989–1991 by providing a standard by which to judge governmental performance in the human-rights and political areas. With this revolution came the evolution of the CSCE. The watershed event in this evolution was the November 1990 summit meeting, at which the thirty-six CSCE states signed the "Charter of Paris for a New Europe." The CSCE was seen as a unique body, which could build a sense of community and cooperation based on democratic principles among all the states of Europe while preserving ties with the U.S. and Canada. Three new institutions were created: the Prague-based Secretariat; the Warsaw-based Office for Free Elections (subsequently expanded and renamed the Office for Democratic Institutions and Human Rights [ODIHR]); and the Vienna-based Conflict Prevention Center (CPC). The CSCE also established a system of accelerated political consultation, including biannual meetings of government heads and annual ministerial meetings.

In 1993, realizing that Europe faced potential instability in several locations, the CSCE attempted to move into the field of operations for early warning, conflict prevention, and crisis management (including fact-finding and rapporteur missions and CSCE peacekeeping), for conflict within participating states as well as between states. Reports submitted include ones on the Kosovo region and Tadjikistan. An outgrowth of the fact-finding mission to Kosovo was the establishment of what is known as a mission of long duration. This small group of CSCE diplomats is engaged in an unusual exercise of what could be called emergency preventive diplomacy. A large portion of its efforts is to convince minorities that they have certain legal rights that can be exercised even in the face of what they perceive to be outright discrimination.

Reflecting the growth of a permanent staff, the CSCE was redesignated in 1994 the Organization for Security and Cooperation in Europe (OSCE). Though limited in power, the OSCE remains important as the only pan-European body. U.S. membership in OSCE is a concrete expression of European acceptance of the U.S. security role in that continent. The size and cumbersome nature of its decision-making process probably ensure that OSCE will remain only a framework for political consultation and consensus-building. However, in 1995, the OSCE sponsored a high-level planning group to begin a peacekeeping mission to the Nagorno-Karabakh region of Azerbaijan; it also tried to mediate in the Chechnya

conflict and established a monitoring presence in Bosnia. Efforts to go much beyond fact-finding and monitoring missions into large-scale peacekeeping operations would be risky; a major failure in this field might, unfortunately, hurt the OSCE's potential for fulfilling its vital political role.

Asia Pacific. Prior to 1990–91, the nature of the regional-security environment in the Asia Pacific region was such that it favored neither the birth nor the growth of international organizations. For the preceding decade, the nations of Southeast Asia had been focused primarily on the internal, domestic aspects of national security. The Association of Southeast Asian Nations (ASEAN), which was the major international organization in the Asia Pacific region, reflected this. The regional military presence of the United States, mandated by its rivalry with the former Soviet Union, provided guarantees of external security. The U.S. military presence remained a major factor in maintaining regional stability.

After 1991, however, conditions changed. Years of impressive economic growth in Southeast Asia helped to reduce destabilizing internal pressures. Prosperity also prompted the discovery of new interests and the means to pursue them more effectively. At the same time, there was also a growing suspicion that the end of the Cold War would mark the decline of the U.S. military presence. In the Northeast Asia subregion, domestic factors again had less force. But, because the powers of the subregion share concerns about the future military presence of the United States, they too are receptive to the idea of organizing to better achieve their economic and security interests. Since 1980, however, no less than eight new multilateral organizations or agreements have emerged. Of the eight, two—the Asia Pacific Economic Cooperation (APEC) accord and the ASEAN Regional Forum (ARF)—qualify as international organizations in the true sense of the term.

The success of APEC shows that the region (with the possible exception of China) has embraced multilateralism as an effective means of managing issues related to economics and trade. Concerned as it is with security matters, the ARF is progressing

A U.S. M–113A2 on lease to the U.N. rolls out of a USAF C–141 at Entebbe Airport in 1994 for use in Rwanda.

more slowly. However, an extremely successful forum in August 1995 indicates that the concept of multilateralism is finding increasing favor as an approach to security issues as well. In the future, the force of economic and security imperatives will increase. As a result, it is likely that the scope and scale of international organizations within the region will also increase.

If the impulse toward multilateralism results in a larger number of stronger international organizations, the regional-security environment would be transformed, thus raising two major considerations for Washington's position and leadership. Many economic and security decisions that have traditionally been made on a bilateral basis will have to be made in a far more complex, multilateral setting. Certainly the influence of the Asian pole of the trans-Pacific relationship will grow as the regional powers perfect the mechanisms of coordination and control. It is also important to remember that the starting point for any new emphasis on international organizations is, in part, a desire to hedge against a perceived decline in U.S. power and will. Whether this perception is encouraged or disarmed will depend upon the approach that is adopted during the initial stages.

Western Hemisphere. The principal U.S. objective in this hemisphere has been to have a peaceful southern flank, one in which political stability and economic growth could be managed on equitable terms. Historically, the notion of a U.S. special relationship with Latin America has been greeted with reserve by governments in the south. The record of U.S. interventions in local affairs, economic domination, and cultural arrogance is difficult to overcome. Influenced by close proximity to overwhelming U.S. power and Washington's Cold War propensity to use it in the hemisphere, the history and traditions of the inter-American system place emphasis on national sovereignty, self-determination and regional solutions to security problems instead of submitting to decisions of others, such as the great power veto system of the Security Council.

Defending Latin American security interests has given rise to several institutions and arrangements known as the Inter-American Defense System. The system's authority, the Inter-American Defense Board, has been headed by a U.S. general. The board has languished, but it remains a mechanism through which the Rio Pact members could cooperate militarily if they were so inclined.

The Organization of American States (OAS) is the oldest regional security organization. Tension between the United States and the other members of the OAS has been a dominant theme of OAS politics, arising from a perception that the United States has attempted to use the organization as a Cold War instrument or a cover for unilateral action, for example, in the 1965 Dominican Republic intervention.

Regional solutions at the height of U.S. unilateralist foreign policy in the Americas during the 1980s tended to bypass the OAS as an ineffective political body. Latin American governments often coalesced into ad hoc focus groups, such as the Central American Esquipulas Group and the Rio Group, to resolve specific transnational problems. When states found it beneficial to introduce an "honest broker" to facilitate peace negotiations, as in the Salvadoran and Guatemalan civil wars, they turned to the United Nations.

Whether in reaction to a growing awareness of mutual and heavy economic interdependence, or to the growing con-

OAS and U.N. Multilateralism in the Haitian Case

The OAS and U.N. cooperated imprecisely over Haiti, in a way that underscores the differences in their respective interests and competencies. Although the Security Council met on September 30, 1991, the day that President Jean-Bestrand Aristide was overthrown, it did not formally convene because a majority of the members felt the coup was entirely a domestic matter. The OAS Permanent Council, however, was obligated to meet by its recently adopted Resolution 1080, which called for automatically convening in the event of an interruption of legitimately elected government in any member state. The council met swiftly on September 30, condemned the coup, and convened an immediate Meeting of Consultation of Foreign Ministers, which met twice in eight days and, in effect, shaped the international response to the crisis. A subsequent meeting of the U.N. Security Council followed the OAS lead in condemning the coup but adopted no formal resolution because China would not concur. In Washington, the OAS dispatched a special mission, led by the Secretary-General, with a mandate to press for restoration of the democratically elected government. When that mission failed, the foreign ministers reconvened, froze all assets of the Haitian state held in any OAS member country, and imposed a trade embargo, which it tightened in May 1992.

Soon, it became apparent that the year-long nonbinding OAS sanctions were being ignored by non-Western Hemisphere countries and even some Latin American countries. Increasingly concerned about the political consequences of a growing exodus of Haitian refugees, the U.S. government in November 1992 sought the involvement of the United Nations. The resultant joint OAS/U.N. mediation effort, led by a former Argentine foreign minister, introduced a large mission of civilian human-rights observers but failed to mediate a political agreement. In June 1993, Haiti was placed on the agenda of the U.N. Security Council by France and three OAS states—Venezuela, Canada, and the United States. The council, acting under Chapter VII of the U.N. Charter, imposed a worldwide mandatory oil and weapons embargo on Haiti, as well as a freeze on the state's assets abroad.

After another year with a failed agreement to lift the economic penalties and return President Aristide, followed by reimposed and intensified U.N. sanctions, including the deployment of American naval vessels to enforce the U.N. near-total trade embargo, the Security Council in July 1994 authorized states to form a multinational force and use all necessary means to facilitate the departure from Haiti of the military leadership. This step led, two months later, to the peaceful arrival of U.S. combat forces in Haiti and the subsequent presence of a U.N. peacekeeping force known as UNMIH—the U.N. Mission in Haiti.

Some observations can be drawn from the experience of the Haitian case. First, the basis for OAS and U.N. action is different but compatible. The OAS responded to Resolution 1080, which calls for member states to defend democracy. That was not grounds for U.N. action. The Security Council justified its decisions on the argument that the Haitian situation was a threat to international peace. However, that was the first time that an internal political crisis having to do with democratic governance provoked such drastic measures on the part of the U.N.

Secondly, there is no legal basis within the OAS to escalate from diplomatic and economic sanctions to military action in order to reverse a coup, nor for armed peacekeeping to assist in the restoration of democracy. Latin American officials are also reluctant on domestic political grounds, and have concerns about who would control the use of force in an asymmetrical hemispheric context. For the foreseeable future, the OAS needs to work closely with the United Nations, which has the mandate and the expertise to engage in peace operations.

Lastly, it is important to recognize that the OAS has been successful in the defense of democracy. Its prompt condemnation and the diplomatic (and possibly economic) isolation this portended worked effectively in more recent Peruvian and Guatemalan crises.

sensus in the region on constitutional democracy as the desirable political model, or both, the Organization of American States has reemerged as a positive and increasingly proactive hemispheric player. In 1991, a key milestone was reached with the adoption by the 21st General Assembly of Resolution 1080, which created an automatic procedure for convening the region's foreign ministers in the event of an interruption of legitimately elected government "to look into events collectively and adopt any decisions deemed appropriate." For the first time in the organization's history, a domestic political event was declared to be grounds for collective action. The resolution provided the legal basis for OAS action in response to a military coup in Haiti less than four months later.

A larger role for the OAS in peace operations is dependent on mutual understanding between the United States and its hemispheric neighbors. The post-Cold War era offers an opportunity to reach such an understanding, especially in light of the spread of democratic government, regional economic integration, and strong OAS support for democracy. In the 1990s, there has been an increase in hemispheric interaction and cooperation in such diverse areas as control of population movements, counterinsurgency, narcoterrorism, disaster relief, extradition of criminals, and cooperation among military establishments.

Private Voluntary Organizations

Humanitarian organizations doing work in the developing world are known as nongovernmental organizations (NGOs) or, especially in the United States, as private voluntary organizations (PVOs). Most major international and American PVOs came into being during the period around World War II: the International Rescue Committee (1933), the Catholic Relief Services (1942), Oxfam/UK (1942), World Relief (1950), Church World Service (1946), and World Vision (1950). However, recent years have seen considerable growth in the number of PVOs that respond in any given international crisis, e.g. 200 PVOs were active in Bosnia in late 1995.

In 1994, PVOs in the Western democracies spent nearly $9 billion on relief and sustainable development programs in the developing world, half of this being attributable to American PVOs alone. The profile of PVOs has grown as they have attempted to influence foreign policy decisions affecting complex emergencies. As the number and extent of complex emergencies have increased, so too have the PVO efforts. Through their advocacy efforts, the PVOs influence the decision makers who direct American foreign policy and by educating the public and engaging its active support through financial contributions to relief efforts. Further, the increasing activity of PVOs in international crises, combined with the greater role of the U.S. military in peace and humanitarian operations, means that PVO activities have become vital components of operations in which the U.S. military is involved. To understand the change in the interaction between PVOs and the U.S. military, a useful contrast is between the Vietnam war, where the interaction was small (and at times unfriendly), and the Bosnia operation unfolding in late 1995, where PVOs are central to the success of the mission.

PVOs' operational work in complex emergencies focuses on the five saving interventions that make up the relief discipline: food distribution, shelter, water, sanitation and medical care. To these disciplines may be added in-depth grassroots organizational skills at the community level, which PVO's use as much in relief efforts as in their longer-term sustainable development work. PVOs know the history, politics, and culture of the society, the religious beliefs, tribal or clan structure, and, most important, they deal on a daily basis with the local and national elites and authority structures that lead the social order.

Because of their sense of geographic place in the villages and cities where they serve, PVO field staff frequently become advocates of the people with whom they work, to such a degree that they lose their objectivity or they see only very localized conditions, which may not be representative of more general societal trends. They sometimes fail to understand the larger political, social, or economic forces at work in the country. Sometimes, their ideological prejudices distort their understanding of what is really happening in a society.

The PVOs are both unlike and similar. Their organizational structures, their philosophical approaches to relief and development and public policy, their sectorial specialization, and their historical roots cover such a wide spectrum that they cannot be easily characterized. Those PVOs that work exclusively on public-policy issues but have no permanent operational presence in the field are known as advocacy groups. These tend to have modest budgets and staffs, and no programs or projects, focusing instead on researching such issues as human-rights abuses, refugee-protection issues, or hunger. Most of the larger PVOs do both relief and development work; a few, such as the International Rescue Committee and International Medical Corps, work only in relief efforts. Some specialize by sector (agriculture, health, or

USAID Development Assistance Funds Channeled Through PVOs
(billions of 1995 $)

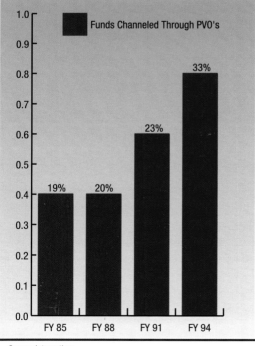

SOURCE: Interaction

education), while others have regional specialization (such as Africare, which works only in Africa).

Many PVOs do not accept or have never applied for grant funding from U.S. foreign-assistance agencies. For some, that is a function of religious principles or their long-standing opposition to American foreign policy; for others, it is a wish simply to be unhindered by the rigorous public-sector procedural and program-design requirements of government grants. Still others, including many smaller PVOs, do not have the expertise to negotiate through the thicket of rules and regulations imposed by these grants. Federal law requires that in order to be eligible to receive grant funding, a PVO must raise at least 20 percent of its aggregate funding from private sources.

Despite the differences among them, PVOs in general have a style of work and an organizational ethos that is markedly different from that of the U.S. military, e.g., less hierarchy among staff, more emphasis on consensus than on command, and more concern about involving locals in decisions. The differences between PVOs and the U.S. military is a challenge to working together smoothly. Yet both parties increasingly need to cooperate to accomplish their separate missions—the PVOs need the military's infrastructure support and the protection from hostiles, and the military needs the PVOs ability to get local civilian institutions functioning again.

Most PVOs, both American and international, help in several ways to implement the foreign policy of the United States, sometimes unintentionally:

● By providing humanitarian assistance to people most vulnerable to starvation and disease in a country governed by a rogue regime in which economic sanctions have been imposed, PVOs avoid the adverse human consequences of sanctions, which might render them politically unacceptable to public and congressional opinion in the U.S.

● By improving basic human services in a country following a civil war through their rehabilitation and reconstruction programs, PVOs help to create public support for whatever regime is in power. If stability of the regime is a foreign policy interest of

the U.S., then PVOs serve that interest. Likewise, PVO human-service programs ensure services are not interrupted in a nation with an authoritarian past while it is democratizing, a process that can at times be chaotic.

● By ensuring a safety net of human services, PVOs can mitigate the consequences of economic reform and structural adjustment in developing countries and thus increase their chance of success. Most economic reform involves the elimination of budget deficits through reduction of the public payroll, human-service programs, and subsidized food prices measures that can create political unrest and destabilize governments that impose the reforms.

● By acting as mediating institutions, faith-based PVOs working through the churches, and secular PVOs working through other grassroots organizations, can act in conflicts as neutral, intermediary institutions between opposing sides and promote pluralism in nondemocratic or newly democratic societies.

Conclusions

International organizations have the potential to serve as useful instruments in pursuit of U.S. foreign policy objectives. They establish conduct to which all states can be held, thereby providing a framework for intrusive, coercive enforcement on rogues. They provide ready-made fora in which common purposes and goals can be hammered out. They are important fora for undertaking conflict-resolution initiatives, as well as for sanctioning multilateral U.S. military operations that might be contemplated, such as economic sanctions. When recourse to military instruments is needed, they provide a foundation for burden-sharing. Furthermore, they provide the venue for organizing international cooperation in response to growing transnational problems, such as terrorism, uncontrolled migrations of large populations, weapons proliferation, and narcotics. They serve as neutral or impartial bodies that reinforce U.S. efforts in such critical areas as proliferation of weapons of mass destruction. In addition, there are practical matters on which cooperation is needed, such as air-traffic security, telecommunications, and postal standards.

On the other hand, international organizations have certain intrinsic drawbacks:

● They often have their own bureaucratic agendas which may or may not be consistent with U.S. interests.

● They have limited rapid-response capabilities as crises materialize.

● With some notable exceptions, their bureaucracies are encrusted with procedures that inhibit innovation or rapid adaptation to changing circumstances.

● Consensus-building on major policy initiatives contemplated by the United States is slow to evolve and decisions taken tend to represent ambiguity arising out of compromises.

The United States can play a major role in efforts to improve the performance of many of these international and regional organizations by establishing clear U.S. policy objectives and concentrating its effort on those agencies and institutions deemed essential to the attainment of those objectives. In particular, the United States will be more effective if it finds ways to accommodate itself to the eccentricities of regional organizations that are prepared to engage in sustained conflict-resolution initiatives.

Key elements within the U.S. government have yet to reach agreement on the relevance and importance of international organizations in the attainment of U.S. security-policy objectives. While there is agreement that priority should be accorded agencies that address issues such as proliferation of weapons of mass destruction, humanitarian needs, and, to a lesser extent, peace operations, the U.S. government has not provided a broad perspective on the roles and relationship of international organizations to vital U.S. security interests.

CHAPTER FIVE

Economics

Introduction

In recent years, economic issues have risen in priority among U.S. foreign policy interests, reflecting two major developments: a relative decline in security concerns, resulting from the end of the East-West struggle; and the American public's dissatisfaction with U.S. economic performance. As concern over economic issues has risen, interest has grown in the use of economic instruments to promote U.S. economic and security interests alike.

Economic Interests as an Issue. During the Cold War, national security concerns took precedence over economics. Differences with Japan or Europe over market access were generally settled in the spirit of the greater common endeavor of advancing collective security. By contrast, the predominant attitude in the post-Cold War era, irrespective of administration, holds that U.S. security depends upon a strong economy in two senses: first, a strong foreign policy requires a strong economic base; and secondly, security in its broadest sense includes economic well-being sufficient to provide prosperity for most and assurance of a safety net for all.

Many Americans are more worried about the economic aspects of security than about the military aspects. Since the mid-1970s, the U.S. economy has not delivered the growth in incomes that Americans have come to expect. Many people believe the economy suffers because the United States has not faced a level playing field in international economic competition, and because Washington has not supported U.S. business interests as strongly as other governments have supported their firms.

Public dissatisfaction with the U.S. economy is fed by the fall in the U.S. relative standing since the early post-World War II years. The U.S. share of world economic output dropped from a peak of perhaps 45 percent in 1945 to 25 percent in 1980, creating a sense that the United States has lost its position as the world's unquestioned economic leader and now is but one of several economic power centers. Less well known, and thus less influential in public opinion, is the fact that the U.S. share of world output has remained stable at about 25 percent during the last fifteen years. Indeed, in the years since the end of the Cold War in 1989, the U.S. GNP has grown as fast as those of Japan and the European Union. Besides maintaining its share of world output, the United

States has also increased its lead in the information industries, including the crucial software industry that gives it a commanding position in the technologies central to future economic growth and modern warfare.

Economics as an Instrument. At different times, the U.S. public endorses inconsistent principles for guiding the instruments of international economic policy. Support for the proposition that all benefit from free trade is contradicted by support for the view that economics is the principal field of competition among nations and the United States must therefore take all necessary steps to ensure it comes out on top. The view adopted tends to depend on circumstances. In the late 1980s, when Japan's economy looked to be on a path to surpass that of the United States, some Americans viewed Japan as a threat; after four years (1992–95) of recession there, the U.S. public has adopted a more relaxed attitude toward Japan.

Whatever principles Washington chooses to adopt, its ability to wield economic instruments, on behalf of either economic or security goals, has been subject to contradictory forces. The effectiveness of economic instruments has become more circumscribed than it was in the heyday of U.S. economic power during the early Cold War era, owing to the decline in the relative weight of the United States in the world economy. Also, the sophistication of many nations' economies has grown, so that they can produce a wide range of industrial goods, which undercuts U.S. unilateral restrictions.

On the other hand, the new world order enhances the effectiveness of economic instruments in two ways. First, during the Cold War, the Soviet Union stood ready to step in whenever the U.S. tried to isolate another nation economically. For example, when Washington applied economic pressure against Cuba, Moscow provided the massive subsidies that kept Havana afloat. No country now possesses the combination of hostile interests and economic might to provide that kind of alternative. Secondly, national economies have become more dependent on international trade and world financial markets. Trade in goods and services across national borders in 1970 amounted to about 15 percent of world output; by 1995, this figure had grown to about 25 percent.

Instruments

Trade Policy

During the Cold War, Washington subordinated the use of trade as a policy instrument to military and diplomatic concerns. One example was the granting or withholding to the USSR and East European countries of normal trade terms, misleadingly known as most favored nation (MFN) status. More often than trade privileges, however, the issue was trade sanctions, especially for what were seen as unfair trade practices. Starting in the 1970s, Congress enacted tougher and tougher legislation mandating antidumping duties and countervailing duties for subsidies. Section 301 of the 1974 Trade Act, which authorizes retaliation for unfair trade practices, requires rapid action by the U.S. on claims filed by U.S. firms and facilitates the imposition of stiff penalties—to the dismay of many economists, who see little basis for the law's view of what constitutes unfair trade. Successive administrations did not place as high a priority on unfair trade, as defined by U.S. law, as on foreign policy issues. Time and again in the late 1970s and early 1980s, proposals by the U.S. Trade Representative (USTR) to impose sanctions on Japan over its mounting trade surplus with the United States were overridden by the State Department and the Pentagon out of fear that such measures would imperil Washington's security ties with Tokyo. Trade actions were more frequently imposed when they could advance national security interests.

In addition, the Washington foreign policy establishment downplayed trade policy as an instrument of national power. Despite aggressive trade promotion efforts in 1994–95, the U.S. still trails its economic rivals in export promotion expenditures. In 1994, the U.K. spent on export promotion about $.25 per $1,000 of GDP; France spent

ECONOMICS

U.S. Exports
(billions of 1995 $)

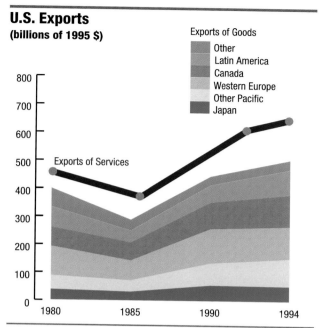

Exports of Goods
- Other
- Latin America
- Canada
- Western Europe
- Other Pacific
- Japan

Exports of Services

SOURCE: International Monetary Fund
NOTE: There are no comprehensive data on the destinations to which services are exported. The exports of services are the gap between the top line and the colored-in area.

$.17; Japan, $.12; and the U.S., $.03. Also, a position at the Commerce Department rarely commanded the same prestige as a comparable one at the State Department, and foreign service officers believed that promotion came more quickly to those who focused on traditional foreign policy concerns than to those who specialized in economics.

Trade policy has gained prominence since the end of the Cold War, owing in part to the growing importance of the international sector for U.S. prosperity. In 1994, the growth in exports provided a third of the growth in GDP, and exports supported 11 million jobs. The Commerce Department estimates that by 2000, exports will support 16 million jobs. And those are good jobs: one study showed that employment in the export sector in 1988–1995 paid 13 percent more than the average wage.

Many members of the Bush administration recognized the importance of this phenomenon and attempted to reshape U.S. policy accordingly—beefing up the Commerce Department's Foreign and Commercial Service to promote U.S. exports, and encouraging the formation of the Asian Pacific Economic Cooperation (APEC) forum to link the U.S. economy more closely with the dynamic economies of Asia. But these attempts were often hamstrung by internal disputes over the proper role of government in such efforts.

The Clinton administration brought an unprecedented focus on international trade policy as an instrument to promote U.S. economic interests. The administration pushed through Congress both the North American Free Trade Agreement (NAFTA) and the Uruguay Round GATT accord, which established the World Trade Organization (WTO). These two agreements were the centerpiece of the administration's strategy for lowering the cost to U.S. consumers of imports while increasing U.S. jobs by expanding markets for U.S. goods.

At the same time, the administration made sweeping changes in the way government works with business to increase U.S. exports. The Trade Promotion Coordinating Committee, which is chaired by the Secretary of Commerce and includes all the U.S. government agencies involved in trade, formulated a National Export Strategy to help American business compete and win overseas. The Commerce Department created an Advocacy Center to track large foreign infrastructure projects and assist U.S. exporters facing logjams; for example, the center helped AT&T win a $4 billion contract to modernize Saudi Arabia's telecommunications system. The Commerce Department has also targeted more than a dozen large, emerging markets—China, Brazil, South Africa, and others—the better to focus government export promotion activities. U.S. government financial assistance to exports—including feasibility studies, export credits, and aid related to exports—has amounted to $19 billion per annum in the mid-1990s. Although in 1995 Congress, led by the Republican majority, considered abolishing the Department of Commerce, it supported continuing the government's trade promotion activities, though the exact organizational structure for doing so remains unclear.

To mesh its economic efforts with traditional policy concerns, the Clinton administration created the National Economic Council (NEC), a White House-based coordinating group equivalent to the National Security Council (NSC). With powerful leaders and many staff members holding joint NEC/NSC positions, the new council has helped broker economic and foreign policy interests. However, balancing trade priorities with other foreign policy concerns has proven difficult. One issue has been whether MFN status—that is, access to the U.S. market on normal terms—should be

China Trade

China's economy has grown at an average annual rate of 10 percent since the end of the Cold War, and its foreign trade has similarly grown by leaps and bounds. This growth has depended in good part on China's access to U.S. markets, which in 1995 absorbed $80 billion in Chinese goods, including about half of all Chinese exports of manufactured goods. The United States benefits from China's exports, as well: inexpensive consumer items from China comprise an important part of mass merchandisers' sales, providing a significant benefit to lower-income Americans. Despite problems in penetrating the Chinese market, which absorbed only $30 billion in U.S. goods in 1994, sales to China offer excellent prospects for growth. U.S. firms have high hopes for substantial investments in China.

Since the brutal crackdown on pro-democracy demonstrations in 1989, there has been pressure, especially in Congress, to withdraw China's MFN trade status, which would render uneconomical a large portion of Chinese imports. Both the Bush and Clinton administrations argued that there was little evidence that the withdrawal of trade privileges would increase Chinese respect for human rights. They also noted that the U.S. and China have discussed certain human rights issues, such as the release of political prisoners. In 1994, in response to entreaties from the U.S. business community, the Clinton administration announced it would henceforth decouple trade and human rights issues in policy making concerning trade with China.

In 1994–95, the United States blocked China's entry into the World Trade Organization (WTO) as a founding member, because Washington insisted on trade-opening measures that Beijing resisted. It is not clear what U.S. pressure will gain in opening the Chinese market and at what geostrategic cost. If a policy secured free access for U.S. goods but convinced Beijing that Washington is a strategic enemy against which China needs thousands of ICBMs, the policy would have served the U.S. poorly.

In 1995, relations with China grew strained over a host of issues, particularly Taiwan. Concern increased in Washington that the United States and China might enter into a strategic competition. Disturbing signs have appeared that China is pursuing an old-fashioned sphere-of-influence policy, including a military buildup to assert Beijing's claims to dominance in the South China Sea and to discourage any move toward independence for Taiwan. It is by no means clear that an assurance of access to U.S. markets would induce China to abandon its saber-rattling and instead compete for influence on the economic field.

made conditional on progress in human rights, most especially for China. An example more closely related to security issues is to what extent U.S.-Japan trade differences can and should be isolated from the bilateral security relationship. In early 1995, as the USTR implemented a get-tough policy with Japan, the Defense Department released its annual report on U.S. security interests in Asia. While the report did little more than restate the U.S. commitment to Asia's defense, Tokyo interpreted the timing of its release and its formulation of the grounds for U.S. troop strength in Asia as signals that U.S. trade concerns remained

separate from, if not necessarily subordinate to, military and diplomatic interests.

The use of regional trade agreements as a policy instrument has a side effect on security interests, because such agreements may implicitly link integration with the U.S. economy to security commitments by Washington. For example, Washington has always demonstrated a profound interest in the political and economic stability of Mexico. By further integrating the U.S. and Mexican economies, NAFTA deepened Washington's sense of responsibility for developments in Mexico, making the Clinton administration's move to bail out the crumbling peso practically inevitable. Similarly, in discussions with Asian nations regarding APEC, Washington has explicitly linked access to the rapidly growing Asian markets with a continued commitment to Asian security. Implicit in this is the suggestion that free trade in the Pacific rim will anchor U.S. interests in Asia and maintain the U.S. security umbrella over the region.

Trade policy will likely serve increasingly as an instrument of U.S. power. However, while at times trade policy can advance foreign-and security-policy interests, trade issues can also complicate those interests. The challenge ahead is to forge a workable balance between these various interests.

One aspect of trade policy has been controls on high-technology exports with potential for military use. Such controls are discussed in the chapter on Arms Control.

Financial and Macroeconomic Policy

Among the economic instruments for affecting foreign governments, by far the bluntest are financial and macroeconomic tools: intervention in exchange rate markets, controls over loans and investment (into or out of the U.S.), interest rate changes, and tax and government expenditure policy. During the Cold War, these instruments were used in part to deny resources to the communist world (e.g., strict limits on loans to the USSR) and in part to push allies (e.g., financial leverage over Great Britain and France to cut short their

ECONOMICS

1956 invasion of Egypt during the Suez Canal nationalization crisis). However, the main Cold War use of financial and macroeconomic instruments was to preserve the unity and promote the joint prosperity of the Western alliance, for instance by running large budget deficits during the 1974–75 oil-price recession to provide an engine for Western economic growth.

Changing Circumstances. In the increasingly interdependent world of the 1990s, any attempt to use financial and macroeconomic instruments to influence a foreign government is fraught with risk. Indeed, many economists are sceptical about the ability of macroeconomic and financial policies to achieve economic goals, much less foreign policy aims. Four reasons may be mentioned.

● Purely national economies no longer exist, if they ever did. Policymakers are constrained by globalization, which has changed financial markets, at least, into truly international markets. Thus, raising short-term interest rates, imposing capital controls, and coordinating monetary policy with other countries prove less effective than they once did because of greater capital mobility and the ability of traders to circumvent national economic regulations.

● International capital flows have become vastly larger than government resources available to defend currencies. This has greatly weakened the ability to use what was once among the most powerful of international financial instruments, namely, the exchange rate. Whereas during the sterling crises of the 1960s the British government could mobilize reserves equal to several weeks (or, in some cases, several months) worth of trading on international currency markets, the volumes those markets now

handle daily exceed the reserves of all countries combined. In 1994, the world's foreign exchange markets handled an estimated one trillion dollars each business day. In the face of such volume, coordinated actions by the G7 countries can be only symbolic, a signal of the intent to change monetary policy.

● Since the late 1970s, the trend has been toward the idea that governments should create a predictable environment within which economic decisions can be made, without getting involved in finetuning the economy, which had been popular during the heyday of Keynesian economics in the 1960s and early 1970s. Governments are less willing to use tax and expenditure policies, which were once seen as central instruments to affect both domestic and world economies. Declining confidence in the government's ability to manage productive assets has only reinforced this trend. In many countries, privatization has replaced nationalization as the trend of the day.

● The size of the U.S. budget and trade deficits places tight constraints on international economic policy. The Federal Reserve has to retain interest rates high enough to finance these deficits, which limits its ability to stimulate the economy with lower rates as some domestic critics would want. In its interest rate policy, the Federal Reserve also has to be concerned about the exchange rate of the dollar for foreign currencies (the lower the interest rates in the U.S., the more attractive to take money abroad, which reduces the value of the U.S. dollar). Besides its effects on capital flows, the exchange rate also affects trade: the lower the value of the dollar is relative to other currencies, the cheaper are U.S. exports and the more expensive to U.S. consumers are imports. When the value of the dollar drops, that can exacerbate tensions with Japan (which worries that its products will no longer be competitive) and with Europe (which worries that capital flows will disrupt the EU's Exchange-Rate Mechanism).

Consequences of Change. That macroeconomic policy coordination among the G7 nations is difficult, and speculators can circumvent exchange-rate agreements, does not mean that cooperation among the advanced

Foreign Assets Held by U.S. Banks
(in billions of 1995 $)

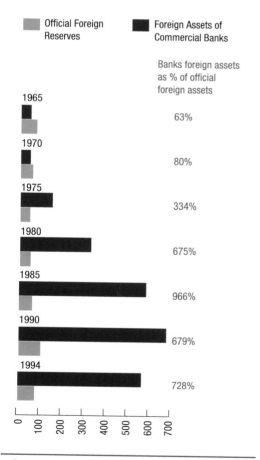

Official Foreign Reserves

Foreign Assets of Commercial Banks

Banks foreign assets as % of official foreign assets

Year	%
1965	63%
1970	80%
1975	334%
1980	675%
1985	966%
1990	679%
1994	728%

SOURCE: International Monetary Fund

**World leaders at the 1995
G7 Summit, Halifax, Canada.**

industrial countries will be abandoned. Macroeconomic coordination, even if only as meetings to air concerns, offers a means to promote openness and reduce the potential that countries will retreat into economic blocs. Such economic blocs might be less inclined to pursue common interests and more inclined to practice beggar-thy-neighbor policies, such as competitive devaluations, that undermine global economic prosperity and drive interstate tension. The formation of closed economic blocs centered around great powers could pose a substantial threat not only to global prosperity but ultimately to world peace.

It is significant that macroeconomics, not national security, led the heads of the Western powers to start meeting annually. While the G7 meetings were initially limited to finance, they evolved into a general consultation on foreign policy issues, such as how to respond to developments in the former Eastern bloc and to challenges from rogue states. In effect, the G7 summits became a way to draw non-NATO Japan—and perhaps one day Russia—into a common security dialogue.

Foreign Aid

During the Cold War, foreign aid was often used to counter potential Soviet influence by supporting governments friendly to the United States, enticing nonaligned governments towards a pro-Western stance,

and ameliorating social conditions that could feed radical anti-Western movements. Some funds went to countries in which the U.S. maintained bases (principally the Philippines, Portugal, Greece, and Turkey), and other funds assisted countries facing communist insurgencies (such as El Salvador). In the 1990s, as the Soviet system has lost its appeal to developing countries and the Soviet threat disappeared, foreign aid has become an instrument to influence governments on a host of issues from labor rights to environmental pollution.

Since the end of the Cold War, there has been strong public pressure to cut spending on foreign aid, even though the aid budget has been shrinking in real terms for twenty years. In inflation-adjusted dollars, aid peaked in the early 1960s, at about twice the 1995 level. As a share of GNP, aid in 1995 was less than one-fourth its level of thirty years earlier.

One of the principal limitations on the effectiveness of foreign aid as a policy instrument is that the goals set for it are overly ambitious, which dissipates what could be more powerful influence if it were more narrowly focused. The legislation that guides the disbursement of foreign aid, the Foreign Assistance Act, is burdened with thirty-three objectives and seventy-five priority areas, which impedes USAID from rewarding governments that shift policy in directions desired by the U.S. Furthermore, Congress earmarks much of the aid, that is, directs how much is to be spent in each country. While earmarking lets the elected representatives rather than career officials decide how to spend the taxpayers' money, it leaves little flexibility for USAID to direct aid to good development and foreign-policy partners and away from poor performers.

Foreign Policy Aid and Economic Development Aid. Foreign aid has many components, which can be grouped for analytical purposes into two categories. First is the foreign policy aid, consisting primarily of military aid and cash payments to foreign governments (more or less equal to the budget category called Economic Support Funds, ESF). Second is development aid, which consists of food aid (PL 480), disaster relief, projects like roads and schools

U.S. Foreign Aid
(Billions FY 1996 dollars)

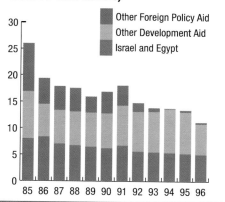

Other Foreign Policy Aid
Other Development Aid
Israel and Egypt

U.S Foreign Policy Aid
(Billions FY 1996 dollars)

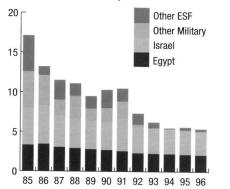

Other ESF
Other Military
Israel
Egypt

NOTE: For other mililtary aid, debt repayments exceeded new aid for countries other than Israel and Egypt after FY 93, so what is shown is zero aid. Data excluded aid classified by INSS as development aid.

U.S. Development Aid
(Billions FY 1996 dollars)

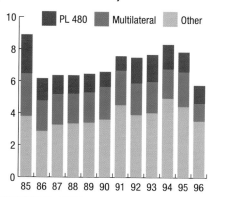

PL 480   Multilateral   Other

NOTE: Data exclude aid classified by INSS as foreign policy aid, e.g., all aid to Israel and Egypt.

SOURCE: USAID
NOTE: Aid is net of some, but not all repayments. Classification of aid data refers to budget authority.1996 Budget is request.

built by USAID, U.S. contributions to international aid institutions, and a variety of smaller programs, such as the Peace Corps. While USAID is the principal foreign aid agency, it is responsible for administering only about one-third of the U.S. foreign assistance funds, and the allocation of its funds is decided in an inter-agency process in which general foreign policy interests weigh heavily.

Since the end of the Cold War, Israel and Egypt have gotten most of the foreign policy aid. Between them, they receive $5 billion a year (including $3.1 billion in military aid), a level set by the 1978 Camp David peace accord between the two countries. (Inflation has cut the value of this assistance by a third since then.) The governments of Egypt and Israel see the aid as part of a U.S. commitment to their respective security, an absolute precondition for the peace between Cairo and Jerusalem. The aid has also helped cement close cooperation on a wide range of issues, including facilities and logistical assistance for the U.S. military.

In 1995, for all countries other than Israel and Egypt, less than $100 million was allocated for military aid grants, while $365 million was allocated for ESF. Foreign policy aid has been particularly hard hit by the decline in aid since the mid-1980s. At FY 1996 prices, foreign policy aid averaged $4.5 billion in 1986–88, $3.5 billion the three years after that (1989–1991), and then fell steeply to an average of less than $.5 billion in 1993–95.

In contrast to the decline in foreign policy aid, economic development has not been as hard hit. Economic development aid—which includes contributions to multilateral organizations, food aid, and direct U.S. aid programs—was relatively stable from 1986 thru 1994, at constant 1996 prices. The annual average for those nine years was $7.3 billion (at 1996 prices), and most years saw a slight growth compared to the year earlier. However in 1996, economic development aid was substantially below the average for the previous decade..

In other words, the reduction in the total aid budget in the late 1980s and early 1990s came entirely out of the foreign policy aid, while economic development aid stayed relatively constant. In 1986, the foreign policy aid was twice the size of the economic development aid. To be sure, much of the foreign policy aid went to Israel and Egypt; setting that aside, the foreign policy aid was still three-fourths the size of the economic development aid. In 1995, the foreign policy aid was less than the economic development aid; indeed, without aid to Israel and Egypt, the foreign policy aid was 5 percent the size of the economic development aid.

Economic development aid, the traditional focus of interest among aid personnel, is said to serve U.S. interests through job creation programs that reduce the pool of alienated youth who could be attracted to radical anti-Western ideologies; family planning and environmental protection programs that ameliorate pressures on the world's resources; and economic development that diminishes the risk of ethnic strife and the collapse of states (which can create humanitarian disasters so massive that the United States intervenes). Two such interventions—Somalia and Rwanda—cost more than Washington spent on development assistance to all of sub-Saharan Africa between 1992 and 1995.

Development assistance has become a less potent instrument of U.S. influence as the proportion of aid dispensed by Washington has declined relative to that of other donors. In 1970–71, the United States provided 40 percent of the world's official development assistance as defined by international agencies (which exclude military

Official Development Assistance from OECD and OPEC Members
(Billion 1996 dollars)

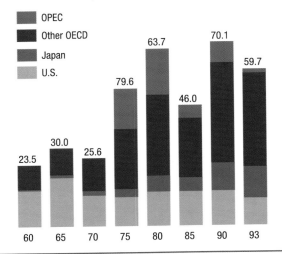

SOURCE: OECD. Data are net flows, that is, after repayment of loans. OPEC 1975 estimated. The reduction in other OECD aid in 1985 reflects primarily the low value of other currencies relative to the dollar.

Military Aid by the U.S.
(Billion FY 1996 dollars)

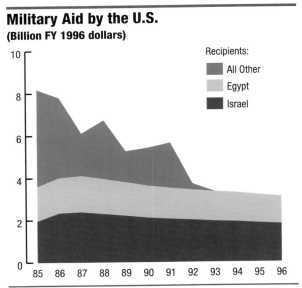

SOURCE: USAID

NOTE: Aid is net of some, but not all, debt repayments. Debt repayments exceeded new aid for countries other than Israel and Egypt after FY 93, so what is shown is zero aid. Data refer to budget authority.

aid from their data). In 1993, the U.S. supplied 16 percent. Not only had Japan become by 1993 the world's largest donor in absolute terms, but Japanese aid to Latin America—an area of traditional U.S. interest—exceeded U.S. aid in that region.

Overall, foreign aid's importance as a source of development financing is shrinking in a world with more open economies and better information about opportunities in developing nations. Countries with sound policies attract private foreign capital that dwarfs available foreign aid. In 1994, private capital flows to developing nations totaled $173 billion—about three times the level of official aid.

Organizational Issues. Debate arose in 1995 about the best organizational structure through which to deliver foreign aid. USAID has been actively cutting its costs. In 1995, USAID closed twenty-one overseas missions and reduced its staff by 1,200 personnel (about 30 percent), partly in response to the criticism that, per dollar of aid distributed, it maintained ten times as many employees abroad as did its British counterpart. Proposals have been made to consolidate USAID with the State Department, which might cut costs but could also reduce the visibility of aid and subordinate development to other foreign policy objectives. Other proposals suggest increasing the responsibility of private voluntary organizations, which already distribute about 30 percent of project funds. However, such plans would not resolve the problem of extensive congressional mandates that establish so many priorities that the impact of aid is diffused, weakening its effectiveness.

In light of the tight resource situation, U.S. policymakers are using innovative means to mobilize funds. Long-established institutions are being tapped for new purposes; witness the use of $20 billion from the Exchange Stabilization Fund to finance the U.S. part of the package to avert a Mexican financial crisis in 1995 (other industrial countries provided $10 billion; the IMF, $8 billion; and commercial banks, $3 billion). Another method of leveraging U.S. money that may be used more in the future is to form international consortia to finance foreign policy initiatives. In 1994–95, the U.S. negotiated an agreement in principle with North Korea for the construction of a nuclear power plant in that country in return for Pyongyang's taking a variety of non-proliferation steps. The cost of that nuclear power plant may be $4 billion to $5 billion, depending upon what associated facilities are also provided and on what restrictions the North Koreans put on the construction process. Little of that money will come from the U.S., which persuaded South Korea and Japan to bear 90 percent of the cost. An international organization, the Korean Peninsula Energy Development Organization (KEDO), was set up to carry out the project. While the U.S. role in resolving this issue and in KEDO might seem disproportionate based on the money the U.S. is contributing, Washington's voice on the matter reflects the U.S.'s nuclear umbrella over Japan and South Korea and its 37,000 troops in South Korea.

In addition to administering foreign aid directly, Washington provides about $2 billion a year for international aid agencies. Most of this money represents the U.S. share in international financial institutions (IFIs), such as the World Bank, the Inter-American Development Bank, and the

Aid to the Former Soviet Union

When the former Soviet Union (FSU) began its transformation from communist economics to the market system in the early 1990s, Western nations responded by promising extensive foreign aid. Their aim was to reinforce those in the FSU who supported democracy and free markets. In 1990–95, however, actual disbursements of aid were modest: $20 billion from all sources, including loans on commercial terms, over six years. Most of the money has come from the IFIs (the IMF, World Bank, and European Bank for Reconstruction and Development), and about half of that money has gone to FSU countries other than Russia.

Aid to the FSU has engendered much debate in the United States. Despite claims in the early 1990s that mobilizing aid for the FSU topped the U.S. political agenda, political support has been minimal. The amount of U.S. aid disbursed to the FSU over four years (1990–93) was less than one-fifth the $51 billion Washington mobilized (from its own resources and from international institutions) for Mexico in the year of its peso crisis.

Western aid has not played the prominent role in either economics or politics that both Western and FSU observers expected in 1990, in part because the need for aid was not as great as had been projected. The concern about widespread starvation in 1992–93 was misplaced, and FSU economies have proven more capable of meeting their citizens' needs than originally forecast. Furthermore, aid programs required the usual long lead times to establish, despite promises of quicker disbursement.

Instead of aid, economic performance in the FSU has depended on domestic factors. Those countries like Estonia with sound economic policies have attracted foreign capital while inducing their own citizens to keep their money at home. Compared to flows of private capital, aid has been small or even insignificant. For example, Russia has experienced $50 billion in capital outflow since the dissolution of the Soviet Union, as Russians have sought to invest abroad rather than at home, thereby exceeding inflows of aid several times over.

Western aid may have encouraged the move toward normal market economies by providing technical assistance and financing pilot projects. On the other hand, unfulfilled promises for massive aid have created unrealistic expectations that, when disappointed, fed antipathy toward and disillusionment with the West. Overall, little conclusive evidence exists that general economic support to the FSU (as distinct from security aid, like the Nunn-Lugar program for safeguarding and dismantling nuclear weapons) has advanced Western interests.

Asian Development Bank. The United States is the largest shareholder, or among the largest, in every IFI.

While Washington alone cannot determine policy in any IFI, it has a strong voice in all of them, which it uses to advocate economic policies that advance U.S. policy interests. For instance, when the collapse of the Mexican peso in late 1994 led to worries about social unrest in that country and about a contagion effect (frightened foreign investors withdrawing funds from otherwise healthy economies) on many smaller developing and ex-communist countries, the IMF stepped in with $18 billion, allowing the U.S. to share the burden of rescuing the Mexican government. In the former Soviet Union, the World Bank and the IMF distributed about $10 billion in loans in 1991–95, dwarfing U.S. aid efforts. Worldwide, the IFIs lend about $60 billion a year, with the World Bank group lending about $40 billion a year, the regional development banks about $10 billion, and the IMF another $10 billion (although IMF lending fluctuates sharply, rising when recession threatens and falling when business booms). That makes these institutions the largest sources of official funds to the developing world. However, most of these funds are provided at market interest rates, while most bilateral aid, including nearly all USAID projects, are grants.

In many countries that borrow from them, the IMF and World Bank have encountered strong criticism for infringing on national sovereignty, for imposing harsh burdens on the poor, and for insisting on doctrinaire conservative free-market policies. The two institutions have acquired a negative reputation among nationalists, especially in Africa and the former Soviet

Union. The IMF and World Bank response is that they are asked in when times have turned tough, so it is hardly surprising that they must prescribe bitter medicine, and that only such medicine will cure the patient. The U.S. government is of two minds about the strong measures that the IMF in particular prefers. On the one hand, necessary as it may be for the medium term, shock adjustment may cause social instability that undermines a friendly government. On the other hand, to the extent that the government concerned needs to be pressured into taking reform steps it resists, then it is in Washington's interests to have the bad news brought by the IMF rather than by U.S. representatives.

One indicator of the usefulness of the IFIs in the post-Cold War period is the pressure to set up additional such institutions. The European Bank for Reconstruction and Development (EBRD), established in 1990, has helped consolidate the transition from communism by financing privatization and private sector firms. The Middle East Bank, formation of which was announced in November 1995, will facilitate roads and other infrastructure (e.g., telephone systems) that might strengthen the Arab-Israeli peace process, for example, by improving conditions of the West Bank and Gaza.

While the IFIs have been important instruments for advancing U.S. economic development goals, such as the promotion of free markets, they have not been as useful for Washington in bringing pressure to bear on regimes unfriendly to the West. Other IFI shareholders have vigorously resisted U.S. efforts to have the IFIs consider non-economic foreign policy concerns when disbursing loans, exhibited in Washington's attempts to block loans to countries that abuse human rights or support terrorism. The United States has, however, often persuaded the IFIs not to lend to rogue states because of their poor economic records. For example, Syria is over $300 million in arrears to the World Bank, and the World Bank is not considering new loans to Iran.

In conclusion, the effectiveness of aid as a tool of U.S. national power has been undermined by a lack of focus, by goals that are too numerous for the resources provided. The political climate in the U.S.

suggests that funding for aid will be cut and restrictions on its use will be increased. More use will be made of alternative techniques to mobilize funds for foreign policy initiatives, such as relying on international financial institutions or specially formed international consortia, as in the case of the power plant for North Korea.

Sanctions

The term "economic sanctions" can refer broadly to the curtailment of any customary trade or financial relation, or narrowly to measures against states that have violated obligations under international agreements. This chapter discusses broad bans on trade or finance. The chapter on arms control considers denial of military and dual-use technology, while the chapter on limited military intervention discusses the enforcement of sanctions with military measures, such as a naval blockade.

The modern interest in sanctions focuses on them as an alternative to war. While the U.N. Charter envisaged sanctions as a major instrument of the Security Council, the Cold War prevented agreement among the council's five permanent members in the face of most threats to peace. A trade ban was imposed on Rhodesia in 1965 (after the white residents declared independence from Britain), and more limited bans (particularly on arms) were used in a few other cases. In addition to these international sanctions, the United States imposed its own trade bans on several communist countries, including North Korea, China, Cuba, and Vietnam. In 1986, the U.S. Comprehensive Anti-Apartheid Act banned new investments and trade with South Africa in a number of goods; in 1988, the U.S. forbade financial transactions with the Panamanian regime of Manuel Noriega.

In the post-Cold War era, internationally mandated sanctions have become a more common instrument, in part because the permanent Security Council members can agree more readily on their use. In 1990–95, the United Nations imposed sanctions on Iraq, Libya, the successors to the former Yugoslavia, and Haiti, all but the latter two of which were still in place

Sanctions on Iraq

Within days of Iraq's invasion of Kuwait in August 1990, the U.N. Security Council imposed a comprehensive ban on trade and financial transactions, other than imports of food and humanitarian goods. A vigorous debate ensued about whether sanctions alone would force an Iraqi withdrawal from Kuwait. In retrospect, the sanctions seem unlikely to have had that effect, given that continued sanctions have not even secured Iraq's cooperation with the U.N. arms control regime.

After the war, Security Council Resolution 687 laid down the terms for ending the sanctions. It was expected that Iraq would expeditiously move to fulfill those conditions. But this expectation has not been met. Because each of the five permanent Security Council members holds a veto over any move to lift the sanctions, Iraq must satisfy the United States—not just a majority of the Council—that its actions merit lifting the sanctions. The Security Council reviews the sanctions at regular sixty-day intervals, but some hold that Washington will insist on maintaining sanctions so long as Saddam Hussein is in power.

It is not clear what impact the sanctions have had on Iraqi behavior. Iraq has cooperated with the U.N. arms control mission on many points, but its continuing revelations about what it previously hid from the U.N. raise the suspicion that other mass destruction weapons programs remain concealed. Furthermore, Iraq's cooperation may result from the demonstrated willingness of the United States and its allies to secure compliance through force as much as from the sanctions. And Iraq has made little headway in areas such as accounting for Kuwaiti POWs and respecting the human rights of its Kurdish and Shiite minorities.

The sanctions have hurt the Iraqi people far more than they have hurt the ruling elite. Saddam cynically used the adverse effects of the sanctions on the most vulnerable members of the Iraqi public to generate support for lifting the sanctions, irrespective of Iraqi compliance with Security Council directives. The Security Council made four separate offers to ease sanctions in order to finance humanitarian imports: in August 1991, to permit sale of $1.6 billion in oil; in February 1993, to unfreeze $300–500 million in Iraqi assets abroad; in March 1994, to generate $500 million by flushing the slowly gelling oil out of the pipeline from Iraq to Turkey; and in April 1995, to generate $2 billion from oil sales. Saddam rejected each offer, demonstrating his indifference to the suffering of the Iraqi people.

Leaks in the sanctions have been small compared to Iraq's $15 billion a year in prewar exports. But the leaks, totalling approximately $1 billion a year, have kept Saddam afloat. The largest leak is trade with Jordan, which has the tacit approval of the United Nations and the United States because of the importance of Jordan's participation in the Arab-Israeli peace process.

Given Saddam's behavior through late 1995, it is difficult to imagine him complying fully with the relevant Security Council resolutions, though he may comply sufficiently to lead some Security Council members to call for ending the export ban (some interpretations of the resolutions hold that the ban should be lifted in return for cooperation on arms control alone). Perhaps Saddam will be overthrown, which would most likely lead to a lifting of sanctions. Dissatisfaction with his government appears to be growing within Iraq, as evidenced by the May 1995 revolt of tribes that traditionally supported him and the August 1995 defection of two top aides married to his daughters.

in late 1995. The sanctions on the former Yugoslavia were suspended by Security Council Resolution 1022 in November 1995. They would be reimposed, without action by the U.N. Security Council, if either the Commander of IFOR (the NATO-led force) or the civilian High Representative (chosen by the OSCE) informed the Council that Serb authorities are significantly failing to meet their obligations under the peace accord. Beyond the U.N.-mandated sanctions, the United States in late 1995 had comprehensive sanctions on Cuba and Iran, as well as partial trade bans on the areas of Angola held by UNITA rebels and, despite the early 1995 easing in relations, on North Korea.

Sanctions' record of success depends upon what they are expected to accomplish. They have been least successful at promoting the fall of regimes or the overthrow of dictators, in part because the elites who could engineer a coup are well insulated from the hardship that sanctions create. Sanctions have also had little success in changing governments' fundamental policies—with some obvious exceptions, such as the end of South African apartheid. More likely, sanctions can persuade governments to change policies to which they are not firmly committed, or which are peripheral to their basic interests. For example, the mid-1980s sanctions of certain Japanese firms for selling militarily useful technology to the USSR encouraged the Japanese government to tighten its controls over dual-use exports. Sanctions can also tip the balance when a government is only considering changing its policies, as occurred in 1995 when the

The Mexican Financial Crisis and the Fall of the Dollar

The Mexican financial crisis of early 1995 and the subsequent decline in the value of the dollar illustrate the complexities associated with using economic means for foreign policy ends. U.S. policymakers sought to prevent a crisis from ballooning into a complete collapse of the Mexican economy. Such a collapse would have reverberated throughout the United States, creating problems for overexposed U.S. banks, precipitating increased illegal immigration across the southern U.S. border, and crippling economic reform in Latin America.

President Clinton first requested Congress to act, but when it became clear that the legislative branch would not provide the desired loan guarantees for Mexico in a timely manner, the president cobbled together a package within the constraints of his own power. The United States provided $20 billion from the Exchange Stabilization Fund (ESF), a $25 billion pool of foreign currency reserves to prop up the dollar in a crisis. While the president can utilize this fund without congressional approval, the $20 billion for Mexico constituted the largest amount ever drawn from the ESF to support a foreign currency. Another $18 billion of the package came from the IMF, $10 billion came from industrial country central banks via the Bank for International Settlements, and $3 billion came from commercial banks.

Mexico's crisis originated with its large current-account deficit (the excess of imports over exports). In 1994, this deficit equaled 8 percent of Mexico's GDP. While current-account deficits do not necessarily indicate a weak economy, they create problems when they are large relative to GDP and are financed by speculative investments in equities and short-term deposits, rather than by foreign direct investment. The former are far more subject to market vicissitudes. Thus, an event that shakes the confidence of investors may lead to capital flight, precipitating a crisis.

This seems to be what happened in Mexico. Political unrest in the Mexican state of Chiapas apparently caused capital flight from Mexico. The government responded by permitting what was intended as a one-time 13 percent devaluation of the peso. But the depletion of Mexico's foreign reserves panicked investors (both Mexican and foreign), and the government was forced to float the currency, which then fell from 3.45 to 5.57 pesos to the dollar in less than three weeks.

The U.S.-led relief effort helped avert a debt crisis such as the one that afflicted Latin America in the 1980s. In addition, reforms in Mexico—balancing the budget, reducing inflation, and approving NAFTA—mitigated the worst consequences of the crisis. But the relief effort seems to have contributed to the type of unintended consequences—in this case, a weakening of the dollar—that beset the realm of international finance with increasing frequency.

The dollar began to fall precipitously shortly after the president acted to relieve the pressure on Mexico. The dollar had already begun its slide at the end of 1994, but the Mexican bailout accelerated the trend. While speculators against the dollar were doubtless motivated by many beliefs, they may have concluded that the Federal Reserve would hesitate to raise U.S. interest rates, which would add to Mexico's debt-service burden. Believing that U.S. interest rates had peaked, speculators apparently dumped dollars in favor of the D-mark, believing that German interest rates would surpass U.S. rates.

The Mexican debt crisis and its consequences recall the statement of Nobel laureate Friedrich von Hayek that economics is "the study of the unintended consequences of human action."

hope of securing an easing of sanctions certainly contributed to the reduction in the Serbian government's support for the Bosnian Serbs and its strong pressure on them to agree to the peace accord negotiated in Dayton, Ohio in late 1995.

In addition, sanctions have often weakened a target government's ability to carry out aggressive plans, by depriving it of resources.

According to a widely cited 1990 Institute for International Economics study by

Gary Hufbauer, Jeffrey Schott, and Kimberly Elliott—*Economic Sanctions Reconsidered*—sanctions achieve greater success in modifying the target country's behavior when their goals are relatively modest, the target is much weaker than the countries imposing sanctions, the target and the nations imposing sanctions conduct significant trade, sanctions are imposed quickly without time for adjustment, and the sanctioning countries avoid high costs to themselves. To this list can be added: that the effectiveness of sanctions increases when the nations imposing them can sustain them for as long as necessary and are willing to use military force to enforce them.

While they may influence governments, sanctions inflict collateral damage on vulnerable civilians. This problem is exacerbated when the target government cares little about the well-being of its people, or will even use their suffering to pry concessions from countries imposing the sanctions. Another shortcoming of sanctions is the cost to the U.S. economy. Unilateral U.S. trade bans may shift business to other countries, though the target country will still probably sustain some losses. The issue is whether the economic loss for the United States is a reasonable price to pay for the damage inflicted on the target. For example, the 1995 ban on dealing with Iran forced the U.S. firm Conoco to cancel an oil investment. Iran renegotiated the deal with the French firm Total on less attractive terms, meaning less revenue for Tehran, which may therefore have to postpone arms purchases during lack of cash.

As noted, in the immediate post-Cold War period, cooperation among the permanent members of the U.N. Security Council facilitated passage of sanctions resolutions. In 1994 and 1995, however, disagreements grew among the permanent five over several of the sanctions it had imposed. For example, the U.S. Congress voted to unilaterally lift the restrictions on arms to Bosnia, the Russian Duma voted to lift trade restrictions on Serbia, and the French and Russian governments expressed unease over the conditions they thought Washington tied to lifting export restrictions on Iraq. In light of the growing differences over existing sanctions, it may become more difficult for the Security Council to approve new ones.

Despite their mixed record, sanctions will remain a popular policy instrument. Their benefit-to-cost ratio usually compares favorably to those of other policies, and they are often seen as more appropriate than the alternatives: military action or diplomatic protest. Sanctions can also signal U.S. displeasure, cautioning that Washington may take additional steps. Furthermore, they warn other nations of the price they will pay for future misbehavior.

However, sanctions can also provide an excuse for inaction. They may placate public demands for action when Washington wants to evade responsibility, and thus they may fail to convey a firm message to the target country, which may see the imposition of sanctions as an indication that stronger measures are unlikely. If that is the case, sanctions can weaken U.S. influence.

Conclusion

Economic policy will continue to grow in importance as the world becomes more economically integrated. The greater the growth in international trade and financial flows, the greater the role the U.S. economy will play in international economic developments. Unlike the Cold War world of ideological conflict, in which traditional security concerns dominated policymakers' thinking, governments now emphasize the pursuit of material prosperity.

Nevertheless, the increasing prominence of economic issues does not necessarily translate into a greater ability to use economic instruments of U.S. power. Economic instruments are often blunt in two senses. First, like a blunt instrument, they work only if swung hard, in which case they can inflict so much damage that they can be destructive. For instance, sanctions are most effective when they are universal, applied by all countries and affecting all trade—but in that case, the sanctions inflict considerable suffering on the innocent civilian population. Another example is the use of economic pressure on an ally with which the U.S. maintains a close security relationship, such as Japan. The difficult task is how to achieve the U.S. economic goals without damaging the security relationship.

Economic instruments are blunt also in the sense that they are not sharp, that is, they are not especially effective. Foreign aid has a mixed record at achieving general foreign policy goals; for instance, the assistance to Russia has done little if anything to improve U.S.-Russian political and security relationships. And foreign aid is becoming a less powerful instrument as budget pressures reduce the funds available. As for economic sanctions, despite specific successes, such as South Africa, and Serbia, the general rule remains that governments are unlikely to change their policies in response to sanctions; the best sanctions can usually do is reduce the target government's income, which may hinder its ability to carry out plans that would damage U.S. interests.

The most powerful economic instruments that the U.S. government wields are those that shape the behavior of the private sector. Rather than spending taxpayer resources, Washington can often affect the economies of other nations more efficiently by offering guidance to the private sector about overseas political risks, and by establishing the framework and incentives to promote private trade and investment overseas. The recognition that the private sector is crucial to international economic relations may in part underlie the declining importance of budget-based instruments such as foreign aid and the growing emphasis on trade policy.

CHAPTER SIX

Intelligence

Introduction

The activities of the intelligence community range from providing the President with timely and accurate information (especially during crises) to monitoring its customary array of targets; and from forecasting new problem areas to undertaking covert actions when traditional instruments of policy are deemed unsuitable or have proven ineffective.

Prior to World War II, the United States lacked a significant intelligence capacity, as that term is understood today; such a capacity—both military and civilian—developed during the war. Then, with the advent of the Cold War came the creation of a new, permanent intelligence infrastructure. The National Security Act of 1947 established the Central Intelligence Agency (CIA), headed by the Director of Central Intelligence (DCI), who was given the responsibility of coordinating all the agencies of the national intelligence community. In the mid-1990s, these agencies include the National Security Agency (NSA), the Defense Intelligence Agency (DIA), the individual military service intelligence agencies, the State Department's Bureau of Intelligence and Research, the

counterintelligence unit of the FBI, and the offices—including the National Intelligence Council—that support the DCI, who has direct administrative control over the Community Management Staff and the CIA. In all, some thirteen federal agencies, most embedded in cabinet departments, are part of the intelligence community.

Although the current budget and personnel size of the intelligence community are classified, both budgetary and personnel figures are headed downward. Each agency is smaller in the mid-1990s than it was in the late 1980s, and Congress has mandated further cuts from what the press speculates was a $28 billion 1995 budget, so that levels by the year 2000 will be only about 75 percent of 1985–89 levels.

While the resources devoted to intelligence are shrinking, the objects of interest to the intelligence community and the demands for intelligence by decision makers are becoming more far-ranging and diverse. With the end of the Cold War, the overriding threat of the Soviet Union has been replaced by an increasing array of smaller threats, each requiring attention from the intelligence community. These threats were set forth as follows in the

Clinton administration's 1995 statement, *A National Security Strategy of Engagement and Enlargement:*

Because national security has taken on a much broader definition . . . intelligence must address a much wider range of threats and dangers. [It] will continue to monitor military and technical threats, to guide long-term force development and weapons acquisition, and to directly support military operations. Intelligence will also be critical for directing new efforts against regional conflicts, proliferation of WMD, counterintelligence, terrorism, and narcotics trafficking. In order to adequately forecast dangers to democracy and U.S. economic well-being, the intelligence community must track political, economic, social, and military developments in those parts of the world where U.S. interests are most heavily engaged and where overt collection of information from open sources is inadequate. Finally, to enhance the study and support of worldwide environmental, humanitarian, and disaster relief activities, technical intelligence assets (principally imagery) must be directed to a greater degree towards the collection of data on these subjects.

Thus, the post-Cold War world poses unprecedented challenges for the U.S. intelligence community: it must function effectively, against a broad range of threats, in an environment of unparalleled openness and oversight, but with dwindling resources.

As of late-1995, three major studies of the U.S. intelligence community were underway—the first by the Aspin Commission, headed by former Defense Secretary Harold Brown. This commission was charged with reviewing the efficacy and appropriateness of community activities, including, among other issues, the community's roles and missions in providing support to the defense and foreign policy establishments; whether the community's roles and missions should extend beyond these traditional areas of support; whether the existing organizational and management framework of the community provides the optimal structure for executing the missions; whether existing principles and strategies concerning collection capabilities should be retained; whether intelligence analysis as structured and executed adds sufficient value to information already available to the government to justify its continuation; whether there is significant waste or duplication; and whether counterintelligence policies and practices are adequate to ensure necessary security.

The report of this commission is due in March 1996.

The second review is being conducted by the House Permanent Select Committee on Intelligence, the oversight committee that deals with the broad range of intelligence issues for the House. This report is scheduled for completion in January 1996, two months in advance of the Aspin report.

The third study, organized by The Twentieth Century Fund, is being done by a bipartisan panel of distinguished former State and Defense Department officials, senior intelligence officers, and members of Congress who have joined the private sector. The focus of the commission is an examination of the relevance of the National Security Act of 1947 in light of post-Cold War circumstances; the nature of the threat facing the U.S. intelligence community after the Cold War; the strategic role of intelligence in a time of growing openness; and the question of whether the proposed organizational reforms go far enough to ensure that the nation's intelligence capabilities are going to be effective in the world of the next century. The report of this commission is to be ready by June 1996.

Instruments

Strictly speaking, the analytical side of intelligence is not an instrument of policy but serves as a support for policy. Unlike diplomacy or military force, intelligence analysis does not directly influence the behavior of foreign states or entities. Instead, its practitioners work intimately with the practitioners of persuasion and coercion who are striving to achieve such influence. Strategic intelligence services provide national security decision makers with the following:

■ Early warning of war and other developments that could threaten core U.S. interests, especially when such developments occur in countries restricting the access of U.S. diplomats and journalists.

■ On-going information about foreign countries' compliance with arms control and other international treaties.

■ Support for negotiators.

■ Support for ongoing or anticipated military operations.

National Security Agency, Fort George G. Meade, MD— SIGINT and information security missions.

Collection

The term "collection" embraces the multiple means of gathering intelligence information. Human intelligence (HUMINT), the oldest type of collection, derives from operatives in the field. The Directorate of Operations within the CIA is principally responsible for clandestine HUMINT collection; DIA, the State Department, and the military services also contribute extensively to HUMINT. Signals intelligence (SIGINT) is the collection and processing of foreign communications, noncommunications electromagnetic radiations, and foreign instrumentation signals. SIGINT is the domain of NSA. Photography, infrared sensors, lasers, electro-optics, and synthetic aperture radar produce imagery intelligence (IMINT). CIA and the Department of Defense (DOD) share imagery tasking and exploitation, although the actual launch and maintenance of satellites has been handled by the National Reconnaissance Office (NRO). Lastly, measurement and signature intelligence (MASINT) comprises intelligence obtained by analyzing the distinctive features of a source, emitter, or sender utilizing acoustic, seismic, particle, multispectral, or other data associated with it.

As the Cold War developed, U.S. intelligence became increasingly proficient in the development and deployment of collection systems using advanced technology—SIGINT, IMINT, and MASINT. HUMINT achieved some spectacular successes, but these were offset by the USSR's penetration of a number of Western intelligence agencies and the subsequent compromise of valuable assets. For example, it has recently come to light that most of the Cubans whom the CIA recruited during the Cold War were actually double agents working for Cuban intelligence. Similarly, Aldrich Ames's disclosure of the names of assets providing intelligence to CIA led to the death of a number of individuals at the hands of the Soviets.

Collection and New Technologies. A profound question for the future of U.S. intelligence is the degree to which technology-based collection systems will retain their effectiveness. Several developments cast a long shadow of doubt:

- Independent assessments of emerging situations and problems, including economic and political developments in key countries and regions.

- Access to data about emerging technologies.

- Protection against hostile intelligence services and others seeking classified information about U.S. government activities (counterintelligence).

- The ability to undertake covert action—specifically, to influence foreign leaders, intervene in foreign conflicts, and alter foreign political organizations—without leaving visible evidence of the U.S. government's involvement. (Covert action differs from other intelligence community activities in that it *is* an instrument of policy, designed to fill the void between diplomacy and military force.)

Given the multiple roles of intelligence, its instruments fall into four categories. One—collection—prepares the intelligence community to support policy makers and military commanders. One—analysis and reporting—is the act of providing such support. One—counterintelligence—supports U.S. personnel and agencies by protecting them from the harmful efforts of foreign intelligence agencies and other hostile groups. One—covert action—subsumes any instrument of influence when it is wielded in such a way as to keep secret the role of the U.S. or at least to provide U.S. leaders with plausible deniability.

● Target countries and entities increasingly implement countermeasures as they become more knowledgeable about the capabilities (and limitations) of U.S. intelligence systems. For example, to preclude the collection of intelligence from space, many countries calculate when satellites are over their territories, and at those times curtail or enshroud activities that they wish to hide.

● Advances in telecommunications and information systems, and the growing prevalence of sophisticated commercial encryption technologies, complicate the collection of data from communications and computer networks. The essence of the basic algorithms for encrypting messages beyond what all but the most powerful computers can break can be obtained from the Internet. Using such publicly posted algorithms as "Pretty Good Privacy," even strangers can exchange traffic secure in the knowledge that their transmissions cannot be interpreted without extraordinary effort.

● The sheer cost of upgrading and maintaining space-based collection systems constitutes an obstacle in light of diminishing intelligence budgets. The press speculates that the U.S. is spending billions of dollars to upgrade its intelligence satellites.

Collection and New Targets. A still more telling question for the intelligence community is the degree to which it can adapt to new targets. From the outset of the Cold War until after the break-up of the Soviet Union, intelligence resources and manpower were focused heavily on the Soviet Union and its spheres of influence. Over the course of forty-five years, the intelligence community built an extensive data base on the activities of the Soviet Union's military, economic, civilian and military leadership, and relations with foreign governments. Analysts watched the other Warsaw Pact countries as well, noting, for example, how they performed during military exercises. In the developing regions of Africa, Asia, South America, and the Middle East, Soviet client states received some attention, and the intelligence community also analyzed Soviet influence in nonaligned countries where conditions appeared ripe for an increased Soviet presence and the replacement of regimes committed to neutrality by leaderships actively hostile to the United States.

Other major Cold War intelligence targets included the People's Republic of China, North Korea, and Cuba—both because of their ties to the Soviet Union and because of the threat they posed to U.S. interests in their regions. Areas of instability such as the Middle East, Africa, and Latin America received periodic surges of attention in response to regional conflicts. Lastly, the intelligence community devoted resources to economic and political developments in countries where the United States had considerable interests, including many outside the Soviet bloc for which open sources were inadequate.

The question has arisen whether the sources and methods of collection cultivated during the Cold War can be translated to the collection challenges of the post-Cold War era. For example, the intelligence community developed unequalled expertise in counting and tracking nuclear weapons, but monitoring the dismantlement of such weapons and the disposal of fissionable materials presents some different problems.

Shifts in the realm of political analysis also lie ahead. During the Cold War, intelligence agencies developed a keen sense of how communist systems functioned. In contrast, the challenge for political analysts in the post-Cold War world is to discover what factors may strengthen democratic political forces in post-communist societies.

In the area of economic intelligence, the methods used to develop human sources and elicit information about the economic weaknesses of socialist systems and Cold War adversaries have little relevance to post-Cold War challenges. The acquisition of information about commercial practices and transactions, and the expertise to interpret financial and business data, require different sources and skills. The personnel most knowledgeable about these subjects are also sought by the private sector, against whose salaries government cannot compete. Furthermore, a host of ethical and methodological questions has arisen over the possibility of the intelligence community's sharing its information with U.S. business—aiding them, for example, in their pursuit of a level playing field in in-

Intelligence Community Structure

Department of Defense elements
Independent agency
Departmental intelligence elements (other than DOD)

- Department of State
- Central Intelligence Agency
- Defense Intelligence Agency
- Department of Energy
- National Security Agency
- Department of the Treasury
- DIRECTOR OF CENTRAL INTELLIGENCE (DCI)
- COMMUNITY MANAGEMENT STAFF
- NATIONAL INTELLIGENCE COUNCIL
- Army Intelligence
- Federal Bureau of Investigation
- Navy Intelligence
- National Reconnaissance Office
- Air Force Intelligence
- Central Imagery Office
- Marine Corps Intelligence

SOURCE: CIA

ternational commerce. Former DCI R. James Woolsey said clearly as he was stepping down from his position in early 1995 "We are not in the business of spying for private firms." Thus far, the policy remains unchanged. But the intelligence community sometimes does pass U.S. firms information about illicit activities taken against them by foreign companies and governments. Commerce Secretary Ron Brown stated that in 1994 "the intelligence community detected foreign firms using bribery to undercut U.S. firms' efforts to win international contracts worth $45 billion" and that in almost every case, the U.S. government informed the U.S. firm about the bribery attempt.

Other new targets—such as international terrorism, crime, and drug trafficking—present their own problems. For instance, counterterrorism operations seek to prevent terrorist acts. Yet taking preemptive action usually entails revealing that the U.S. government was in a position to know of a terrorist organization's plans, which in turn jeopardizes intelligence sources and meth-

ods. Intelligence professionals must work closely with law enforcement officials to ensure that these sources and methods are not compromised in the process of providing foreign intelligence to the law enforcement community. The same holds true for counternarcotics operations.

Environmental monitoring is another new target. Vice President Al Gore led an effort to make available hundreds of thousands of reconnaissance satellite images. Some 800,000 declassified images processed by the National Reconnaissance Office between 1960 and 1972, released in February 1995, are available on the Internet. Similarly, both France and Russia are offering satellite imagery for sale to commercial and other customers, a practice likely to spread. Environmental targets are becoming part of the tasking of imagery satellites. But intelligence personnel who interpret such images may find that expertise in identifying the signatures of Soviet military forces does not necessarily translate into a facility for addressing environmental issues.

Some new targets seem to fit a traditional mold yet actually differ drastically. For example, the intelligence community traditionally supported U.S. intervention operations by providing early warning of volatile situations. But this role is greatly complicated to the extent that the issues driving U.S. foreign policy are unclear. As Les Aspin, the late chairman of the Commission on Roles and Capabilities of the U.S. intelligence community, noted, "Using the military to protect our values overseas . . . drives the intelligence community crazy because there is no way to anticipate where values issues might crop up next."

Another example is the use of satellite photos to detect a new kind of suspicious military activity, namely, war crimes, as in Bosnia. Such use creates great pressure to reveal photo data, which the U.S. has traditionally been extremely reluctant to do. Indeed, after revealing evidence of mass graves dug by Bosnian Serb forces, the U.S. was not willing to provide all of its intelligence on the subject to the international tribunal judging war crimes in the former Yugoslavia.

Possible Mass Graves
Kasaba/Konjevic Polje Area, Bosnia

Unclassified

Jul 95

Recently disturbed earth
Vehicle revetment

Unclassified

Overhead photo of possible Serb war crimes site, displayed to the U.N. Security Council.

While adaptation to these circumstances has been reasonably successful, it has not been without problems. Most means of collection—in particular, satellite imaging—were designed to cover the Soviet Union. Within the constraints of physics, satellites have been adapted through new technologies to cover targets for which they were not originally designed. According to John Pike of the Federation of American Scientists, the new satellites can cover a wider area than the old. However, certain targets remain outside their range and must be accessed by alternative collection means, sometimes with the assistance of foreign partners who are unproven allies.

Open-Source Information. The opening up of the former Soviet Union, combined with the information revolution, has provided a wealth of unclassified data that was hitherto unavailable. The explosion in open-source information creates yet another set of conceptual challenges for intelligence analysis.

Some experts estimate that more than 80 percent of the data used by the intelligence community comes from open sources, and CIA and NSA are probably the only U.S. government agencies that have the technical capability to handle the vast quantities of information available. Such volume puts enormous strains on the systems designed to filter the intake and on the analysts who must process what is left.

Another effect of greatly increased open-source information is the decreasing dependence on the intelligence community in some segments of the national security community. CNN is available in most operations centers and other government offices, as is increasingly the Internet, to satisfy multiple information needs. Some intelligence consumers prefer to probe their own sources and private contacts—either academics or foreign counterparts or colleagues whom they trust. One reason is that such information does not necessarily come with the cumbersome restrictions on use that accompany the output of the intelligence community. As a result, the intelligence community will in the future have to compete for customers as it never did when much information about the Soviet Union could be acquired only through sensitive sources, and such competition will require that the community add intelligence value to information it obtains from open sources.

These facts have led some to question the need for maintaining an elaborate and expensive intelligence establishment at all. But aside from the issue of information not available from public sources, major distinctions still exist between information and intelligence. Journalists—the primary purveyors of information—generally describe what they have observed or have been told, often without the time, experience, and expertise to analyze or evaluate the implications of this information. Intelligence, however, constitutes information from a variety of sources that has been analyzed by specialists and tailored to the specific needs of the user. Thus, it will remain true that some key questions of policymakers and military commanders will be answerable only by the intelligence community. And those who take advantage of the community's capabilities will find that no media organization, think tank, or academic research can match the intelligence community for timeliness, responsiveness, and access to otherwise unavailable information—particularly when analysts understand their customers requirements.

Analysis and Reporting

For reasons of economy and security, national intelligence agencies were dispersed during the Cold War. While most remain in and around the Washington area, their geographic separation has made it difficult to develop a closely knit group of experts who could convene easily to deal with intelligence issues. Fortunately, new technology makes virtual meetings using audio-visual technology a reality. This also permits analysts deployed in the field to interact more productively with their Washington counterparts.

The intelligence community's principal analytical organizations are the Directorate for Intelligence within the CIA, most of DIA, and the Bureau of Intelligence and Research in the State Department. These agencies have produced some impressive results, such as the analysis that sustained the Western effort to control exports of sensitive technologies to communist countries during the Cold War. But some post-Cold War concerns—for example, crises requiring the deployment of U.S. forces for brief periods—are short-lived, unlike the enduring concern over the Soviet Union. Even though budgets are declining, the intelligence community is still expected to produce timely and accurate intelligence on these situations, some of them involving countries about which little previous data has been developed.

Outside Expertise. While information data bases can be built up over time and updated if resources allow, it is not cost-effective or even possible to maintain a cadre of specialists with the expertise to cover all possible contingencies. Therefore, the community has occasionally had to find ways to acquire the expertise it needs through non-traditional means. A case in point is the use of Kuwaiti students studying in the U.S. during the build-up to Desert Storm, when the number of capable Arabic linguists in the U.S. military and the intelligence commu-

nity proved insufficient to meet the demand. Similarly, it is occasionally necessary to call upon the academic community for expertise that the intelligence community lacks.

The United States' growing involvement in U.N. operations, and Washington's commitment to provide intelligence to support allied operations other than war, has led not only to greater sharing of intelligence with foreign governments but also to increased reliance on foreign expertise. The result so far is mixed. The United States still contributes the preponderance of intelligence to such operations; some coalition partners have been unwilling to provide their input on other than a bilateral basis with the United States. The storage and protection of intelligence documents have been problematic, as exemplified in the Somali operation by the discovery of classified material in an unguarded U.N. area. Intelligence support for U.S. military forces deployed in U.N. operations poses special problems. Deployments often occur in regions where neither the United Nations nor the United States has a complete picture of conditions on the ground. Such situations increasingly require cooperation with the private sector—private voluntary organizations (PVOs), for example—to gather information about infrastructure, language, customs, culture, and other subjects useful for humanitarian and peace operations. Some PVOs have been traditionally reluctant, if not averse, to cooperating with military forces or intelligence organizations and only recently have warmed somewhat to these interactions.

Changes in Customer Support. Within the intelligence community, major changes have occurred in customer support since the end of the Cold War. However, these changes did not result from the altered strategic environment as much as from the increased integration of intelligence professionals into policy and military staffs and from dramatic changes in technology.

By virtue of the changes in information technology, users of intelligence information, from policymakers to military commanders and their staffs, can retrieve some material directly from community data bases. Rather than waiting for the results of standing or special intelligence

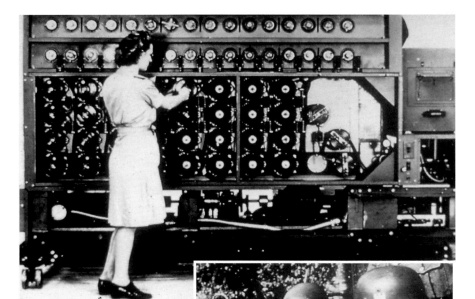

Turing Machine— The successful cryptanalytic effort against the "Enigma" depended on the Turing Machine.

German soldiers in WWII use the "Enigma," an electromechanical cipher machine.

decisions. For example, during the buildup to the Gulf War, one of the earliest and most challenging problems facing the intelligence community was limiting the intelligence sent to Riyadh. Without pre-selection, customers would have been overwhelmed by data and unable to pick useful material out of the mass of information.

But no amount of technological advance will matter if customers are unaware of the availability of intelligence, or choose not to use it. While this is a timeless problem, it has acquired added importance in the information age. In Desert Storm, one U.S. division commander executing the "Hail Mary" to flank Iraqi forces from the west was fully informed of Iraqi military activities throughout the operation, while another, executing a parallel mission, operated without such intelligence. The former had experts who knew how to obtain and use the relevant intelligence, something which the latter apparently lacked. Such situations will prove increasingly detrimental to the performance of coordinated operations in the future. To optimize intelligence, therefore, policymakers and military commanders must have experienced, well-trained intelligence officers and should understand the basics of the intelligence community and how it can serve their needs. Ideally, customers should also hold periodic meetings with the intelligence officers who support them. In such instances, the quality of intelligence support increases immeasurably.

Support to Military Commanders. While each military service has its own intelligence organization, U.S. planners have long recognized the value of independently produced national intelligence. Such intelligence can serve as a check on the work of operational commanders' own intelligence units and add both breadth and detail to the strategic picture. Moreover, though military intelligence personnel may train for a wider range of contingencies, the services concentrate on tactical intelligence unique to their needs. They cannot devote sufficient resources to develop expertise for all possible operations. And when the expertise of their own intelligence agencies falls short, military commanders will look to the broader intelligence community to provide the required expertise.

requirements, customers can acquire tailored intelligence almost as easily as they can access information from the Internet and other unclassified data bases. In addition to established hard copy intelligence publications, the Defense Intelligence Network provides televised reports of intelligence-based news events to senior levels in the Pentagon and the field. Intelink, the intelligence professionals' Internet, provides access to an expanding array of intelligence products and data bases and represents a powerful new tool in their analytical kit.

But just as insufficient intelligence can pose a problem, too much unfiltered information can also impede sound policy and decision making. While technology also addresses this problem, it remains the responsibility of the intelligence community, particularly in a crisis, to deliver only the information needed to make timely, sound

Intelligence Quotations

Those who use technical intelligence almost always do so with preconceptions that they bring to the analytical process. There is rarely disagreement over what a picture shows, for example, but what it means is often the subject of intense debate.

—William E. Burrows, *Deep Black*

No combat commander has ever had as full and complete a view of his adversary as did our field commander. Intelligence support to Operations Desert Shield and Desert Storm was a success story.

—General Colin Powell,
former Chairman, Joint Chiefs of Staff

The reason the enlightened prince and the wise general conquer the enemy whenever they move and their achievements surpass those of ordinary men is foreknowledge.

—Sun Tzu, *The Art of War*

It is not easy to define counterintelligence. Practitioners themselves disagree about the meaning of the concept. At a minimum, however, counterintelligence can be defined as the identification and neutralization of the threat posed by foreign intelligence services, and the manipulation of those services for the manipulator's benefit.

—Roy Godson, *Intelligence Requirements
for the 1980s: Counterintelligence*

In the past, however, some intelligence support to military commanders has been inconsistent in quality, presented in a form or at a time that made it difficult to use, pitched at so general a level that it frustrated commanders making concrete decisions, or provided from too many technical sources to offer a coherent picture. "Good intelligence," DCI John Deutch noted in an address to the 1995 graduating class at the National Defense University, is "particularly important at a time when we have a smaller military that is being asked to take on a wider number of different challenges in remote and unfamiliar areas of the world." But to make a difference, Deutch continued, the national agencies "must be clearly focused on the needs of the warfighter." Thus, intelligence collection and analysis organizations must continue to provide information for military commanders that is more timely, accurate, attuned to the specific needs of operational commanders, and presented in a form tailored to battlefield situations.

According to the DCI, intelligence promotes battlefield awareness by providing "joint force commanders real-time, or near real-time, all-weather, comprehensive, continuous surveillance and information." A newly established Associate Director of Central Intelligence for Military Support is to ensure that, despite their multiple priorities and consumers, intelligence agencies continue to meet the special needs of the military and the circumstances of the battlefield. This requires closer attention to how the intelligence community disseminates its data during wartime conditions and how it receives feedback from its military customers.

Press reports speculate about organizational changes to improve the coordination among analysts of satellite imagery, including use of the same data for intelligence analysis and map making. In 1995, eleven separate agencies did their own imagery analysis, according to press reports unconfirmed by official sources. In October 1995, a reorganization of the imagery activities into one consolidated agency was announced.

Commanders, in turn, must strive to articulate better how national intelligence can serve their tactical needs. For instance, the traditional written intelligence report has been supplemented and complemented by a growing array of multimedia products that often help in the planning and execution of combat operations. Technologically, this intelligence can be transmitted simultaneously to the commander and the individual soldier in the field, which, from the commander's perspective, creates problems for maintaining command and control. That is a new dimension in information the services have yet to understand fully.

As former CIA Deputy Director for Intelligence Douglas MacEachin described in a 1994 working paper to the Washington-based Consortium for the Study of Intelligence, the community must ensure that the needs of the customer are the driving factors in the production of intelligence and that analytic tradecraft emphasizes both the facts and the findings derived from them. Opinions must be linked to "what is known, how it is known, and with what level of reliability"—in short, the rigorous application of principles of analytic tradecraft.

Overseas collection site with covered antennae.

Counterintelligence

Counterintelligence aids national security by protecting U.S. forces and government agencies and their personnel against espionage, sabotage, assassinations, and terrorism conducted on behalf of foreign powers and organizations.

In 1995, despite the end of the Cold War, the United States remains the primary intelligence target for many countries, including some traditional allies who have increased their attempts to acquire economic and corporate secrets. What has changed in the post-Cold War world is the ease with which foreign intelligence services can operate in the United States. The relaxation of security concerns, plus advances in penetration techniques, has made it increasingly difficult for the United States to implement successful counterintelligence measures.

Porous international borders and market-driven decisions create pressure for the national security community to relax limitations on the export of hitherto restricted technologies. A growing number of countries thus have access to advanced technology that previously was difficult to acquire outside of the United States and its allies.

As a result, U.S. systems that protect sensitive information are increasingly vulnerable to exploitation. The steady expansion of computer networks, the growth in corporate and political intelligence stored in networked computers, and the continuing internationalization of the public phone system, private communications networks, and the Internet have created new challenges in protecting information. Software tools to break into and read sensitive information are freely available all over the world. In addition, the challenge of protecting sources and methods, the pressure to downgrade and declassify information, declining security standards, and leaks and espionage have produced vulnerabilities that are increasingly difficult to counteract.

On the other hand, though Aldrich Ames was a Cold War spy, his arrest in 1994 did dramatize for the country the serious problems that can result from lax security and ineffective counterintelligence. This scandal prompted the Clinton administration, at the insistence of Congress, to alter counterintelligence structures and to require the FBI and CIA, with assistance from other intelligence agencies, to work together more closely to define current and future threats and implement countermeasures. As part of this renewed emphasis on counterintelligence, the National Counterintelligence Center, created in 1993 by Presidential Decision Directive 24, maintains an extensive data base on foreign intelligence activity and provides intelligence support to the counterintelligence operations of the FBI and CIA.

Covert Action

Covert action uses intelligence assets and capabilities to influence foreign governments, events, organizations, or persons in support of foreign policy objectives while concealing the actions' sponsor, or at least allowing plausible deniability. Covert actions are the responsibility of the intelligence community, which may draw for support on other government agencies, such as the military's special operations forces.

Covert action became a staple of the four-decade struggle between the communist East and the democratic West. The KGB's covert action typically tried to subvert noncommunist governments and political movements—in Europe, Latin America, Africa, and Asia, as well as the United States. A CIA covert-action capability developed primarily to counter these initiatives, giving U.S. policymakers an effective option in situations where diplomacy or foreign aid were insufficient, but the use of military force or overt political or economic intervention was inappropriate. Such action was a key element in the immediate postwar struggle for political power in southern and western Europe. Over subsequent years, CIA covert operations ranged from small, discrete efforts, such as sneaking banned publications into communist states and bankrolling selected noncommunist politicians, to supporting large-scale conflicts in such theaters as Afghanistan and Angola. In rare instances, most notably in the Iran-Contra affair, the White House assumed control of covert action, effectively taking it out of the hands of the CIA.

As an instrument of policy, covert action has always generated controversy. Its supporters stress the importance of expanding the range of instruments available to policymakers and the utility of an option that does not bear the fingerprints of the U.S. government. Detractors focus on the difficulty—which approaches impossibility as operations grow large—of keeping covert action secret, and the damage to U.S. credibility and interests that can accompany the exposure of these actions. Critics also point out the inherent tension between the world of covert action and the world of democratic government. Secret operations are susceptible to abuse unless carefully overseen. This danger has been highlighted recently by public allegations concerning a CIA connection with a Guatemalan intelligence officer involved in serious human-rights abuses.

President Clinton on the Future of Intelligence, July 14, 1995

Today, because the Cold War is over, some say that we should and can step back from the world and that we don't need intelligence as much as we used to; that we ought to severely cut the intelligence budget. A few have even urged us to scrap the Central Intelligence service. I think these views are profoundly wrong. I believe making deep cuts in intelligence during peacetime is comparable to cancelling your health insurance when you're feeling fine.

Following the Cold War, instead of a single enemy, we face a host of scattered and dangerous challenges . . . There are ethnic and regional tensions that threaten to flare into full-scale war in more than thirty nations. Two dozen countries are trying to get their hands on nuclear, chemical, and biological weapons. As these terrible tools of destruction spread, so too spreads the potential for terrorism and for criminals to acquire them. And drug trafficking, organized crime, and environmental decay threaten the stability of new and emerging democracies, and threaten our well-being here at home.

Earlier this year, I set out in a presidential decision directive what we most want [the intelligence community] to focus on. . . . First, the intelligence needs of our military during an operation. If we have to stand down Iraqi aggression in the Gulf or stand for democracy in Haiti, our military commanders must have prompt, thorough intelligence to fully inform their decisions and maximize the security of our troops.

Second, political, economic, and military intelligence about countries hostile to the United States. We must also compile all source information on major political and economic powers with weapons of mass destruction who are potentially hostile to us.

Third, intelligence about specific transnational threats to our security, such as weapons proliferation, terrorism, drug trafficking, organized crime, illicit trade practices, and environmental issues of great gravity.

Let me say that I know the Ames scandal has colored a lot of the current debate over the future of the CIA. . . . It's important that we don't minimize the damage that Ames did or the changes that need to be made to prevent future scandals. But Aldrich Ames was a terrible exception to a proud tradition of service—a tradition that is reflected in the fifty-nine stars that shine on the CIA's memorial wall in honor of those who gave their lives to serve our country.

The end of the Cold War renewed the debate over whether a significant need for such a capability remains. But the emerging missions for the intelligence community—particularly the interconnected threats of proliferation of weapons of mass destruction, international terrorism, and international organized crime—suggest strongly that the need for covert action persists. The next critical challenge will be to develop a covert capability whose operations can be monitored by overseers in the executive and legislative branches, while still proving effective against the sophisticated networks run by international criminal syndicates, illicit arms merchants, and rogue governments.

Conclusions

An intelligence community is always suspect in an open society, but during the Cold War the U.S. intelligence community established itself as a major element of national security. With the end of the Cold War, that positive perception has begun to fade, and not only because of a traditional aversion to secrecy. There have also been the Ames scandal; questions about the quality, accuracy, timeliness, and relevance of intelligence; concerns over the control of covert activities; a belief that the intelligence community needs to be restrained and streamlined; and a conviction that tax dollars should go to undertakings that more directly serve the U.S. public.

The numerous proposals that have been made to re-examine the structure and functions of the intelligence community in light of the dissolution of the Soviet threat have ranged far and wide, but a common theme is that the community needs to be streamlined, downsized, refocused on new targets, and generally made more efficient. Some argue that the expensive systems required to support intelligence, to say nothing of the organizations that produce it, are costly excesses in the post-Cold War world and that public funds should not be spent to acquire information available in the public domain. The current reviews in the executive and legislative branches as well as the private sector may well reach the same conclusion, although it is not clear the various recommendations coming out of these studies will be acted on in an election year.

If recent crises are predictive of the future, a substantial increase in HUMINT collection will be needed to answer the intelligence questions posed by the crises of today and the future. Among the most important intelligence needs in Bosnia-like conflicts are insights into the intentions of the leaders and their warring factions, for which the human collector is critical. Emplacement of sources and their cultivation take many months if not years, and the U.S. intelligence resources may not be sufficient to meet the demand.

Technology and automation can offset some of the loss of personnel, but trained, analytical expertise remains beyond the capacity of the computer. Community analysts have learned over many years not to be bound by rigid intelligence requirements but to anticipate where resources must be reapplied to meet emerging intelligence needs. Even before the end of the planned downsizing, it is clear that more selectivity will be required, despite the risk that priority will be given to the wrong targets and techniques.

The next decade will be an unsettling time. The U.S. intelligence community will not receive funding sufficient to achieve the levels of expertise it enjoyed during the Cold War, and the principal challenge will thus be to identify the level of effort that will produce the most useful intelligence at the lowest cost. As its funding shrinks, the size of the community will also shrink, and the community will likely be reorganized, resulting in some amalgamation of functions at the national level and perhaps the elimination of others. The argument that today's threats require more, not less, intelligence has not been persuasive thus far.

CHAPTER SEVEN

Productive and Technological Base

Introduction

The productive and technological base of a nation is the foundation of its national power. As Hemocrates noted 2400 years ago, the ability to wage war—as well as to influence events in the world without using military power—depends to a large degree upon a nation's wealth. A strong productive base provides the means and leverage for action and can significantly enhance a nation's prestige and ability to influence the outcome of international events.

The view that the productive and technological base is the foundation of national power was expressed in 1989 by Harvard scholar Paul Kennedy in *The Rise and Fall of the Great Powers*:

[The] historical record suggests that there is a very clear connection in the long run between an individual Great Power's economic rise and fall and its growth and decline as an important military power... Technological and organizational breakthroughs... bring greater advantage to one society than another.

For over forty years, U.S. strategic policy was directed at maintaining a technological edge over the USSR. The Cold War was, to a significant extent, a contest between the superpowers' productive and technological bases. The United States and the Soviet Union devoted large portions of their respective national wealth and productive capacity to wage the Cold War. As the conflict progressed, the productive bases from which these nations' power arose diverged significantly.

Although the rate of increase of U.S. gross domestic product (GDP) slowed considerably after the mid-1960s, all except three of the thirty years between 1965 and 1995 saw real growth in the economy. While it is difficult to secure reliable GDP data for the former Soviet Union, it seems clear in retrospect that the Soviet productive base suffered some long and serious setbacks in the last decades of its existence. The declining Soviet productive base could not support both the demands of the military establishment and the demands of the Soviet people. Perhaps more than any other single factor, this poor economic performance led to the demise of the Soviet Union as a superpower and its subsequent dissolution as a state. Had the GDP of the Soviet Union expanded at a rate of 3 percent annually instead of declining, the superpowers might still be waging the Cold War.

This chapter examines the major forces affecting the U.S. productive and technological base in the mid-1990s, and addresses the question of what role the U.S. government can play in reinforcing important sectors of the productive base and in translating industrial might into an effective instrument of national power. The forces examined are:

● The relationship between manufacturing and services.

● The impact upon national power of increased globalization.

● The rise of information technology as a strategic industry.

● The effects of downsizing on the defense industrial base.

Instruments

Manufacturing and Services

The most basic distinction in the productive base (construction, agriculture, and mining aside) is between manufacturing and services, though the dividing line has become blurred as manufacturers increasingly rely upon services from outside firms.

The shift from a manufacturing to a more service-based economy may be seen in changes in employment. In 1970, 27 percent of the U.S. nonagricultural work force was employed in manufacturing. By 1993, the figure was only 16 percent. During the same period, service-sector employment increased from 67 to 79 percent. Manufacturing employment fell from 19.4 million to 17.8 million workers; and employment in services increased from 47.3 million to 87.2 million workers.

Although this shift is not a new phenomenon—as long ago as 1900, more Americans worked in services than in manufacturing—the magnitude of the shift has given rise to a number of concerns. Most pertinent here, this shift raised doubts as to whether a nation can wage war without a strong manufacturing base. But these doubts may be premature, for

the strength of a nation's manufacturing base cannot be determined solely on the basis of employment trends, and waging war has become less dependent on large numbers of classical military instruments.

In fact, employment data is downright misleading: despite a decline in manufacturing employment, total U.S. manufacturing *production* almost doubled between 1970 and 1993—an increase of over 3 percent annually. The durable-goods sector—of which producers of military hardware are a part—more than doubled its production during the same period. Since 1982, durable-goods production increased more rapidly than total industrial output. Declining employment combined with increased output suggests that improvements in productivity have been proceeding apace.

Productivity, although an increasingly elusive quantity to measure, is the single most telling indicator of the performance of a nation's productive base. And sustained increases in productivity over time are a crucial foundation of national power. Indeed it is the *relative* productivity of a nation's productive base that counts, that is, not simply how productive the U.S. economy is in absolute terms but how well it is doing compared to its competitors. In addition to relative productivity performance, the sheer size of the U.S. productive base provides foundational support for national power. To take an extreme example, a super-productive small economy, such as Luxembourg, could not match the military power of a huge but generally inefficient power, such as Russia.

Between 1965 and 1995, Germany and Japan made significant strides to close the productivity gap with the United States but have not yet caught up. A 1992 McKinsey study comparing U.S. manufacturing and service productivity with that of the United States's international peers found that the U.S. still maintained an edge in overall productivity compared to Britain, Germany, France, and Japan—despite Japan's much-touted dominance in certain high-profile industries, such as metal products, automobiles, and electronic equipment.

The manufacturing sector continues to be the workhorse of productivity improvement for the United States. Regardless of

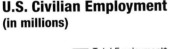

U.S. Civilian Employment
(in millions)

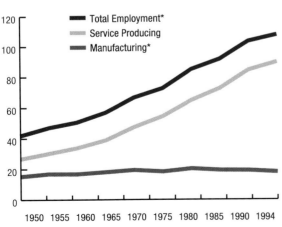

SOURCE: *Economic Report of the President 1995*
* NOTE: Excludes mining and construction

U.S. Workforce in 1993

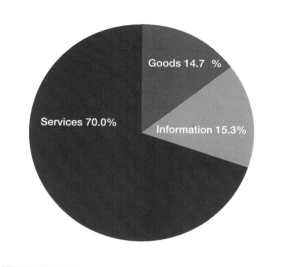

Goods 14.7 %

Information 15.3%

Services 70.0%

SOURCE: *Business Week,* November 7,1994

NOTE: **Goods** include mining, manufacturing, and most utilities. **Services,** include people-oriented jobs such as hotels/restaurants, banking, most health care, government, and elementary education. The **information** sector is narrowly defined to include communications, computers, software, entainment, and higher education.

its apparently poor productivity performance, the service sector too has great potential as an instrument of national power. It includes among other industries transportation and communications, both of which are significant force multipliers in the event of conflict. For example, many of the world's manufacturers have been substituting transportation and communications assets for large inventories, resulting in so-called just-in-time inventory—a process that the military can adopt, and to some degree already has.

In the past, the essential link between the productive base and national power was the ability to increase production runs of weapons. World War II and the Korean War provide prime examples of when the time necessary to close the gap between productive output and military requirements was paid for in blood and territory. However, many analysts suggest that future wars will be of short duration and will therefore be fought with on-hand weapons and munitions, obviating the need for a massive industrial mobilization.

Thus, the more relevant questions may be whether the industrial base can, on an ongoing basis, supply the new technologies and weapons that will ensure an overwhelming advantage for U.S. and allied forces, and whether the military can rapidly incorporate these new technologies into its inventory. The answers are not clear.

When the Department of Defense (DOD) was the major buyer of high technology in the marketplace, it was assured first access to leading-edge technologies. DOD no longer enjoys this position in most high-tech markets: its expenditures for the latest computers, electronics, and telecommunications technology have been surpassed by a rapidly expanding civilian

marketplace. This raises the issue of whether the defense-acquisition system can respond to changing needs and changing technologies fast enough so that front-line warriors have at their disposal the latest and best technology that industry can provide. The present acquisition system may be unable to shorten its delivery lead time (seven to fifteen years, as of 1995) and thus unable to take advantage of high-tech production commercial-development cycles of two to five years. The Clinton administration's Federal Acquisition Streamlining Act (FASA) of 1994 made some significant steps toward simplifying the acquisition system, but, to a large degree, the focus of FASA was on the many small procurements the government makes rather than on the acquisition of major weapon systems, where there are few actions, but each involves much money. The agenda of Vice President Gore's National Performance Review (NPR) also included the objective of streamlining procurement. FASA and NPR have thus far failed to produce significant acceleration of major systems procurement. Those undertaking acquisition reform have to overcome serious political, cultural, and organizational obstacles.

As an example, DOD's continual reliance upon outdated military specifications (milspecs) is seen by some as evidence of the acquisition system's inability to aggressively provide the best and latest technologies to U.S. warriors. While this allegation has the ring of truth, it is important to remember that in a manufacturing environment, specifications are one of the foundations of production. Additionally, there are many areas of military equipment production where there are no commercial specifications available. The issue is not simply avoidance of milspecs, but rather the identification and use of the latest and best specifications to describe the requirement.

There are many examples where the DOD acquisition system was adjusted to accommodate new threats and new realities: the Polaris missile program, the nuclear-power program, and the many secret ("black world") efforts. If the productive base is to be used effectively as an instrument of national power in this era of rapid development and obsolescence of technologies, the acquisition system will be sorely challenged to be an enabler, giving the military access to the dynamic developments in computing and telecommunications, rather than a hindrance. In a future conflict or arms race, the nation with the shortest acquisition lead time and product-cycle time will have a distinct advantage.

Globalization and U.S. National Power

The environment in which the U.S. productive and technological base operates has changed dramatically since the end of World War II. That changing environment has affected the ability of the United States to use its productive and technological base as an instrument of national power.

The environment may be characterized as one of increasing global economic interdependence, that is, globalization. Both the work force and the manufacturing base are increasingly global. Capital flows over national borders essentially unimpeded. Globalization has been greatly facilitated by the peace among the major industrial nations since 1945, the revolutions in telecommunications and transportation, technological changes in the manufacturing processes, and the rapid increase in world trade.

Globalization has advantages and costs. On the one hand, it promises ever improving levels of efficiency and quality—provided that trade barriers are not erected by those nations that perceive themselves to be at a disadvantage. On the other hand, it is perhaps the single most important threat to national sovereignty in the mid to late 1990s. There is an inherent conflict between the idea of economic openness and the desire for national control. The continued reluctance of the nations of the European Union to embrace a single currency and a single central banking system,

despite much rhetoric favoring such institutions, is a clear example of this conflict.

Indicators of Globalization. In 1959, U.S. exports accounted for 4.2 percent of GDP. By 1993, this figure had grown to 10.4 percent. Of this, about one-quarter is services and one-tenth is agricultural products. Services is the fastest growing portion of U.S. exports. At the same time, advanced technology products account for more than 23 percent of total U.S. exports. Between 1990 and 1993, the U.S. trade in advanced technology products increased by more than 16 percent.

Perhaps the most significant change in the nature of U.S. trade is the substantially increased role of multinational corporations and intrafirm trade. In 1990, multinational firms accounted for more than 75 percent of the total U.S. trade in goods. It is estimated that about one-third of U.S. exports goes to multinational firms' own subsidiaries abroad. Another one-third is exported from foreign-owned companies in the United States to their parent firms' own countries. To further compound the confusion over national production and trade, the import content of U.S. exports rose from 10 percent to 14 percent between 1987 and 1992.

While the United States and the world have seen rapid growth in trade, increases in international financial transactions and investment have been even more significant. In 1993, about $1 trillion per day was traded around the world in a globalized exchange market that never closes. The rapid increases in capital movements and market influences on exchange rates have done much to circumscribe the power of national central banks. The September 1992 failure, in the face of market opposition, of the Bank of England's efforts to maintain the prescribed value of the pound sterling within the European Exchange Rate Mechanism illustrates the point.

Foreign direct investment in the United States grew from $83 billion in 1980 to more than $445 billion in 1993. Japan has 22 percent of the total, compared to 59 percent for the European Union (including 21 percent for Britain and 15 percent for the Netherlands). Thirty-eight percent of for-

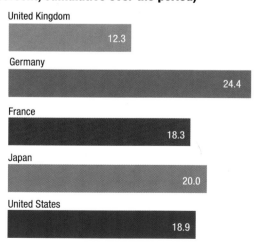

Real GDP Growth 1989–96
(in percent, cumulative over the period)

United Kingdom 12.3

Germany 24.4

France 18.3

Japan 20.0

United States 18.9

SOURCE: International Monetary Fund
NOTE: Data compare 1996 projected GDP to 1988 GDP at constant price.

Distribution of Internet Hosts by Region of the World, July 1995
(in millions)

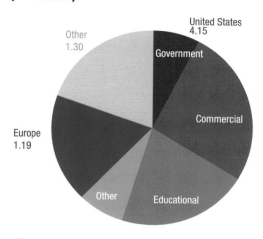

[Number of users is approximately 10 times the number of hosts.]

SOURCE: ZONE program run by Mark Lotter, Network Wizard.

Worldwide Information Technology Sales, 1993

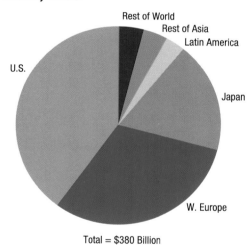

Total = $380 Billion

SOURCE: *Computer Industry Report*, August, 1994.
NOTE: Includes hardware and software other than network services.

eign direct investment is in manufacturing, 9 percent in petroleum, 10 percent in finance, and 16 percent in retail and wholesale trade. U.S. affiliates of foreign companies accounted for almost 6 percent of U.S. GDP in 1992, compared to 4 percent in 1987.

By contrast, from 1980 to 1993, U.S. direct investment abroad grew from $215 billion to $548 billion, of which 18 percent is invested in Britain and 13 percent in Canada. Europe remains the most popular location for newly acquired affiliates, which indicates that access to well-ordered and established integrated markets seems to outweigh access to low-wage labor markets in direct U.S. investment decisions. Thirty-eight percent of U.S. direct investment abroad is in manufacturing, while petroleum accounts for 11 percent, and finance 26 percent.

Manufacturing, petroleum, and finance interrelations raise the possibility of one government's using leverage in other countries to influence the outcome of global issues. On the surface, it may appear from the relative balance of U.S. and foreign direct investments that other governments may have as much potential leverage as the United States. However, this is not the case. For while total direct foreign investments in the U.S represent 6.6 percent of U.S. GDP, the United States has considerably larger relative investments in other countries. For example, 1991 U.S. direct investment in Britain represented about 7.7 percent of their GDP, while British investment in the U.S. was only 1.8 percent of U.S. GDP. The same can be said of almost all other coun-

tries except Japan, whose direct investment in the U.S. is 1.6 percent of U.S. GDP, while U.S. investment in Japan is only 0.7 percent of the Japanese GDP.

Globalization and U.S. National Influence. Use of any economic leverage power to influence international outcomes needs to be country specific and industry specific. The U.S has potentially more influence in some countries than in others and is clearly more vulnerable to return influence by certain countries.

The same specificity may be required if trade is to be used as a lever of national power. The U.S. relationship with Japan and China are perhaps extreme examples. China's exports to the United States grew from $2.8 billion in 1987 to $22.8 billion in 1993, giving the U.S. perhaps some influence not previously held with China. By contrast, the large and pervasive trade deficit with Japan places U.S. national power in some question. Some suggest that the U.S. enjoys the perverse power of the debtor over the creditor who threatens nonpayment.

Nonetheless, because of its historic position favoring free trade, the size of its market, and its industrial power, the United States is in a unique position to use the global marketplace as an instrument of national power. In some contexts, the promise of access to U.S. markets or the threat of exclusion may have an impact on the outcome of events. However, it is important to recognize that this form of U.S. influence has declined relatively as other nations—particularly Japan and the European Union—have acquired significant wealth and productive power.

Any exercise of U.S. power in the industrial realm must recognize the increasing influence of multinational firms in the global market. The international firms operating within the global marketplace are major new stakeholders in the quest for global stability and therefore are potential allies to which the United States may turn in a variety of situations. The goals of multinational firms often coincide with those of the U.S. government. Both are interested in global stability, the peaceful transition of political power, the creation

Growth of U.S. Information Industry

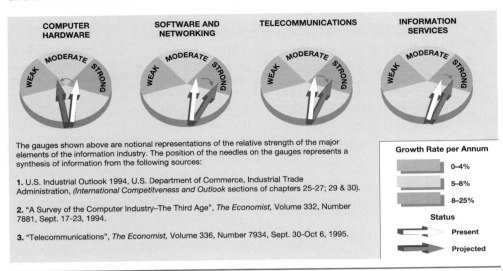

COMPUTER HARDWARE

SOFTWARE AND NETWORKING

TELECOMMUNICATIONS

INFORMATION SERVICES

The gauges shown above are notional representations of the relative strength of the major elements of the information industry. The position of the needles on the gauges represents a synthesis of information from the following sources:

1. U.S. Industrial Outlook 1994, U.S. Department of Commerce, Industrial Trade Administration, *(International Competitveness and Outlook* sections of chapters 25-27; 29 & 30).

2. "A Survey of the Computer Industry–The Third Age", *The Economist*, Volume 332, Number 7881, Sept. 17-23, 1994.

3. "Telecommunications", *The Economist*, Volume 336, Number 7934, Sept. 30-Oct 6, 1995.

Growth Rate per Annum

0–4%

5–8%

8–25%

Status

Present

Projected

and maintenance of free markets, free access to raw materials, access to the global manufacturing base, the removal of trade barriers, and the establishment of internationally applied product standards and rules of ownership.

There is not only a global marketplace but—of greater national security interest—a global manufacturing base. It is increasingly difficult to identify a manufactured product as "Made in America." The U.S. military has become more dependent upon items with significant foreign content, especially as more and more defense hardware is purchased from commercial sources rather than traditional defense-industry sources. Still, reliance on foreign sources may be less militarily significant now than it would have been in the past. As discussed below, future wars are likely to be fought with the equipment on hand rather than with weaponry produced during a long, extensive mobilization of the domestic industrial base.

Information Technology as a Strategic Industry

Certain industries are generally considered to be more important than others to a nation's economy, power, and prestige. There is a debate in the United States over how to identify such industries and what—

if anything—the U.S. government should do to support them and to ensure they are fully exploited to the national advantage.

A strategic industry may be defined as one that causes significant economic growth in excess of its own value. History provides many examples of strategic industries: railroads and agriculture in the United States; textiles, railroads, and coal in Britain; and the chemical industry in Germany. Each of these cases suggests a connection between new technology and strong economic growth not just in the strategic industry itself but in related industries as well.

For example, the U.S. railroad industry, with heavy government support, spurred growth in the steel industry with its demands for massive amounts of steel for rails, bridges, and equipment; it also substantially stimulated the machine tools industry, the telegraph industry, and the coal industry. Moreover, the growth of the railroads provided a cheap means to move bulk agricultural products to market, thus substantially reducing the cost of these products and providing consumers with a better diet. Similarly, railroads provided cheap transportation for coal and pig iron, thus indirectly stimulating heavy industries.

Strategic industries also exist today. Whether government takes a role in fostering them is essentially a political decision. Historically, the U.S. government has supported strategic industries in a variety of ways: through outright ownership, as with the Tennessee Valley Authority and the National Aeronautics and Space Administration; protection from some of the rigors of free markets, as with agriculture; subsidies for research and development support, as with semiconductors; and provision of a market for new technologies before they are commercially viable, as with DOD support of computers.

The information industry today holds the most convincing claim to the status of a strategic industry. As an element of national power, the U.S. information indus-

Percentage of Households with PCs and Modems, 1994

	PC	Modem
Japan	7.4%	3.2%
W. Europe	24.9%	3.0%
USA	37.0%	17.1%

SOURCE: International Data Corporation, IDC Global IT Survey, Households (1995).

try generates considerable wealth in its own right. It also provides foundational support to the whole of the U.S. information economy, estimated by some at 36 percent of U.S. GNP in the mid-1990s. The information economy is defined as the confluence of computer hardware, software, telecommunications, and the value-added information-provider sector. Historically, there were clear boundaries between hardware, software, telecommunications, and service providers. Such is no longer the case. Now, they are inextricably linked to form a very powerful source of economic and productive energy that can be leveraged at the national and international level.

The question of what role Washington should play in supporting strategic industries in the information age usually divides respondents into two camps: those who want the government to allow the free markets to work, and those who favor government support for strategic investments in the most promising future technologies.

The historical record suggests that the government can play a constructive role. But success in supporting railroads, agriculture, mining, and air transport, for example, is counterbalanced by Washington's tendency to become a captive to those industries as they mature and become politically powerful. The challenge is to identify and support dynamic, emerging industries that are a potential source of national power and wealth and avoid long-term capture.

U.S. firms have long been at the forefront of the information industry. Microsoft's MS–DOS or Windows operating systems run over 80 percent of the world's personal computers. The software industry grew by 11 percent in 1994, making it the fastest-growing service business in the United States. With the deregulation and privatization of telecommunications markets around the world, U.S. telecommunications firms are becoming strategic part-

ners with newly privatized telephone providers in foreign markets. More important, joint ownership or access to foreign telephone markets provides an entree for a plethora of information-service providers. Distinctly American information-service providers (Prodigy, America Online, Compuserve, Dun and Bradstreet, and others) offer a variety of services that instantaneously link customers with far-flung sources of information. The United States maintains a huge $3 billion trade surplus in information-related services, including those of information providers such as Mead Data Central, the company that runs Lexis and Nexis.

Measuring the Information Economy

Most economists agree that the production and dissemination of information are playing an increasing role in the United States and other advanced economies. However, there is no widely accepted methodology for calculating the size of the information economy. A handful of economists have attempted to measure the size of the information sector of the U.S. economy by means of various complex methodologies. In 1962, Fritz Machlup (*The Production and Distribution of Knowledge in the United States*) calculated that in 1958, 32 percent of the U.S. work force was engaged in knowledge-producing activities. In 1977, Marc U. Porat and Michael Rubin (in a nine-volume report for the U.S. Department of Commerce entitled *The Information Economy*) concluded that in 1967, the sector in which information was the main output accounted for 25.1 percent of U.S. GNP, and information activities within noninformation industries accounted for 21.1 percent. Lastly, in 1986, Michael Rubin and Mary Huber (in *The Knowledge Industry in the United States, 1960–1980*) concluded that in 1980, 36.5 percent of the U.S. GNP could be attributed to knowledge production.

Even if one narrowly defines the economy's information sector, the industrial and service sectors are increasingly dependent upon the use of information in their productive activities. For instance, the capital spending on information machines in the U.S. economy has exceeded spending on traditional industrial equipment.

In the late 1980s, some analysts predicted that Japan and Pacific Rim countries would dominate high-tech markets. This has not happened, nor is it likely to occur in the foreseeable future. U.S. companies are still the foremost innovators, standard-setters, and market leaders of the information revolution. Five of the top six computer makers are headquartered in the United States. Intel leads the semiconductor business, Microsoft tops the PC software market, and Motorola is the international leader in cellular technology. Further, the United States leads the world in connectivity, household computing power, household connectivity with external information providers, electronic commerce, and other facets of the information industry.

U.S. policy can influence the behavior of nation-states or regional geopolitical jurisdictions by establishing policies that influence who may participate in and have access to the opportunities available in the United States. Additionally, influence can be brought to bear by employing the principle of reciprocity. If country X does Y, then U.S. policy will permit that country to accelerate its development of a technically advanced information infrastructure.

As an element of national power, the U.S. capability to leverage its edge in the information industries depends upon the ability of U.S. providers to establish de facto technical standards by dominating worldwide markets, and to innovate future generations of information products and services. For example, in 1995 Microsoft's MS–DOS and Windows software functioned as a standard for PC operating systems throughout much of the world. Application software developers therefore had to develop programs that operated within Microsoft's environment if they hoped to penetrate world markets. Japanese firms did much the same in the less strategic VCR industry.

Underpinning the development of future generations of information-technology applications and products is the ability to innovate. Technological development is, in turn, dependent on access to the requisite intellectual capital. Technological innovation will migrate, physically or electronically, to areas, regions, or countries where the intellectual capital resides. Maintaining a leadership position within the global-information industry therefore requires a world-class educational and cultural infrastructure to produce the human capital to develop new generations of information-technology products and services. It also requires the creation and maintenance of the structural capital—that is, the networks, information systems, and information repositories—that is the foundation for innovation.

The Defense Industrial Base

The current wisdom holds that future conflicts will be fought with off-the-shelf systems and technologies, and the major challenge for the U.S. defense industrial base will be to replace forces lost in conflicts rather than to handle massive, sustained production runs. Given the inventory and age of defense hardware in 1995, coupled with the unlikelihood of a serious conflict, the capabilities of the defense industrial base will probably not be tested seriously until obsolescence begins to threaten defense capabilities early in the next century. The crux of the argument over support of the defense industrial base beyond current needs is the issue of whether what remains of the base in the future will be able to respond in a timely manner to the requirement to replace obsolescent equipment or, indeed, to support a long, hot war if predictions of relatively short conflicts prove wrong. It is unclear what would be the cost in time and money to reconstitute the once highly prized skills that are being allowed to languish.

The defense base reaches more deeply into the U.S. industrial base than is often understood. For example, it supported much of the high-tech research performed in the United States since the Second World War. As recently as 1990, it directly or indirectly employed about a quarter of all engineers, consumed about 15 percent of durable-goods output, and supported half of all computer research.

The decline in U.S. defense procurement spending began in 1985 and continued in the first half of the 1990s. The re-

US soldier demonstrating laptop use in the field.

duced military spending hit hard at the defense industrial base. Defense procurement went from a FY 1985 peak of $136 billion to $42 billion in FY 1996 (in FY 1996 dollars), that is, from the equivalent of 2.4 percent of GDP to 0.6 percent. And these numbers understate the problem for defense firms, since procurement of goods with a large civilian market, like food and personal computers, fell proportionately less than the purchases of major weapons systems, which is the key issue for the traditional defense industrial base.

The response by defense firms to the decline has focused on mergers and consolidations in order to ensure a competitive position. The essential question is whether U.S. defense firms, despite the very significant decline in defense procurement, remain capable of satisfying the materiel requirements to support the use of national power.

Contrary to popular belief, the defense industry is not simply a few large contractors that work exclusively to supply weapons for the Department of Defense. True, there are some cases in which only a single or a few suppliers of a particular system exist; but such suppliers typically engage some 800 to 1,000 subcontractors, who contribute about 60 percent of the value of delivered systems. Additionally, the vast majority of companies that do business with the DOD also undertake significant commercial work. John Alic and Harvey Brooks reported in *Beyond Spinoff* that the 67 largest prime contractors obtained only about 9 percent of their revenues from de-

fense work, even during the height of the Reagan buildup.

Thus, the prime firms in the defense industry have a more varied customer base than is generally supposed. Subcontractors do not usually rely solely upon defense work either. Rather, most defense contractors are prepared to adapt to market forces as military orders dwindle, and most will probably continue to be capable of providing needed goods.

However, certain industrial segments and technologies are so unique to defense that no commercial market for them exists or is likely to exist. Thus, despite the overall health of the manufacturing base, there are some very critical defense industrial activities where no commercial applications would sustain a company or production line between defense orders. In this category are laser guidance, stealth technology, and submarine construction, among others. These specialized items can be produced only with direct government support.

Thus, Washington has to face the policy dilemma of which companies to support, and why. Ideally, the government would make these decisions based on a clearly articulated, high-priority military requirement, coupled with an extensive cost/benefit analysis. But the connection between grand strategy, military requirements, and actual production is tenuous in the best of times. During a significant reduction in forces and the subsequent contraction of support facilities and the defense industrial base, the question of what to save ultimately will be decided on Capitol Hill as part of the political debate. The decision process surrounding the Seawolf submarine is a case in point—regardless of the decision's merits.

The defense base faces at least two major challenges: continued restructuring to ensure survival in an era of modest defense spending, and competition in the global marketplace with foreign suppliers that are vying for a declining export market. The most overt response to these challenges has been an increased effort among defense firms to collaborate in the development and production of new systems so as to reduce risks, increase access to technologies, and share up-front costs. Such collaborations include the teaming of U.S. prime contractors for the duration of a project, as well as international collaborations, sometimes with government-owned foreign companies.

This collaborative trend within the United States may ensure the survival of a viable U.S. defense industrial base. But when partnerships between U.S. and foreign firms are involved, new concerns emerge. International collaboration implies either sharing or partitioning information so that neither party can make the unit individually. Partitioning arrangements may significantly affect U.S. ability to exercise unilateral action in pursuit of its national security goals. For example, General Electric (GE) and SNECMA of France jointly manufacture the CFM–56 aircraft engine,

which is used in military (the KC–135R air-refueler) and many civilian aircraft. Neither company manufacturers the complete engine. Rather, GE makes the "hot section" and SNECMA makes the "cold section." Each company assembles complete engines using the other's sections and then delivers them to customers. Although France's status as an ally makes disruptions in the exchange of sections unlikely, this example illustrates the vulnerabilities that can be incurred by cross-border defense ventures: U.S. capability to expand its air-power projection could be severely hampered if France chose not to allow cold section shipments to the United States. GE could, of course, manufacture CFM–56 cold sections given sufficient time and resources.

The Seawolf Submarine

At the height of the Cold War, the Navy's plan had been to buy three Seawolf submarines a year for six years, costing some $33.6 billion. President Bush in May 1992 called for cancellation of the Seawolf submarine production program except for the one boat under construction at the General Dynamics electric boat (EB) division in Groton, Connecticut.

The opponents of the cancellation decision included the congressional delegations from Connecticut and Rhode Island, who were concerned with the cancellation's economic impact. Besides the loss of thousands of jobs, they argued that loss of Seawolf production would place in grave jeopardy one of the nation's two nuclear-capable shipyards. EB strongly maintained that it could not continue to make submarines without at least one new order a year. Additionally, responding to a future military threat would be more costly if EB were to lose its highly trained, specially skilled work force.

President Bush's supporters argued that Seawolf was no longer needed and was too costly, particularly in light of the demands for tax cuts, reduced federal spending, and the need to balance the budget. The Seawolf

Sea Wolf submarine.

Washington could also exploit such arrangements by blocking shipments to a collaborating company if doing so would serve some compelling national interest. Collaboration is more and more common as increasing numbers of U.S. and foreign companies develop arrangements for development and production. The usual arrangement is similar to the GE/SNECMA model: each makes part of the product, while sharing as little technical data as possible. These commercial arrangements are usually undertaken to share costs and risks, to obtain technology, and to facilitate market penetration.

As defense firms continue to downsize and embrace international collaborative efforts to ensure survival, the U.S. defense industrial base loses some of its unilateral ability to respond to sovereign interests.

Washington has the power to reverse these trends through direct intervention in the defense industry, but economic and political realities run counter to creation of a policy broadly supporting the declining base.

Besides a diminished threat and rapidly declining defense dollars, there has been a fundamental shift in the way DOD approaches acquisition. Defense is increasingly relying on commercial products for major portions of its high-technology equipment. The old system of heavy DOD R&D funding followed by procurement is gone. In its place is a reduced DOD presence in the R&D market. The need is to capitalize upon rapidly changing market-driven products so that DOD can take advantage of the latest technologies and commercial economies of scale. The old, unique defense supplier base is unaffordable. It lacks the means to exploit rapidly new technologies and fails to take advantage of commercial-sector production economies.

The government's challenge is to adapt its acquisition system to make the defense market more commercial friendly in order to gain maximum advantage of commercial technologies and prices while maintaining required defense-unique capabilities. Specific military mission analysis can assist in identification of necessary defense-unique products. Formulating policies to protect and foster unique capabilities is no trivial task, being fraught with political difficulties and serious trade-offs: for example, national versus collaborative development and production, domestic versus foreign sourcing, current capability versus future capability, and

had long been a target of criticism from Senator John McCain (R—Arizona), a staunch supporter of defense, who maintained that the submarine was too expensive and the money could be better spent on other Navy needs. The House and Senate eventually agreed on funding a second Seawolf, which was acceptable to President Bush.

In September 1993, President Clinton—who had announced in March 1992 during the Connecticut primary his support for either two or three Seawolfs—confirmed a third submarine would be built at a cost of $2.3 billion at EB. Newport News, the other nuclear-capable yard (in Newport News, Virginia), was slated to receive an order for a new aircraft carrier.

After the November 1994 election, the Seawolf was again under attack, with Senators McCain and John Warner (R—Virginia) identifying as wasteful some $8 billion in spending, including Seawolf production. The Congressional Budget Office in May 1995 lent support to the critics of Seawolf when it questioned the military need for a third Seawolf and stated that construction of the third submarine would do little to help the vital subcontractors in the submarine industrial base. Virginia Senators Charles Robb (D) and Warner joined forces and strongly objected to the Navy's plan to continue to bypass competition by giving the order for the third Seawolf to EB. The Navy, however, maintained that by preserving the nuclear shipbuilding base in the mid-1990s—with orders to both EB and Newport News—competition to build nuclear-powered ships would exist for the next decade.

In June 1995, the House voted to cancel the third Seawolf and use the savings to improve the second Seawolf and start the new line of advanced—more affordable—submarines. However, Congress accepted in November 1995 the proposal crafted by Senator Warner, under which the third and final Seawolf would be built by EB, which would also get the order for the lead boat of the new submarine class in 1998, but Newport News would get the order for the second new-class boat in 1999. From then on, there would be competition for the planned twenty-eight follow-on orders. This plan preserves the skill base at EB until the next-generation order is received, and provides for future competition between EB and Newport News.

The Seawolf debate was a mixture of many different elements, but most emphasis was on preserving jobs. Apparently, less consideration was given to Russia's continued submarine-building program. A troubling aspect of the Russian defense structure since the end of the Cold War is the emphasis on submarines. Production of the improved Akula class has continued at much the same pace as in the late 1980s. Additionally, construction of a new ballistic submarine class began in December 1993. In the new boats, the Russians—thanks to their own technical skill and to borrowed Western technology—have largely closed the gap with the U.S. in quietness, one of the major measures of submarine quality. By 2000, the Russian nuclear submarine force may be 80 boats, most of which will be about as quiet as the 70 boats the U.S. will have then.

competition versus sole sourcing. The alternative is to let the political process or the marketplace decide. That alternative may, in fact, be more efficient than generally credited.

Conclusions

The U.S. productive and technological base is quite strong and doing well in comparison with its foreign peers, providing a solid foundation for the exercise of national power. Yet, the base is constantly changing. The major forces affecting the base include:

● A sharp rise in the service sector coupled with a steady growth in manufacturing production.

● A greater reliance upon trade as a source of national income.

● Increased globalization of information, manufacturing, and finance.

● Expansion of the role of international firms in world affairs.

● The rise of information technology dominated by the United States.

● Reduced defense expenditures for R&D and procurement, resulting in a downsized defense industrial base.

● A significant change in defense acquisition focus toward increased use of commercial items and technology.

The issue of the proper role and goals of the government to foster and protect the productive and technological base as an instrument of national power is unresolved. The challenge for the United States is how to harness the economic growth capacity of new technologies and industries so as to remain the world's premier power. The debate continues over the appropriate goals and role of the government in preserving manufacturing skills unique to defense requirements.

Despite the debate, the productive and technological base remains a firm foundation of national power against which a number of instruments may be leveraged to influence the outcome of world events. These instruments include:

● The control of access to the U.S. domestic market and U.S. technology, including information technology.

● Use of the foreign affiliates of U.S. firms to influence local events, at least by demonstration of "enlightened" policies.

● Maintenance of the appearance, if not the reality, of great industrial might (including the defense industry) to forestall potential adversaries.

● Efforts to demonstrate, if no other way than by example, the promise of greater economic and political well-being through participation in the global marketplace, which requires political stability, maintenance of free markets and sources, removal of trade barriers, establishment of international standards, and rules of ownership enforceable under law.

The U.S. productive and technological base is inextricably woven into the fabric of the global marketplace. It cannot retreat without incurring serious costs. As in the past, economic interrelationships offer the promise of increased stability and peace in the world. The productive and technological base can be used as an instrument to support and enhance U.S. interests globally, but not without consideration of the enablers and limitations resulting from the global nature of the base itself.

CHAPTER EIGHT

Arms Control

Introduction

Before the end of World War II, arms control had not experienced significant success. Modern arms control had its roots in the nuclear age, when the technology of war advanced to the point where humanity possessed the means to destroy itself. At the start of the Cold War, the focus was on eliminating dangerous weapons, e.g., the Acheson-Lillienthal Report calling for eliminating nuclear weapons. This attitude persisted, resulting in the 1968 Treaty on the Non-Proliferation of Nuclear Weapons (NPT) and the 1972 Biological Weapons Convention (BWC). But during the middle of the Cold War, the theory of arms control rested in large part on the notion that adversaries could cooperate in creating force postures that would place less pressure on political leaders to use their forces or lose them. Hence the emphasis was on preventing a first-strike posture with nuclear weapons, and on measures to reduce the risk of inadvertent conventional conflict as well as to complicate the task of military planners who might see some advantage in a surprise military attack. At the end of the Cold War, the emphasis shifted back to eliminating weapons, even whole classes of weapons, which was the centerpiece of the two Strategic Arms Reduction Talks (START) treaties and the Treaty on Conventional Armed Forces in Europe, signed in 1989–92.

A fundamental question for arms control is what the disappearance of the special circumstances that prevailed during the Cold War will mean for the theory and practice of arms control. One open issue is to what extent control of their respective weapons will remain an important part of the U.S.-Russian relationship. Another important question will be how to develop arms-control mechanisms for volatile regions, or for the globe as a whole, when the underlying political situation is more complex and multisided than in the relatively straightforward East-West Cold War confrontation.

Instruments

Nuclear Arms Control

By the middle of the Cold War, U.S. thinking about arms control had moved from an emphasis on reducing numbers of weapons to a focus on stabilizing the U.S.-Soviet strategic relationship. In 1969, bilateral negotiations began between the superpowers on limiting the delivery systems of strategic nuclear weapons. The Strategic Arms Limitation Talks (SALT) were conducted on the premise that a "first-strike" posture should be eschewed in favor of a "second-strike" posture. The resulting SALT I Interim Agreement, the first negotiated limitation on strategic nuclear delivery vehicles, entered into force in October 1972, essentially freezing strategic offensive ballistic missile systems at their then current levels for five years.

The United States continued to seek a stable force posture through the negotiation of the SALT II Treaty, which was signed in 1979 but never ratified. This treaty implemented the 1974 Vladivostok Accord, in which the United States and the Soviet Union agreed on the principle of equal aggregate limitations on strategic offensive-delivery vehicles, that is, intercontinental ballistic missiles (ICBMs), submarine-launched ballistic missiles (SLBMs), and heavy bombers. Both the SALT I Interim Agreement (beyond its five-year term) and the SALT II Treaty were observed through an informal arrangement until 1986, when President Reagan discontinued this observance in response to Soviet violations.

U.S. Secretary of Defense Perry and Russian Defense Minister Grachev watch the destruction of a U.S. missile silo.

President Reagan shifted the U.S. approach to arms control back in the direction of disarmament, proposing to cancel the deployment of U.S. intermediate-range nuclear missiles in Europe in exchange for the elimination of similar Soviet weapons, and opening the Strategic Arms Reductions Talks (START). The Intermediate-range Nuclear Forces (INF) Treaty, signed in 1987, eliminated an entire class of nuclear-weapons delivery vehicles—ground-launched missiles with ranges of 500–5,500 kilometers. This treaty also contained a precedent-setting verification regime, allowing for short-notice, on-site inspections that had previously been unacceptable to the Soviets. The INF Treaty was the first agreement that provided for the actual elimination of existing nuclear-weapons delivery systems.

In September 1991, President Bush offered to destroy all U.S. nuclear artillery shells, stand down ICBMs scheduled for elimination under START I, end the twenty-four-hour runway alert status for nuclear bombers, and remove nuclear weapons from U.S. surface ships, land-based naval aircraft, and attack submarines. As a result of this initiative, 90 percent of U.S. tactical nuclear weapons have been eliminated. Soviet President Gorbachev responded within a week with a similar initiative, promising to destroy Soviet nuclear artillery shells, take USSR bombers off alert, confine mobile missiles to their garrisons, and cancel several new weapons programs. Both countries also committed themselves to significant cuts in their strategic nuclear arsenals, pursuant to the conclusion of the START Treaty—which mandated reductions in the total number of deployed warheads to 6,000 each—on July 31, 1991.

In the wake of the Soviet Union's dissolution, Presidents Bush and Yeltsin signed the Joint Understanding on Reductions in Strategic Offensive Arms, which obligated both sides to cut their strategic nuclear forces below START I levels. The ensuing START II Treaty will, when ratified and implemented, reduce each side's nuclear warheads to between 3,000 and 3,500. START II also places eliminates heavy ICBMs and Multiple Independently-targetable Reentry Vehicles (MIRVs) on land-based missiles, promoting stability by focusing on weapons that lend themselves to first-strike use. Once START II is in force, the United States and Russia have pledged to consider further reductions in strategic forces.

Even if relations between Washington and Moscow remain cordial, arms control will remain an important instrument for promoting U.S. national interests as long as states retain nuclear weapons. Maintaining current treaties serves the interests of strategic stability: a unilateral change in any of these agreements would almost certainly destabilize the U.S.-Russian strategic relationship. In the future, the strategic nuclear arms control instrument may cease to be a U.S.-Russian monopoly and instead become multilateral with the inclusion of China, Britain, and France.

Cooperative Threat Reduction

The dissolution of the former Soviet Union had a dual impact on the arms control instrument of U.S. policy. On the one hand, it opened the door to the possibility that former Soviet nuclear weapons or weapons-usable material could fall into the hands of rogue states or terrorists. On the other hand, it created arms control possibilities that were impossible during the Cold War beyond the field of "traditional" strategic nuclear arms control. The opportunity exists to greatly enhance the national security of both the United States and Russia through cooperative measures, but there are no guarantees that this opportunity will last.

During the Cold War, the Soviets went to great lengths to protect their nuclear weapons and materials from loss, theft, or misuse. The demise of the former Soviet Union left nuclear forces and weapons-production facilities spread across new international borders, while the central government that had imposed stringent administrative control over these forces and facilities ceased to exist. Military morale and cohesion have declined, as have the living standards of former Soviet nuclear weapons scientists. Homeless military officers and nuclear physicists whose children are hungry struggle to maintain strict accountability for nuclear weapons and materials, but they are faced with diminished resources to perform this function and the lure of the significant economic benefits they could receive from selling weapons, material, and expertise to criminal elements. The possibility that nuclear weapons or weapons-usable material could fall into terrorist hands has increased. As a result, the United States may face a greater nuclear danger today, albeit of an entirely different type, than it did during the Cold War.

These new dangers have created the opportunity for a new type of arms control emphasizing cooperative efforts. The threat is different; the governments of the newly independent states of the former Soviet Union share with the U.S. an interest in protecting the security of the nuclear weapons and materials in their territories. The U.S. can work with them in ways it could not work with the former Soviet Union. For example, Washington and Moscow are cooperating to enhance the security of nuclear weapons and fissile material, as discussed in the next chapter. Both sides are reducing their nuclear arsenals as quickly as possible. Transparency measures are being implemented to increase the confidence of both sides that the agreed reductions are taking place. Furthermore, steps will be taken to prevent unauthorized seizure of nuclear warheads or fissile materials by non-government entities. Measures under negotiation include declarations of quantities and types of warheads and fissile material, spot checks to confirm the accuracy of these declarations, and mutual inspections of dismantled warheads in storage facilities. Other measures to promote nuclear security focus on building a storage facility for dismantled warheads, improving the security of material in transit, tightening export controls, and improving the physical protection of—and accounting measures for—warheads and fissile material.

In the mid-1990s, the United States has implemented innovative cooperative measures to protect nuclear materials that would have been impossible during the Cold War, using both economic incentives and security arguments. For example, in Operation Sapphire, the U.S. government airlifted 600 kilograms of highly enriched uranium (HEU), enough for dozens of bombs, from Kazakhstan to the United States for safe disposition. Similarly, Washington forged a deal with Russia to purchase 500 metric tons of HEU from dismantled weapons, blend it down into low-enriched uranium for use in reactor fuel, and ship it to the United States. The U.S., Russia, and Ukraine also negotiated a tripartite agreement for the commercial use of the nuclear material in Ukrainian weapons, which was central to securing from nationalist Ukrainian politicians the agreement that Kiev would give up its nuclear weapons. However, these latter two arrangements remain beset by problems, including economic worries (the U.S. uranium

Conventional Armed Forces in
Europe (CFE) Treaty Inspection Team.

CFE Article V Flank Limits on Former Soviet Union

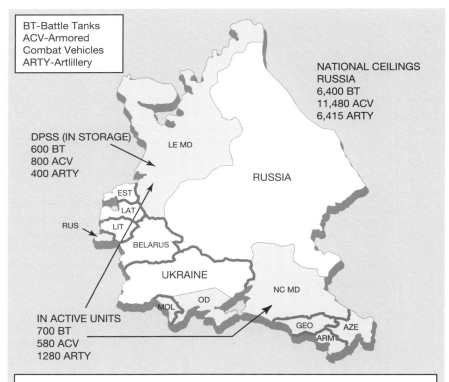

BT-Battle Tanks
ACV-Armored
Combat Vehicles
ARTY-Artlillery

NATIONAL CEILINGS
RUSSIA
6,400 BT
11,480 ACV
6,415 ARTY

DPSS (IN STORAGE)
600 BT
800 ACV
400 ARTY

LE MD

RUSSIA

EST
LAT
RUS
LIT
BELARUS

UKRAINE

NC MD

MOL OD

GEO   AZE
ARM

IN ACTIVE UNITS
700 BT
580 ACV
1280 ARTY

LEGEND
LE–Leningrad Military District (Russia)
NC–North Cacasus Military District (Russia)
OD–Odessa Military District (Ukraine)
☐ –Area of Former Soviet Union Constrained by Article V "Flank" Limits. Includes all of Moldova, Georgia, Armenia, Azerbaijan, and portions of Ukraine and Russian Federation
DPSS–Designated Permanent Storage

SOURCE: Jeff McCausland, U.S. Army War College
NOTE: Article V flank limits also apply to Bulgaria, Greece, Norway, Romania and Turkey. Estonia, Latvia, and Lithuania are not parties to CFE.

mining industry is concerned about the competition from cheaper Russian and Ukrainian materials, and there are worries that the deals may jeopardize the price Washington will get for selling the reprocessing company it owns). It is far from clear whether the U.S.-Russian partnership is solid enough to sustain the kind of cooperative effort that these measures require.

Conventional Arms Control

The U.S.–NATO proposals on Mutual and Balanced Force Reductions (MBFR) in 1973 sought to create equality between NATO and Warsaw Pact manpower in a narrow zone in central Europe. The Treaty on Conventional Armed Forces in Europe (CFE) of 1990 was designed to regulate, in a verifiable way, the levels of key types of military equipment—including tanks, armored personnel carriers, attack helicopters, artillery, and fixed-wing combat aircraft—held by NATO and the Warsaw Pact in the Atlantic-to-Urals zone of application. Thus, the CFE Treaty limits the deployment of the kinds of equipment necessary for combined arms attacks. By providing for verification that these limits are being observed through intrusive, on-site inspections, CFE increases the confidence of its parties that no one is massing forces for an attack. The CFE and its implementing body, the Joint Consultative Group, provide an effective framework for stabilizing the conventional arms situation among its parties in Europe. Through the October 1994 deadline for achieving 60 percent of the total reduction called for in the treaty, more than 18,000 items of treaty-limited equipment had been destroyed, including 6,000 by Russia. The full reduction was required by November 1995, with an additional four months allocated to verify the residual levels, and then a review conference is to follow, probably in Vienna in May 1996.

Europe has changed dramatically since CFE was signed in 1990. Most notably, the Soviet Union and the Warsaw Pact, the Eastern parties to the CFE regime, have dissolved. This complicates the treaty's application. For example, the CFE set ceilings for deployments in four subzones, which were to be reached by late 1995. Russia—and, to a lesser extent, Ukraine—want adjustments in some CFE provisions that limit deployments in the flank zones around the Black and Baltic Seas, claiming that the breakup of the former Soviet Union and instability in the Caucasus generate requirements unanticipated during the negotiations that shaped the treaty. As it had warned since September 1993, Russia did not meet the November 1995 original treaty requirements. Most of the various solutions proposed by Russia in 1993–95 would require a significant change to the CFE Treaty. Shortly before the November 1995 deadline, the CFE signatories agreed to a framework to ease the CFE flank caps, despite dissatisfaction by Norway and Turkey over allowing more Russian weaponry in the zones near their borders. While by no means a final deal, the framework agreement represented major progress towards resolving the dispute about CFE flanks. Failure to resolve the CFE Treaty compliance issue could complicate approval of START II by the Russian Duma and the U.S. Congress.

Missile Defense: Consensus and Controversy

The Anti-Ballistic Missile (ABM) Treaty, which entered into force in 1972, sought to prohibit deployment of large-scale strategic defenses. The ABM Treaty followed the premise that defensive systems are inherently destabilizing: if a country deploys effective defenses against ballistic missiles, it could launch a first strike with impunity because whatever retaliatory enemy forces survived the attack would be no match for the attacker's defensive systems. By limiting defensive systems, the ABM Treaty thus reduced the imperative for rapid growth in offensive systems necessary to overwhelm missile defenses.

During the 1980s, President Reagan's desire to provide for a space-based national missile defense through the Strategic Defense Initiative (SDI) led to attempts by his administration to reinterpret the ABM Treaty to allow for defenses based on "other physical principles" than those anticipated when the treaty was negotiated. The debate was rendered moot by the collapse of the former Soviet Union.

The military and political utility of theater-range ballistic missiles was demonstrated during the Gulf War, when Iraq launched SCUD missiles against targets in Israel and Saudi Arabia. Since that time, a strong consensus has been forged in the United States concerning the need for active theater missile defenses (TMD) to counter missiles with ranges up to 3,500 km. This consensus has been bolstered by the continued proliferation of ballistic-missile technology in Asia and the Middle East. U.S. policymakers have taken steps to improve the Patriot and system missiles for point defense, to develop Theater High Altitude Area Defense for wider-area defense, and to expand the AEGIS system for tactical missile defense from the sea.

While improving TMD capability is a priority shared by the Clinton administration, Congress, and the armed forces, the development of a national missile defense (NMD) is a far more divisive issue. The debate over NMD centers on differing perceptions of the threat to U.S. territory posed by nuclear, biological, and chemical weapons, and differing views concerning the utility of the 1972 ABM Treaty in the post-Cold War world. Illustrative of the controversy are the divergent approaches taken by the Bush and Clinton administrations on the NMD issue.

The Bush administration believed proliferation of NBC and missile capabilities to be a near-term threat to U.S. territory. In response, President Bush looked to strengthen active U.S. defenses against limited ballistic-missile attacks. The Strategic Defense Initiative of the Reagan administration was reoriented to deal with limited ballistic-missile threats. The new program, named Global Protection Against Limited Strikes, sought to create and deploy a limited, layered national missile defense without undermining the deterrent effect of the Cold War nuclear balance. The existing terms of the 1972 ABM Treaty, however, stood as an obstacle to the creation of a national missile defense. Describing the treaty as "an outdated relic of the Cold War," the Bush administration looked to amend the treaty's terms to correspond with what it believed to be the new security requirements of the post-Cold War world.

In contrast, the Clinton administration's policies reflect a belief that the short-term possibility of a missile attack on the United States is highly unlikely. While TMD continued to garner attention, the Bush administration's priority of establishing a national missile defense was downgraded. Instead, President Clinton chose to preserve the existing terms of the ABM Treaty, calling it "the bedrock of strategic stability." The Clinton administration considered maintenance of the strategic nuclear deterrence provided by the ABM Treaty during the Cold War to be a crucial and sufficient hedge against post-Cold War uncertainties.

Following the 1994 mid-term elections, the political tide again turned on the issue of national missile defense. The "Contract with America" of the victorious congressional Republicans promised to speed development of anti-ballistic missile defenses on both the theater and national levels. With Republican majorities in the House and the Senate, 1995 witnessed congressional approval of funding for a national missile defense project. Congress also rejected language recommended by the White House stipulating that this NMD program would not abrogate the ABM Treaty as it is currently written. The Clinton administration has threatened to veto any legislation that breaks with the terms of the ABM Treaty.

The effectiveness of any military technology must be evaluated not only against the standard of its economic and opportunity costs but also in terms of likely countermeasures potential adversaries will develop. Effective defense of U.S. cities and troops abroad against WMD would be a massive benefit. National missile defense may be available only at significant cost. The establishment of an effective national missile defense could lead potential adversaries to circumvent such a system by delivering their weapons through unconventional means.

Parties to the NPT, BWC, CWC

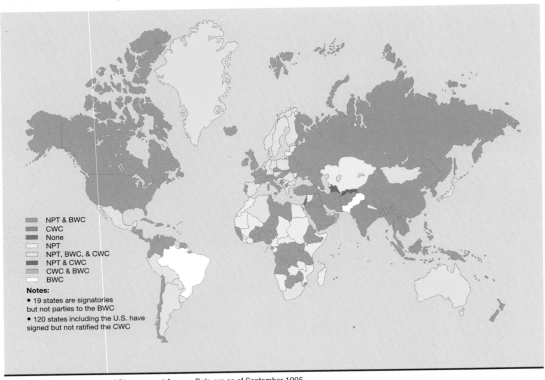

Legend:
- NPT & BWC
- CWC
- None
- NPT
- NPT, BWC, & CWC
- NPT & CWC
- CWC & BWC
- BWC

Notes:
- 19 states are signatories but not parties to the BWC
- 120 states including the U.S. have signed but not ratified the CWC

Source: U.S. Arms Control and Disarmament Agency. Data are as of September 1995.

Conventional arms control on the model of CFE holds potential for increasing stability in regions of tension throughout the world. A particularly important application of the CFE's lessons is the Dayton accords ending the fighting in Bosnia, which set forth target dates for agreement on verifiable reduction in the same types of military equipment covered by CFE. The CFE holds lessons for the Korean Peninsula, where an effective conventional arms control regime would have to be an important part of any lasting package to replace the 1953 armistice agreement. Conventional arms control could also be used to make conflict less likely in the Middle East, South Asia, and Latin America.

Confidence- and Security-Building Measures

Confidence- and security-building measures (CSBMs) are another instrument by which negotiations with potential adversaries can serve the U.S. interest to reduce the risk of conflict. They are used to clarify intentions rather than limit weapons. When neither side of a dispute wants war, it is possible to mutually enhance confidence that neither side will start a war by making the actions of both militaries more transparent. CSBMs aim to create less-threatening force postures in this manner. While such measures do not eliminate the risk of attack, they reduce the risk that precipitous incidents or inadvertent escalation will lead to war. CSBMs clarify the intentions of certain military operations (such as field exercises), enhance communications between potential belligerents, and establish guidelines concerning military operations susceptible to misunderstanding. Restraints on military operations may also play a role in confidence- and security-building regimes.

Like other arms control instruments, CSBM regimes depend on political will. All parties must agree that the agreement serves their interests. Thus, CSBMs can only be effective when none of the parties intends to launch an attack. If and when this necessary condition fails and military planners on one side prepare to launch an attack, they must choose between openly renouncing the regime or simply violating it. The unwillingness of CSBM regime members to fulfill their obligations acts as a trip-wire, alerting other members that the regime is failing and must be adjusted or abandoned.

Europe has been home to the most fully developed CSBM program since 1975, owing to the efforts of the Conference on Security and Cooperation in Europe (CSCE)—now known as the Organization for Security and Cooperation in Europe (OSCE). Along with all European countries, the U.S. participated in the CSBM regime of Vienna Document 1999 and in the Vienna-based Forum on Security Cooperation. Over the last thirty years, however,

CSBMs were first tested in the Middle East, in connection with the Israeli-Egyptian agreement on the Sinai. CSBMs of a sort are in place between Pakistan and India, and have been the subject of thus far fruitless discussions between North and South Korea. CSBMs can only be effective when all parties want them to work. When crises become acute, CSBMs have already failed.

Nonproliferation

Nonproliferation is the means by which countries are discouraged from acquiring certain types of weapons through negotiated agreements and the establishment of international norms in order to prevent the spread of weapons of mass destruction (WMD) and their delivery vehicles, as well as related dangerous technologies. Judging that it is in the vital interest of the United States to keep nuclear, chemical, and biological weapons out of the hands of additional countries as well as terrorists, the United States has aggressively pursued nonproliferation measures for several decades.

While now widely accepted, the international norm against nuclear proliferation did not spontaneously appear. Estimates in the mid-1960s were that there might be as many as thirty countries with nuclear weapons by the late 1970s. To forestall this possibility, the 1968 Treaty on the Non-Proliferation of Nuclear Weapons (NPT) was negotiated. The NPT struck a bargain between the nuclear weapon "haves" and "have nots." The non-nuclear weapons states pledged to forgo such weapons (Article II) and to accept internationally monitored safeguards on their nuclear programs (Article III). In return, the nuclear weapons states pledged to offer the non-nuclear weapons states assistance in the development of the peaceful uses of nuclear energy (Article IV) and to "pursue negotiations in good faith on effective measures relating to the cessation of the nuclear arms race at an early date and to nuclear disarmament, and on a treaty on general and complete disarmament under strict and effective international control" (Article VI).

Five countries had openly developed nuclear weapons before the NPT was negotiated, but after the NPT came into force in 1970, this trend stopped abruptly. India

tested a nuclear device (euphemistically called a "peaceful nuclear explosion") in 1974, Israel developed a nuclear arsenal of at least several dozen weapons, and it is likely that Pakistan has the capability to constitute nuclear arsenals on short order. However, even these three nuclear threshold states, who have never signed the NPT, have not openly deployed nuclear arsenals. South Africa clandestinely built a small nuclear arsenal, but dismantled it and joined the NPT. Other states have taken actions that indicate an interest in a nuclear weapons option, but none has gone as far as the four mentioned above. The NPT attached a political cost to nuclear proliferation, even for countries not party to the treaty. It also established incentives not to proliferate, like peaceful nuclear cooperation for treaty parties and enhanced confidence that neighboring states are not developing nuclear weapons.

The international nonproliferation environment changed with the end of the Cold War. The end of the superpower arms race increased the relative importance of smaller nuclear threats just as the nonproliferation discipline the superpowers had imposed on their client states was evaporating. This change was highlighted after the Gulf War, when Iraq's program for developing WMD was discovered to be of much greater scope than previously believed, despite monitoring of the Iraqi program. In response, the International Atomic Energy Agency (IAEA)—the body responsible for monitoring safeguards on civil nuclear programs to prevent diversion to weapons programs—upgraded its safeguards program and became more aggressive in its pursuit of information, reaffirming its right to conduct special inspections wherever it chose.

One of the great post-Cold War successes of U.S. nonproliferation policy was the persuasion of Ukraine, Kazakhstan, and Belarus to return the nuclear weapons on their soil to Russia and to join the NPT as non-nuclear weapons states. If these states had not renounced the former Soviet nuclear weapons on their territories, significant strategic nuclear arsenals would have remained in their possession, which might someday have threatened the United States.

Examining Scud missile remains northwest of Riyadh.

Further, if these states had chosen to retain nuclear weapons, START I could not have been brought into force, and further strategic arms reductions between the United States and Russia would not be possible.

When the NPT was negotiated several countries were unwilling to accept a permanent treaty, demanding instead a review conference after twenty-five years. In May 1995, the nearly 180 parties to the NPT met in New York and decided to extend the NPT indefinitely. The treaty called only for a majority of the parties to decide, but the United States and its allies had engaged in a global diplomatic campaign to gain widespread support for the treaty, which resulted in a consensus decision to extend the NPT without conditions. A limited extension had been suggested by many developing states as a way to lever further arms control progress from the nuclear weapons states.

Next Steps on Nuclear Nonproliferation. In addition to indefinitely extending the NPT, the 1995 conference endorsed the IAEA's "93+2" plan for strengthened safeguards and increased cooperation in peaceful uses of nuclear energy. It also set forth a series of goals on continued reductions in nuclear arsenals in the direction of ultimate abolition, pursuit of an agreement on the termination of production of fissile material for weapons purposes, pursuit of the cre-

ation of more nuclear weapon free zones, and achievement of a comprehensive test ban treaty (CTBT) by the end of 1996.

The United States no longer produces fissile material for nuclear weapons purposes and has placed a significant quantity of nuclear material under IAEA safeguards. President Clinton has urged that a fissile material cutoff treaty be negotiated by which other countries would commit to do the same under an international verification regime. Such a treaty would cap the amount of material available for nuclear explosives. More important it could bring the nuclear programs of non-NPT states—specifically, India, Israel, and Pakistan—under international safeguards for the first time. These states, which refuse to sign the NPT in part because of the perception that it is discriminatory (allowing some states to possess nuclear weapons while forbidding others), may be more willing to sign a cutoff treaty that applies to all states.

The United States is party to one nuclear weapon free zone (NWFZ), the one in Latin America established by the Treaty of Tlatelolco. The five nuclear-weapons states are party to its protocols, in which they pledge to observe the nuclear-free status of the zone by not deploying nuclear weapons within it and promising never to use nuclear weapons against a state (a negative security assurance) that is a party to the zone and is in compliance with its treaty obligations. The 1986 Treaty of Rarotonga established a nuclear-free zone for the South Pacific and included a pledge not to test nuclear weapons in the zone. Thus far, only Russia and China, among the five nuclear weapons states, are parties to this treaty. French nuclear tests at Mururoa Atoll within the zone have sparked severe international protests.

Completion of a CTBT in 1996 is considered by many a litmus test of the compliance of the nuclear weapons states with their NPT extension commitments. In August 1995, President Clinton decided that, rather than seeking to conduct very small nuclear tests which might have been allowed under a CTBT, the United States would seek a zero-yield CTBT. The President made this decision based in part on a

ARMS CONTROL

report by the JASONs, a group of senior scientists and nuclear weapon designers, which determined that a high level of confidence in the safety and reliability of the U.S. arsenal could be maintained in the absence of nuclear testing through a sophisticated, science-based stockpile stewardship program. This decision was made with the caveat that the U.S. could withdraw from a CTBT if this level of confidence could not be maintained, a development that President Clinton views as very unlikely.

The United States is seeking a CTBT for several reasons. First, it would make nuclear proliferation more difficult by imposing a verifiable international ban on nuclear testing. Secondly, it would support the global nuclear nonproliferation regime by demonstrating the good faith of the nuclear weapons states. Thirdly, the United States has already conducted over a thousand nuclear tests, and it is questionable if further testing would be worth the political costs.

Biological and Chemical Weapons. The U.S. is one of 175 signatories of the Biological Weapons Convention (BWC), which entered into effect in 1974. The treaty sought to eliminate a type of weapon thought, at the time of the treaty's signing in 1972, to be militarily useless because of its unpredictability, and therefore suitable only for terrorists. However, with advances in research, this assessment may be changing. Thus, an ongoing international effort strives to enhance the BWC's verification provisions.

Nearly 160 states have signed the 1993 Chemical Weapons Convention (CWC). It will come into force once it is ratified by sixty-five states. The United States has not yet ratified the CWC, and many other nations are waiting to see what Washington will do before proceeding with ratification. Through the ratification of this treaty, the United States will gain a prohibition on the so-called poor man's atomic weapon. However, there is concern about the cost, excessive intrusiveness of inspections in the United States, and the ultimate effectiveness of inspections.

Export Controls

Controls over exports of arms and military equipment are administered by the Department of State, whereas controls over exports of "dual-use" items—that is, commodities and technology primarily of a civilian nature but with some military applications or possible use in the development of weapons of mass destruction (i.e., nuclear, chemical, biological, or missiles)—are administered by the Department of Commerce.

The collapse of the Soviet Union and rising concerns over the future economic prosperity of the U.S. have resulted in substantial changes in the administration of the controls on dual-use items. The regulatory authority under the Export Administration Act (EAA) was not extended by Congress before it expired in 1995, and these controls are administered under the provisions of the International Economic Emergency Powers Act (IEEPA).

Although the terms under which Congress will ultimately renew the EAA are still uncertain, no one seriously questions the need for continuing to impose export controls on dual-use items or the justification

U.S. and Soviet/Russia Warhead Levels, 1974–1994
(thousands)

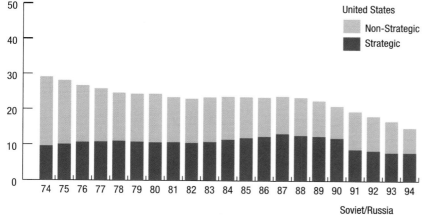

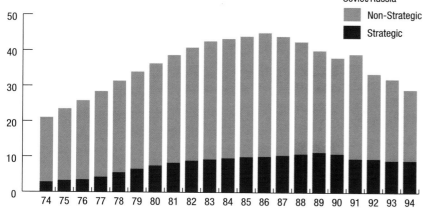

SOURCE: Natural Resources Defense Council.

for changing the manner in which these were administered during the Cold War. In short, in 1995, these controls were in a state of transition, with many changes already in effect, others in process, and some hinging on future congressional decisions.

In response to the emergence of regional stability concerns as presenting the most likely threats to world security, emphasis has shifted from controls primarily designed to restrict conventional military buildup of communist nations to those primarily designed to curtail the proliferation of WMD in Third World nations. Export controls alone cannot prevail against a state determined to build or obtain WMD. Such controls can, however, make proliferation more costly, time-consuming, or visible. By

Safeguarding Nuclear Technology

Distinguishing between a peaceful energy program and one that can produce nuclear weapons is often a difficult task. The responsibility for ensuring that NPT parties' nuclear activities are subjected to safeguards and are directed toward peaceful purposes lies with the IAEA. IAEA safeguards are a comprehensive system of accounting and reporting procedures, on-site inspections, nuclear material measurements, and containment and surveillance techniques. As a result of the discovery of the wide scope of Iraq's nuclear weapons development program, the IAEA strengthened its safeguards system. The new safeguards enhancements, known as the "93+2" program, require increased access for IAEA inspectors and reaffirmation of the IAEA's right to conduct "special inspections" of undeclared sites, more information provided to the IAEA on nuclear activities, environmental monitoring to detect nuclear materials and facilities, increased cooperation by states, and greater use of advanced technology, including unattended surveillance and measurement instruments and remote transmission of data.

Reactor Technology. The most common type of nuclear reactor is the light-water reactor (LWR). LWRs use ordinary water as a moderator (a component of nuclear reactors that slows neutrons, increasing their chances of fissioning) and as a coolant (a substance circulated through a reactor to remove or transfer heat), and use LEU as fuel. Light-water reactors must also be shut down to be refueled, which makes it easier to ascertain that no materials have been diverted for military purposes.

Another type of reactor that is in widespread use is the heavy-water reactor (HWR). It uses water that contains more than the natural proportion of heavy hydrogen atoms (also known as deuterium) to ordinary hydrogen atoms as both a moderator and coolant. Heavy water absorbs fewer neutrons than normal water, making a chain reaction easier and allowing the use of natural uranium as fuel. The most popular type of HWR is the CANDU (Canadian deuterium-uranium reactor). These reactors do not need to be shut down in order to be refueled, which makes it more difficult to determine if materials have been diverted. Fortunately, the IAEA has developed safeguards that allow such diversions to be detected, and since the CANDU uses natural rather than enriched uranium, the danger of materials being used for weapons purposes is somewhat lessened.

A third reactor type, high-temperature gas-cooled reactors (HTGRs, or gas-cooled reactors—GCRs), uses graphite as a moderator and helium rather than water as a coolant. HTGRs use HEU for fuel, which makes them more efficient than reactors that use LEU or natural uranium, but also makes them an obvious source of nonproliferation concern.

Another type of reactor, the breeder reactor, uses plutonium as fuel and actually produces more plutonium in its operation than it consumes. The large amounts of plutonium that would result from a commercial breeder reactor program have serious consequences for any attempts to stem proliferation. In 1995, only Japan had plans to use breeder reactors on a large scale.

The greatest dangers of proliferation come from enrichment and reprocessing facilities. As noted above, uranium enriched to various levels is often used as fuel in reactors. Some states have built their own means of enriching uranium rather than rely on outside sources of fuel. This raises the worry that in addition to producing only LEU for use in reactors, these states could also produce HEU or plutonium for weapons purposes. There are four different enrichment techniques in use or being researched: gaseous diffusion, gas centrifuge, aerodynamic, and laser. Gaseous diffusion was developed in the 1940s as part of the Manhattan Project. It requires huge plants and enormous amounts of electric power to operate, making it unlikely that it would be used to covertly develop material for use in a weapon. Gas centrifuge technology, on the other hand, requires only a fraction of the power and can be built in a much smaller facility. This makes it efficient for use in the nuclear power industry, but also lends itself to clandestine development of weapons. Aerodynamic methods (the two primary being the "Becker Nozzle" and "Helikon") require less space than the gas centrifuge process, allowing them to be easily hidden, but demand even more power than gaseous diffusion plants, making them an unattractive means for secretly developing weapons. A new technique using lasers to separate isotopes is being experimented with that would consume very little energy and could be carried out in a single step, requiring only a small facility in which to operate. The laser enrichment process could easily be adapted for covertly producing weapons-grade material, but the complex and difficult technology needed to build it represents a significant barrier.

Reprocessing plants are designed to recycle the residual U–235 and plutonium from spent fuel, usually through chemical means. Several countries operate reprocessing plants because it provides an alternative to storing nuclear waste. Reprocessing is cause for great concern in regards to proliferation because it produces uranium and plutonium that are highly purified and in convenient chemical forms. Although the purified uranium would not be weapons grade, any plutonium emerging from a reprocessing plant would be suitable for direct use in nuclear weapons.

raising the political and economic costs of proliferation, export controls can complement diplomatic efforts to discourage proliferation. By slowing or exposing would-be proliferators, export controls can buy time for counterproliferation efforts.

With the growing concerns over maintaining economic security as a large component of national security, the Trade Promotion Coordinating Committee's National Export Strategy led to the elimination of restrictions on exports of many commodities, particularly in the sectors of chemicals, software, computers, and telecommunications equipment. The strategy focused on the adverse economic impact on U.S. firms and industries of denying export authorizations. It called for expediting procedures to ensure prompt insurance of the licenses, simplifying Export Administration Regulations to make these more user friendly, and reducing the fragmentation of administration responsibilities among several U.S. government agencies.

During the Cold War, Congress allowed the executive branch broad authority to administer export controls on dual-use items. The trend is clearly moving toward limiting this discretion. Whereas in the past, export control decisions have always been exempt from judicial review, under the pending bills to renew the EAA, including the administration bill, the exporter would be afforded the right of redress in the courts.

The spread of high technology across the world makes unilateral controls less effective than before, and these are particularly damaging to U.S. exporters. Accordingly, unilateral controls are being eliminated, except in limited circumstances (such as with Iran), while the U.S. takes the lead in increasing the effectiveness of multilateral controls.

Principal export control regimes and groups are:

● *NPT Exporters Committee, or Zangger Committee,* as it is often referred to, was created to coordinate implementation of the NPT's Article III.2. This article requires each NPT party to ensure that IAEA safeguards are applied to their exports to non-nuclear weapons states of source or special fissionable nuclear material and "especially designed or prepared" equipment and material. One of the main activities of the Zangger Committee since its creation has been to produce and clarify the control list, often called the "trigger list." Membership of the NPT Exporters Committee consists of twenty-nine states, whose representatives meet twice a year.

● *Nuclear Suppliers Group (NSG)* was created to coordinate nuclear export controls in a multilateral forum not directly tied to the NPT. NSG guidelines require that a recipient non-nuclear weapons state accept safeguards on all its nuclear activities, not just the exported item, as a condition for the supply of nuclear material, equipment, and technology. The guidelines also emphasize the importance of exercising restraint in the export of sensitive commodities and technology, such as enrichment and reprocessing, and call for consultation in cases where such exports might increase the risk of conflict or instability. The NSG meets several times a year and has thirty-one members.

● *"Australia Group"* is an informal forum of states, chaired by Australia, whose goal is to discourage and impede CW and BW proliferation by harmonizing national export controls on CW precursor chemicals, BW pathogens, and CBW dual-use production equipment; sharing information on CBW proliferation developments; and seeking other ways to curb the use of CBW. The group has established common export controls for CBW and has issued an informal "warning list" of dual-use CBW precursors, bulk chemicals, and CBW-related equipment.

● *Missile Technology Control Regime (MTCR).* The purpose of the MTCR is to arrest missile proliferation worldwide through export controls on missiles and their related technologies. It is neither a treaty nor an international agreement; rather, the MTCR is a voluntary arrangement among twenty-seven countries that share a common interest in stemming missile proliferation and controlling exports of missile-related items in accordance with common guidelines and a technology annex. The MTCR originally controlled missiles and unmanned air vehicles capable of carrying a 500 kg payload to a range of

300 km; it has since been extended to cover missiles capable of delivering any weapon of mass destruction (nuclear, biological, or chemical) of any weight to any range.

● *Coordinating Committee for Multilateral Export Controls (COCOM)* was a multilateral export control regime established in 1949 to maintain common controls on items that could enhance the military capabilities of the then Communist Bloc nations. Presidents Clinton and Yeltsin agreed at the Vancouver summit to eliminate export control relics of the Cold War and to establish in their place a partnership between the East and West in this area. COCOM formally ended on March 1994, but members agreed to keep national controls on former COCOM-controlled items until the new regime is established. On the basis of a September 1995 meeting in the Hague, the "New Forum" post-COCOM regime is scheduled to come into existence in January 1996, with Russia and several East European states among the twenty-eight founding members. It is based on the principle of exchanging information about the transfer of arms and sensitive dual-use goods and technologies.

In addition to stopping the transfer of technology with military applications to potential adversaries or aggressive states, U.S. export control policy also aims to monitor technology flows that are acceptable in themselves but that need to be tracked to prevent diversion and to ensure that U.S. forces recognize the military capabilities they might face in any given region. Occasional attempts have been made to control the conventional arms trade, the most recent being the 1991 agreement among the five permanent members of the U.N. Security Council to notify each other of arms sales to the Middle East. This agreement collapsed in the wake of China's withdrawal after the United States announced that it would sell F–16s to Taiwan in 1992.

Conclusions

While successful arms control agreements can limit the spread and reduce the number of weapons and otherwise enhance security and stability, standing alone they seldom prevent a state that is determined to acquire such weapons from doing so. They can, however, raise the political or economic costs to such a degree that many states will forgo the use or acquisition of these weapons. In this regard, the NPT is a shining example of the effectiveness of U.S. arms control efforts. It has codified and strengthened the international norm against nuclear proliferation such that no state has been willing to openly violate the treaty, and very few states have attempted to skirt it even covertly.

Whereas arms control agreements at the height of the Cold War were designed to cap or limit buildups and modernizations, the post-Cold War role of arms control agreements is to manage weapons reductions that are already underway, because countries are cutting spending in what they perceive as a less threatening environment.

Despite the end of the Cold War, Russia remains indispensable to successful arms control on such issues as dismantling the nuclear weapons legacy of the Cold War and working out new arrangements for European security to supplement the CFE Treaty. A major issue is adjusting Cold War-era agreements to retain their arms control accomplishments while permitting responses to the changed post-Cold War threats, e.g., permitting defenses against rouges with missiles within the framework of the ABM Treaty and promoting stability in the Caucasus while preserving CFE limits on conventional forces.

In zones of regional conflict, the pressing arms control problem is to prevent the spread of advanced weapons technology. Global regimes to contain or roll back weapons of mass destruction are more or less in place, with the exception of a comprehensive test ban treaty and confirmation of signed treaties. Progress has been made to safeguard nuclear technology and material, as well as to limit the spread of missile technology. Efforts are underway to supplement these agreements with cooperative security-building measures. But the success of these regimes may depend on progress towards resolving regional conflicts, such as those in Northeast Asia, the Middle East, and South Asia.

CHAPTER NINE

Defense Engagement in Peacetime

Introduction

Defense engagement is a term that is being used by the Office of the Secretary of Defense (OSD) to describe the long-standing political-military issue of the nature, scope and scale of noncombat military and defense support of U.S. foreign policy in peacetime, a role that has evolved from many changes in political and professional thinking.

The Cold War national strategy of containment demanded the presence of a modern, trained U.S. military capability worldwide, maintenance of its readiness for combat, and help to friendly and allied countries around the globe to develop stronger national defenses. The United States initially provided a bargain-basement shortcut to military modernization with its World War II and Korean War stocks of inexpensive but reliable arms and a wide range of associated military equipment. Under the Mutual Defense Assistance Program, which became Security Assistance in the early 1960s, the U.S. provided on a grant basis or sold a wide range of defense articles and services, including professional education and technical training. By the early 1980s, however, Security Assistance had be-

come a prisoner of its own bureaucracy, leading one Unified Commander to observe that its programs "satisfy the requirements of trying to deal with Congress, but do not necessarily help us as we work with our regional allies in carrying out our [national security] responsibilities."

During the Cold War, the United States also conducted low-cost and low-profile political-military activities in other regions of the world, such as the provision of humanitarian and advisory assistance, and maintained service-to-service contacts. Yet, these initiatives remained marginal in DOD's resource-allocation process and the military's doctrinal thinking. For years, the armed services minimized these nonstandard programs and criticized them for diverting resources and undermining force readiness.

As of the mid-1990s, however, the situation has begun to change. The defense community's past resistance to using noncombat means to project U.S. influence is slowly giving way. The difference has been a post-Cold War national-security strategy emphasizing active leadership and involvement worldwide, also known as engagement and enlargement (of the community of democracies). This strategy challenges the Defense Department not only to ensure that the armed forces maintain the capability to protect U.S. interests with force but also to employ the department's civilian and military organizational, professional, and institutional assets to support the National Security Strategy's goals of security, economic prosperity, and democratic growth—goals that do not translate easily into classical defense and military concepts.

Faced with these new realities, the 1995 *National Military Strategy*, prepared by the Joint Chiefs of Staff, identifies "peacetime engagement" as one of three sets of tasks for achieving the military objectives of promoting stability and thwarting aggression. This term, the publication says, describes a broad range of noncombat activities undertaken by U.S. armed forces, which demonstrate commitment, improve collective military capabilities, promote democratic ideals, relieve suffering, and in many other ways enhance regional stability.

A little-noticed trend toward greater innovation in selectively using military forces and defense resources in peacetime outside of the traditional framework of military assistance had already emerged in the Americas during the 1980s, as U.S. Southern Command developed more immediately responsive and effective forms of defense involvement in order to support the Reagan administration's Central American policy. These included using active duty, reserve, and National Guard units to conduct engineering exercises and military humanitarian deployments for training in the Caribbean Basin. By 1987, Southern Command had a catalogue of twenty-seven defense activities, including security-assistance programs, to offer U.S. country teams in the Americas. Other unified commands have since adopted, and adapted, many of the same activities and programs.

Instruments

This chapter examines two groups of initiatives under the conceptual umbrella of defense engagement. The first comprises Foreign Military Interaction (FMI), which includes military assistance, military education, and joint planning, exercises and operations. The second group combines DOD programs that constitute "defense diplomacy."

Military Assistance

The United States offers grant and commercial-sales programs to enable friendly nations to acquire U.S. military equipment, services, and training for legitimate self-defense and burden-sharing purposes. Adequate military capabilities among allies decrease the likelihood that U.S. forces will be

---

Foreign Military Interaction

Early in 1995, the Joint Staff defined foreign military interaction as "initiatives whereby U.S. defense personnel—by direction of US Defense authorities and in coordination with the US country team—interact with foreign defense personnel on a systemic and cooperative basis to achieve national security objectives." Most of the instruments examined in this chapter fall under the heading of Foreign Military Interaction (FMI), and several were on a 1995 Joint Staff list identifying sixteen separate FMI programs. However, the Joint Staff's list is not all-inclusive; for example, it excludes the Excess Defense Articles and Direct Commercial Sales programs.

Successful FMI programs depend upon close cooperation between Defense and State personnel at the regional and national levels. Ideally, the geographic CINCs, working within policy guidelines set in Washington and collaborating with U.S. ambassadors and country teams within their areas of responsibility, tailor programs and activities to meet changing local and regional requirements, thus anticipating trends rather than reacting to events as they occur.

FMI Programs and Activities Grouped by Funding Source*

Department of State:
Foreign Military Sales (FMS)
International Military Education and Training (IMET)
Foreign Military Financing (FMF)

Department of Defense:
Combined Planning and Exercises
Traditional CINC Programs (TCP)
Regional Study Centers
Special Operations Forces (multiple activities)
Defense Attaché System (DAS)
Army Foreign Area Officer (FAO) Program
Personnel Exchange Program (PEP)
Schools of Other Nations (SON) Program
Port Calls, Visits, Deployments, and Demonstrations
Cooperative Threat Reduction (CTR) Program

Cofunded by State and Defense:
Partnership for Peace
Humanitarian De-mining
Counterdrug Programs

* Source: Director for Strategic Plans and Policy (J–5), "Foreign Military Interaction: Strategic Rationale," (Overseas Presence Joint Warfighting Capabilities Assessment), January 1995.

Arms Deliveries to Developing Nations by Recipient, 1987–94
Deliveries to the leading recipients
(in millions of current US Dollars)*

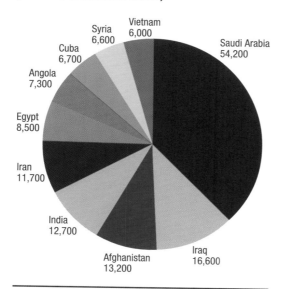

- Vietnam 6,000
- Syria 6,600
- Cuba 6,700
- Angola 7,300
- Egypt 8,500
- Iran 11,700
- India 12,700
- Afghanistan 13,200
- Iraq 16,600
- Saudi Arabia 54,200

SOURCE: Richard Grimmett, Congressional Research Service
NOTE: Data refer to deliveries from all supplier countries combined.

Arms Deliveries to Developing Nations by Supplier, 1987–94
(billions of current dollars)

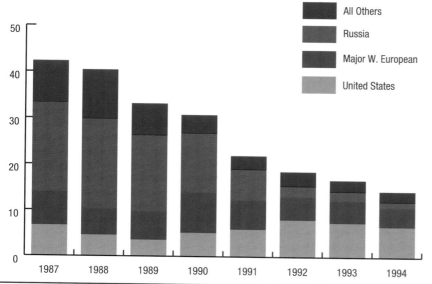

Legend:
- All Others
- Russia
- Major W. European
- United States

1987, 1988, 1989, 1990, 1991, 1992, 1993, 1994

SOURCE: Richard Grimmett, Congressional Research Service.
NOTE: Major West European is France, U.K., Germany, and Italy.

called on to intervene in a crisis and improve the odds that U.S. forces will find a favorable (interoperable) situation should intervention prove necessary.

DOD manages a number of congressionally authorized military-equipment programs. Known during the Cold War as Security Assistance, these programs are now called Foreign Operations Assistance. This term also refers to a range of nondefense programs discussed in other chapters, such as the Economic Support Fund (ESF), migration and refugee assistance, and international narcotics control. This section discusses two elements on the Joint Staff's FMI list—Foreign Military Financing (FMF) and Foreign Military Sales (FMS)—as well as Excess Defense Articles (EDA) and Direct Commercial Sales (DCS). To avoid confusion with the nondefense aspects of the Foreign Operations Assistance, the term "military assistance" is used here.

Since the mid-1980s, trends have developed in four areas that affect military assistance programs:

● *Congressional interest.* A trend toward greater congressional oversight of national security policy begun in the 1970s continues in the mid-1990s. Increasingly, Senate and House authorization committees oriented toward foreign policy, as well as appropriation subcommittees, use legislation to delimit and guide implementation of military assistance programs. They direct, for example, the inclusion (or exclusion) of specific countries and earmark the level of funding for specific states. These four legislative bodies often require the executive branch to provide notification before specific military assistance initiatives can be implemented, such as before lethal equipment and air frames are provided or sold to particular countries, and when there is an intent to give or sell excess defense articles to any foreign government.

● *Foreign interest.* The success of the United States in the Persian Gulf war has significantly increased foreign interest in U.S. military doctrine, equipment, and training. Many governments share the expanded, post-Cold War U.S. security policy agenda—covering such issues as democracy, drugs, and peacekeeping—leading to many requests for military equipment, technical training, and professional education.

● *Funding.* Since the mid-1980s, congressional funding of the two principal military assistance programs, FMF and International Military Education and Training (IMET), has steadily declined. Foreign governments today, freed from the ideological constraints of the Cold War, have become more price conscious and often shop for the best arrangements to purchase equipment and training. This has resulted in a shift toward FMS and DCS; toward alternative U.S. sources, like the Excess Defense Articles program; and toward the use of other suppliers, such as Russia, France, and the United Kingdom.

● *Arms transfers.* Over the seven-year period from 1987 to 1994, the value of international arms deliveries to developing nations steadily declined. In 1994, the trend reached its low point of $14.4 billion (of which $6.7 billion were U.S. sales), slightly more than a quarter of the 1987 total. This pattern reflects the conclusion of the Iran-Iraq War, the end of the Cold War, and the winding down of other regional conflicts. While many major U.S. arms clients in the Middle East ordered substantial amounts of equipment after Desert Storm, deliveries are proceeding slowly, partly because of the need to absorb equipment but mostly because of budget difficulties.

Foreign Military Financing (FMF). FMF has long been the primary means by which the U.S. government finances the purchase of U.S. defense articles and services by select friends and allies. However, Washington has changed its procedures from a loan system at near market interest rates, the norm in the mid-1980s, to a grant arrangement. The latter method is intended to help governments receiving FMF to devote scarce financial resources to economic development.

The initial force and effectiveness of this program worldwide have been lost gradually since the mid-1980s as a result of

Rapier anti-aircraft missile system in Turkey.

two trends. First, congressional appropriations have steadily decreased from $5.2 billion in FY 1986 to $3.2 billion in FY 1995. Secondly, annual legislation has fenced increasingly larger percentages of this funding. In 1995, more than 98 percent of FMF was for Israel and Egypt, the main recipients ($3.1 billion), and for several small, specialized programs, such as aid to build democracy in Haiti ($3 million). This left only $25.7 million available in 1995 for discretionary allocation among eligible countries. Foreign Military Financing aided twenty-eight countries in 1984; eleven years later, it assisted nine nations and a demining program. The termination of most country programs has had a debilitating influence on the quality and scope of U.S. defense relations with many Latin American, East Asian, and Middle Eastern countries.

Foreign Military Sales (FMS). The FMS program enables friendly nations to buy U.S. military equipment, services, and training. Purchases are made with some U.S. financial assistance for eligible countries. As measured by agreements signed rather than by deliveries, FMS averaged $11.5 billion annually between FY 1984 and FY 1992. After a one-year jump in FY 1993 to $32.4 billion due to sales to the Middle East, FMS returned to a lower level of $13.2 billion in FY 1994 and an estimated $8 billion in FY 1995. FMS also covers the sale of professional military education, which is consistently high, accounting for well over 50 percent of the international students in DOD schools. By providing foreign forces with U.S. hardware, using U.S. military personnel to familiarize foreign officers with its operation and maintenance, and by educating future military leaders in the United States, FMS fosters and reinforces the idea of interoperability with the U.S. armed forces. DOD also benefits from the tendencies of foreign sales to keep important production lines running and lower the unit costs of key weapons systems.

The FMS program is affected by a congressional restriction on the transfer of FMS-purchased material to third parties, which hinders the disposal of obsolescent material and the purchase of new equipment to replace it. In addition, the Arms Export Control Act requires that the costs of implementing the FMS program be paid by FMS customer countries. An administrative surcharge of 3 percent is applied to most sales. A 5 percent rate is applied to nonstandard items and services. In addition, a logistics-support charge of 3.1 percent is also applied on certain deliveries of spare parts, equipment modifications, secondary support equipment, and supplies.

Direct Commercial Sales (DCS). Some states prefer to rely on direct commercial purchases of U.S. military hardware, training, and technical assistance from defense contractors. These companies must first obtain export licenses, which require State Department approval. Estimated commercial sales in FY 1995 were $5.9 billion. During the period 1989–1995, DCS purchases averaged about 31 percent of purchases through the FMS program. The trend in the mid-1990s is toward growth in DCS relative to FMS. Depending on the type of equipment or services purchased as well as possible legal or policy limitations, this approach offered cheaper arrangements and fewer bureaucratic obstacles.

Excess Defense Articles (EDA). Defense articles no longer needed by the U.S. armed forces—ranging from rations and uniforms to used vehicles, cargo aircraft, and ships—may be sold to eligible countries and international organizations under the FMS program, or transferred without cost under provisions of the Foreign Assistance Act of 1961. An elaborate framework of rules governs the EDA. A joint Defense-State EDA Coordinating Committee, for example, matches requirements with assets and U.S. policy priorities, trying to ensure some equity in distribution of items among countries. Several Central and Eastern European countries are eligible to receive only nonlethal EDA. A limit exists on the annual value of EDA that a foreign government may acquire by sales or grant—in fiscal year 1995, this limit was $250 million (although exceptions are made for high-cost items, such as ships). And Congress must be notified of all EDA sales or grants. In fiscal year 1994, total EDA amounted to $1.1 billion, a decrease compared with the average of $1.5 billion in FY 1991–93. The decline reflects the existence of budgetary constraints in many countries interested in EDA, as well as a certain amount of frustration with the bureaucracy surrounding

this program. Morocco, Turkey, Greece, and Israel were the largest recipients of grant EDA in 1994. Given the ineligibility of most countries for FMF funding, both State and DOD are seeking ways to make better use of EDA as an instrument of policy, particularly the program's ability to support developing countries with limited defense budgets. As the downsizing and modernization of the U.S. armed forces continues to slow down, fewer articles will be available in the immediate future, increasing the competition for EDA.

In sum, military assistance programs reflect increasing congressional involvement in the direction and details of U.S. foreign policy through its control of the foreign-operations budget. When the executive and legislative branches agree on objectives and the concept for using FMF and EDA as instruments of policy, proactive assistance tends to take place, although affecting fewer countries and at lower levels of funding than during the Cold War era. Many foreign governments, becoming aware of Congress's influential role, have begun to make their case strongly on Capitol Hill as well as to U.S. ambassadors. There is flexibility in this DOD category of policy instruments, but it is found in programs that are outside the formal Foreign Operations budget process: in Foreign Military Sales and, particularly, in Direct Commercial Sales—programs over which State and Defense can exercise more independent control.

Military Education

International Military Education and Training (IMET). The premise underlying IMET is that educating younger foreign military officers in the United States invests in the future promotion of U.S. interests. Graduates may rise to positions of prominence within the military, government, or business community of their countries, and Washington desires access to these future leaders. Furthermore, the United States wants to help emerging leaders utilize their defense resources more effectively and encourage self-reliance in national defense.

International Military Education and Training by Region
(in millions of current year dollars)

SOURCE: Defense Security Assistance Agency

More than 100,000 students from 114 countries have attended IMET courses in 1976–1995, averaging 5,500 annually in 1976–1989 and 3,800 annually in 1990–95. The attraction is twofold: grantees gain insight into U.S. combat techniques as well as learn how the armed forces fulfill their role in a functioning democracy. Schooling

is highly sought after by foreign governments: interest far exceeds funding levels and available classroom seats.

In 1991, Congress legislated a variant of IMET for education on resource management, civilian control, military law, and regard for human rights. This initiative, entitled Expanded IMET (E–IMET), allows civilians with defense-related interests from foreign government agencies, legislatures, and nongovernmental organizations to participate in IMET programs. The legislation has also fostered a popular and highly effective series of courses taught overseas by mobile education teams. E–IMET shows great promise in its ability to bring senior civilian and military officials together in their own country, often for the first time, for shared, confidence-building educational experiences. The introduction of E–IMET, however, has decreased the amount of money available for traditional professional military education.

Regional Study Centers. This relatively inexpensive FMI program, begun in 1993, allows regional unified commanders to offer academic courses on defense planning and management in democratic societies for mid- to senior-level foreign military personnel and, when possible, civilians. The first regional study facility chartered by the Secretary of Defense was the U.S. European Command's George C. Marshall Center in Garmisch, Germany. It focuses on instructing personnel from Central and Eastern Europe and the former Soviet Union. In 1995 an Asia-Pacific Center was being established in Hawaii to support the U.S. Pacific Command. The aim of this facility is to foster a broader understanding of U.S. military, diplomatic, and economic interrelationships in the Pacific.

In sum, these two initiatives are solid investments in the future—the future stability of many friendly countries worldwide and future U.S. access to and interaction with senior government officials in these countries.

Joint Planning, Exercises, and Operations

A group of loosely related, relatively new Defense Department programs for joint planning, exercises, and operations existed on a small scale during the Cold

IMET Country Programs FY 1985–96

Fiscal Year	Thousand FY 96 $	Number of Countries	Number of Students
1985	79,269	91	6,600
1986	74,106	96	6,200
1987	74,480	96	6,300
1988	60,672	98	5,600
1989	58,302	95	5,300
1990	55,932	94	4,500
1991	53803	97	4,900
1992	49,476	99	4,400
1993	45,900	105	4,500
1994	23,585	103	2,100
1995	27,140	114	2,800 (estimated)
1996 (planned)	39,781	113	

SOURCE: Defense Security Assistance Agency

War, although they became more common in Central America in the 1980s. These programs have become common practice with many more countries since the end of the Cold War.

Combined Planning and Exercises. Sponsored by either the Chairman of the Joint Chiefs of Staff, unified commanders, or the military services, combined planning and exercises focus on improving U.S. military readiness while fostering interoperability between U.S. forces and potential military partners. These high-profile events build interpersonal contacts and force collaboration among participants, outcomes that are integral to successful coalition operations. The roots of the spectacular allied achievements during the Gulf War can be found in a series of increasingly more sophisticated regional exercises during the 1980s, which built a foundation of operational and logistical planning and cooperation. The trend in the mid-1990s toward reduced forward-basing of U.S. military forces worldwide increases the importance of the relationships that grow out of combined planning and multilateral exercises. These opportunities also become important confidence-building measures among neighboring states.

This category includes exercise-related construction, a dimension that provides a tangible example of U.S. commitment to a country and can facilitate subsequent U.S. deployments in response to regional crises. U.S. Southern Command used exercise-re-

lated construction strategically in the 1980s to develop Honduran airfield and port capabilities to deter Nicaraguan aggression against its neighbors, while creating the transportation infrastructure needed to support a U.S. military response. Joint and combined planning and exercise activities tend to be expensive and often, because of their strategic importance, drain funding intended for other defense programs.

Traditional CINC Activities (TCAs). The five regional Unified Commanders conduct a variety of FMI activities to promote regional stability and support other national security goals. While programs vary based on each command's requirements, TCAs share common characteristics. Planning is responsive, flexible, and transparent, and accomplished in coordination with U.S. diplomatic missions. Examples of major TCAs include U.S. military liaison teams working in former Soviet-bloc countries; the activities comprising "cooperative engagement" in the Asia-Pacific region; staff exchanges with Middle Eastern countries; training deployments for reserve and National Guard units in the Caribbean Basin; and the peacetime Psychological Operations program worldwide. (See chapter on unconventional military instruments.) Unified commanders have two major concerns about TCAs: internal DOD funding has tended to fluctuate from year to year, making a consistent program difficult to achieve; and, in this regard, a mechanism is needed to weigh different CINC requirements against the funds apportioned within DOD.

Cooperative Threat Reduction (CTR) Program. Also known as the Nunn-Lugar program after its congressional sponsors, CTR focuses on the states of the former Soviet Union that retain nuclear weapons: Russia, Ukraine, and Kazakhstan. The program's broad goals include facilitating safe disposition of nuclear weapons and other weapons of mass destruction; preventing proliferation of such weapons; maintaining regional stability; and avoiding the return of a Cold War-type rivalry with Russia. CTR-funded activities include Russian-U.S. peacekeeping exercises and the establishment of high-level communication links between the Defense Department and ministries of defense in Russia and Ukraine.

United States and Royal Thai Marines fast rope from a CH–46 Sea Knight helicopter during Exercise Cobra Gold '95.

Combined forces from the United States and Thailand head for the beach in U.S. Marine Amphibious Assault Vehicles during Exercise Cobra Gold '95.

FMI activities involving former Soviet states do not come under the auspices of a geographic CINC, being instead managed by the Office of the Secretary of Defense and the Joint Staff. Therefore, CTR does not fall under the TCPs funded by the military departments; nor do CTR activities include formal military education under IMET.

Partnership for Peace (PFP). This post-Cold War initiative aims to build working ties between NATO and the militaries of its former Warsaw Pact adversaries, with an eye to developing possible future members of NATO and maintaining cordial relations with the militaries of nations that opt to remain outside of NATO. Exercises under this program will focus on improving the capability of PFP militaries to work together in peacekeeping, search and rescue, and humanitarian-assistance operations, particularly in NATO-led combined joint task forces.

Twenty-six states have joined the Partnership since the January 1994 NATO summit when the initiative was announced. But as of late 1995, participation in PFP activities, not to mention interoperability with NATO, is hampered by chronic resource problems, equipment obsolescence, operational incompatibilities, and leadership deficiencies. Once these problems are overcome, interaction between NATO and its PFP partners should lead to better military coopera-

tion and greater burden-sharing, which should improve U.S. strategic flexibility.

Funding by the United States is critical to the success of this fledgling program. Eastern PFP partner states are unlikely to have the fiscal wherewithal to fund their own activities, and enthusiasm among other NATO countries for assisting with the program is doubtful. To help jump-start partner integration into PFP and initial participation in small-scale military exercises, President Clinton announced while visiting Warsaw in July 1994 a bilateral initiative to provide $100 million in assistance to PFP member countries in 1996—$25 million of which would be earmarked for Poland. The Departments of State and Defense will most likely share this funding using a 60/40 split.

Counterdrug Programs. In 1989, Congress directed DOD to take charge of detecting and monitoring maritime and air transit of illegal drugs bound for the United States. Four years later, the President's strategy shifted the emphasis from fighting drug transit to supporting countries where the drugs originate so these countries can better conduct their own counterdrug operations. DOD provides resources in five areas: support to source nations; detection and monitoring of transit zones; support for domestic drug law-enforcement agencies; initiatives to dismantle cartels; and demand-reduction programs. In addition, the State Department uses FMF to sustain its own fleet of military aircraft in two major source countries and fund a small military education program. (A more detailed discussion of these programs can be found in the chapter on unconventional military instruments.)

In sum, the true measure of U.S. defense involvement abroad is not only the forces deployed worldwide but also the wide array of programs used to associate and work with other countries to achieve different shared goals. This strategy will be successful in each region of the world to the degree that each unified command's persistent, low-profile, and long-range programs reduce the need to deploy forces in emergency situations.

Defense Diplomacy

In contrast to FMI programs that geographic CINC's use within their overseas areas of responsibility, the category of defense diplomacy includes professional contacts involving the Secretary and his principal civilian and military assistants, the Chairman of the Joint Chiefs of Staff, members of the Joint Staff and the three military departments, or their representatives. Also an integral part are policy-related, outreach activities by DOD's academic and research institutions, such as the National Defense University and the Defense Resource Management Institute, and by various DOD agencies, such as the Defense Mapping Agency and the U.S. Army's School of the Americas. Most frequently, initiatives in this category take place in the United States. Defense diplomacy and FMI differ in other ways as well. The former is not an official term. As used in this chapter, it groups different defense and service activities whose relevance and importance as instruments of policy either have not been recognized or have been taken for granted. Consequently, these initiatives tend to occur without a plan to create synergy or to guide their development and exploitation over time. Lastly, they lack the established funding sources and bases in legislation that undergird FMI.

Defense diplomacy is not new, but it has long been downplayed as routine. Defense officials often do not think of their interactions with counterparts from other countries or the initiatives taken by their agencies that engage foreign personnel as instruments of foreign policy. In the past, such activities have been presumed part of

NDU's Role in U.S-China Defense Diplomacy

Official relations between U.S. and Chinese national defense universities were established in 1987. The 1987 agreement actually put the seal on informal ties that had been developing steadily since the early 1980s.

Both sides were eager to advance relations. At the height of the Cold War, the United States wanted to consolidate military-to-military relations with China, which were considered significant in the continuing struggle with the Soviet Union. Moreover, relations with the Chinese National Defense University (NDU) fit neatly within the overall framework of military-to-military ties, which, at that time, embraced high-level visits, working-level exchanges, and so-called military/technical cooperation, or the transfer of certain types of military and dual-use technologies to China.

For their part, the Chinese, although not unwilling to send a signal to Moscow about their position in the Cold War, were more interested in gaining information relevant to their military modernization program. Beijing emphasized such priorities as assessing U.S. military technologies, professional military education and training, and concepts of operations and doctrine. Despite differing priorities, the relationship developed because both sides decided that such ties served their respective interests.

Relations came to a halt, however, in the wake of the Chinese military's violent suppression of the demonstrators in Tiananmen Square in June 1989. Relations remained in limbo until January 1994, when the president of the U.S. NDU visited his counterpart and agreed, in principle, to reconstruct institutional ties. That effort progressed reasonably well, despite a pause in mid-1995. In late 1995, the president of the U.S. NDU visited China's NDU, and further advances in the institutions' relations are planned for 1996.

Despite the ups and downs of the relationship, the United States derived considerable benefit from links between the two national defense universities. Bonds established between the leaders of the institutions have been maintained, despite retirements and transfers on both sides. Also, interactions at lower levels of the faculties and staffs produced a self-sustaining cadre of military and civilian professors and researchers who gained insight into the strategic priorities and methods of their counterparts. For example, the U.S. gained access to information on China's assessment of the regional security environment, the military budgeting process, Chinese thinking about doctrine and operational art, and Chinese perceptions of the requirements of professional military education. Lastly, relations between the two institutions form a network that supports continued communication, despite problems in overall bilateral relations. The link between the two military establishments embodied in the ties between the NDUs may forge a new strategic basis for U.S.-Chinese ties in the future.

Two major lessons can be drawn from the experience of the inter-NDU relationship. First, defense engagement is a dependent variable; the scope and scale of defense relations are influenced by the tenor of overall relations. In the case of China, defense relations were the first to lapse and the last to be restored. Although defense engagement enhances bilateral ties and may help to slow a decline, its role in shoring up strained relations is less than clear. Secondly, in the absence of shared strategic objectives, defense engagement is difficult to establish and sustain. For example, as of the mid-1990s, China is suspicious of U.S. strategic intentions. In these circumstances, defense-related initiatives designed to build confidence and a basis for improved relations encounter some difficulty. Great care and sensitivity are required in defining the engagement agenda to include areas of common interest and mutual benefit.

U.S. medical readiness exercise in Ecuador.

the job, and not always one that was welcomed.

In the post-Cold War era, however, there is an important niche in DOD's participation in peacetime engagement for defense diplomacy. For one thing, certain strategic relationships and issues do not fit easily into the unified-command-based model of overseas presence. For example, Mexico, Canada, and the states of the former Soviet Union do not fall under a geographic CINC. The Office of the Secretary of Defense and the Joint Staff are better positioned in Washington to manage most of the delicate defense-policy interactions in these countries. Likewise, some security issues—alliance policies, weapons of mass destruction, arms transfers, and confi-

U.S. Army exercise-related construction project in Honduras, creating a farm to market road where only a trail existed.

dence-building, for example—are so politically sensitive that they are handled directly by the Pentagon.

Also, the norm in military relationships worldwide is the association of counterparts—ministry to ministry, service to service, joint staff to joint staff. While some foreign governments appreciate the CINC's potential as a patron within the U.S. system of military assistance and are willing to work closely with him, others

prefer to deal directly with their counterparts in Washington.

Furthermore, DOD has developed an unprecedented capacity to educate and train its civilian officials, as well as to build functional staff expertise in several specialized areas, such as resource management, public affairs, and emergency management. During most of the Cold War, there was little interest in exporting any defense know-how outside of the United States. Today's security environment and policy to promote democracy make sharing such abilities more feasible and desirable.

The department's defense-diplomacy activities tend to fall into five categories with somewhat fuzzy boundaries, some of which are long-standing practices and some of which are new to the 1990s:

● *High-level contacts:* official visits overseas, counterpart visits to the United States, defense ministerial meetings, bilateral-security working groups, contact with the Washington diplomatic corps, and personal associations with senior foreign leaders that mature over time.

● *Staff talks:* bilateral Joint Staff talks, multinational service conferences, and both joint and service expert exchange opportunities (relating to subjects such as military law, simulations, and force development).

● *Sharing professional expertise:* OSD briefing (teaching) teams from such staff offices as Program Analysis and Evaluation, the Emergency Planning Directorate, and the Defense Intelligence Agency; the U.S.–U.K. Kermit Roosevelt exchange military lecture series; NDU's collaboration with the Inter-American Defense College; and various DOD outreach programs.

● *Developing an understanding of defense issues and requirements among civilian defense officials:* foreign attendance of courses in service and defense education systems for DOD's civilian professionals; meetings between visiting government and legislative officials and DOD's civilian functional area experts; and short workshops in Washington designed to address this need.

● *Academic/research support of policy:* formal affiliation with sister institutions for military education; counterpart exchange visits by directors of military colleges and universities; roundtable discussions and workshops to share ideas with visiting civilian and military dignitaries, academics, and journalists on topics of their interest; and the distribution of magazines, reports, and other professional literature published by service and defense academic and research institutions—ideally material published in foreign languages.

Thus far, there is no formal network of programs for defense diplomacy similar to FMI, no funding sources other than existing representational and regionally focused service "cooperation" funds, and no management structure within OSD, the Joint Staff, or the service staffs. There is no one in offices devoted to international political-military affairs who attempts deliberately to meet the security or governance needs of a country or subregion by crafting programs that draw upon activities in one or more of these categories. The outlook for this multifaceted instrument as a means of U.S. influence is continued ad hoc use and failure to realize defense diplomacy's potential. As a minimum, OSD should develop regionally oriented matrices characterizing the key security and defense policy issues and identifying different defense-diplomacy initiatives to be used (or created) to address them. Ideally, each region's matrix would mesh with, reinforce, and, in turn, be reinforced by the CINC's strategy for using FMI assets.

Repelling Aggression in El Salvador

The activities of the Department of Defense in support of U.S. policy in El Salvador during its twelve-year civil war (1980–1992) fall somewhere between "defense engagement in peacetime" and "limited military intervention." DOD went beyond a normal combination of foreign military interaction programs—FMF, IMET, and TCPs—and defense diplomacy by deploying highly specialized mobile training teams under security assistance, sharing a wide range of intelligence products, and supporting the country's large military management requirements, particularly in a military emergency. Washington went to great lengths to keep the U.S. military presence in El Salvador small, limiting the number of trainer/advisors to fifty-five, and to ensure that its overall approach to military support did not replicate earlier Cold War experiences.

By the end of the Salvadoran civil war, the Pentagon and individual U.S. services had provided a myriad of programs, services, and suggestions to their Salvadoran counterparts in an effort to help the government of El Salvador defeat the FMLN insurgency. The only resource purposefully withheld was the direct involvement of American warfighters. A large military assistance program, mobile training teams, out-of-country training of units, periodic visits by the CJCS and other high-level U.S. military leaders, assistance with intelligence collection, intelligence sharing, civic action assistance, IMET training in the U.S.—all were tried. Some were successful in advancing U.S. interests, others had no effect one way or the other. A few had negative results.

What worked. The smartest move the U.S. made in helping El Salvador repel aggression was to resist the temptation of direct U.S. military involvement in the fighting. The preponderance of U.S. assistance was spent on teaching the Salvadorans to teach themselves, i.e., on training the trainers. Also, what advanced U.S. interests best was assistance uncluttered—and carefully crafted for the Salvadoran situation and culture. The resident presence of U.S. military personnel, officers and enlisted, was also extremely beneficial when those assigned represented the best of the U.S. professional force, i.e., role models. The exposure of the Salvadoran military, and of civilians who harbored a distrust of their armed forces, to what a professional military acting under civilian leadership is all about was the most effective method of conveying those concepts.

What seldom worked. The U.S. put enormous effort into intelligence sharing. With a multitude of platforms and other data gathering mechanisms, the U.S. tried to pass information that could be of use to the Salvadoran allies. This seldom had effect. First, it was most often too little, too late. Secondly, Salvadoran expectations as to what the all-knowing U.S. intelligence community could produce far outstripped reality. As a result, the Salvadoran military never understood or accepted the importance of intelligence. In a similar vein, the U.S. effort to demonstrate the importance of PSYOP, particularly in counterinsurgency warfare, was wasted. The assignment of PSYOP trainers with no in-depth knowledge of Salvadoran culture or the mindset of its military had either no discernable impact or was, as in one case, an unmitigated disaster.

What always failed. The delivery of messages by high ranking U.S. military or Defense civilian visitors, especially the delivery of messages having nothing to do with military matters, never had the desired result. The distinguished status of the visitor never made up for a necessarily limited personal knowledge of the environment into which the message was being delivered. Thus, messages were inevitably mangled and misunderstood. Worse yet, the U.S. often then proceeded on the false assumption that the message had gotten across. Activities that the U.S. employed to encourage attitudinal and institutional reforms within the Salvadoran military almost always came to naught. The U.S. rarely, if ever, had sufficient knowledge of how the Salvadoran military truly functioned, or what its institutional mindset was on any given subject. The U.S. practice of conditioning all or part of military assistance funds each year to coerce changes within the armed forces was largely counterproductive.

Army tank conducting live fire exercise in Egypt.

Conclusion

The conclusions of two 1995 studies underscore the importance of defense engagement today and for the future. First, the Commission on Roles and Missions of the Armed Forces argued that engagement in peacetime is a sound and relatively inexpensive investment in the promotion of regional stability and the nurturing of democratic norms. It encouraged measures further to integrate and coordinate defensive engagements within DOD and other government agencies. Secondly, a study of the effectiveness of one education program, IMET, conducted by the Institute for National Strategic Studies, concluded that this form of defense engagement has had a positive effect on many foreign civilian and military leaders who have participated in U.S. programs, frequently causing them to to be more favorably inclined toward the United States and its policies.

While the United States has made considerable progress in adapting how military resources are used in peacetime today, beyond solely maintaining readiness for combat, three general patterns are emerging that may shape the future of defense engagement in peacetime.

● *Reliance on DOD's resources.* Funding for foreign policy initiatives is shrinking, even as defense civilians and units of the armed forces demonstrate that technical-military expertise and professionalism can be an effective diplomatic tool, particularly in peace operations, and while FMI programs and defense diplomacy increasingly support U.S. security policies worldwide.

● *Decreasing personnel.* In addition to a growing shortage of officers and non-commissioned officers with foreign-area expertise, the particular active duty units that participate in most FMI programs—engineers, military police, communications, and medical—are shrinking in number at a more rapid rate than the services as a whole. The immediate impact is to increase competition among the geographic Commands for the use of remaining units.

● *Appearance of defense contractors.* New actors in peacetime defense engagement are defense contractors who negotiate agreements directly with foreign governments. They typically advertise corporate military expertise in such areas as streamlining security assistance, force management, modernization, training, and military transition assistance programs for emerging democracies. The appearance of these companies is too recent for an informed judgement to be made about impact on defense engagement. But the arrival of such independent parties suggests the direction in which this instrument of U.S. power might travel in the future.

CHAPTER TEN

Security Relationships and Overseas Presence

Introduction

Security relationships and overseas presence have come under increasing scrutiny since the end of the Cold War. Despite this scrutiny, or perhaps because of it, both the Bush and Clinton administrations have made a strong case for preserving commitments to core allies, engaging potential coalition partners, and continuing a credible military presence in Europe, the Asia Pacific, the Middle East, and the Western Hemisphere.

The end of the U.S.-Soviet rivalry has left the United States with a global network of multilateral and bilateral relationships without a rationale clearly understood by the public. Regardless of the absence of a menacing global threat, which provided a stable cohesive for past U.S. security relationships, the United States has an enduring and fundamental interest in preserving close ties with powerful states. Such ties can deter regional aggressors, reassure allies and their neighbors, and ensure rapid and effective military response in the event of conflict. However, the recent security environment has led some to question America's alliances as: too rigid to respond swiftly to today's less conventional secu-

rity challenges, unnecessarily benefitting the U.S.'s major economic competitors, and easily supplanted by less binding relationships that entail fewer political and physical costs.

Although there is no simple typology for organizing the complex variety of security relationships and forces deployed overseas, this chapter organizes these diverse and at times overlapping instruments of national power into four types of security relationships—the North Atlantic Treaty Organization (NATO), other formal alliances, de facto alliances, and coalitions—and three types of overseas presence—forward-deployed forces, military exercises, and pre-positioned military materiel.

Instruments

NATO

America's Cold War strategy of containment was predicated on an extensive array of alliance commitments and forward-stationed military troops. Of all those commitments, none was so instrumental in bringing the Cold War to a peaceful and successful end as was the transatlantic alliance, led by the United States and embodied in NATO, with the United States, Canada, and eventually fourteen western European nations including Britain, France, Germany, and Italy.

NATO's genesis was the wreckage left in Europe after the Second World War: an imperial, totalitarian regime in Moscow threatening an exhausted European continent. Only the United States could balance the West European democracies against Soviet hegemony. In response, the U.S. led its European allies in erecting an economic, political, and military bulwark to defend the west against the East. As the military instrument, NATO became the most im-

portant and visible pillar of Western solidarity. The key dates were the 1949 founding of NATO; the 1955 decision of the Federal Republic of Germany to join NATO rather than choose a course of neutrality, an action that led to the creation of the Warsaw Pact nine days later; and the 1967 adoption of a new military strategy of flexible response.

NATO's vitality as an instrument of U.S. power derived from the unwavering American commitment to Europe, U.S. leadership, common interests and values, and the gradual, decades-long development of mechanisms for cooperation and consultation. The incremental institutionalization of NATO—with the North Atlantic Council, the many political committees, the Military Committee, the civilian and military international staffs, and numerous agencies and integrated commands—led to a truly integrated combined military capability that has endured many intra-alliance crises, deterred Soviet aggression, and continues to prove its capabilities in the post-Cold War era.

In the mid-1990s, NATO remains the anchor of American engagement in Europe and the linchpin of transatlantic security. However, the most successful political-military alliance in modern history faces a number of crucial choices with regard to its future. Among these are the difficult issues associated with NATO's membership and mission.

NATO's post-Cold War membership debate is sometimes simplified as a conflict between broadening or deepening the alliance. The former would try to preserve the gains of the Cold War's end by moving quickly to incorporate the fledgling democracies of Eastern and Central Europe that achieve certain basic criteria. The latter would concentrate on maintaining cooperation among the sixteen members of NATO and delay its enlargement, in particular because expansion would antagonize Russia. NATO has balanced the two goals. First, NATO's London summit declaration of July 1990 proclaimed Russia to be no longer an adversary, and it announced a new program for diplomatic liaison open to all the members of the Warsaw Pact. Next, at the Rome summit in November 1991, NATO's commitment to an inclusive

NATO Enlargement

The NATO enlargement process faces two dangers. The first is that enlargement will proceed too fast, which could upset a delicate political process underway in Russia. The other is that the process slows too much, in which case it could stall.

Impact on Russia. There is not much consensus at present in Russia on anything, but there is consensus among the national security elite against enlargement. Many Russians believe that NATO enlargement would draw a new line in Europe which would create cultural and economic barriers that would be impossible to overcome. Russian observers say that if NATO enlarges, Russia may abandon START II and the CFE Treaty.

Impact on Central and Eastern Europe. Not all of the Central and Eastern European states may be ready to join NATO at the same time. The 1995 NATO study on enlargement concluded that decisions should be made on a case by case basis. While the NATO study makes clear that there are no fixed criteria, it does provide some guidelines, including that ethnic and border disputes need to be settled. Progress on democratic reform and civil-military relations will also be an important factor.

As NATO proceeds, it risks separating Central Europe from Eastern Europe and creating a strategic vacuum in the East. States in this region are concerned they will have no firm security framework and that they may have to deal with a Russia which is more aggressive in response to enlargement.

Impact on Western Europe. Western Europe is somewhat divided on the enlargement issue, with Northern Europe generally more interested than Southern Europe. A West European consensus could form around the proposition that NATO enlargement should be tied to EU enlargement. But that may take too long for some in the U.S. and Germany.

Impact on NATO. The 1995 NATO study focuses on enlarging in a way that strengthens rather than weakens NATO. A minimum degree of military interoperability will be needed on the part of candidate countries so that NATO can operate smoothly. The extent of the modernization required has already generated a debate about the danger of extending hollow commitments which could cost NATO tens of billions of dollars to fix. The study also concludes that NATO has no *a priori* need for forward deployment of either troops or nuclear weapons into any candidate country, but it would reserve the right to do so.

HMS *Gloucester* alongside USS *Niagara Falls* and USS *Fife* during Desert Storm.

Europe was further manifest in its creation of the North Atlantic Cooperation Council (NACC), which established a new institutional framework for consultation and cooperation on political and security issues between NATO and the non-NATO states of the Conference on Security and Cooperation in Europe (CSCE, later OSCE). Then, at the January 1994 NATO summit, President Clinton launched the Partnership for Peace program aimed at drawing interested countries closer to the alliance through individual political and (especially) military partnership programs.

As of late 1995, officials from NATO member countries continue to struggle with the issue of defining the criteria for expanding full membership in the alliance. Even if some Central European countries should meet such criteria for NATO membership, their entry into the alliance—still subject to unanimous consent of the members under the Washington Treaty—could be held up by widespread concerns about Russia's reaction. The notion of a strategic understanding with Russia over NATO expansion seems

as desirable as it is difficult to achieve. The challenge is to define the NATO-Russian relationship in a way that strengthens NATO reassures the Central and Eastern European states, and satisfies Russia that its security is in no way diminished.

The debate over NATO's mission has concerned whether and how to transform an alliance traditionally focused on the defense of members' territory into an alliance that is also capable—and willing—to respond to the crises that threaten the allies' collective interests near their territory, or even farther away. Some observers have summarized NATO's post-Cold War prospects by the phrase "out of area or out of business."

In 1991 NATO allies agreed for the first time on the importance of addressing security threats beyond the NATO area, and established crisis management operations as important NATO missions. In 1993, the allies added peacekeeping to their crisis response missions by agreeing to respond to both CSCE and U.N. calls for peacekeeping on a case-by-case basis. In

The Purposes of Security Relationships

First and most fundamentally, alliances augment military power. Rather than unilaterally building up military power, nations may opt to join a security relationship with other nations.

Secondly, alliances are usually threat-based; that is, they are formed with specific antagonists in mind. Thus, alliances—and other less formal security relationships—are aimed primarily *against* a potential threat, and only derivatively *for* something. The offensive alliance, in which aggressive nations band in the avaricious expectation of being able to share the spoils of an offensive victory, is far from the norm.

Throughout history, states have entered into alliances for a variety of other reasons, such as ideology (holy alliances) or political penetration (satellites or client states subverted, for example, through significant political, financial, or technical assistance). Moreover, Otto von Bismarck's diplomacy of constantly shifting among alliances in the latter half of the nineteenth century was predicated more on considerations of maintaining order in the international state system than on balancing threatening power.

Thirdly, the common bond holding alliances together is each ally's perception that its national interest is served by the alliance. Alliances are rooted in common interests. But unlike individuals, nations cannot have friends. Because alliances are founded on common interests, it follows that when interests change, alliances are affected. This goes a long way toward explaining some of the difficulties in alliance management since the demise of a common global opponent, the Soviet Union.

Some scholars offer less hard-nosed views of the purposes of alliances. Idealists believe that alliances can be a step toward permanent collective-security regimes, such as the United Nations, or regional-security communities rooted in common values and respect for international law. Neoliberals emphasize how interlocking networks of relations can provide countries with a stake in accepted international norms, customs, and practices. Hence, neoliberals suggest that alliances are relevant not simply for addressing threatening power (collective defense) but also for more positive objectives, such as buttressing international order (collective security).

1994, NATO agreed to form Combined Joint Task Forces (CJTF) as a means of modifying the Cold War vintage Integrated Military Structure to achieve the flexibility and mobility needed for crisis response. In 1995, in its first actual military operation, NATO military forces unleashed massive, sustained air strikes in support of major new diplomatic effort to bring peace to war-torn Bosnia-Hercegovina. At this writing (November 1995), such military intervention appeared to have been largely successful at protecting safe haven zones and advancing the peace process. The mere decision to deploy NATO forces outside of its members' territory marked a milestone on the path of transforming NATO into an effective transatlantic alliance for the post-Cold War era.

The CJTF initiative holds the most significant promise to date for genuine re-orientation of the alliance's military capabilities for new missions. By investing in the concepts, standardized procedures, and exercise regimes for CJTF as it did for collective defense, NATO will become the reservoir of multinational expertise and essential infrastructure to conduct the rapid deployment of task forces to respond to a wide array of crises. Not only will this give NATO the means to mount operations as an alliance, but the latent cooperation among its participating nations will provide a nucleus to deploy coalitions of the willing outside of NATO's political-military apparatus as well. In this regard, the Western European Union (WEU) will be a special benefactor of CJTF. Simply the presence of a CJTF capability will go far to reassure NATO's friends and to deter aggression well beyond NATO's borders.

Yet it is no surprise that the political struggle to agree on a concept for CJTF capabilities and employment has been especially difficult. More so than any other post-Cold War initiative, CJTF goes to the heart of the allies' debate over the future of the alliance. While most want CJTF to be at the center of European collective security

U.S. Air Force F–16Cs flank a Republic of Korea F–5 overflying South Korea's Independence Hall.

response to the Dayton peace plan. In Bosnia, theoretical debates over future institutional relationships are yielding to the ealities of political will and military capability. As a result, IFOR's operational links to the EU, OSCE, WEU and UN, as well as to many non-NATO nations, will establish the precent for what works in crisis response.

Approval of IFOR's deployment brought France closer to NATO's military structures. In addition, the late 1995 French decision to re-join NATO's Military Committee and to participate regularly in meetings of defense ministers may prove a most significant turning point in mapping NATO's place in Europe's future security structure. France will be engaged in NATO's military policy planning process for the first time in nearly thirty years.

Within the framework of the North Atlantic Treaty, the United States and Canada maintain an additional defense agreement—the North American Aerospace Defense Command (NORAD). NORAD's primary interest in the 1960s was to defend North America against air attack (meaning bombers from the Soviet Union). By the 1970s, NORAD's objectives had broadened to deterrence against ballistic missile attack through warning and assessment. Then, in 1986, the two nations agreed to upgrade their systems to counter an evolving cruise missile threat. In the mid-1990s, NORAD units routinely assist law enforcement agencies in their efforts to stem the tide of illicit drugs into Canada and the United States. The evolution of NORAD's objectives will undoubtedly continue as new technologies redefine the threats against Canada and the United States. In the final analysis, the NORAD Agreement represents the amicable and enduring relationship between Canada and the United States.

Other Formal Alliances

Besides NATO, the other principal formal alliances are in East Asia and the Western Hemisphere. Unlike multinational NATO, America's alliances in East Asia are chiefly bilateral. Even so, the Cold War's

and crisis management, some see it at the periphery as a backstop to capabilities the WEU hopes to some day obtain. While none see the WEU today as capable of managing, for example, the crisis in Bosnia, those who see NATO's future as a backdrop to Europe's own capability in security and defense want to avoid the creation of a permanent crisis-management tool such as CJTF in NATO. A still more fundamental question remains: Whether NATO will continue to be a collective defense alliance directed at outside threats or whether it will take on a different task as the provider of security to all of Europe, including Russia.

In large part, the answer to that question will be revealed as NATO deploys its implementation Force (IFOR) to Bosnia in

Coalition Organization and Execution

A number of issues will affect how well the coalitions in which the U.S. is likely to participate will cohere and function:

■ *Pre-coalition groundwork.* Advance preparation, such as increased joint training, education, exercises, and exchanges, can introduce U.S. military personnel and civilian counterparts to prospective coalition partners, as discussed in the chapter on Defense Engagement.

■ *Access to foreign facilities.* Because future coalitions are likely to be more flexible and short-lived, the United States cannot count on the same degree of access to foreign military facilities that it enjoyed during the Cold War era. This suggests that U.S. military forces will have to become more autonomous, even if achieving this capability is costly.

■ *The core military group.* In any coalition, some countries inevitably become part of a core group while others remain peripheral to decision making and the execution of operations. In Desert Shield and Desert Storm, the United States and Saudi Arabia were politically and financially at the core, whereas the United States, Britain, and perhaps France were militarily at the core. Combat operations will proceed more smoothly if core nations exclude those that cannot conduct combined operations with similar equipment and doctrine. On the periphery, there are two basic categories of partners: those that can make a useful contribution in the military operation, and those that cannot, but add political cover.

■ *Coalition maintenance.* A robust liaison with militarily and politically essential partners may be necessary to hold together a coalition. In the Gulf War, for instance, the United States saturated the Saudis' and other key partners' defense apparatuses with competent U.S. civilians and officers to ensure a unity of effort. If combined combat operations are contemplated, then it is in the interest of U.S. component commanders to check and double check, rehearse and re-rehearse actions to be undertaken to avoid costly mistakes, including fratricide. Given that coalitions are often symbolic and require much political give-and-take, U.S. leaders may devote much effort to the collegiality and diplomacy required to placate the national sentiments of coalition partners.

lective-security treaty for the Western Hemisphere, the Rio Treaty calls for consultation in the event of a threat rather than invoking an automatic response like Article 5 of the North Atlantic Charter. The absence of such an unambiguous "musketeer principle"—all for one and one for all—has tended to emphasize diplomacy rather than concerted military cooperation among the countries of the Americas, only 22 of which have ratified it. In fact, when the Rio Treaty was invoked by Argentina in its 1982 war with Britain over the Falkland-Malvinas Islands, it proved ineffective in rallying diplomatic and military support. There were no common interests to unite neighboring countries suspicious of each other. Although the Rio Treaty was designed to keep foreign powers at bay and to provide the United States with political and moral legitimacy to wage the Cold War on behalf of noncommunist nations, it was seldom used to significant effect.

It is precisely this looser mutual commitment among countries of the Western Hemisphere that has begun to change in the 1990s, as a result of unprecedented cooperation in economic matters and the almost universal acceptance of democracy as the political ideal. U.S. defense diplomacy as well as military interaction with counterparts have made important contributions in the areas of Latin American political-military cooperation and respect for human rights. While the Rio Treaty itself has had no impact, trust and confidence among neighbors is growing on several levels. This can be seen in the 1994 Summit in Miami; the first-ever 1995 Defense Ministerial in Williamsburg, Virginia; the extensive involvement of regional police and military forces in bring peace and stability to Haiti; and the hemisphere's collective success in ending sustained combat in 1995 between Peru and Educador as well as setting the stage for negotiations to resolve this long-standing border dispute. These events, and particularly the supportive, low-profile role played by U.S. civilian and military defense officials, underscore the potential for greater confidence and security building within the American neighborhood and the prospect for more effective collaborative engagement abroad.

De Facto Alliances

While any nation could potentially become a coalition partner with the United States in a time of crisis, some countries have security relationships that are alliances in all but name. That is, although they may lack a formal treaty of alliance, the variety of military, political, and other interactions with these countries make them de facto allies. Particularly important are the relationships with three Middle Eastern states because of the vital U.S. interests at stake and the level of threat they face.

Recent Coalitions

Since the end of the Cold War, the United States has found coalition partners from all over the globe. Some of the more significant recent coalitions were:

■ *Desert Shield/Storm:* In 1990, the U.S. deployed 500,000 troops to the Persian Gulf as part of a U.S.-led coalition force to defend Saudi Arabia. In January 1991, the U.S.-led coalition commenced a six-week military campaign that liberated Kuwait and crushed the Iraqi armed forces. Coalition forces, particularly from key NATO allies, such as Britain and France, played an important military role in the victory.

■ *Southern Watch:* Since 1992, U.S. and coalition aircraft have enforced a no-fly zone over southern Iraq.

■ *Provide Comfort:* Under way since the end of the Gulf War, this operation maintains a secure environment that permits humanitarian assistance to flow to the endangered Kurdish population of northern Iraq. Multinational operations include approximately 1,500 U.S. military personnel and some 50 aircraft sorties per day, on average, from NATO bases in Turkey.

■ *Vigilant Warrior:* In October 1994, after two Iraqi Republican Guard divisions massed on the Kuwaiti border, the U.S. deployed a Marine Expeditionary Unit, elements of a heavy Army division, a carrier task force, and additional land-based aircraft to reinforce security partners Kuwait and Saudi Arabia.

■ *Uphold Democracy:* In September 1994, the United States entered Haiti peacefully to oversee the return of the country's popularly elected government (ending President Jean-Bertrand Aristide's three-year exile) and the departure of the nation's military leaders. The use of U.S. military power in an effort to restore a democratically elected government was the first such operation in the Western Hemisphere ever authorized by the United Nations. Various regional nations pledged support to help provide civil control after the U.S. military operation reined in the armed forces, police, and paramilitary groups.

■ *Deny Flight:* Beginning in April 1993, about 1,700 U.S. military personnel stationed in Europe participated with NATO allies to enforce a ban on military flights over Bosnia, monitoring the U.N. protection areas and providing close air support to U.N. peacekeepers in Bosnia when called upon.

■ *Able Sentry:* Since the spring of 1993, about 500 U.S. troops have participated in the U.N. observer force, now called the U.N. Preventive Deployment in the former Yugoslav republic of Macedonia, providing a stabilizing presence and preventing the conflict in other regions of the former Yugoslavia from spilling over into Macedonia.

■ *Sharp Guard:* Starting in April 1993, three U.S. naval vessels and approximately 7,800 U.S. personnel participated regularly with NATO allies in maritime enforcement of sanctions against Serbia in the Adriatic Sea, with intermittent support from other assets of the U.S. Sixth Fleet. As with Deny Flight, Sharp Guard was teriminated in December 1995 with the establishment of IFOR.

■ *Support Hope:* From June through September 1994, some 2,000 U.S. military personnel from Europe deployed to Africa to organize and carry out emergency humanitarian relief operations for refugees fleeing a brutal civil war in Rwanda. While the U.S. operation was unilateral, it directly supported multinational governmental and nongovernmental efforts at providing humanitarian support. Moreover, as the U.S. pulled out in the autumn of 1994, its major Asian ally, Japan, dispatched peacekeeping forces to support refugee camps in Zaire.

■ *Provide Relief:* From August 1992 until March 1993, the U.S. conducted a military airlift from Mombasa, Kenya, to deliver goods to Somali refugees. The U.S. also led the Unified Interim Task Force from December 1992 to May 1993, which was a large-scale coalition effort to stem mass starvation.

Israel. U.S. interests are tightly interwoven with those of Israel for historic, political, and moral reasons. Ever since President Harry Truman promptly recognized the new state, the United States has been pledged to its survival. During the Cold War, Israel was an essential partner in the Cold War struggle to limit Soviet influence in the region. In the post-Cold War era, the U.S. supports Israel's security through a combination of means, not the least of which is major security assistance so that

Responsibility Sharing

The United States has increasingly expected its allies to assume greater responsibility for regional security. From the mid-1980s to 1993, U.S. annual defense outlays declined in real terms by over 15 percent ($60 billion). Post-Cold War changes in the international environment have enabled other U.S. reductions, with active duty end strengths dropping 20 percent since the end of the Cold War, and major force components down 15 to 25 percent from 1990 levels. Since 1990, the U.S. has reduced troop levels permanently stationed overseas by over 225,000 (44 percent)—mostly out of Europe—and its estimated real annual stationing costs (including military pay) have been reduced—through negotiated agreements as well as lower forces levels—by nearly $10 billion (33 percent).

U.S. allies in Europe, East Asia, and the Middle East provide a wide array of host-nation support to the United States. DOD estimates that the U.S. receives more than $10 billion annually in cost-sharing and cost-avoidance from European and East Asian allies, which equates to roughly 40 to 50 percent of the extra costs of deploying those forces overseas. Japan's contribution is the highest of any ally, and a new host-nation agreement and special-measures agreement worked out in late 1995 committed Japan to approximately $5 billion in direct and indirect support for each of the next five years. The Republic of Korea, which provides land and facilities for U.S. use, logistics support and manpower augmentees, contributes about $3 billion a year in direct support, indirect support, and foregone revenue. Estimates of Germany's direct support, indirect support, and foregone revenues are in the range of $2 billion a year.

Summary of Estimated Defense Cost-Sharing/Host Nation Support to the United States for 1994
($ in millions)

Host Nations	Direct Support[a]		Indirect Support		Total Support (other than forgone revenue)	
	Low	High	Low	High	Low	High
Germany	$ 242	$ 249	$1176	$1300	$1418	$1549
Japan	3403	3857	766	766	4169	4623
Republic of Korea	265	266	1368	1368	1633	1634
Other European and Pacific[b]	18	35	796	823	814	858
Europe and Pacific Subtotal	3928	4407	4106	4257	8034	8664
Kuwait	186	186	4	4	190	190
Total	4114	4593	4110	4216	8224	8854

SOURCE: Secretary of Defense, *Report on Allied Contributions to the Common Defense 1995*.
NOTES: Excludes some Middle East contributions. Excludes foregone revenues.
  a. Direct cost-sharing estimates (low range) reflect pledged contributions.
  b. Other Host Nations include: Belgium, Canada, Denmark, France, Greece, Italy, Luxembourg, the Netherlands, Norway, Portugal, Spain, Turkey, and the United Kingdom.

Israel can maintain its qualitative edge over any likely combination of aggressors. Moreover, the United States supports Israel in its pursuit of a peaceful and stable regional framework with its neighbors for the long-term.

Saudi Arabia. Saudi Arabia, as the largest Gulf state supportive of Western interests, sits atop a critical region of the world for its oil and yet is adjacent to two major security concerns in Iraq and Iran. The security of Saudi Arabia is not guaranteed by a formal treaty of alliance; however, successive American Presidents over several decades have reiterated the U.S. interest in its safety. The Gulf War and the Vigilant Warrior deployment of 1994 demonstrated the firmness of this and similar commitments. It was Saudi Arabia's decision to gradually buildup a vital military infrastructure during the 1970s and 1980s that enabled the United States to deploy overwhelming military force against Iraq. Since 1991 a continuing U.S.-led operation to keep watch on Saddam Hussein has been based in the region, and Saudi Arabia and Kuwait have borne much of the deployment's cost. Some Saudis are concerned about these costs and about he continuing presence of U.S. soldiers in what is a conservative Muslim society. Of course, as the U.S.-led coalition to defend Kuwait suggested, aggression against any of the six members of the Gulf Cooperation Council (Saudi Arabia, Kuwait, Qatar, Bahrain, the United Arab Emirates, and Oman) would be likely to compel an American response.

Egypt. For nearly two decades during the Cold War, Egypt, the Arab world's most populous country, led an anti-Western, pan-Arab movement that supported Soviet objectives in the Middle East. From the 1970s onward, however, Egypt became a stalwart Western supporter, first in the Cold War and then in the establishment of an Arab-Israeli peace process. Egypt's willingness to make peace at Camp David was the first major breakthrough in the peace process. Cairo continues to take a leading part in promoting interests shared with the United States throughout the Middle East, whether in rallying Arab League backing for Kuwait after the Iraqi invasion, providing two divisions to Desert Storm, or offering key support to the Middle East peace process.

Coalitions

Alliances, whether de jure or de facto, represent the traditional security commitment of the Cold War era. Since the breakup of the East-West contest, however, rigid ideological alignments have given way to far less structured and more ad hoc arrangements. In response to crises, coalitions of the willing have formed. Of these various coalitions, it is useful to distinguish between those led by the United States, albeit perhaps authorized by the United Nations or regional collective-security bodies, and those directed by the United Nations in which the U.S. participates.

For the foreseeable future, Washington will continue to insist that it lead and direct any operation that may involve U.S. military forces in combat or prospective combat situations. Conversely, if the situation can be characterized as posing little risk of combat—as is the case in traditional peacekeeping operations, such as in Cyprus—then the United States is likely to encourage other nations to carry the burden of leading and directing the coalition operation. In short, in combat situations in which the National Command Authorities have decided to intervene, the United States will seek U.N. authority but abjure U.N. direction. Besides domestic political opposition to U.S. troops under U.N. command, a basic reason for this distinction is that any effective military operation requires a unity of command and effort.

Coalitions and formal alliances both offer the same potential benefits, although the chief benefit of a coalition is typically different from that of an alliance. Whereas both types of security relationship offer political legitimacy and an aggregation of military power, the emphasis in a coalition is on the former, whereas the emphasis in an alliance—which, after all, is a latent war community—is on the latter.

Another advantage of both types of association is the aggregation of finances and resources to support military operations. Also, both coalitions and alliances can serve a restraining function by limiting the actions of allies and coalition partners—for example, by eliminating the chance that a given nation will join an opponent's coalition.

Whatever the benefit of any given coalition, its relative merits need to be weighed against the potential costs of creating it. The fundamental risk in setting up or joining a coalition is that national objectives may become submerged, diverted, or derailed. An identity of common interests and objectives is rare enough among two or three countries. Disparities are magnified geometrically, however, when even larger groups of nations are involved. Agreement in international organizations or among large groups of coalition partners usually represents something like the lowest common denominator of interests. This can make a coalition's objectives murky. From an operational perspective, it can sharply restrict the scope, pace, and flexibility of operations.

In short, the political and diplomatic imperative to seek consensus within a coalition often stands at odds with the military imperative to achieve results through the threat or use of unrestrained force. Thus, in some instances, the impulse to form a restrictive or binding coalition should be suppressed in order to maintain maximum flexibility. Future coalitions, like their predecessors, will cohere principally in proportion to the level of perceived threat. Given that starkly different scenarios for the future are plausible, U.S. alliance and coalition policies will have to remain, above all else, flexible.

Clemenceau–class aircraft carrier
Foch during exercise Distant
Drum.

This chapter has implicitly assumed that the United States will largely remain a status quo power, and that its primary objectives in participating in military coalitions will be to enhance stability in general and to defend specific national interests in particular. Like most states, the United States tends to view its own behavior as benevolent and defensive. Yet, U.S. decision makers should not assume that others share this view. Even governments that Washington does not regard as hostile worry about the uses to which U.S. power might be put, and even traditional U.S. allies may not always approve of U.S. policies or actions. These facts suggest that when thinking about future alliances and coalitions, Washington also needs to think about preventing future arrangements from forming against the United States.

Forward-Deployed Forces

The most critical military aspect of U.S. engagement strategy is forward deployment. Post-Cold War reductions are nearly complete, and as of mid-1995, the United States sustained an overseas presence of about 255,000 personnel (or 15 percent of the total active force). That figure represented a 50 percent reduction, down from 510,000 personnel stationed overseas just six years earlier.

Often, even a token presence can serve like a cooling rod in a nuclear power plant. This is particularly true in Asia, where a power balance among China, Japan, and the members of the Association of Southeast Asian Nations has yet to be struck. The roughly 100,000 U.S. military personnel stationed in East Asia stabilize the balance, reassure U.S. security partners, and prevent unnecessary regional military buildups. Most Asians recognize this more readily than Americans, which is why they wish U.S. forces to stay and why Japan is willing to contribute a high level of host-nation support. Although the U.S. Government remains committed to current force deployments in Japan and South Korea for the foreseeable future, future events and evolving political debates may encourage Washington to focus more on capabilities than quantities. For instance, the alleged rape of a Japanese schoolgirl by American servicemen crystallized debate over plans to reconsolidate U.S. facilities on Okinawa, which houses some 28,000 or 62 percent of the U.S. troop presence in Japan. If the bilateral commission established in late-1995 to review America's 40 facilities on Okinawa is perceived as stonewalling the local Okinawans, then it is highly likely that U.S. presence in Japan will remain a volatile political issue. Hence, especially if there is a diminution of the threat from North Korea, subsequent U.S. security planners may find it prudent to focus less on the number 100,000 and more on essential missions and types of leading-edge forces, especially naval and air, which adequately convey the seriousness of America's commitment to the region.

Reassurance also remains important in Europe, where most want Germany to retain its non-nuclear status and defensive posture.

Forward-deployed forces are fundamental to America's ability to react to crises around the world that affect vital interests or humanitarian concerns. In Desert Storm, about 95 percent of the airlift arrived via Europe. A review of twenty-seven operations mounted between March 1991 and October 1994 reveals that more

CJCS Exercises, FY 1995

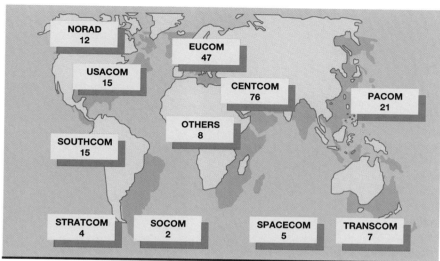

NORAD
12

EUCOM
47

USACOM
15

CENTCOM
76

PACOM
21

OTHERS
8

SOUTHCOM
15

STRATCOM
4

SOCOM
2

SPACECOM
5

TRANSCOM
7

SOURCE: Joint Staff
NOTE:: Data indicate the location of the 212 Exercises in the FY 95 CJCS Program

than half were staged from Europe. Without forward-staging areas, America's ability to react would be severely constrained.

Each service struggles with a portion of forward deployment:

● Many in the Army would prefer to bring home the two heavy divisions in Europe while only retaining a "reception cen-

ter" infrastructure. There may be a case for replacing armor with more mobile light units. Similarly, should the threat from the North disappear on the Korean peninsula, the 2nd Infantry Division in South Korea might also be reduced or removed, although there appears to be mounting interest in retaining at least a residual U.S. ground presence, and perhaps an enhanced naval and air presence, for regional reassurance and crisis response well into the next century.

● The Navy finds it increasingly difficult to retain a significant presence in the Caribbean, Mediterranean, Atlantic, Pacific, Indian Ocean, and Persian Gulf with a fleet two-thirds the size of a decade ago. As Marine Expeditionary Units increasingly provide a mobile presence for crisis management, there do not seem to be enough forces to go around.

● More than the other services, the Air Force emphasizes the coercive impact of all military assets, not just those deployed overseas. Thus, while the Air Force agrees that forces stationed overseas are the most tangible form of U.S. presence, its global-presence concept contends that space assets, ICBMs and bombers in the U.S., aircraft carriers, and airborne units all

USAREUR forces being loaded for pre-positioning afloat, Antwerp, Belgium.

U.S. Forces Pre-positioning

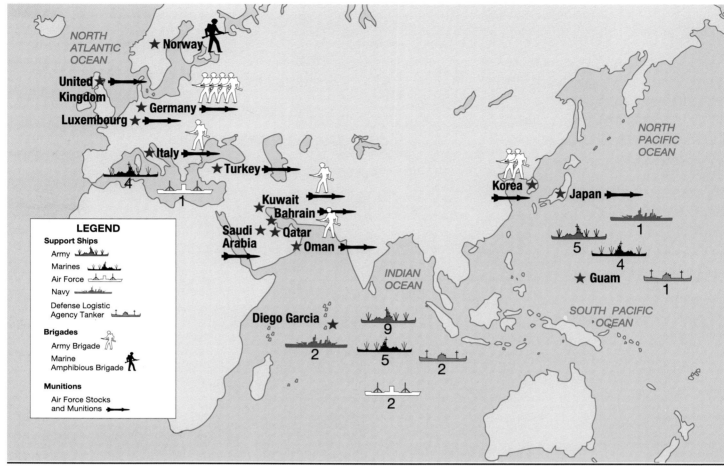

SOURCE: DOD

NOTE: The Army brigade for Qatar and the second brigade for Korea is planned.

exert influence on or coerce U.S. adversaries to varying degrees.

Closer to home, the United States maintains an important military presence on foreign territory within the Western Hemisphere, in Panama and Cuba. Although the U.S. will honor the 1977 Panama Canal treaties, which call for the complete withdrawal of all U.S. military forces from the country before the beginning of the year 2000, both sides agreed in late 1995 on the need to retain a forward U.S. presence into the next century. Thus, even after relocating America's Southern Command to Miami, Florida, the U.S. armed forces stationed in Panama at the

beginning of the next century could be in the range of 5,000 troops. In addition, the United States retained forces based in Guantanamo, Cuba.

The post-Cold War decline in America's overseas military presence has increased U.S. reliance on long-range transportation to project power. Throughout the course of any given year, the United States Transportation Command (USTRANSCOM) shows the flag on every continent and in most countries of the world. Moreover, USTRANSCOM is essential to all U.S. military operations, as well as many global humanitarian and peace operations. For instance, in 1995, USTRANSCOM moved 5,000 British troops and their equipment to

Russian Marines debark from *USS Dubuque's* LCU near Vladivostock during combined exercises.

the Bosnian theater. While unremarkable in and of itself, the airlift was yet another demonstration of how the capability to project power overseas has become an integral part of America's long-term commitment to allies and security partners around the world.

Military Exercises

The Goldwater-Nichols Department of Defense Reorganization Act of 1986 placed greater emphasis on joint training and exercises. Accordingly, the emerging role of U.S. Atlantic Command as the Joint Force Integrator and the start-up of the Joint Warfighting Center contribute to this emphasis through a higher degree of integration of joint training, exercises, and doctrine than existed during the Cold War.

The Chairman of the Joint Chiefs of Staff (CJCS) Exercise Program remains the Chairman's principal vehicle for achieving interservice and multinational operational training. Exercises also demonstrate U.S. resolve and the capability to project military presence anywhere in the world, and they provide an opportunity to stress strategic transportation and C⁴I systems and to assess their readiness.

CINC-sponsored exercises, a large subset of the CJCS Exercise Program, are continuing their transition in the post-Cold War environment to reflect emerging security relationships, evolving theater strategies, and increased joint task-force training. The emphasis of CINC-sponsored exercises has shifted from a few large-scale exercises focused on global contingencies and conflicts to an increased number of smaller-scale exercises focused on regional contingencies. As a result, CINC-sponsored exercises have increased in number from ninety in FY 1990 to two hundred in FY 1995, but they have decreased in size and scope. As the permanent overseas presence of U.S. forces has been reduced, joint exercises have increasingly been used to maintain regional access and presence and to demonstrate U.S. resolve. Other exercise trends include increased use of modeling and simulations in exercises; the enhancement of military relations and interoperability with allies and security partners; containerization of ammunition and unit equipment; the exercising of pre-positioned equipment; and special-forces participation in CINC-sponsored exercises.

As operational deployments continue to increase and resources to decrease, U.S. forces are finding it more difficult to support exercise requirements. For this reason, the Joint Staff launched a review in 1995 of the entire CJCS Exercise Program, with an eye toward combining scheduled CJCS exercises or integrating CINCs' requirements with existing component exercises to reduce the overall number of exercises while increasing their quality. The military is also looking at the opportunities to use simulations, computer-assisted exercises, or command-post exercises to replace or complement current field-training exercises.

Pre-positioned Military Equipment and Materiel

Affordable and rapid crisis-response capabilities cannot rely exclusively on airlift—which is expensive and limited by available aircraft—or on sealift, which is relatively slow. A comprehensive *Mobility Requirements Study* in 1992 estimated what combination of lift and pre-positioned arms and supplies would best yield a "strategically prudent force that is fiscally responsible." As a result of this study, as well as a March 1995 *Mobility Requirements Study Bottom-Up Review Update,* an increasing emphasis has been placed on pre-positioning to help improve U.S. mobility and crisis-response capabilities.

Pre-positioning Afloat. Ships filled with military materiel are based in foreign ports where formal agreements specify U.S. basing rights. These "floating depots" may leave without host-country permission and proceed through international waters wherever and whenever directed, before full-blown crises develop, if desired. Ships sometimes may reduce vulnerabilities by maneuvering out of harm's way, and the cargoes they carry may be tailored to satisfy requirements in more than one theater. However, optimum locations are not always available. Thailand, for example, rebuffed U.S. requests to tie up in its waters midway between Diego Garcia and Guam, where U.S. squadrons are stationed. In addition, even under the best circumstances, costs for afloat pre-positioning are higher than for stocks pre-positioned ashore.

In 1980, in response to concerns about the Persian Gulf, the Navy acquired seven commercial ships configured to carry cargo for 11,200 Marines. Various shortcomings associated with this initial force were corrected when thirteen Maritime Pre-positioning Ships (MPS) were leased until the year 2010. A five-ship squadron, together with a Fleet Hospital Ship, is homeported in Diego Garcia in the Indian Ocean, earmarked for duty in the Persian Gulf. One four-ship squadron is based at Guam/Saipan; another roams the Mediterranean. Each squadron is prepared to outfit tailored Marine formations up to and including a 17,300-man Marine Air-Ground Task Force, which it can sustain for thirty days with ammunition, water, rations, and supplies. Plans call for three more MPS to enter the inventory, one per squadron.

The Army Pre-positioned Afloat program postdates the Cold War. Since November 1993, a heavy combat brigade, in-cluding 123 M1A1 tanks and fifteen days of essential supplies aboard five roll-on/roll-off (RO/RO) ships has been stationed at Diego Garcia, together with a Heavy Lift Prepo Ship for port operations and three Lighter Aboard Ship (LASH) vessels loaded mainly with munitions. The Army also has five LASH vessels in Guam. The plan is to modernize and expand by two ships by FY 1998, including replacing seven aging ships with eight new Large Medium-Speed RO/ROs.

Pre-positioning Ashore. Since the 1950s, pre-positioning programs ashore have been intended primarily for use by Army armored and mechanized brigades. The Berlin crisis of 1961 prompted Pre-positioned Overseas Material Configured to Unit Sets (POMCUS), which provided for three divisions plus support in Germany at the Cold War peak. Sets for four brigades remain, although critics consider them anachronistic. Most agree that the Army brigade sets in Korea, Kuwait, and Italy are more relevant to the post-Cold War environment. In addition to the brigades sets, significant amounts of Air Force and Army materiel are stored in Southwest Asia, some of it left over from Desert Storm. In particular, the October 1994 *Operation Vigilant Warrior* validated the need for pre-positioned ground combat equipment in the Persian Gulf. Subject to congressional approval of construction funding, a second armored brigade set with a division base will be pre-positioned in Southwest Asia by FY 1998, and another armored brigade set will be pre-positioned in South Korea in FY 1996.

In summary, pre-positioning has become an increasingly important part of U.S. defense plans for ensuring rapid mobility in the event of a crisis. Recent initiatives will significantly enhance the U.S. deterrent posture, deployment response time, and warfighting capability in volatile regions. At the same time, however, contentious issues—such as command and control arrangements, local security, and maintenance requirements for pre-positioned stocks—will continue to require constant negotiation and oversight by senior defense officials.

Marine F/A–18, Japanese F–1 and Air Force F–16 during Cape North 94–1.

Conclusions

America's complex network of security relationships and various types of overseas presence has been profoundly affected by the end of the Cold War, and there remains a widespread consensus that these instruments of national power remain important for preserving U.S. influence in the world.

Security Relationships. In the last few years of the twentieth century, America's formal alliances are likely to face continuing challenges to their existence. Policymakers will continue to be pressed to articulate clear rationales for alliances, both to persuade public opinion of their relevance in the post-Cold War era and to provide fundamental stability to alliances in spite of periodic economic competition or other disputes. Shoring up NATO's mission and credibility without recreating a Russian threat to the east will remain a paramount challenge for U.S. decision makers; likewise, adapting and making more equal America's alliances in East Asia, especially with Japan and South Korea, will be critical tasks in the next few years.

America's other security partners, its de facto allies, will represent an even greater range of challenges. On the one hand, the United States is likely to face a growing array of relationships that require specialized expertise to maintain; on the other hand, the United States will be unlikely to extend to these countries the kinds of formal commitments Washington was eager to make during the 1950s, when it created its global network of Cold War alliances. In short, the U.S. will have to juggle these security relationships, using troop rotations, exercises, and information exchanges to shore up key partnerships and retain a vast set of friendly relations that would enable an effective coalition to be built in the event of a conflict or crisis. In the longer term, the question of proliferating weapons of mass destruction, especially relatively inexpensive systems, such as cruise missiles and biological warheads, is apt to pose increasing challenges to all U.S. security partners and allies, underscoring the importance of counterproliferation measures, including active defenses, as means of retaining the requisite political will to endure.

In the foreseeable future, the United States is unlikely to fight a major conflict except as part of a coalition. If that coalition is led by the United Nations, then the U.S. is apt to steer clear of direct and massive combat support and instead confine its role to rear-area support. The international response to a major conflict would probably not be led by the U.N. but by some executive agent, whether the United States, another major power, or a military alliance like NATO. If the coalition is led by the United States, then it needs to focus on the nucleus of other capable allies, de jure or de facto, who will form the nucleus of its warfighting potential; other security partners will need to be brought into the coalition on the basis of their strategic value, whether on the battlefield or in symbolic political value.

Overseas Presence. Just as alliances and other security relationships will face many challenges in the next few years, so, too, is overseas presence likely to face increasing scrutiny, especially if significant military threats fail to materialize.

Forward deployments are sure to face increasing questions from members of Congress, many of whom will be confronted with further base closings in their home states or other competing motivations, such as reducing the federal deficit. Even so, the consensus behind maintaining an active presence in Europe, East Asia, and the Middle East seems unlikely to break in the foreseeable future. While sudden changes cannot be ruled out—for example, the collapse of North Korea—the likely challenge will not be to forward presence per se but more to the appropriate size of the military overall.

Recent trends in exercises are likely to continue to accentuate the importance of smaller, more varied efforts, designed not for massive land or blue-water threats but oriented to multinational cooperation for other military operations, including peace operations and humanitarian assistance.

Lastly, as force structure declines and support for large overseas bases continues to diminish, the importance of pre-positioned forces ashore and afloat is likely to expand. Nonetheless, the difficulty in winning support to base such stocks can be a delicate political matter, as the United States found out when such support was rejected in Thailand in early 1995. Consequently, policymakers might expect to spend increasing amounts of time winning local support for such pre-positioned military equipment and materiel, which will be critical to timely and effective efforts to respond to crises.

CHAPTER ELEVEN

Peace Operations and Humanitarian Support

Introduction

Peace operations is a subset of the broader category of operations other than war (OOTW). It refers to a form of military intervention short of full-scale war, in support of diplomatic actions, and conducted by, or with the endorsement of, a collective security organization in order to maintain or restore stability to a region or a state. In addition to "defusing and resolving international conflicts," as proclaimed by Presidential Decision Directive 25, *Reforming Multilateral Peace Operations* (PDD 25), peace operations also address civil strife and humanitarian crises within individual states.

This study discusses four distinct instruments or capabilities: 1) peacemaking and conflict prevention; 2) peacekeeping; 3) expanded peacekeeping and peace enforcement; and 4) humanitarian operations. The taxonomy of peace operations is organized according to a combination of four pivotal factors: the breadth of the mandate or rules of engagement; the presence or absence of an accord among the disputants; the degree to which the operating environment for the peace force is characterized by basic consent or by armed opposition; and the size and complexity of the mission. This chapter does not discuss major conflicts such as Korea (1950) or the Persian Gulf (1991), even though they were endorsed by the U.N. Security Council. This chapter also excludes unilateral U.S. operations, such as Lebanon in 1958 and Grenada in 1983, where there was no international endorsement.

Since the late 1980s, many peace operations have combined traditional military and diplomatic activities with humanitarian support for civilian populations conducted by military units, usually to save lives and alleviate suffering on a large scale. Such support can entail conducting, assisting, or safeguarding the delivery of food and medical supplies; protecting civilian populations; and so forth. Humanitarian support operations have also been conducted by the armed forces alone, independent of other actors. These have taken place in various sizes, under various mandates, in both permissive and hostile environments.

On occasion (e.g., Somalia and Bosnia), the protection of humanitarian activities by peacekeeping forces has evolved into peace enforcement on a large scale. For these reasons, humanitarian support is discussed as a separate category. Nation assistance or peace-building activities—disarmament of factions, conduct of elections, rebuilding of local administration,

Typology of Humanitarian Support and Peace Operations

	Mandate Roes	Peace Accord	Degree of Opposition	Size & Complexity
Peacemaking	Self-defense only (Ch. VI)	No; Incipient	None: peace force seen as impartial	Small (under 500) Observers/Mission Support
Peacekeeping	Self-defense, observation, verification	Yes	None: peace force seen as impartial	Medium (500–6,000) Observers; some peace building
Expanded Peacekeeping	Force in support of diplomacy	Not normally	Episodic clashes: peace force seen as ambivalent	Large (20,000+) Some combat capability; peace building
Peace Enforcement	Use of all necessary means (Ch. VII)	No	Peace force seen as antagonist	Large. Offensive combat capability
Humanitarian Support	Variable (Ch. VI or VII)	Variable	Variable	Variable

NOTE: Chapter numbers refer to which chapter of the U.N. Charter is invoked for the operation.

and other measures to strengthen a weakened or collapsed state—have also been frequently incorporated. However, they will not be discussed as a separate instrument since they have not been conducted independently of other operations. Moreover, most are performed by civilian specialists, although the U.S. military has on occasion contributed civil or military expertise and other specialized skills.

Between 1945 and 1988, there were thirteen U.N. peace operations, limited mostly to the Middle East and aimed at discouraging the renewal of conflict after a cease-fire between hostile states. The Middle East actions took place with the blessing of both the United States and the Soviet Union, both of whom wished to avoid escalation that might precipitate unwanted great power confrontation. Most other proposals for U.N. action ran into Soviet veto power, thus severely limiting the number of peace operations. Few U.S. military personnel and no U.S. units participated.

Between 1988 and 1995, there were some twenty-six new and separate peace operations authorized and commanded by the U.N. Starting in 1987–88, a positive attitude emerged in Moscow toward both U.N. peacekeeping and cooperation with Washington in resolving regional conflicts. The ensuing cooperation produced a much

more assertive approach by the U.S. and key U.N. members toward peace operations. In addition, the United States organized, outside the formal U.N. framework, two major coalition peace operations (Restore Hope in Somalia and Uphold Democracy in Haiti) as well as a more limited multinational mission (Provide Comfort in Iraq). France and Russia also organized and led peace operations outside the U.N. framework but with its concurrence: France in Rwanda in 1994, and Russia in Georgia and Tajikistan in 1994–95 (using the CIS). In addition, involvement of regional and subregional organizations in peacekeeping increased markedly during this period (e.g. OAS in Haiti, NATO in Bosnia, OAU in Burundi, ECOWAS in Liberia).

As a result, the U.S. military has become heavily involved in peace operations around the globe, both through direct participation and as a source of transportation, logistical support, and equipment. As of end-September 1995, 3,239 U.S. military personnel were part of U.N. operations, according to U.N. definitions. Twenty-thousand U.S. military personnel were being dispatched to Bosnia as part of a NATO peace operation. The participation of U.S. military units in post-Cold War peace operations qualitatively boosted multilateral effectiveness. U.S. C^{3}I capabilities and experience in managing coalitions have proven to be major assets in planning and coordinating multilateral operations, and valuable specialties—such as civil affairs, psychological operations, special forces, engineering, and advanced logistics (including tactical and strategic airlift)—have been contributed by the U.S. Few other military establishments can provide such assets to the U.N. When there has been danger of conflict, U.S. combat units participating in U.N. peace operations have remained under the operational command and control of U.S. senior officers, as in Somalia and Haiti. On occasion, for temporary duty, U.S. military personnel are under operational or tactical control of other military commanders, including NATO.

In keeping with the growth of operations, the number of U.N. peacekeeping personnel increased from 8,000 in 1988 to some 62,500 in 1995, and assessments for

U.N. peace operations rose from approximately $200 million in 1988 to $3 billion in 1995. (Moreover, these figures do not cover the costly, U.S.-led operations in Iraq, Somalia, and Haiti.)

Starting in 1994, however, the U.N. and U.S. both adopted a more cautious attitude. Haiti, Angola, and Tajikistan were the only new U.N. peacekeeping missions undertaken in 1994–95, along with the reinforcement of the U.N. Protection Force in the former Yugolsavia (UNPROFOR) and the creation of the NATO-led implementation Force (IFOR) in Bosnia. No new expanded peacekeeping operations were authorized, and six earlier operations were completed or terminated, including expanded ones in Cambodia and Somalia and medium-size missions in El Salvador and Mozambique; UNPROFOR was scheduled to end in late 1995. Simultaneously, a strong movement arose in Congress favoring a drastic reduction in U.S. contributions and support for future U.N. peace operations, as well as tight limits on the use of U.S. forces. The backlash generated by the failed mission in Somalia, the agonizing dilemmas of the operation in Bosnia, and the need for deep cuts in the overall U.S. budget generated serious concerns over the utility of U.N. peacekeeping and made it an inviting political target. The Clinton administration has favored tighter restrictions upon the UN but opposed drastic cuts and overly restrictive constraints, and argued for the continued utility of selective, more effective, and usually less costly peace operations. At the same time, it assisted in substantial improvements in the peacekeeping capabilities of the U.N. Secretariat, particularly in the areas of logistics, planning, and C³I.

Repeated use of this rapidly evolving instrument of national policy has confronted military thinkers with a host of nettlesome doctrinal, training, financial, and operational issues, while policymakers have been forced to grapple with an array of novel political and diplomatic challenges.

According to Congressional Research Service data, the cost to the U.S. for peacekeeping jumped in FY 1995 to approximately $1.5 billion in incremental operating costs and $1.2 billion in contributions to the U.N. peacekeeping budget, as well as $680 million in humanitarian aid more or less associated with the crises that led to the peacekeeping operations. The need for effective interagency as well as international coordination has become more important as civilian functions and agencies—including scores of private voluntary organizations—have been integrated with military forces in peace operations. Managing the interaction and interdependence of political, military, humanitarian, and economic activities is an essential element for success.

Instruments

Conflict Prevention and Peacemaking

Intended to forestall the outbreak of hostilities or to facilitate resolution of an armed dispute, conflict prevention and peacemaking missions are conducted with strict impartiality, almost always with approval of the disputants. They are comprised of primarily diplomats and other civilians, including humanitarian workers, human rights monitors, etc. Limited numbers of military personnel, usually unarmed, often assist in liaison with the belligerents, implementing confidence-building measures or arranging a cease-fire. A recent innovation in this category of peace operations, known as preventive deployment, stations lightly armed troops as a trip-wire to deter the spread of conflict. The only example of this, to date, is Macedonia, where some 1,000 U.N. military observers (half from the U.S.) have contributed to deterring a spill-over of hostilities from Bosnia or Croatia.

During the Cold War, prevailing U.N. practice and Soviet opposition restricted the number of U.N. peacemaking missions. With the exception of the Congo in the early 1960s, the U.N. avoided addressing domestic unrest. Since the end of the Cold War, the Security Council has been increasingly

Number of Major Peace Operations

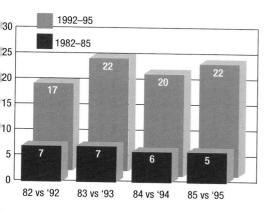

SOURCE: Stinson Center
NOTE: Not all operations are by the U.N.

Paradoxes of Peace Operations

A clear mandate is vital to effective execution of any peace mission. However, U.N. Security Council resolutions are often ambiguous political documents to accommodate divergent national interests (e.g., over eighty separate resolutions on Bosnia).

Unity of purpose and an integrated political, military, and humanitarian relief strategy are vital for success in major peace operations. However, unity and integration are often vitiated during execution of the mission because nations and organizations comprising a multilateral peace mission pursue their own views and interests at the expense of the overall mission.

To avoid mission creep, contain costs, and generate domestic support, it is best to establish in advance an exit strategy and departure date. However, the ultimate success of the mission can be jeopardized if parties to the dispute exploit them, or if circumstances change so that they are no longer feasible.

The U.N. is incapable of conducting the more demanding types of peace operations (e.g. peace enforcements), thus, U.S. participation will often be essential for success. However, these are also the most challenging and costly operations, with the greatest risk of casualties, which renders U.S. participation problematical.

Scenes of mass starvation or genocide can generate powerful initial public support for humanitarian operations. However, unless the underlying causes are also addressed effectively, humanitarian relief may merely be a palliative or lead to deeper or more dangerous involvement, accompanied by loss of public support—as in Somalia and Bosnia.

inclined to approve peace operations. Since 1995, the U.N. Secretary General has been able to authorize conflict prevention missions on his own initiative. Most of the new operations have been explicitly concerned with internal conflicts.

As a result, the United Nations has undertaken scores of conflict prevention or peacemaking missions, (mostly initiatives by the Secretary General) and demands for military personnel to assist these diplomatic activities have also increased. Since 1989, such operations have been conducted in Afghanistan, Angola, Western Sahara, Rwanda, Somalia, and the Aouzou strip in Chad. These missions generally involved domestic rather than interstate conflict (except for Afghanistan and the Aouzou strip). The mandates essentially involved monitoring cease-fires, movements of forces, and weapons deployments. Several carried additional objectives: registering voters and supervising a referendum on the disputed territory in Western Sahara; protecting the delivery of relief supplies in Somalia; and assisting with a cease-fire, demobilization, and election in Angola. Operations in Georgia and Tajikistan by the CIS and in Liberia by ECOWAS had U.N. observers assigned to them.

Mission results have been mixed, determined primarily by the willingness of warring parties to pursue peace and honor the agreements reached. Clear and realistic mission objectives, a good comprehension of the local political situation, adequate resources, and strong outside political support from key states also contributed to success. In the Bosnian, Somalian and Rwandan cases, local disputants were not sufficiently receptive to international mediation, and the peace forces lacked the power, cohesion, and will to bring an end to those conflicts. The same was true in Liberia for five years. On the other hand, Libyan troops did withdraw from Aouzou, as did Soviet troops from Afghanistan, facilitated by U.N. observers. The first Angola mission failed due to inadequate understanding of the local situation, an undermanned U.N. mission, an unrealistic timetable, and continued differences between the two disputants. A subsequent mission successfully corrected these deficiencies.

The United States has provided political, logistical, and financial support to almost all these conflict prevention/peacemaking operations and on occasion has also contributed a small number of military observers. Despite mixed results, Washington has regarded such operations as a useful, low-cost means of collectively pursuing secondary interests. Governments and nongovernmental organizations are directing a great deal of attention to developing a rapid-response capability for quickly mobilizing trained, multinational teams of diplomatic, humanitarian, and military personnel in response to international crises. This capability could increase the effectiveness of efforts at prevention or containment thus avoiding much larger and more costly security and humanitarian problems if crises continue unchecked.

Peacekeeping

Peacekeeping operations occur after disputants have achieved a tentative resolution to their conflict, whether international or intrastate. In such missions, impartial military observers verify implementation of a cease-fire or monitor the separation of forces. The number and success of these operations have increased substantially since the end of the Cold War, as has the operations' complexity. Recent peacekeeping operations have frequently involved some aspects of peace-building, as well as support for humanitarian operations.

Prior to 1989, U.N. peacekeeping missions were limited to observing and patrolling demilitarized zones and force-limitation zones, and monitoring cease-fire agreements. Such operations had mixed results. The 1956 mission in the Sinai helped prevent war for a decade but was compelled to withdraw at Egypt's insistence in 1967, powerless to prevent another Arab-Israeli war. A subsequent Sinai mission in 1973 facilitated the successful transition to the Camp David peace treaty in 1979. The Golan mission has helped Israel and Syria avoid even a single incident since it was constituted at U.S. instigation in 1974. On the other hand, the operation in South Lebanon, begun in 1972, proved impotent to prevent conflict. Its continued presence follows the Security Council's judgment that the situation would be even more volatile if it were withdrawn. This is also true for the Cyprus operation, which began in 1964, was upset by a major war in 1974, and continues at a lower level of force and expectation.

In 1962, a U.N. General Assembly action created a Unique Temporary Executive Authority for West New Guinea to avoid an impending war. It successfully provided security and an interim administration for the territory, turning it over to Indonesia after seven months and organizing "an expression of popular opinion" on the future. This prefigured the more complex and challenging sort of peacekeeping operation that has arisen in the post-Cold War period.

Outside of the formal U.N. framework, the Israel-Egypt peace treaty established the Multinational Force and Observer (MFO) mission for the Sinai in 1981. With some 2,000 personnel from eleven countries (about half from the United States) and an annual budget of $50 million, it is still in existence. Its usefulness is illustrated by the absence of subsequent incidents in the Sinai. In 1982–85, the U.S., Italy, and France undertook a multinational operation to calm the situation in Lebanon.

It was successful in 1982, but crossing the line between impartiality and partisanship in 1983 led to extensive U.S. casualties. U.S. and other forces subsequently withdrew.

In late 1989, a peacekeeping operation was deployed in Nicaragua to monitor a cease-fire, verify the concentration of Contra guerrillas in security zones and the concurrent concentration of the Nicaraguan army, and oversee Contra disarmament and demobilization. The number of sea, air, and ground observers gradually decreased from 1,200 in early 1990 to 300–400 during 1991. By June 1990, most of the 22,000 Contra personnel had been demobilized, and the Nicaraguan army had disengaged. Elections were held, and the operation was officially terminated in January 1992.

A separate U.N. peacekeeping operation for El Salvador was established in 1991, involving some 1,000 personnel. Its tasks were to monitor respect for human rights, the separation of combatants, demobilization of Soviet- and Cuban-backed guerrilla forces, restructuring of the Salvadoran military and police forces, and the conduct of elections, as stipulated in the Chapultepec accords. Also successful in achieving its aims, the operation was terminated in 1995.

Several Iraq-related U.N. operations were established in 1991 stemming from the Gulf War, including a peacekeeping mission with some 1,000 lightly armed military personnel that continues to monitor the Iraq-Kuwait border and demilitarized zone against hostile Iraqi actions. A smaller operation demarcated the border to the satisfaction of Kuwait and disbanded.

In Mozambique, a larger and more complex peacekeeping force of between 5,000 and 7,000 personnel (ONUMOZ) was established in December 1992. Its mandate was to monitor the cease-fire between government and guerrilla forces, verify the subsequent separation and demobilization of forces, oversee elections, and facilitate the return of refugees. Its annual budget was some $250 million. The original implementation period was lengthened to provide more time to accomplish its tasks and to persuade the warring parties to respect both their previous agreements and future election results (including certain prior understandings on power sharing). The

Troop Contributions to U.N. Peacekeeping
Operations as of September 30, 1995.

UK	8,575
	TOTAL 62,498
France	7,884
Pakistan	3,964
USA	3,239
Bangladesh	3,172
Canada	2,271
India	2,198
Norway	1,760
Malaysia	1,655
Russia Fed.	1,525
Others	26,255

SOURCE: U.N.
NOTE: Based on U.N. records. The U.S. uses a different definition of which of its troops are part of U.N. peacekeeping operations.

Major World Peacekeeping Operations

U.N. Operations:

1. U.N. Truce Supervision (UNTSO).
Mission: Supervise the observance of the truce in Palestine called for by the Security Council. At present, UNTSO assists and cooperates with UNDOF and UNIFIL; military observers are stationed in Beirut, South Lebanon, Sinai, Jordan, Israel and Syria.
1994 cost: $ 30 m.
Strength: 220 (15 US observers).

2. U.N. Military Observer Group in India and Pakistan (UNMOGIP).
Mission: Observe the cease-fire between India and Pakistan along the line of control in the state of Jammu and Kashmir.
1994 cost: $ 8 m.
Strength: 39.

3. U.N. Peacekeeping Force in Cyprus (UNFICYP).
Mission: Supervise 1974 ceasefire and maintain a buffer zone between the Cyprus National Guard and the Turkish and Turkish-Cypriot forces.
1994 cost: $ 47 m.
Strength: 1,212.

4. U.N. Defense Observer Force (UNDOF).
Mission: Supervise the ceasefire between Israel and Syria, and to establish an area of separation and verifying troop levels.
1994 cost: $ 35 m.
Strength: 1,036.

5. U.N. Interim Force in Lebanon (UNIFIL).
Mission: Confirm the withdrawal of Israeli forces from southern Lebanon, restore international peace and security, and assist the government of Lebanon in ensuring the effective return of its authority in the area.
1994 cost: $ 138 m.
Strength: 4,963.

6. U.N. Iraq/Kuwait Observer Mission (UNIKOM).
Mission: Monitor demilitarized zone between Iraq and Kuwait. Deter violations of the boundary and observe hostile or potentially hostile actions.
1994 cost: $ 73 m.
Strength: 1,100 (14 US observers).

7. U.N. Mission for the Referendum in Western Sahara (MINURSO).
Mission: Verify ceasefire in Western Sahara. Supervise referendum on future of region.
1994 cost: $ 40 m.
Strength: 377 (30 US observers).

8. U.N. Angola Verification Mission III (UNAVEM III).
Mission: Assist in the disengagement of forces; set up verification mechanisms; establish communications links between government UNITA and UNAVEM; start process on mine clearance.
1994 cost: $ 25 m.
Strength: 4,109.

9. U.N. Assistance Mission for Rwanda (UNAMIR).
Mission: Establish a demilitarized zone in northern Rwanda; act as intermediary between warring parties to achieve a ceasefire; protect refugees and assist in humanitarian relief missions; assist with demining and police training.
1994 cost: $ 98 m.
Strength: 2,776.

10. U.N. Observer Mission in Georgia (UNOMIG).
Mission: Verify compliance with ceasefire agreement; investigate and resolve violations; observe CIS peacekeepers; monitor withdrawal of Georgian forces from Kodori valley; encourage orderly return of refugees and displaced persons.
1994 cost: $ 5 m.
Strength: 142 (4 US observers).

11. U.N. Observer Mission in Liberia (UNOMIL).
Mission: Investigate all reported violations of ceasefire agreement; observe and verify election process; assist in coordination of humanitarian activities; develop a plan for the demobilization of combatants; train engineers in mine clearance; coordinate with ECOMOG.
1994 cost: $ 65 m.
Strength: 52.

12. U.N. Mission of Observers in Tajikistan (UNMOT).
Mission: Monitor ceasefire between government forces and Islamic opposition, and coordinate with CIS peacekeeping force.
1994 cost: $ 65 m.
Strength: 39.

13. U.N. Confidence Restoration Operation in Croatia (UNCRO).
Mission: Create conditions of peace and security required to negotiate settlement of overall Yugoslav crisis; ensure demilitarization and protection of UN Protected Areas; assist in monitoring and reporting the crossing of military personnel, equipment and supplies over international borders of the former Yugoslavia.
1994 cost: figure not available.
Strength: 14,034.

SOURCE: Data provided by U.N., State Department, and Council for a Livable World Education Fund. Strength as of August 1995.

peacekeeping operation was successfully completed in December 1994. By August 1995, more than 1.7 million refugees had returned with the assistance of the U.N. High Commission for Refugees (UNHCR) and PVOs.

In Angola, a renewed U.N. operation (UNAVEM III) deployed in 1995. The plan was to reach a level of 5,000–6,000 forces, building up gradually while testing the willingness of both government and opposition guerrilla groups to disarm, accept the 1993 elections, and prepare for a second round of elections. Thus far, progress has been fitful, but a power-sharing agreement based on the 1993 elections has been reached, and renewal of hostilities has been avoided.

On March 31, 1995, UNMIH replaced a U.N.-sanctioned expanded peacekeeping operation in Haiti (the Multi-National

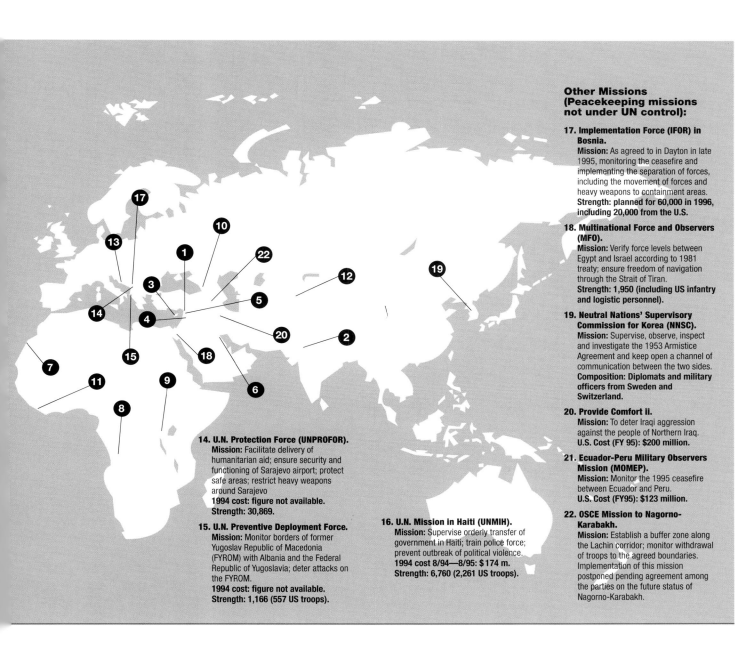

Other Missions (Peacekeeping missions not under UN control):

17. Implementation Force (IFOR) in Bosnia.
Mission: As agreed to in Dayton in late 1995, monitoring the ceasefire and implementing the separation of forces, including the movement of forces and heavy weapons to containment areas.
Strength: planned for 60,000 in 1996, including 20,000 from the U.S.

18. Multinational Force and Observers (MFO).
Mission: Verify force levels between Egypt and Israel according to 1981 treaty; ensure freedom of navigation through the Strait of Tiran.
Strength: 1,950 (including US infantry and logistic personnel).

19. Neutral Nations' Supervisory Commission for Korea (NNSC).
Mission: Supervise, observe, inspect and investigate the 1953 Armistice Agreement and keep open a channel of communication between the two sides.
Composition: Diplomats and military officers from Sweden and Switzerland.

20. Provide Comfort ii.
Mission: To deter Iraqi aggression against the people of Northern Iraq.
U.S. Cost (FY 95): $200 million.

21. Ecuador-Peru Military Observers Mission (MOMEP).
Mission: Monitor the 1995 ceasefire between Ecuador and Peru.
U.S. Cost (FY95): $123 million.

22. OSCE Mission to Nagorno-Karabakh.
Mission: Establish a buffer zone along the Lachin corridor; monitor withdrawal of troops to the agreed boundaries. Implementation of this mission postponed pending agreement among the parties on the future status of Nagorno-Karabakh.

14. U.N. Protection Force (UNPROFOR).
Mission: Facilitate delivery of humanitarian aid; ensure security and functioning of Sarajevo airport; protect safe areas; restrict heavy weapons around Sarajevo
1994 cost: figure not available.
Strength: 30,869.

15. U.N. Preventive Deployment Force.
Mission: Monitor borders of former Yugoslav Republic of Macedonia (FYROM) with Albania and the Federal Republic of Yugoslavia; deter attacks on the FYROM.
1994 cost: figure not available.
Strength: 1,166 (557 US troops).

16. U.N. Mission in Haiti (UNMIH).
Mission: Supervise orderly transfer of government in Haiti; train police force; prevent outbreak of political violence.
1994 cost 8/94—8/95: $174 m.
Strength: 6,760 (2,261 US troops).

Force, or MNF) that had been led by the U.S. Its mandate stemmed from Chapter VI of the U.N. Charter, and the military component was limited to 6,000 personnel (2,400 from the U.S.). Overtly hostile elements had been neutralized before deployment. The operation's objectives were to provide security for elections and other peace-building activities, including creation of a new police force, training the judiciary, monitoring human rights, and promoting economic revitalization. The U.S. headed the military component, thereby retaining effective command and control. So far, UNMIH has been successful in fulfilling its mandate to provide security and restore civil institutions to Haiti, although the conduct of the first round of parliamentary and municipal elections in June 1995 was badly flawed. The involvement of U.S. military

Cost to the U.S. of Selected Peacekeeping and Humanitarian Operations
($ millions)

	DoD Incremental Costs	Humanitarian Assistance	Assessment for U.N. Peacekeeping	Total
FY94				
Angola	2.6	87.3	16.3	106.2
Cambodia	5.0			5.0
Haiti	371.0	106.6	.2	477.8
Iraq	124.8	1.0		125.8
Lebanon			43.0	43.0
Mozambique			110.7	110.7
Rwanda Regional Crisis	134.8	166.3	34.0	335.1
Somalia	528.0	39.0	330.9	897.9
Sudan		94.8		94.8
Yugoslavia	292.0	387.0	459.7	1138.7
Other			55.9	55.9
Total FY 1994	1458.2	882.0	1050.7	3390.9
FY95				
Angola	4.5	99.3	69.2	173.0
Cambodia				
Haiti	595.0	34.3	56.2	685.5
Iraq	579.0	8.4		587.4
Lebanon			44.8	44.8
Mozambique			26.7	26.7
Rwanda Regional Crisis	17.0	286.0	72.6	375.6
Somalia		12.5	166.9	179.4
Sudan		53.8		53.8
Yugoslavia	311.9	185.0	659.8	1156.7
Other			86.0	86.0
Total FY 1995	1507.4	679.3	1182.2	3368.9

SOURCE: Congressional Research Service

forces has been broader, more prolonged, and costlier than anticipated, in part because civilian agencies in the U.S. and U.N. have been slow to muster the required resources, and in part due to administrative deficiencies of the Aristide government. An upsurge of violence in late 1995 and questions about the capacity of the fledgling Haitian police force to maintain order when UNMIH departs illustrates the challenges confronting such missions.

Peacekeeping has become increasingly complex and more likely to deal with internal instead of interstate, strife. Despite this, its overall record since 1991 has been positive. Failures have arisen from inadequate

planning and resources, lack of political sophistication, or insufficient political support from key states. Above all, peacekeeping missions have foundered when the warring parties lack a commitment to peace (as in Somalia). Post-Cold War successes in internal peacekeeping operations—including very substantial peace-building and humanitarian activities in Namibia, Central America, Mozambique, Angola, and Haiti—demonstrate the possibilities for future peacekeeping operations.

With political support from major powers and key regional actors, bloody civil strife that had endured for a decade or more in Southern Africa and Central America has ceased. Prospects for more representative government and democracy have improved greatly in both regions. Indirect benefits have also been substantial, including South Africa's peaceful transition to a multiracial democracy and a reinvigorated economy. In the Middle East, more traditional peacekeeping operations continue to serve very important U.S. interests: maintaining peace between Israel and its neighbors and forestalling renewed Iraqi aggression.

Extensive support from the U.S. and others has helped the U.N. Secretariat improve its capability to plan, deploy, command, and sustain peacekeeping operations of modest scale, and to prepare for still larger operations. For example, by mid-1995, the U.N. Peacekeeping Office had over one hundred experienced military officers on loan to its staff, including a German lieutenant general, a Dutch major general, and a dozen Americans. In contrast, it had a staff of three in mid-1993. It also had established a twenty-four-hour command-and-communications center and consolidated previously dispersed logistics functions.

The Secretariat has developed a preliminary roster of earmarked or standby units from member states, and work is proceeding on a deployable headquarters unit; however, limits on these capabilities clearly remain. Shortfalls in financial support from member states, chief among them the United States, impede further improvement. Entrenched bureaucratic inefficiencies and rivalries within the Secretariat, and between the Secretariat and

Expanded Peacekeeping and Peace Enforcement in Somalia

Expanded peacekeeping in Somalia began after the failure of UNOSOM I accompanied by the specter of 500,000 Somalis dead from famine by the fall of 1992 and hundreds of thousands more in danger of dying. The U.S.-led coalition approved by the Security Council in December 1992 had a mandate of protecting humanitarian operations and creating a secure environment for eventual political reconciliation. At the same time, it had the authority to use all necessary means, including military force. By March 1993, mass starvation had been overcome, and security was much improved. At its peak, almost 30,000 U.S. military personnel participated in the operation, along with 10,000 personnel from twenty-four other states. Despite the absence of political agreement among the rival forces, periodic provocations, and occasional military responses by UNITAF, the coalition retained its impartiality and avoided open combat with Somali factions—blending its coercive powers with political dialogue, psychological operations, and highly visible humanitarian activities.

On May 4, 1993, UNITAF was succeeded by UNOSOM II, but the transition was badly managed. Basic U.N. deficiencies in planning, C³I, and political acumen were compounded by an expanded and intrusive mandate; greatly diminished military capabilities; more aggressive Somali opposition; uncertain support from the United States; differences within the coalition; and uncertainty by the Security Council, the Secretariat, and others. Subsequently, UNOSOM II crossed the "Mogadishu (or Beirut) line" and became a badly flawed peace enforcement operation. (In Beirut in 1983 and Mogadishu in 1994, military forces came to be seen by parties to the local conflict as co-belligerents rather than impartial peacekeepers.)

In Somalia, peace enforcement was only an implicit element of the original U.N. mandate, which focused on peace-building (disarmament, political reconciliation, and economic rehabilitation). However, after a confrontation between the Somali National Alliance (SNA) and the U.N. led to the killing of twenty-five Pakistani peacekeepers, the Security Council made the operation's peace-enforcement mission explicit. It was executed by both U.N. forces and a 1,000-man U.S. rapid-reaction force under U.S. operational control, with the authority of the United Nations. (There was also a 3,000-man U.S. logistics unit under U.N. operational control.) A lack of decisiveness, cohesion, and command and control by the undermanned U.N. mission (half the strength of UNITAF, with some 20,000 personnel) and a series of armed clashes between U.S./U.N. forces and the SNA created a virtual state of war and undermined the effectiveness of the U.N. operation. Confusion over the dual-command relationship between the U.S. and UNOSOM II was another complicating factor, with a U.S. general officer serving as both the U.N. deputy forces commander and commander of U.S. forces. A clash on October 3–4 left eighteen U.S. personnel dead and seventy-eight wounded, along with over one thousand Somali casualties. Public outcry in the United States contributed to the decision to withdraw U.S. forces in March 1994. That, coupled with continued internal strife and SNA hostility toward the U.N., led to a total U.N. withdrawal in March 1995. This was executed skillfully, without casualties, in a carefully planned combined U.S.–U.N. action.

separate U.N. agencies, significantly inhibit coordination and rapid reaction. Continued improvement of U.N. capabilities, particularly logistics, training and C³I, will reduce the amount of support requested from the U.S., lower costs, and enhance operational effectiveness.

Expanded Peacekeeping and Peace Enforcement

Expanded peacekeeping operations go beyond even the more complex peacekeeping operations considered in the previous section. They are larger in magnitude (20,000 personnel or more), more costly ($1 billion or more), and confront a potentially more hostile operational environment because consent from disputants may be nominal, incomplete, or, at times, nonexistent. Accordingly, they have involved more assertive mandates and rules of engagement, including the use of force under authorization of Chapter VII of the U.N. Charter.

The only Cold War era U.N. operation in this category—in the Congo—resulted from an unplanned expansion of the mission's original mandate, activities, and personnel between 1960 and 1964. Eventually, the mission abandoned impartiality and employed military force to help achieve a political outcome deemed desirable by the United States.

Between 1992 and 1995, expanded peacekeeping operations were undertaken in Cambodia (UNTAC), Bosnia (UNPROFOR), Somalia (UNITAF), and Haiti (MNF) in response to serious internal political and military strife and critical humanitarian and human-rights conditions. The United States was, in all cases, a leading advocate and active participant in generating these missions, but had no units involved in UNTAC and UNPROFOR. Initially, all carried primarily humanitarian and peace-building objectives (e.g., saving lives, repatriating refugees, organizing elections, rehabilitating the local economy, monitoring human rights, reforming civil administration, disarming and demobilizing militias, and training a new cadre of police), as opposed to merely providing military assistance to a diplomatic mission or monitoring the military aspects of an interstate accord. However, the dynamics of implementation meant that the dominant issue and key determinant of success became the use of military power and its relationship to other activities.

The mandates, objectives, and uses of available military power varied among the four operations. The MNF in Haiti and

Expanded Peacekeeping in Haiti and Cambodia

Haiti. The U.S.-led Multinational Force for Haiti (MNF) began on September 19, 1994 with the approval of the Security Council, which, at the same time, approved the follow-on U.N. operation. The credible threat of overwhelming force—combined with skillful, eleventh-hour diplomacy—enabled U.S. forces to land unopposed and avoid the negative consequences that combat would have brought. The MNF initially employed over 20,000 U.S. military personnel, plus some 2,000 personnel from a dozen other countries. The mission was to restore democracy by removing the de facto military regime, return the previously elected Aristide regime to power, ensure security, assist with the rehabilitation of civil administration, train a police force and judiciary, help prepare for elections, and turn over responsibility to the U.N. A prior but unfulfilled political agreement between the parties on Governor's Island (New York) in 1991 served as a template to shape objectives. There was a major commitment to peace-building by civilian agencies of the U.S. government, particularly USAID, closely coordinated with the U.N. and numerous other international, regional, and non-governmental organizations. The mission was successfully completed on March 31, 1995, thanks to well-executed political, military, diplomatic, and humanitarian activities. U.S. special operations forces played an essential role in establishing security and assuring de facto public administration in rural areas.

Army Rangers aboard USS Roosevelt for Operations Restore Democracy off Haiti.

Advanced planning and coordination for the transition were well managed by the U.S. and the U.N., as were the selection and training of senior leaders to sustain continued cooperative international action. In contrast to the Somalia transition, the U.N. deployed an advance headquarters element to Haiti six months prior to the change of command. On March 31, 1995, a smaller U.N. peacekeeping mission in Haiti (UNMIH) succeeded the powerful MNF, with a March 1996 deadline for completion, after a newly-elected President is scheduled to take office.

Cambodia. This mission originated with a 1991 Paris agreement amongst the five permanent members of the UNSC, aimed at getting Vietnamese troops out of Cambodia and curbing the power of the Khmer Rouge. The objectives of the 20,000-person military and civilian force were: reform of civil administration and police forces; relief and repatriation of over 500,000 refugees and internally displaced persons; clearing of mines; the demobilization of militias; monitoring the departure of foreign military forces; and managing the organization and conduct of elections. U.S. military personnel were present only as observers. Initially, the mission sought to assume de facto administrative control over Cambodia and disarm all combatants; however, facing serious armed opposition from the Khmer Rouge, it cut back its intrusive mandate and kept the channels of dialogue open rather than creating an adversarial relationship (as in Somalia). This decision avoided what would have been a very bloody and disruptive conflict, putting the mission at serious risk. It allowed free elections to be held in 90 percent of the country. The mission was successfully terminated in September 1993.

UNITAF in Somalia had Chapter VII enforcement authority from the outset, which explicitly authorized them to use force, not merely in self-defense, but as needed to achieve their objectives. In practice, force was used sparingly and essentially in self-defense rather than systematically and coercively; yet both missions maintained a clear upper hand over actual or potential opponents and created an acceptable degree of security for the local population. UNTAC, operating under Chapter VI, achieved essentially the same objective by stressing political dialogue. Basic impartiality was maintained in all cases. UNPROFOR in Bosnia was given Chapter VII authority for specific, limited objectives in 1994, which were shared in a confused, dual-key arrangement with NATO. Coordination problems between the U.N. and NATO and confusion amongst key governments severely hampered operations until August 1995, at considerable expense to the credibility of both organizations.

When norms of international conduct have been egregiously violated, the U.N. Security Council may decide upon peace enforcement action. Peace enforcement is most likely to meet its demanding objectives when coercive military force is employed on a sustained basis without necessarily adhering to the principles of consent or impartiality. Nevertheless, the military objectives are limited in nature, such as protecting safe areas, enforcing no-fly zones and cease-fires, or compelling disarmament.

In the cases of UNOSOM II in Somalia and UNPROFOR in Bosnia, expanded peacekeeping operations produce considerable conflict with local parties and evolved into peace enforcement on the ground, in part due to confusion by the U.N. Security Council and key governments as well as in the execution of operations on the ground. In the cases of Cambodia and Haiti and UNITAF in Somalia, the potential for conflict was present, but a skillful combination of force and diplomacy allowed the operations to proceed successfully, avoiding conflict and the need for peace enforcement on the ground.

U.N. Secretary General Boutros Boutros-Ghali frankly admitted in his January 1995 report to the General Assembly and Security Council that the United Nations lacks the resources and capabilities to manage complex peace operations properly, especially those involving large military forces in a combat environment. For its part, the United States must also consider many issues—such as financial cost, diversion of national military resources from other missions, the risk of casualties, and the fragility of domestic and international support for peace operations—in the context of whether participating furthers important national interests. Doubts have also been raised about the efficacy of using military force to pursue a durable political agreement in states where political institutions have been destroyed, and the wisdom of using force in conflicted situations when impartiality and consent are vital to success.

Whatever the frequency of future expanded peacekeeping or peace-enforcement operations, U.S. involvement in them will continue to be critical. In missions that enjoyed strong, consistent backing from the United States—such as Cambodia and the U.S.-led operations in Somalia and Haiti—there was a unity of purpose and cohesive command. They established a dominant position at the outset and maintained it, skillfully combining political, military, and humanitarian activities. In contrast, the U.N. missions in Somalia lacked a realistic mandate and coherent support, politically or militarily, from those states with the most influence and interest in the area. They also suffered from internal U.N. weakness in the face of tough opposition.

Operations in Bosnia were also plagued for two years by indecisiveness and internal dissension (compounded by dual-command arrangements), owing to limited and uncertain support by the United States and others; the U.N.'s inherent weakness; and ruthless, calculating opponents who felt threatened but not cowed by the U.N. presence and tried to exploit it.

When expanded operations are under consideration, the issues to consider include: how to set the objectives clearly and with as narrow limits as possible; what resources are likely to be required over the anticipated duration of the mission and how much support can be expected from other countries and organizations; whether the resultant degree, duration, and cost of a U.S. commitment is merited by the national interests involved; how these interests can be articulated persuasively; and the likelihood of sustained domestic political support. Humanitarian motivations can generate very strong initial pressures for U.S. involvement; however, in the absence of a coherent policy and a politically salable rationale that has been communicated effectively, public support typically fades soon after difficulties arise. Indeed, nation-building—that is, de facto trusteeship—requires such a long-term commitment of large-scale resources that the U.S. is likely to avoid this responsibility unless there is an overwhelming U.S. interest in the country.

A variety of steps can be taken to limit the resources required from the U.S. The size of the operation can be minimized if the mission avoids direct confrontation with opposing parties, seeks to contain rather than eliminate conflict, avoids excessive intrusion into internal affairs such as nation-building or externally created political reconciliation, and phases operations out after an initial period—if necessary, even if total success has not been achieved. The U.S. need not play a major role in every operation; in some, it may contribute a minor share of the personnel and resources by emphasizing its unique and specialized capabilities and encouraging others to provide the bulk of military forces required. In instances where a major U.S. contribution is required, the U.S. can

IFOR Areas of Responsibility in Bosnia

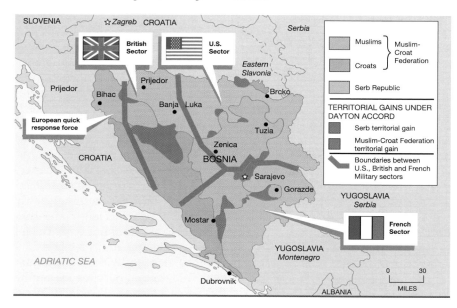

capabilities of any of the parties to the conflict, the mission will likely become enveloped in major hostilities. At this stage, it must pull out or shift from peace operations to virtual war. To be successful, future operations will have to navigate this potentially dangerous situation. Furthermore, peace forces are much more likely to be successful in such situations when they possess overwhelming military superiority and good C³I, are not deployed in exposed positions or vulnerable to retaliation, have a good understanding of the local political scene, and maintain political dialogue with all sides.

Humanitarian Support Operations

Humanitarian support operations entail conducting, assisting, or safeguarding the delivery of food and medical supplies, protecting civilian populations, and so forth. During the Cold War, they were occasionally conducted in conjunction with peace operations (e.g., in the Congo and Dominican Republic), but only infrequently and usually as an afterthought.

Since the end of the Cold War, humanitarian operations have been undertaken with increasing frequency and scope by the international community, primarily to reduce the number of deaths and alleviate human suffering on a massive scale. Military forces have been a major component

still reduce the longer-term burden by planning at the outset for other nations to contribute follow-on forces once threatening initial obstacles have been overcome (as in Haiti).

Peace-enforcement missions are normally given strictly limited objectives. Protection of safe or no-fly zones and of relief deliveries can often be achieved by combined military and political activity without abandoning impartiality. However, if actions become so intrusive that they jeopardize the core interests or major military

Expanded Peacekeeping and Peace Enforcement in Bosnia

The U.N. operation in the former Yugoslavia was originally concentrated in Croatia and then separated in early 1995 into three loosely connected forces—in Croatia, Macedonia, and Bosnia. U.N. military personnel in Croatia, who arrived in March 1992, numbered 15,000. Moderately armed, they were charged with monitoring an existing cease-fire. In Macedonia, the U.N. undertook the first preventive deployment in its history, with a force of 1,150 lightly armed personnel, half of them from the United States. In Bosnia, the mission's initial objective was support for a major humanitarian relief operation by the U.N. High Commissioner for Refugees.

No U.S. military units participated in the U.N. Protection Force (UNPROFOR), although U.S. aircraft and naval vessels provided the bulk of the NATO naval blockade and air attack forces, plus logistics and C³I acting in its support. The USAF also mounted a separate humanitarian airlift and airdrop for Bosnia.

In 1994, the U.N. mission for Bosnia was given an expanded mandate by the Security Council: to enforce weapons exclusion and no-fly zones, and to deter attacks on designated safe areas for civilians. Enforcement was to be shared with NATO air units, subject to U.N. approval. Use of military force was hamstrung by major differences, however, both within NATO and the Security Council, and among NATO, U.N. field commanders, and U.N. headquarters. Serbian actions also proved daunting (e.g., hostage taking of U.N. personnel), while Bosnian government forces exploited safe areas to launch raids on Serb forces UNPROFOR was not given the resources needed to carry out its expanded mission as set forth in numerous UNSC Resolutions. The Serb capture of U.N.-protected safe havens in July 1995, the Croatian capture of Serb-held areas, and the brutal expulsion of of several operations—some of which were conducted in association with peace operations—providing logistical support, assisting the activities of civilian organizations, delivering food and health care directly to refugees, rescuing emigrants at sea, and protecting humanitarian operations undertaken by the international community. On occasion, as in Bosnia and Somalia, the protection of humanitarian operations by military forces under Chapter VI of the U.N. Charter (i.e., operating with the consent of the parties concerned) evolved into peace enforcement under Chapter VII (with authority to use force).

In April 1991, Operation Sea Angel—a joint task force led by the U.S. Marine Corps—provided emergency assistance to a million Bangladeshis stricken by a devastating cyclone.

In Somalia, Operation Provide Relief began in August 1992. A dozen Air Force C–130s delivered 48,000 tons of food and medical supplies in six months to international humanitarian organizations, trying to help over three million starving people. When this proved inadequate to stop the massive death and displacement of Somali people (500,000 dead; 1.5 million refugees or displaced), the U.S. in December 1992 launched a major coalition operation to assist and protect humanitarian activities. The operation was successful in stopping the famine and saving an estimated 200,000 lives, as well as de-escalating the high-intensity civil war into low-level, local skirmishes.

In 1992, UNPROFOR was established in Bosnia primarily to protect relief operations. UNHCR was the lead agency in coordinating the effort. Later, U.N. forces—with no direct U.S. participation—attempted to provide safe havens and protection for relief convoys. The U.S. played a major role in the relief operation by conducting an airlift/airdrop of 69,000 tons to Sarajevo. These activities alleviated but did not stop the massive human suffering in Bosnia. UNPROFOR's humanitarian operations led to clashes with most of the disputants, especially the Serbs. UNPROFOR eventually became a peace enforcement operation.

In late July 1994, the U.S. military undertook Operation Support Hope to supply food, medicine, vehicles, water-pumping and purification equipment, and other items to an international effort led by UNHCR to assist a million Rwandan refugees. Six other countries also deployed military forces for this purpose, among them Japan, France, Israel, and the Netherlands.

Another type of humanitarian operation has been conducted by the U.S. over the past several years in the Caribbean. Operation Distant Shore intercepted Haitians and Cubans fleeing their countries in flimsy craft destined for Florida. Though it can be considered a humanitarian operation insofar as it rescued people

---

Serbs in August 1995 led to a full-scale reassessment—by the United Nations, the United States, and NATO—of the Bosnian mission's role and mandate. The 30,000-man force in Bosnia was reinforced by a 10,000-man, heavily armed rapid-reaction force from the U.K., France, and the Netherlands. The force in Croatia was ordered withdrawn by the Security Council, since Croatian military success had vitiated its role of monitoring the lines between Croatians and Serbs.

Until August 1995, despite blatant provocations, force had been used by NATO hesitantly, weakly and not at all by UNPROFOR. As a result, credibility was lost by the U.N., NATO, and the U.S. By mid-August, the U.N. and NATO had greatly improved their coordination and strengthened their political will. Following Serb attacks on Sarajevo in late August, NATO undertook a well-planned air action, reinforced on the ground by the rapid reaction force, in responding to Serb attacks. At this point, UNPROFOR, as well as NATO, crossed the key threshold of impartiality; UNPROFOR became a peace enforcement operation.

Using momentum generated by the August–September 1995 joint Croat-Bosnian offensive and the powerful NATO air strikes, the U.S. launched a new diplomatic peace initiative. On September 8 in Geneva, the foreign ministers of Bosnia-Herzegovina, Croatia, and Serbia signed an agreed statement of basic principles on ending the conflict in Bosnia. On October 12, a cease-fire officially came into force. In November, proximity talks in Dayton brokered by the U.S. led to an eventual peace agreement. President Clinton announced his intention to deploy 20,000 U.S. personnel as part of the 60,000 person NATO-led force that would replace UNPROFOR to enforce the peace agreement, and to work with civilian agencies, coordinated by the High Representative of the international community called for by the Dayton accords, to facillitate resettlement of over a million displaced persons and the holding of elections.

Humanitarian Emergencies, 1995

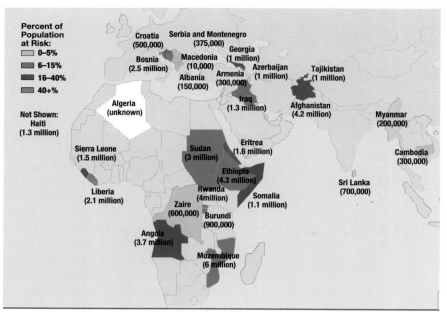

SOURCE: CIA
NOTE: Numbers in parenthesis are the number of people affected by the humanitarian emergency.

at risk on the open seas, the operation's principal purpose was to prevent the intrusion of hundreds of thousands of illegal aliens into the country, a highly charged political issue. By intercepting these refugees before they reached U.S. soil, it was possible to return them to their country of origin or confine them in temporary detention centers. In some instances, Cuba and Haiti deliberately encouraged emigration in order to apply pressure on the U.S. Thus, Operation Distant Shore can be seen as a means of managing a security problem, as well as humanitarian support.

Each relief operation with a potential requirement for military support is likely to be assessed in more than just the terms of the U.S. interests involved. The immediate and long-term need for U.S. help, the availability of other assistance, probable costs, and attainability of objectives will also be evaluated. Whenever civilian agencies are given the job, perhaps with military logistics support, the potential that disputants might control or manipulate food distribution and that the operation

could become entangled in unresolved domestic power struggles must be considered as well. Without proper oversight, humanitarian missions can evolve unintentionally into political-military operations with totally different objectives and requirements, as occurred in Somalia and Bosnia.

The military cannot seek to be a replacement for civilian humanitarian organizations. Humanitarian support seems to work best when the military relinquishes operations to civilians as soon as the latter are able to manage them. Owing to their unmatched logistical and organizational capabilities, however, the armed forces are uniquely able to provide a massive, rapid response to crises in remote locations and will likely continue to do so in partnership with civilian organizations. Given the inclination of the U.S. public to support humanitarian causes, continued use of military assets for such missions seems probable.

Conclusions

Peace operations provide a useful array of instruments for the pursuit of important U.S. interests and values—notably the preservation or restoration of stability, the enhancement of democracy and human rights, and the alleviation of humanitarian crises. Even if U.S. security is not immediately threatened, instability, violence, and large-scale human suffering often pose a long-term menace to important U.S. political and economic interests. Under proper circumstances, the various forms of peace operations have demonstrated a capacity to preclude, limit, or resolve conflict and to relieve human suffering. Collective action offers an alternative to inaction or unilateral action, with the added advantage of a reduction in material and financial costs for the U.S. and an increase in political effectiveness.

The least militarily intensive peace operations—conflict prevention and peacemaking operations—have had a mixed record of success. Yet they remain a viable instrument of policy because of their relatively low cost, small size, and sustainability. Such preventive measures may be used more frequently in the future, especially given the favorable contrast with costly extended peacekeeping operations and the

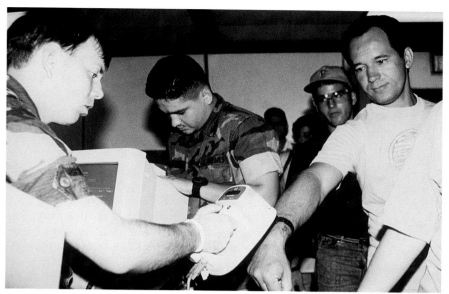

A U.S. serviceman identifies a Cuban migrant by using the computerized Defense Mass Personnel Identification and Tracking System at the U.S. Naval Base, Guantanamo Bay, Cuba, on June, 1995. The worker scans a bracelet worn by the migrant which contains a computer chip with positive personal identification.

degree of U.S. participation can be minimized. Thus, continued U.S. active support rests upon a calculation of national interest versus cost.

Coordination among interested member states, the United Nations, regional organizations, and PVOs has become even more pivotal to success for both the political and military dimensions of peacekeeping. The Organization of American States has gained experience in peacekeeping; the CIS is developing a capability; serious projects are underway to improve the peacekeeping capabilities of the Organization of African Unity; and the OSCE is interested in developing its peacekeeping role. NATO is for the first time deeply involved in peace operations. Numerous Asian, African, Latin American, and European armies (including those from the CIS) are improving their own peacekeeping potential, in some cases with help from the U.S. International and non-governmental organizations are following the same approach. This trend deserves encouragement since it will tend to make other countries both more receptive and more effective when needed for peace operations. For the U.S., this means further improvement in its own interagency capabilities and its coordination with PVOs. It also means more work in helping the U.N. Secretariat, regional organizations, and individual countries become more proficient. In particular, the U.S. can provide valuable help in improving planning, logistics, training, and C^3 capabilities. U.N. and regional organization approval will continue to be very important as legitimization, enhancing the prospects of participation or support by more states. This means closer, sustained attention to diplomatic and military-to-military efforts aimed at strengthening U.S. relations with other countries.

increased efforts by the U.N., many member states, and PVOs to make them more effective and more rapidly responsive. Still, greater U.S. military and civilian cooperation with others in this effort is fully justified by the low level of expenditure, the potentially high benefits, and the anticipated cost savings.

Peacekeeping operations have generally worked best when the warring parties have reached an enduring settlement, although the presence of peacekeeping forces, coupled with capable diplomacy, can also provide a valuable face-saving cover needed to forge a cease-fire and other agreements. With the end of superpower rivalry, peacekeeping operations have generally focused on resolving internal conflicts in individual states rather than cross-border aggression. The missions are thus more complicated, since there is less control over armed elements and, in some cases, virtually no administrative structures or organized leadership with which to work. As a result, the operations have become multidimensional, incorporating such considerations as human rights, police training, election monitoring, and institution-building. Such versatility has led to a steady demand for their deployment, and continued use in the future seems inevitable, given the troubled state of the world. Moreover, they are of modest cost, especially when there is broad, international participation and support, and the

Some degree of U.S. military involvement can frequently make the difference between success and failure for both conflict prevention and peacekeeping operations. U.S. special skills—supplied by small numbers of specialized personnel for headquarters, C^3I, psychological operations, civil affairs, and special operations functions—can provide the essential extras to

United Nation troops patrol the streets around Kigali Airport.

ensure success. In addition, U.S. participation in an operation will often inspire others to contribute, while U.S. absence is apt to deter others, as well as harm the overall conduct of operations and erode U.S. influence. This means a greater U.S. concentration on how to enhance prospects for success with limited participation, rather than assuming that the U.S. will play the dominant role. Whatever role the U.S. plays, it is essential to pay close, continuing attention on the ground and in Washington to articulating U.S. objectives and interests, and explaining clearly how operations are proceeding. Such measures will help build and sustain support at home.

The prognosis for expanded peacekeeping and peace enforcement is less certain. By its own admission, the United Nations lacks the capability to manage these ambitious missions, and the serious problems of the operation in Bosnia and the failure of the Somalia mission, plus very high costs, have undermined support for such activities. Thus, additional operations, involving large military forces under U.N. command, are not likely to be undertaken any time in the near future, unless Washington decides that an expanded peacekeeping or peace enforcement mission

would serve important U.S. interests and opts to form a coalition to undertake the action (as in Bosnia, secceeding UNPROFOR). The U.S. government might seek a Security Council or regional endorsement to mobilize international support for an effective coalition under U.S. or perhaps under NATO leadership and C³I, as it did for IFOR.

The number of military establishments capable of engaging seriously in peace enforcement is not likely to increase significantly in the near term, despite U.S. military assistance. Therefore, future coalition-formation efforts may focus primarily on countries that already possess advanced military capabilities. Other countries are more likely to be considered for supporting, rather than principal, tasks in such a coalition. Operational effectiveness in rapidly changing situations is likely to be impeded if arrangements are made with an eye to political symbolism. Dual-command arrangements (e.g. U.S.–U.N. in Somalia, NATO–U.N. in Bosnia) are an example of arrangements that pose serious operational difficulties. Moreover, UNSC Resolutions are not always realistic in their operational implications for forces on the ground.

Humanitarian operations continue to receive a great deal of attention in Washington and around the world. Military support has proven its utility as a partner in such operations in northern Iraq, Somalia, Bangladesh, and on the Zaire-Rwanda border. A number of other countries are expanding their military as well as civilian capacity to support humanitarian operations. Similarly, important work continues within the U.S. armed forces, other government agencies, and some NGOs to institutionalize and improve military-civilian cooperation in humanitarian operations.

CHAPTER TWELVE

Unconventional Military Instruments

Introduction

The unconventional threats to national security are not based on the ability to seize territory and defeat military forces; rather, they affect U.S. interests through less direct means and often take advantage of, or are directed by, non-state actors or forces. Terrorism, insurgency, subversion, narcotics trafficking, and refugee flows, for example, are all means that foreign adversaries may employ or manipulate to their advantage and at the expense of U.S. national interests. Such unconventional threats are distinct from the threat posed by the military forces of other nations and the routine political and economic competition that mark interstate relations.

The importance of unconventional threats to national security is often debated. Some hold that unconventional threats do not challenge vital national security interests and do not typically evolve into major threats to peace. Others, however, maintain that the cumulative effect of unconventional threats is a slow but steady erosion of the U.S. security posture, and that it is best to deal with these threats while they are smaller and more easily managed.

The end of the Cold War produced two countervailing effects on unconventional threats to U.S. national security. On the other hand, the dissolution of the Soviet Union eliminated a primary source of support for international terrorism, regional subversion, and insurgency directed against U.S. interests. On the other hand, with the passing of the bipolar world, many regional, intrastate, and transnational antagonisms that had been held in check by the Cold War have erupted, and some have precipitated unconventional challenges to U.S. policy and security. For instance, the withdrawal of superpower support for Siad Barre's regime in Somalia was largely responsible for his fall from power, an event that set the stage for a humanitarian disaster that prompted a complicated U.S./U.N. intervention.

Ironically, the unparalleled success of U.S. forces in the Gulf War has also contributed to the likelihood of unconventional threats. Having witnessed the proficiency of conventional U.S. military forces in Operation Desert Storm, foes of U.S. interests will probably be more inclined to challenge the United States through unconventional means.

Instruments

Conventional threats to national security generally evoke a response in kind. But for legal, moral, political, and practical reasons, the United States usually cannot respond in kind to unconventional threats. More often than not it must use tools other than those adopted by its foes. Diplomatic and military responses are, respectively, the first and last lines of defense against unconventional threats, but the United States may also augment these options with its own unconventional tools, such as nonlethal weapons and special operations.

Managing unconventional threats with unconventional instruments presents problems for the United States, for a variety of reasons. The American tendency to see war and peace as discrete, discontinuous states makes it difficult to build public support for unconventional options, which often employ limited means to obtain limited ends. An unconventional campaign may require restraint, patience, perseverance, and acceptance of ambiguous results, all of which may be unpopular. Because of the political sensitivity attached to such options, they require special management.

Besides being politically sensitive, unconventional options often fall between or beyond the typical mandates and missions of government agencies. For example, encouraging an adversary to desist from destabilizing a government friendly to the United States might involve a covert act of sabotage that requires military expertise resident in DOD and tradecraft skills resident in the Central Intelligence Agency. Negotiating migrant camp rules with Haitian refugees in Panama may require the legal background of Department of Justice personnel but the linguistic and cultural capabilities of special operations forces or diplomats. Delivering large amounts of aid to Bosnian refugees may require DOD logistics and the Agency for International Development's contacts with the humanitarian organizations. Hence, applying unconventional instruments to unconventional security problems requires an unusually high degree of interagency cooperation.

This chapter begins with general response options to the unconventional threats of terrorism, narcotics, and refugee/migrant flows. It then considers a number of unconventional capabilities at the disposal of the United States: special forces, unconventional warfare, nonlethal weapons, psychological operations, and foreign law enforcement and constabulary training.

Combatting Terrorism

By themselves, terrorist organizations have never threatened vital U.S. interests. But when used by states in a deliberate way, they have adversely affected U.S. actions and policies, if only by imposing higher costs. State support gives these terrorists money, weapons, training, diplomatic passports for their travel, diplomatic pouches for their weapons and explosives, intelligence, and safe havens. The terrorists' organizations give them resiliency, durability, and, through the division of skilled labor, expertise in the destructive arts greater than any individual could muster. Thus, state-sponsored terrorist organizations were and are formidable adversaries.

Since the mid-1960s, states have supported and sponsored terrorist attacks against the interests of the United States in an effort to undermine American policies in Europe, the Middle East, and Latin America.

The United States responds to the threat of international terrorism by:

- Encouraging cooperation among targeted countries.
- Refusing to make concessions to terrorists' demands.
- Seizing terrorists overseas and transporting them to the United States for trial.
- Imposing economic sanctions on countries that sponsor terrorists.
- Retaliating against sponsoring countries with military force.
- Attempting to prevent, preempt, and disrupt terrorist activities.

None of these measures alone constitutes a sufficient response. However, when used in combination as part of an integrated, consistent strategy, they can be effective, despite the inevitable exceptions to the strategy that must be made to serve more pressing national interests. The decline in international terrorism between

U.S. Special Operations Forces rehearse counter-terrorist actions.

1985 and 1995 resulted not merely from worldwide political and economic changes but from the application of just such an integrated, consistent strategy toward a number of countries known to sponsor terrorists, especially Libya and Syria.

The last two of the six enumerated methods deserve special comment. The United States has used military retaliation twice: the Air Force, Navy, and Marine Corps raid against Libya in 1986; and the Navy cruise-missile attack on Iraqi intelligence headquarters in 1993. The raid on Libya quieted its leader, Mu`ammar al-Qaddafi, for approximately eighteen months and, according to some experts, has had a residual chastening effect. Yet more Americans died from Libyan terrorism following the raid than before it—even excluding those killed in the bombing of Pan Am flight 103—suggesting a limit to the usefulness of retaliating with overt military force. However, a less public use of force might sacrifice the coercive effect the raid produced on other countries as various as Syria and East Germany.

Preventing terrorism entails the use of defensive measures, such as perimeter security around facilities, as well as efforts to address what are sometimes called the underlying causes of terrorism, such as economic inequalities, injustice, or racial or religious discrimination. The former sort of prevention is the least glamorous but perhaps the most effective way to combat terrorism; the latter, because of limits in our knowledge and resources, is perhaps the least effective.

Preemption does not mean assassination. It means only preventing a specific act of terrorism from taking place. That may be accomplished by sending a démarche to a sponsoring state or by apprehending terrorists before they act. Preemption requires good intelligence, however, which is often not available.

Disrupting terrorist activity means targeting a terrorist organization and taking measures, not to stop one of its particular operations, but to render all its activities more difficult. The ultimate goal is to make the organization completely ineffective. How that is done depends on how the terrorists are organized, but it can include all of the measures mentioned above, especially attacks on the means by which terrorists are supported.

Increasingly, international terrorism has been marked by the appearance of less-organized groups, which coalesce around a leader for a specific operation or series of operations, receiving various kinds and levels of support from different governments and individuals. Such a group carried out the bombing of the World Trade Center. Because they are not tied directly to any one country's political agenda, these groups may be less restrained in their use of violence. For the same reason, it is more difficult for the United States to influence them by pressuring their state sponsors.

It is too early to tell how serious a problem these groups pose. While they are capable of horrendous acts of violence, they generally are more vulnerable to penetration and less capable than terrorists who are more organized. All the measures used against the more highly organized terrorists may be useful to a degree against these groups, but countering them will require that we disrupt the activities of both the operators and their supporters. Tracking and arresting the ringleaders, as was done after the World Trade Center bombing, or having another government seize them are important ways to counter this terrorism. Such anti-terrorist operations will require a continued emphasis on intelligence and close cooperation between intelligence and law enforcement.

UNCONVENTIONAL MILITARY INSTRUMENTS

Counternarcotics Forces

The flow of cocaine, heroin, and marijuana into the U.S. from South American and Southeast and Southwest Asian source nations continues to constitute a critical national security threat to the U.S. The violence accompanying the distribution and sale of these illegal drugs and the societal toll that drug use imposes are national problems that affect every U.S. citizen. Moreover, the violence and official corruption that the narcotics smuggling cartels bring pose significant threats to democratic institutions throughout the world.

The programs used in international counternarcotics operations include, but are not limited to, enforcement measures such as aerial and manual eradication of coca and poppy crops, crop substitution programs, destruction of drug laboratories, and the disruption and dismantlement of major narcotics trafficking organizations through arrests, prosecutions, and asset seizures.

The demise of the USSR has significantly changed the international political and geographical landscape, and the drug industry is responding to an array of new business and criminal opportunities. Traffickers now use new smuggling routes that traverse the poorly guarded borders of the Caucasus, Central Asia, and Eastern Europe, where local law enforcement is poorly staffed and ill equipped to oppose smugglers. In some cases the "new" routes are in fact old smuggling highways that had been blocked by the Soviet Union and Yugoslavia.

To attack this threat, the U.S. has called for a shift of emphasis away from efforts to disrupt the flow of cocaine in transit and toward efforts in source countries, beginning in the Western Hemisphere. Thus, interdiction activities now make up only 8.8 percent of the total U.S. FY 1996 counterdrug budget, while a major effort has been made to assist other nations in developing and implementing policies to destroy narcotrafficking organizations.

Numerous federal agencies are involved in international counternarcotics efforts. The Drug Enforcement Administration (DEA), the lead agency enforcing federal drug laws, has 3,000 agents in 100 offices in the U.S. and 65 countries abroad, and an air wing active both in the U.S. and abroad. The U.S. Customs Service, as the primary border-enforcement agency, plays a key role in interdicting the flow of illegal drugs; it also maintains an extensive money-laundering control program. The U.S. Coast Guard, the principal maritime law enforcement agency, conducts patrols and special operations in maritime areas to intercept drugs, and maintains an intelligence capability on vessels and aircraft engaged in smuggling drugs. The State Department's Bureau of International Narcotics and Law Enforcement (INL) has primary responsibility for the U.S. government's international supply-reduction strategies, in which it is aided by the Agency for International Development.

The Department of Defense's role in anti-drug operations includes domestic activities, such as the use of National Guard forces, as well as an array of international programs, including aerial and ground reconnaissance, detection and monitoring, and administering the distribution of excess military equipment to law enforcement agencies for use in counterdrug operations. Despite budget cuts and competing requirements, DOD has made a concerted effort to enhance programs in source nations, while maintaining a strong presence in the transit zone. For example, DOD provides training and operational support to strengthen foreign police and military counterdrug activities. It also provides a continuum of specialized training teams to other countries' counterdrug forces, both in those countries and in military schools in the United States. This training ranges from aircraft maintenance to small-unit tactics and operational planning. DOD also provides intelligence to other countries' counterdrug forces through the embassy country teams. Tactical Analysis Teams help coordinate intelligence and build tactical-information portfolios on key drug traffickers, which are then passed to the appropriate country team element for dissemination to host nations. Joint Planning Assistance Teams assist foreign forces in developing operational plans around intelligence collection activities. Lastly, DOD assists other countries' interdiction forces by providing their interceptors with essential real-time tracking information on suspected narcotrafficking aircraft.

Partly as a result of international cooperation during 1995, Peru and Colombia have had greater success in intercepting illegal flights between the two countries, significantly disrupting the movement of cocaine base into Colombia. Moreover, cooperative counterdrug efforts with the government of Colombia led to the arrest of six of the top seven Cali mafia kingpins. With U.S. encouragement, Colombia and Bolivia have also launched active coca eradication campaigns.

Although cocaine remains the primary drug threat to the U.S., heroin has reemerged as a major threat. The heroin threat may require a significantly different approach than that prescribed for cocaine. The heroin industry internationally is much more decentralized, diversified, and difficult to monitor for purposes of enforcement operations. Also, in many of the major heroin source and transit countries, particularly in Southeast and Southwest Asia, the U.S. has important security interests that must be taken into account; however, to pursue these other interests, the drug industry and its criminal activities must be dealt with as well.

Forces for Controlling Migrants and Refugees

Large population movements can be intentional tools of statecraft as well as humanitarian problems. By employing emigration as an instrument for creating international friction, regimes are able to embarrass or frighten their enemies, influence other states' domestic and foreign policies, divert another state's resources, negotiate preferred outcomes from international organizations, stabilize their internal politics by expelling dissident groups, and even fill their coffers by extorting payments either from those leaving or states receiving the emigrants. Among the countries that have used this tool successfully in the last two decades are Vietnam, East Germany, Cuba, and Haiti. The use of emigrants as an instrument costs little, is highly effective in attracting international attention, and is readily available to virtually every state, particularly those of the developing world that may lack more traditional tools of statecraft.

Emigration from both Haiti and Cuba in 1994 illustrates many of these general statements. Although not an organized initiative of the junta in Port-au-Prince, the emigrant flow created strong political pressure that affected U.S. policies. Simultaneously, the Cuban regime successfully manipulated mass emigration to extract concessions from the United States on several issues. As in the past, Castro used emigration not only to embarrass Washington but also to gain a favorable change in the annual quota of legal emigration from Cuba to the United States, a move that helped stabilize his own domestic political situation.

Dealing with a sudden emigration crisis requires the diversion of resources from other government activities. In the 1994–95 emigrant operations in the Caribbean, for example, DOD provided a broad range of goods and services, including camp facilities, rations, health care, security, crowd control, and mail delivery. The Navy provided the principal forces for a massive interdiction operation, including the tracking, interception, and inspection of all craft departing either Cuba or Haiti, as well as the transportation of all emigrants to DOD facilities throughout the Caribbean. These activities significantly impaired military operations and readiness. In order to deal with emigrants at the Guantanamo base alone, Atlantic Command had to cease fleet training and base maintenance operations, suspend contracts, halt base construction, and send home all non-essential civilian personnel.

Cuban Refugees at Guantanamo.

Responding successfully to the strategic use of emigration requires, first distinguishing between population movements that are initiated or manipulated for political purposes from those resulting from humanitarian problems. Since the former are largely efforts at extortion, they may multiply if the targeted states repeatedly succumb to pressure and accommodate the objectives of the state from which the movement originated. Countermeasures to stem emigrant flows depend largely on the role of the originating state. If, as in the case of Cuba, a government manipulates an emigrant flow for political gain, countermeasures focus on altering the behavior of the government, through sanctions, blockades, or other diplomatic and/or military means. Interdiction can limit the number of emigrants that reach U.S. territory. Programs for the transport, protection, processing, or repatriation of the emigrants handle those that do.

In cases such as Haiti's, where the emigrant flow is exploited but not originated by the sending country, countermeasures primarily focus upon the emigrants themselves. Measures include interdiction at sea or by land, repatriation, or transfer of migrants to a third location. In addition, psychological operations (PSYOP) can help convince would-be emigrants that they have little or no hope of reaching U.S. territory.

All countermeasures must be applied carefully. For example, sanctions that affect a country's population more than its leadership may only increase emigration by adding a humanitarian exodus to a forced one. Forcible repatriation can serve as a deterrent, but may present legal and political problems. Often, public information campaigns are neccessary to cast the country of origin a bad light and to apprise domestic and foreign citizens of the true character of the refugee problem.

The cases in which forced emigrant flows might affect the United States directly are few in number but, particularly in the case of Cuba, are difficult to handle politically and logistically. Ethnic cleansing in the Balkans will probably suggest to those engaged in ethnic conflicts that forced emigration is an effective tool. It helps attain a war aim, ethnic purity, while causing difficulties for your enemies, who must receive and take care of the emigrants.

Special Operations Forces

Special operations forces (SOF) are an exceptionally flexible instrument for responding to unconventional threats. The small size, unique capabilities, and relatively self-sufficient nature of SOF units often mean that their employment will not entail the degree of political liability or risk of escalation normally associated with the employment of larger, more visible conventional forces. Those traits, in turn, make SOF a particularly attractive option for responding to indirect aggression.

SOF may be used to maximize the effectiveness of conventional forces, for example, by augmenting the Navy and Coast Guard enforcement of sanctions. Or they may be used to provide decision makers with an unconventional alternative to diplomacy or conventional force, such as a hostage rescue operation. Or they may be used to perform a variety of nontraditional military missions, such as emergency medical procedures or de-mining operations, that are especially appropriate for unconventional threats.

SOF as Commandos. In general terms, SOF perform two roles for the National Command Authority that may prove useful in responding to unconventional threats. SOF exercise their commando role when they utilize stealth, speed, precision, and audacity to undertake precision penetration and strike operations against selected targets. Such missions may be designed to seize, damage, or destroy a target; to recover personnel or materiel; or to conduct reconnaissance/surveillance operations. In the context of unconventional threats, SOF commando capabilities can be used for gathering intelligence and evidence against terrorists; recovering valued persons, such as hostages; or destroying an adversary's selected national assets in support of an aggressive sanctions effort.

Dramatic improvements over the past decade in conventional standoff precision-strike and long-range reconnaissance capabilities mean that the undesirable risk of putting SOF personnel on the ground can often be avoided. However, to retrieve personnel or materiel or to make critical on-the-scene judgments still requires putting men on the ground. Moreover, advances in long-range reconnaissance and strike capabilities have been partially offset by improvements in integrated enemy air defenses and the trend toward moving high-value targets underground.

The airborne platforms carrying U.S. advanced reconnaissance and strike systems are not invulnerable. They can be shot down, risking loss of life or the taking of hostages, as well as the embarrassing loss of a high-value platform, as occurred in Lebanon in 1983 and Bosnia in 1995. Depending on the target and circumstances,

---

SOF Definition and Forces

Special operations forces (SOF) consist of Army Special Forces, Rangers, and Special Operations Aviation; Navy Sea-Air-Land (SEAL) and SEAL Delivery Vehicle (SDV) teams and special boat squadrons/units; Air Force special operations units; special operations support units; psychological operations units; and civil affairs units.

In defense planning, decision makers look to SOF to provide a strategic economy of force in support of conventional forces, to expand the range of available options, and to provide unique capabilities. The small, self-contained, and highly trained units can support conventional military forces before, during, and after a conflict. Their skills include intelligence gathering, surgical strikes, and language training and regional orientation, which make them particularly suited to support coalition warfare with advisory and liaison capabilities. Small, self-contained SOF units also provide the United States with rapid, focused military options that avoid the political and military ramifications of a larger, more visible conventional force.

SOF are often defined in contradistinction with conventional or general-purpose forces, with the observation that SOF conduct operations that conventional forces cannot accomplish or undertake without unacceptable risks and commitments of resources. A more technical definition of special operations is that they manifest at least three of the following characteristics.

Unorthodox Approaches. Special operations require tactics, techniques, and procedures that cannot be employed efficiently or effectively by conventional forces. This does not mean that special operations negate the traditional principles of war, but rather that they put a different emphasis on their combination or ranking of importance. For example, in comparison with conventional operations, mass is less important in special operations, while surprise achieved by speed, stealth, audacity, deception, and new tactics and techniques is far more important. Special operations forces can target a conventional enemy's weaknesses through unorthodox approaches or counter unconventional adversaries by meeting them on their own unorthodox terms.

Unconventional Training and Equipment. All military training and equipment, from boot camp to the cockpit of a B–1 bomber or Abrams tank, is to some extent special. Moreover, as General Wayne Downing (Commander-in-Chief, Special Operations Command) noted in 1995, the definition of what is unconventional changes over time. SOF pioneered techniques that today are considered conventional, such as the use of night-vision devices and deep precision-strike capabilities. At any given time, however, there are mission requirements that must be defined as unconventional when compared with existing conventional capabilities. Because special operations are often conducted at great distances from support facilities, beyond the limits of conventional military forces, and using a broad range of specialized skills, they often require special training and equipment compared to their conventional counterparts.

Political Context/Implications. Army special forces doctrine rightly identifies recognizing political implications as an imperative. Political considerations define the general parameters of almost all military operations, but special operations are often conducted in a politically sensitive context that constrains virtually every aspect of the operation. Local mores may dictate methods, and more general political considerations may require clandestine, covert, or low-visibility techniques, as well as oversight at the national level.

Special Intelligence Requirements. Special operations require special intelligence. This may sometimes mean very fine-grained intelligence about a difficult target; other times it may mean in-depth information on political, social, and cultural issues. In certain instances, the intelligence picture will not only help design the special operation but may in fact determine its very feasibility.

SOF used alone or in conjunction with conventional forces to assist in target designation, location, and tracking may reduce the overall risk of a reprisal attack or sensitive reconnaissance mission. To improve their reconnaissance and precision-strike capabilities, SOF are taking advantage of advanced technologies in such areas as thermal imagery, electronic-signals collection, radiation and magnetic-detection equipment, unmanned aerial vehicles, secure real-time communications, and placed, unattended systems that increase the team's survivability and enable it to cover a larger area.

SOF as Diplomat-Warriors. SOF perform their second type of role—sometimes referred to as their indirect, diplomat-warrior, or unconventional-warrior role—when they influence, advise, train, and conduct operations with foreign forces and populations. In this indirect role, SOF may help manage refugee camps, train and advise allied counterinsurgency forces, train and assist allied indigenous forces in unconventional warfare, and help stabilize friendly governments via psychological operations and advice and assistance on civil-sector activities. The quiet deployment of SOF to assist allies can signal U.S. determination and provide a low-risk, high-payoff option for decision makers. Performing the unconventional-warrior role requires not only language and cross-cultural skills but also cutting-edge lethal force capabilities.

SOF in Haiti

Special operations forces (SOF) performed a number of key functions in Operation Uphold Democracy in Haiti. Navy SEALs used their Coastal Patrol Craft to interdict embargo violators and intercept refugees during the long buildup. Special forces and Ranger personnel were prepared to remove the illegal military regime by force (some elements were en route when a negotiated settlement was reached). Capitalizing on their flexibility, SOF changed their plan and made a rapid transition to a peacekeeping role. During the peak of the multinational force phase of the operation, there were approximately 1,350 SOF personnel operating in small teams, based in thirty population centers throughout Haiti. From those centers, SOF visited over five hundred towns and villages, where they were essential to establishing a safe and secure environment.

From their bases in the countryside, Army Special-Forces teams acted as an extension of the larger conventional force. When President Jean-Bertrand Aristide abolished the section chiefs as the chief local authority, Special Forces ensured their removal (and security), then helped establish local government by organizing town meetings and helping restore basic public services. In addition, they provided some limited emergency medical care (for both Haitians and other foreign nationals) and assisted the numerous private volunteer organizations operating in the countryside. Special Forces also provided area familiarization and tactical training to the foreign military members of the multinational forces supporting the U.N. mission in Haiti. In addition, they provided most of the secure tactical communications support required for the U.N. peacekeeping force.

PSYOP forces used radio and TV broadcasts, loudspeaker announcements, leaflet drops, handbills, and other dissemination measures to inform and reassure the Haitian people. With the approval of President Clinton, DOD initiated Radio Democracy, an aircraft-based PSYOP radio broadcast that enabled President Aristide to communicate directly with Haitian citizens. His appeals for restraint and a peaceful return, coupled with his assurances of security and justice for all, were a key element in restraining the population from violence.

Civil Affairs (CA) forces were primarily drawn from the U.S. Army Reserves. A contingent of active CA soldiers from the 96th CA Batallion initially deployed until the reservists could be mobilized and sent into theater. Nearly 97 percent of the U.S. CA capability is in the Army Reserves because it needs to draw heavily on civilian acquired skills, which would be impractical or impossible to maintain in the active force. Such professionals as international bankers, transportation system managers, civilian judges, city managers and others bring their education, training, and years of job experience to assist the local and national community in restoring its services, capability, and infrastructure. By alleviating the civilian problems, CA troops can reduce the demands on the military commander for emergency and humanitarian assistance and allow him to comply with his responsibilities, both legal and moral, to the civilian population. The recent history of this type of assistance ranges from Grenada to Kuwait.

In Haiti these CA reservists provided technical advice and assistance to twelve Haitian government ministries for up to ninety days. The advisors assisted the ministries in assessing priorities for their offices and developing plans to carry out their responsibilities. Other assistance included helping to develop department budgets, establishing an immunization system against rabies and anthrax, identifying timber thefts in the national forest, and assisting ministries in preparing for participation in numerous international meetings and conferences. A special group of fifteen civilian judges, prosecutors, and civil lawyers provided an assessment of the Haitian judicial system, codifying the laws, providing training for judges and law clerks, and passing out legal references and forms to court officials.

Civil affairs personnel also provided direct support to all major subordinate units of the multinational force, staffed the Civil Military Operations Center (CMOC), and manned the Humanitarian Assistance Coordination Center.

Special Operations Funding 1984–1995
(millions of constant 1995 $)

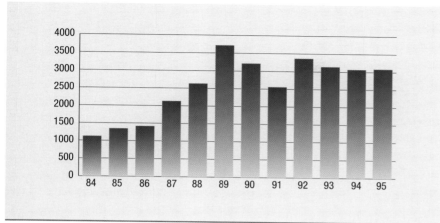

SOURCE: DOD

Nevertheless, there is a nonlethal dimension to SOF's indirect role that is attracting more attention and providing a more balanced view of these versatile forces so long associated in the public imagination with "mission impossible" commando operations.

Immediately following the Gulf War, the relief effort in Northern Iraq, to save the Kurds from Saddam Hussein's wrath and the harsh mountain environment showcased SOF's nonlethal skills. While cognizant of tribal prerogatives and an ongoing insurgency, the civil affairs and special forces soldiers were able to earn the confidence of Kurdish leaders, organize camps, and deliver lifesaving food, shelter, and medical supplies. PSYOP detachments used loudspeakers and on-the-spot newsletters to reassure the Kurds and coax them down from the mountains, and civil affairs units designed way stations and camps that reflected religious, tribal, and family customs. These units also negotiated the transition between U.S. military forces and the U.N. and other international relief agencies.

Other examples of nonlethal applications of SOF in their indirect role include the mine-awareness and de-mining training conducted by Special Forces and PSYOP units in support of U.N. peacekeeping efforts in the early 1990s. The use of civil affairs units to set up and manage the Haitian refugee camps at Guantanamo and to manage rural security and presence for

U.N. forces in Haiti are other examples of the way SOF can be used in response to unconventional security problems.

Special operations forces include civil affairs units, which are largely in the Reserves. They are trained to provide the interface between the military and the civilian population and government in the area of military operations. They are also increasingly taking on a role of coordination with Private Voluntary Organizations (PVOs). An example of the importance of such coordination came during Operation Restore Hope in Somalia. The Civil-Military Operations Center (CMOC), with liaison officers from each of the major contingents in the multinational coalition, including the U.S., worked closely with the Humanitarian Operations Center run by the United Nations, thereby providing a single focal point for all relief agencies in the country. Eventually, nine parallel CMOCs controlled the issue of ID cards and maintained a data matrix on the status of food relief supplies.

Unconventional Warfare

Unconventional warfare is military operations conducted in enemy-held, enemy-controlled, or politically sensitive territory, including guerrilla warfare and support to insurgency, that are carried out by indigenous personnel supported or directed in varying degrees by external forces. There are three ways in which the United States might engage in unconventional warfare: as part of a major regional conflict (MRC); in support of a citizen/partisan defense intended as a deterrent; and as an effort to support an insurgency. Engaging in unconventional warfare as part of an MRC is not always possible, however, because some regimes oppose the arming and training of any significant number of their general citizenry. Preparing and assisting a partisan deterrence force can likewise present political problems by what it may suggest: that the United States believes the partisans' country is unprepared to fight, or will be overrun in any case, or should mount a holding action while the United States improves its negotiating position.

The U.S. experience in the 1980s—for example, in Afghanistan and Nicaragua—proved that support for an insurgency can be an effective way of putting indirect pressure on adversaries. But it also showed that such support can be hard to control, and that once training and equipment have been provided, they can be used in ways contrary to U.S. precepts or interests. Thus, a careful weighing of costs and benefits is necessary to determine the merits of using unconventional warfare against states that support insurgencies against U.S. allies, support terrorism, or acquire weapons of mass destruction, perhaps the three most important future uses of this blunt instrument.

Nonlethal Weapons

Nonlethal weapons are characterized by their ability to disable or incapacitate people or things while minimizing physical harm to them, either because their effects are highly discriminate or relatively reversible. The concept of nonlethal weapons is not new. Tear gas, for example, is a familiar option generally employed to nonlethal effect. For example, tear gas was used during the Vietnam conflict, not only to quell disturbances, but to flush Vietcong guerrillas from underground hiding places. In addition, anti-traction compounds were applied experimentally to sections of the Ho Chi Minh Trail.

Nonlethal Weapons in the Evacuation from Somalia

In early 1995, the U.N. Security Council called for the withdrawal of all U.N. peacekeepers from Somalia by the end of March. The withdrawal—Operation United Shield—was executed by a combined task force commanded by Lt. Gen. Anthony Zinni of the U.S. Marine Corps. Based in part on previous experience, planners knew that unarmed but hostile elements in Somalia could attempt to disrupt the withdrawal. General Zinni determined that nonlethal weapons were needed to help save lives and minimize the impact of any possible confrontation. On an emergency basis, the Marines identified off-the-shelf nonlethal weapons and near-mature developmental nonlethal weapons that showed promise of being useful in this role. The main concerns were: how well the individual devices would perform in the Somali environment; how much time would be required to train individuals with no previous experience in their employment; and how the nonlethal munitions could be fired from weapons already possessed by a marine rifle company, specifically, the M203 grenade launcher, the M–16 rifle, and the 12-gauge shotgun.

With the support of the Los Angeles Sheriff's Department; the Office of the Secretary of Defense; the U.S. Army Armaments Research, Development, and Engineering Center; the U.S. Army Edgewood Research, Development, and Engineering Center; Phillips Laboratory; and Sandia National Laboratory, the Marines very quickly identified, located, tested, and obtained the appropriate systems, which included:

- Nonlethal projectiles (bean-bag rounds, rubber-baton rounds, and rubber-pellet rounds).
- Stinger grenades (which dispense rubber pellets instead of metal shrapnel).
- Sticky foam (dispensed by an operator against an individual human target).
- Barrier foam (resembles soap suds, but laced with irritating gas).

The nonlethal weapons and their operators were brought to Mombassa, Kenya, for training, and shipboard training was also conducted. At the same time, legal and policy reviews to validate these new systems were undertaken in the Pentagon, with generally favorable results, and rules of engagement were developed and approved. Also, Somali clan leaders were warned not to attempt to interfere with the operation, and a press briefing in the Pentagon described some of the nonlethal weapons the Marines would have available. It is known that the Somalis became aware of these systems, and the Marines believe the weapons played a significant role in deterring the Somalis from hostile actions.

The withdrawal operation was conducted with no significant problems with crowds or rioters, and no task-force casualties. Thus, it was not necessary to employ any of the nonlethal weapons directly against Somalis. This experience presented a number of lessons.

- There are significant shortcomings in the Department of Defense's ability to identify, acquire, and deploy nonlethal weapons. In particular, there is no unified process in place to coordinate the fragmented efforts in nonlethal weapons research and development.
- Since the use of nonlethal weapons was allowed only in situations where lethal force would be authorized, current U.S. military rules of engagement with respect to the tactical decision to use nonlethal or lethal means need to be clarified. Thus, the Marines believed nonlethal weapons could not be used readily to control escalation or to apply a graduated response to the threat.
- In training for operations other than war, traditional wartime skills, such as the return of a high volume of fire immediately when fired upon, must be modified, since there is a premium on restraint in the use of firepower and violence.
- A media plan must be carefully crafted and conscientiously followed by commanders and spokesperson, releasing sufficient information to deter, but not so much information that U.S. tactics could be easily defeated by a cognizant adversary.

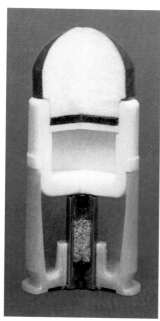

Non-lethal bullet.

Several elements of the post-Cold War era have affected the use of nonlethal force. First, a new political and strategic significance attaches to nonlethal weapons in an era of increasingly comprehensive and instantaneous multimedia global news coverage. Secondly, the increased likelihood of operating in densely populated urban areas and against unconventional foes using human shields has focused renewed attention on alternative applications of force with maximum restraint and minimum violence. Many adversaries understand that the United States is deterred from taking steps that can harm innocent civilians, and so deliberately intermingle with them while engaging in hostile or provocative actions. Nonlethal weapons untie U.S. hands by allowing forces to initiate action against a mixed group of noncombatants, combatants, and agents provocateurs. Even in cases where civilians are consciously abetting foes or acting to disrupt or impede U.S. efforts, it often is inappropriate and counterproductive to respond with indiscriminate lethal force, or sometimes with any lethal force at all.

But not least among post-Cold War developments affecting the use of nonlethal weapons has been the advent of highly advanced and, in some cases, exotic technologies, with subtle damage mechanisms. These weapons can be highly discriminate or relatively reversible. For example, an electromagnetic pulse can short-circuit electronic subsystems within adversary assets such as vehicles or weapons, rendering them useless; but the pulse leaves human beings unharmed. Or a large crowd might be temporarily incapacitated by a powerful, low-frequency acoustic signal without permanent effect. Ideally, no one dies, and all eventually recover fully, suffering no lasting deleterious effects.

In general, nonlethal weapons are an attractive means of expanding the options available to policymakers and commanders in that thin gray area between no application of military force at all and application of lethal force. Nonlethal weapons can stretch out the gray area and control the evolution of situations, providing better management of an escalation. It was precisely that desire to achieve military objectives while minimizing human fatalities

and collateral material damage that led the U.S. Marine Corps to obtain nonlethal weapons to assist in the withdrawal of UNOSOM II forces from Somalia.

Nevertheless, nonlethal weapons are not without problems. Left unqualified, the term "nonlethal" can lead to unrealistic public expectations that no fatalities will result from using such weapons. In fact, there will always be some residual risk of fatalities or permanent physical harm to people or physical assets, even though the U.S. intention is to develop nonlethal weapons that cause no lasting harm. Having nonlethal weapons in the U.S. arsenal may also lead some to believe erroneously that the United States is constrained to try them first in any encounter, and escalate to lethal means only if other measures fail. Others may misunderstand the nature of certain nonlethal weapons and incorrectly infer that they violate arms-control treaties or international legal constraints.

Witness the controversy surrounding anti-personnel lasers, which could be used to blind enemy soldiers. The U.S. program is designed to develop lasers that would take enemy equipment, such as anti-tank-weapon sights, out of commission without causing lasting damage to the eyesight of enemy soldiers. That is consistent with the October 1995 laser weapon protocol to the Convention on Conventional Weapons, supported by the U.S. However, a protocol banning anti-personnel devices has been proposed by the Swedish government, illustrating the political sensitivity of nonlethal weapons.

More to the point, the employment of nonlethal weapons will not always be fully successful. Not all prospective nonlethal technologies will prove technically, legally, or politically feasible. Those weapons that are fielded will require special training and new doctrines, as well as careful planning. Unless the United States is very shrewd in the way it conceives of and employs nonlethal weapons, paying particular attention to the psychological and political dimension of such operations, a military success could be thwarted by political countermeasures. Even a perfectly executed attack in

PSYOP: UH-60 dropping leaflets in Thailand during the Cobra Gold 94.

which nonlethal weapons perform as expected might be countered by ruthless adversaries willing to kill their own compatriots and blame it on the United States.

Thus, while nonlethal weapons appear to provide important advantages to the United States in the post-Cold War environment, they are subject to a number of cautions. Fully realizing their promise requires coordination of the operational needs of military commanders, the political priorities and concerns of top civilian leadership, and the creativity and resourcefulness of the acquisition and technical communities. Since several agencies, including the Department of Transportation and Department of Justice, have a role in countering unconventional threats, such coordination will require an interagency effort as well.

Psychological Operations (PSYOP)

For years, the subject of PSYOP remained shrouded in mystery, despite its use by the U.S. armed forces since the earliest days of the Republic. It was viewed as a black art that employed falsehoods, half-truths, and deception. In fact, to capture an audience, hold its attention, and foster a particular belief or behavior, PSYOP messages normally must be truthful.

The successful use of PSYOP during military operations in Grenada (1983), Panama (1989), the Persian Gulf (1991), Somalia (1993–94), and Haiti (1994–95) helped lift PSYOP's shroud and demonstrated its utility and flexibility across a wide range of military activity.

The U.S. Army's PSYOP force structure, active and reserves, is relatively small: 1,200 active-duty soldiers and civilians and 3,000 reserves. The force is regionally oriented and trained, and recruited according to language skills, cultural awareness, and ethnicity. A core of highly qualified civilians provides the cultural skills so vital in the conduct of successful PSYOP. The force has many highly qualified linguists but usually relies on local hires and Army-wide searches to obtain native-born speakers.

The U.S. Air Force also maintains the capability to deliver leaflets and conduct airborne radio-TV broadcast operations. This capability has been demonstrated, for example, by the deployment of EC–130 aircraft that conducted television and radio broadcasts of PSYOP messages in Haiti.

As a result of the information revolution and the concurrent explosion of global telecommunication capabilities, a degree of international interconnectivity has evolved that was unimaginable even in the mid-1980s. In this environment, cyberspace may become the battlespace of the information warrior. In addition to PSYOP's usual arsenal of printing presses, loudspeakers, radio, and TV transmitters, efforts are underway to use emerging technologies to enhance PSYOP effectiveness. PSYOP payloads in unmanned aerial vehicles, for example, can be used to extend current broadcast and leaflet-delivery capabilities to previously denied areas. Faxes can be sent to recipients worldwide, autodialers can deliver recorded messages to individuals via telephone, and direct broadcast satellites can be used to provide televised "news" to large segments of the world's population. PSYOP billboards can be established on the Internet to send messages to anyone with access to it. The explosion of information and communication technology will continue to offer new opportunities for PSYOP; the challenge will be to incorporate this technology in the most cost-effective manner.

Information systems represent the medium over which messages are carried; it is the job of PSYOP to tailor the message that is received. PSYOP will be more effective to the extent to which its messages are culturally sound, linguistically perfect, and highly persuasive, that is, messages that resonate with and reinforce attitudes that can work to produce the desired behavioral results.

Foreign Law-Enforcement and Constabulary Training

Responding to unconventional threats very often requires working with the law enforcement communities of other nations. Managing refugees, enforcing sanctions, preempting or disrupting terrorists, interdicting narcotics trafficking, or establishing public order after military operations or a natural or man-made disaster all involve working with indigenous security forces. As with the other unconventional instruments described above, foreign police assistance is both politically sensitive and complex in that several U.S. government agencies may become involved in these kinds of activities.

In response to abuses related to police-training assistance programs in Vietnam, Congress passed legislation in the 1970s prohibiting the use of any Foreign Assistance Act funds for the purpose of training or assisting foreign police, a general prohibition that applied to all government agencies. In subsequent years, however, Congress allowed several broad legislative exceptions to this general prohibition, particularly in the area of cooperative international counternarcotics and antiterrorism efforts, which also applied generally to all agencies. DOD, for example, has trained foreign civilian police under the counterdrug program and other special exceptions to the Foreign Assistance Act in Costa Rica, the eastern Caribbean, Honduras, and El Salvador. Under the auspices of the Department of State's Antiterrorism Assistance Program, the Departments of Defense, Justice, Transportation, and Treasury, as well as the CIA, provide antiterrorism assistance to friendly governments. By 1995, more than 16,000 people from 83 countries had received training since the program's inception in 1983. The general trend toward acknowledging the importance of human rights and the rule of law continued in 1986, when the Department of Justice created its International Criminal Investigative Training Assistance Program (ICITAP). ICITAP activities are funded by the Department of

State and structured to provide advice and assistance on the long-term development of law enforcement institutions.

Unfortunately, in military contingency operations where there is little warning or where the environment is not permissive, ICITAP does not have the authority, structure, or capability to quickly reconstitute police forces and police services. Dependent on funding from Congress to pay for consultants or award a contract to a civilian firm to conduct training classes, ICITAP may require several months to establish a training program. ICITAP civilian consultants and contractors generally do not accompany indigenous security personnel on joint police patrols to provide on-the-job training or operate at the precinct/substation level. ICITAP is designed to professionalize existing police forces over an extended period of time by teaching detailed classes in police methods, often in a police academy setting.

Consequently, the Department of Defense often is called upon to shoulder the burden of emergency law enforcement and short-term support of foreign police. Over the past two decades, DOD personnel had to assist in the creation of rudimentary public security forces following short interventions in Grenada, Panama, Somalia, and Haiti. Since military police, civil affairs, special forces, engineers, and other supporting forces normally are already on the ground to conduct U.S. force protection and public safety activities, in some cases it may be possible to extend these capabilities to support for internal security forces. The DOD has been slow to plan for and undertake these potential activities, being concerned about legal constraints, the political sensitivities surrounding public safety issues, and the budgetary implications of assuming even partial responsibility for what ultimately is a job for other government agencies. While acknowledging that it is occasionally required to support foreign internal security forces, the department responded to the 1995 Roles and Missions Commission's recommendations for greater DOD involvement in this area by emphasizing that "the training of foreign constabulary forces is not and should not be a DOD mission."

One barrier to greater DOD involvement in foreign law enforcement training and constabulary operations is that DOD has no role in such activities inside the U.S. The 1868 Posse Comitatus law prohibits the Army and Air Force from engaging in domestic law enforcement; a long-standing order from the Secretary of Navy extends that prohibition to the the Navy and Marines. Despite a few exceptions made over the years, Congress remains extremely reluctant to relax the Posse Comitatus restrictions.

Since 1975, a provision known as Section 660 (of the Foreign Assistance Act) has restricted use of foreign assistance funds for foreign law enforcement, including training. These restrictions were designed to distance the U.S. from controversy over police violatinos of human rights, and they do not apply in countries with longstanding democratic traditions. A variety of execptions to Section 660 have been exacted over the years, but it still restricts DOD's role in foreign law enforcement training.

Despite past and present legal and bureaucratic disagreements over divisions of responsibility, some elements in the Congress and many senior civilian leaders in the executive branch recognize that it is often not possible to pursue U.S. national security interests without working with foreign internal security forces. Civilian police who support democracy, respect internationally recognized standards of human rights and the rule of law, and are free of corruption can support U.S. regional defense strategy by contributing to the restoration of peace and stability following conflicts or crises; countering terrorist acts and terrorist groups; strengthening local authority at the grassroots level; and fighting subversion of their democratic governments. In late 1995, Congress was considering legislation that would relax some restrictions on the use of Foreign Assistance Act funding for police support and training activities overseas under specific conditions.

Conclusions

While the United States must expect more unconventional challenges to its interests in the future, this does not necessarily mean that unconventional threats are growing in importance or that unconventional instruments will be a policy option of choice for U.S. decision makers. With respect to unconventional threats, the extent to which they have a cumulative effect on U.S. security interests, and thus must be taken more seriously, depends in part on how the United States defines its interests and on how one assesses trends in the international security environment. For example, a U.S. national security strategy of engagement designed to preserve a position of world leadership will treat unconventional threats more seriously than a strategy that reflects less concern for developments overseas. Likewise, unconventional threats will be deemed more important if they are directed or manipulated by growing regional powers intent on systematically challenging U.S. interests than if they seem to be isolated and discrete events.

It is also difficult to generalize about the applicability of unconventional instruments to future national security problems. The instruments discussed in this chapter seem to be of increasing importance because they can broaden the range of options open to decision makers reluctant to resort to higher-cost military measures, and they often minimize the collateral damage associated with the use of coercive measures. Nevertheless, all unconventional options will continue to be politically sensitive and hard to manage. Unconventional instruments, which often are slow to produce even limited results, may seem attractive to decision makers who consider all the alternative policy options even less satisfactory, but they may not be sustainable without a carefully managed effort to marshal public support. To the extent unconventional measures are seen as innovative, proportionate, and discriminate responses to real threats, the public is more likely to be supportive. If they are interpreted as unethical and ineffective half-measures, they will receive less support and be difficult to sustain.

CHAPTER THIRTEEN

Limited Military Intervention

Introduction

Military intervention comprises violent and nonviolent operations to protect or advance U.S. national interests. But this chapter includes only those operations in the middle ground above the level of a covert or unconventional action and below the level of a major war. Thus, the limited military interventions analyzed here include such undertakings as:

- Military deployment in support of diplomacy.
- The evacuation or rescue of U.S. and allied citizens.
- The enforcement of sanctions, embargoes and exclusion zones.
- Limited air strikes.
- Noncombat support for allies in small wars.
- Combat operations by U.S. forces in small wars.

Because limited military intervention differs from full-scale war by involving limited numbers of personnel and is often of shorter duration, it also differs politically. Historical precedent and Supreme Court decisions have given the President significant latitude in initiating interventions without prior congressional approval. Of course, Presidents frequently *have* consulted with Congress prior to initiating military intervention, and Congress has been able to terminate such operations, particularly by withdrawing funds. Domestic U.S. politics can play an important role in the success or failure of an intervention; the depth and breadth of public support for the operation can vitally influence decisions about operational matters, such as the numbers and kinds of forces deployed.

Though military intervention is a limited instrument, it remains very much a weapon—an instrument with the potential to injure and to kill. Consequently, military intervention is inherently threatening and as such carries particular risks. No matter how benevolent U.S. intentions may be, the very act of wielding a weapon may produce an adverse reaction in others. Even in the case of military intervention to aid disaster victims, there may be some whose interests are threatened by the amelioration of local suffering or simply by the deployment of U.S. forces. When military intervention takes place with the threat of even a low-level use of force—for example, in the establishment of exclusion zones—the danger of violent opposition increases.

As a result, those proposing military intervention need to answer two separate

USS _Wasp_ off Haiti during Operation Restore Democracy.

but equally important sets of questions: What do they intend to accomplish by their use of the U.S. armed forces, and how do they plan to do it? What are the possible responses of governments and populations in the region where intervention is planned? Once these questions have been answered, planners can decide whether the aim of military intervention would be worth the likely price of achieving it. In this sense, a proposed military intervention needs to be analyzed as if it were a limited war in two meanings of the term: limited as to resources to be invested, and limited as to goals to be achieved. That is true even in the case of nonviolent operations.

Limited military intervention can exert great pressure, particularly against a weak foe. But U.S. military intervention may provoke total resistance on the part of a moderately powerful adversary. Although a commitment to total war on the part of such an adversary does not necessarily guarantee defeat for an intervening power, such a situation does raise the possibility of a military intervention's progressively escalating as the intervening power is forced to commit ever greater resources to accomplish its original aims. Such an increasing commitment can also create a logic of its own, obscuring the goals of the intervention, introducing questions of national prestige and credibility, and evoking a determination to justify heavy casualties by victory. Such a dilemma faced the United States in Vietnam and the Soviet Union in Afghanistan. Nonetheless, such cases are the exception rather than the rule. Generally, military intervention provides a highly flexible weapon that allows a government an option lying somewhere between the extremes of passively accepting injury to national interests and waging all-out war.

Instruments

For the past half century, U.S. military intervention has involved so many activities on so vast a scale that categorizing and analyzing them can hardly be attempted in a few pages. Nonetheless, some general patterns do present themselves. It is more difficult to make educated guesses about how American military intervention may evolve in the post-Cold War world. The fundamental nature of warfare seems in the process of a major shift, what is commonly referred to as a "revolution in military affairs." Even small wars and military intervention short of war seem likely to be affected by such developments.

Military Deployments in Support of Diplomacy

Cold War diplomacy was inextricably linked with the threat of force. The Berlin crises of 1948–49 and 1961 offer prime examples. These were resolved not on the battlefield but in secret exchanges between U.S. and Soviet diplomats over the status and survival of the West Berlin enclave. However, U.S. military deployments were an important factor in the West's diplomatic successes. The deployments offered concrete proof of the United States's ability to sustain Berlin and Washington's resolve to go to war to defend the city, if necessary.

The United States so routinely deployed aircraft carriers to back up its diplomacy during the Cold War that listing all the instances would prove tedious. Still, a number of examples stand out: the introduction of a Marine landing team into the Mediterranean aboard the USS _Midway_ in 1948 to support Greece and Turkey; the movement of the USS _Enterprise_ into the Bay of Bengal during the India-Pakistan war of 1971; and the crossing by Sixth Fleet carriers of the Libyan government's "line of death" in the Gulf of Sidra in the 1980s. On other occasions, the U.S. backed up diplomacy with aerospace assets (e.g., deploying AWACS or fighters to a crisis zone, placing strategic bombers and missiles on alert, and, most famously, organizing the 1948–49 airlift to Berlin). Less frequently, ground forces were employed.

The life-or-death rationale that underlay armed diplomacy during the Cold War is gone. In the post-Cold War world, U.S. leaders must be extremely careful about ensuring public support before threatening or promising the use of U.S. ground forces as a form of diplomatic leverage. To make such declarations, only to discover that Congress does not approve, would be damaging to U.S. credibility. For such deployments to succeed, the President will have to make clear that serious national interests are involved and, thereafter, gain and sustain the support of the public for the duration of the intervention.

Operations in support of diplomacy continued after the end of the Cold War, notable examples being President Clinton's military response to the Iraqi buildup along the Kuwaiti border in October 1994, and similar deployments to Kuwait and Jordan in August 1995. These temporary force movements and exercises demonstrated American resolve to defend Iraq's Arab neighbors against aggression. But one can presume that private warnings conveyed through third parties or secret channels were also important in making U.S. resolve clear to Baghdad.

In striking contrast to the United States's success in deterring aggression against Kuwait were its difficulties in achieving its diplomatic aims in the western Balkans in 1993–94. While U.S. peacekeepers in Macedonia helped prevent the spread of fighting to that country, a lasting cease-fire in Bosnia was achieved only in November 1995 after negotiations in Dayton, Ohio, organized by the U.S. government. Some argue that this delay may have been because Washington announced *a priori* that it would not deploy large-scale ground forces to the region until a peace agreement had been achieved, greatly reducing the power of U.S. diplomacy. The U.S.-encouraged NATO air strikes in the former Yugoslavia in summer 1995 were an important contributing factor to the Serbian side's decision to agree to peace talks. But as a sign of Washington's commitment, they could not substitute for the placement of U.S. military personnel on the ground. Compare the failed 1993 mission of the USS *Harlan County* in Haiti with the success of the 1994 Carter-Nunn-Powell mission to Port-au-Prince (backed up by the imminent arrival of thousands of U.S. ground troops).

Given the far greater control ground forces can exercise in a region, compared to air or naval operations, the threat of their deployment is a powerful tool with which to support a diplomatic initiative. However, introducing ground forces greatly ups the dangers (e.g., of casualties and hostages) and therefore the domestic political stakes of an operation. The American public and Congress displayed great unease over the idea of dispatching U.S. ground forces to Haiti. A similar attitude regarding the use of U.S. ground forces to guarantee the peace settlement in Bosnia was overcome only after considerable efforts by President Clinton to persuade Congress and the U.S. public that the deployment was vital to U.S. interests for leadership in NATO and peace in a volatile part of Europe. One reason is the danger

Secretary Perry's Criteria for Military Intervention

After evaluating the interests at stake and the costs of the operation, the administration will consider many specific factors before deciding whether to commit forces, what objectives to assign to them, and what level of forces to employ. Prominent among these factors are:

■ Existing treaty commitments.

■ The willingness and ability of like-minded nations, particularly those most directly affected by the conflict, to contribute to the operation.

■ Whether, in the absence of coalition partners, U.S. unilateral action is justified.

■ Clear military objectives supporting political objectives.

■ Judgments about the necessary duration and costs of the operation. In other words, can it be achieved in a reasonable amount of time with an acceptable expenditure of resources and concluded in an acceptable manner.

■ The willingness to commit sufficient forces to achieve the defined objectives.

■ The extent to which support for U.S. involvement exists among Congress and the American people, and the extent to which such support can be marshaled.

■ The acceptability, in the case of multilateral operations, of proposed arrangements for command and control of U.S. forces.

The relationship among the size, composition, and disposition of forces committed and U.S. objectives must be continually reasserted and, if necessary, adjusted.

Source: Report of the Secretary of Defense to the President and the Congress, February 1995.

that such deployments could bring casualties to which the American public is increasingly sensitive. Another factor is the degree to which U.S. national interests are seen to be at stake. There was little hesitation in sending ground forces to Saudi Arabia in 1990, despite the risk of casualties, because there was a consensus that important U.S. interests were at stake (in contrast to the congressional debate in January 1991 about whether to liberate Kuwait).

Uses of military intervention such as the force movements in the Middle East during the Clinton administration will likely continue even in an age of decreasing overseas presence, information warfare, and cruise missiles. Nothing so demonstrates U.S. determination to honor a diplomatic commitment as the placing of U.S. military personnel in harm's way to fulfill such a pledge.

Evacuation and Rescue Missions

U.S. armed forces frequently engaged in evacuation and rescue operations during the Cold War: to pull Americans away from hostile mobs during the Middle East wars and crises from 1948 to 1991; to protect missionaries in the Congo during the bloody chaos following independence in the early 1960s; and to evacuate hundreds of thousands of Vietnamese and Cambodians from Indochina in 1975. These missions were in support of humanitarian ideals, the centuries-old European principle of protecting Western nationals abroad (if necessary by armed force), and the U.S. Cold War policy of offering refuge to those who had placed their lives at risk by opposing communism.

More recent examples of this form of military intervention include the evacuations of imperiled foreigners from Liberia, Somalia, and Rwanda. The anarchy that led to these missions adds weight to the widespread expectation that other states

---

Military Intervention in Support of Diplomacy: Korea 1993–95

The U.S. armed forces have played a major role in support of diplomatic efforts to end the North Korean development of nuclear weapons. Through both activity and inactivity, the U.S. military—especially the Army and Air Force units stationed in South Korea—has given the United States special political and psychological as well as military leverage with the Pyongyang regime.

The public phase of the crisis began in March 1993 with the North Korean announcement that it would withdraw from the Treaty on the Non-proliferation of Nuclear Weapons (NPT), and would not allow the International Atomic Energy Agency to inspect its suspected nuclear-weapons program. Throughout the spring of that year, U.S. government spokesmen offered high-level talks with the Pyongyang regime. But these offers seemed to accomplish nothing. Finally, in June, the United States offered to cancel the annual joint military exercises in South Korea—exercises that Pyongyang has long denounced as provocative and as preparatory for an invasion of the North. This concession was rapidly followed by North Korean-U.S. negotiations and the announcement in June 1993 that Pyongyang would continue to honor the NPT.

The following month, President Clinton visited South Korea. American forces were presented for his inspection, and the president reassured the South Korean people that U.S. forces would remain in their country as long as they were needed. In September, in order to reassure America's other major ally in the region, the United States and Japan began talks on developing an antimissile system for deployment on Japanese soil. The talks were in obvious response to North Korean testing of missiles that could be armed with nuclear warheads.

Negotiations between the United States and North Korea continued throughout the fall of 1993, with little result. In December, the Defense Department announced it was considering options to strengthen both American forces in South Korea and the South Korean forces themselves. Within days, Pyongyang declared that it

---

throughout Africa and southwest Asia will fail over the coming decades. If these pessimistic predictions prove correct, U.S. armed forces will most likely be called upon to engage in numerous evacuation and rescue missions for Westerners over the next quarter of a century.

On the other hand, the collapse of the Soviet empire has ended the U.S. policy of rescuing anti-communist refugees. Furthermore, hostility is growing within North American and Western European public opinion to offering assistance to refugees and would-be immigrants from Third World and Fourth World countries. This raises questions about the future willingness of the U.S. government to employ armed forces to rescue non-American citizens or citizens of countries closely allied to the United States.

Other problems facing the implementation of such missions in the future may arise from logistics and transportation availability. The armed forces of the United States and its allies are shrinking. Washing-

ton is also in the process of reducing the number of its overseas bases, so that, in several decades' time, the U.S. military may no longer have bases on foreign soil. For these reasons, the future ability of the American military to launch successful evacuation and rescue missions may be somewhat circumscribed. Particularly large operations may require cooperation between U.S. and foreign militaries.

However, compared to all other countries, the sea and air transport resources of the U.S. armed forces remain enormous, although many Air Force C–141 transports are reaching the end of their operational lives. In order to project military force, the U.S. armed forces is likely to retain such lift capability through modernization and upgrading. It will therefore also be available for evacuation and rescue operations. Thus, U.S. superiority in the ability to evacuate large numbers of people by ship or aircraft is certain to endure for decades to come. In cases where a relatively small number of

would allow inspectors access to its officially disclosed nuclear-program sites. Despite this breakthrough, the U.S. government revealed in January 1994 that it would ship Patriot antimissile batteries to South Korea.

The crisis worsened in the spring of 1994. Pyongyang blocked nuclear inspectors from carrying out their work and renewed its threat to withdraw from the NPT. Washington annouced its intention to seek UN economic sanctions on North Korea, but other major powers were reluctant to support sanctions at that stage. In June, President Clinton began studying plans for a major military buildup in South Korea.

As tensions mounted, former President Jimmy Carter visited both halves of Korea and returned to the United States announcing that he had found North Korean dictator Kim Il-sung reasonable and willing to negotiate. Although Kim died in July 1994, U.S.-North Korean talks continued to press on into the fall, culminating in an agreement in October 1994. Pyongyang would suspend its nuclear program, in return for which the United States would provide oil as a short-term fix to North Korea's energy problems and create an international consortium to provide proliferation-resistant light-water reactors to replace the North's graphite-moderated reactors.

In the spring of 1995, repeating the pattern of the crisis since it had begun, the North Koreans rejected the delivery of South Korean nuclear reactors. These formed an essential part of the aid package assembled the previous fall. U.S. diplomats insisted that the Pyongyang regime accept the reactors, and in May, the North Koreans acquiesced. For the time being, the crisis subsided.

Without knowing the ultimate resolution of the delicate situation on the Korean peninsula, it is still obvious that the U.S. military presence provides the security foundation on which rest U.S. diplomatic efforts to prevent Pyongyang from building nuclear weapons. Looming over every other reality was the unmentioned stick of the U.S. nuclear arsenal. The final argument for American diplomats in their negotiations with the North Koreans was that even if Pyongyang produced a few warheads and married them to ballistic missiles, the United States could obliterate North Korea if it came to nuclear blows.

U.S. Marine on patrol in Somalia during Operation Restore Hope in Somalia.

people are involved, it may be possible for such missions to be conducted by other countries' armed forces. But when a sizable number of people require rescue or evacuation, U.S. participation will be necessary.

The rescue of U.S. military personnel under combat conditions, particularly downed flight crews, will also continue to be carried out on a fairly frequent basis. The June 1995 extraction from Bosnia of Air Force Captain Scott O'Grady by U.S. Marines offers one recent example of this type of operation. Since the United States remains committed to various surveillance, exclusion, humanitarian, peacekeeping, and covert operations involving manned aircraft and special-operations units, the rescue of their personnel will almost certainly be required from time to time. The practice by certain societies of abusing U.S. military prisoners to put psychological pressure on the U.S. government and public will only make such rescue operations more imperative.

Sanctions Enforcement

During the Cold War, the United States generally was not able to gain adherence to sanctions such as exclusion areas, in which certain types of activity (e.g., moving military units) are prohibited, or embargoes, which prohibit the import or export of certain types of materiel (e.g., arms or petroleum). Any U.N. Security

Council resolution to create such zones favored by the United States was almost certain to be vetoed by the Soviet Union. And without U.N. approval, it was virtually impossible to create the legal and moral authority to establish such restricted areas. However, in a few cases in which the Soviets favored such U.N. resolutions and the United States chose to agree, exclusion zones and embargoes were established. The major cases were the embargoes on arms sales to Portugal during the final years of its colonial wars in Guinea, Angola, and Mozambique, and to South Africa because of its policy of apartheid. After its 1965 unilateral and illegal declaration of independence from Britain, the white minority government in Rhodesia was placed under a near-total embargo.

Despite U.S. adherence to these U.N. resolutions, the role of the U.S. military in enforcing them was minimal. In a small number of cases during the decades of East-West confrontation, the United States chose to use its armed forces unilaterally to enforce blockades or exclusion zones, even at the risk of war. The most famous case was the blockade of Cuba in the fall of 1962; another was the counterinvasion patrol in the Formosa Strait from 1950 to 1972.

In the early 1990s, the permanent members of the Security Council cooperated far more, with the result that exclusion-zone and embargo resolutions became fairly common. Examples included the no-fly zones established over Bosnia and Iraq, and the embargo on arms deliveries to Croatia, Bosnia, and Serbia-Montenegro. Decision makers often turn to sanctions because they represent a stronger step than a diplomatic démarche but avoid the drawbacks and risks of military force. Unlike the latter, sanctions can easily be ratcheted up or down. Sanctions also can be used to weaken the military capabilities of a target state, thus improving chances for success should military force become necessary.

Although other U.S. government agencies take the lead on sanctions policy, military forces play the dominant role in enforcing embargoes and exclusion zones. The ever-increasing C^4I and surveillance capabilities enjoyed by the U.S. armed forces make such operations easier from a techni-

Coast Guard intercepts an Iraqi ship, 1990.

cal standpoint. No other military enjoys a comparable ability to monitor the locations, dimensions, directions, speeds, and communications of ships, aircraft, and land vehicles. Similar capabilities from both technical and human intelligence resources allow the United States to keep track of foreign economic and financial activities, giving U.S. forces unparalleled ability to enforce blockades and exclusion zones.

In the enforcement of embargoes, the military's largest responsibility is interdicting goods on land and at sea. In the case of Haiti, for example, the U.S. Navy and the U.S. Coast Guard contributed most of the ships in the U.N.'s maritime interdiction force, while U.S. Army forces, working with their Dominican Republic counterparts, limited smuggling across the land border into Haiti. U.S. forces have also contributed most of the capabilities to enforce the embargo against Iraq imposed in 1990. In the former Yugoslavia, the U.S. Navy helped enforce economic sanctions against Serbia, as well as the arms embargo applying to all the former Yugoslav republics. At the same time, DOD contractors, mostly retired U.S. military personnel, helped monitor border traffic between Serbia and Serb-occupied areas of Bosnia, thereby slowing the flow of fuel, arms, and other war materiel to Bosnian Serbs.

The effectiveness of sanctions could be enhanced by more aggressive interdiction, more precise focus of sanctions within the target state, and mitigation of unintended economic and political consequences. For example, interdiction missions could be strengthened by using nonlethal technologies to stop ships, planes, and other forms of transport. More precise focusing of sanctions within a target state could be achieved through direct action, such as sabotage of transportation nodes, or through forms of information warfare, including the disruption of communications, especially those affecting the banking and trading system. More precise focusing might also be feasible by imposing sanctions in ways that would damage the interests of political elites in the target state more than ordinary citizens. Lastly, psychological operations could be used more effectively to mitigate the unwanted side effects of sanctions by garnering support for U.S. policy from within the target state as well as without. Greater consideration could also be given to using psychological operations as a means of maximizing popular resistance against the leadership of a sanctioned regime.

Sanctions work most effectively when they are accompanied by other, forceful military initiatives. In the case of Haiti, the deployment of U.S. forces offshore helped keep pressure on the Cédras regime via threats of direct U.S. military intervention. Deployment of U.S. forces in Iraq serves a similar purpose, with the U.S. military having the additional important role of protecting the Kurdish population, which is an important source of opposition to Saddam's regime.

When using U.S. forces to support sanctions, U.S. policymakers sometimes face conflicts between political and military objectives. For example, stopping intercoastal smuggling between Haiti and the Dominican Republic was a top U.S. priority. However, devising adequate rules of engagement for the maritime patrols proved very difficult, because most smuggling took place on small boats piloted by Haitian and Dominican civilians. The dilemma was that stopping this trade required strong action, including warning and disabling shots that would have produced conflict and casualties, including casualties for U.S. forces. In the end, the United States decided against strong action to block intercoastal smuggling, because the political and diplomatic fallout could have undermined support for the sanctions.

Lastly, U.S. military forces help mitigate the effects of sanctions so that U.S. policy gains are maximized. In Haiti, for example, U.S. forces delivered aid and improved Haiti's ability to absorb the aid through civil affairs programs, thus significantly improving Haiti's economic condition.

Limited Air Strikes

Bombardment by non-nuclear explosives, particularly air-delivered bombardment, has become increasingly attractive to the U.S. government in applying military force while minimizing risk. Such operations present a smaller likelihood of U.S. casualties than those involving ground forces in contact with the enemy. The chances of U.S. forces suffering loss or capture in bombardment operations have been further reduced since the end of the Cold War. The collapse of Soviet military power has granted overwhelming superiority over any conceivable foe of the U.S. Air Force and the U.S. Navy.

Area bombing, naval gunfire, and rocket fire have been superceded by the use of "smart bombs," cruise missiles, and other precision-guided munitions. Accurate strikes on military targets reduce the possibility of collateral damage, that is, unintended civilian casualties or destruction of non-military targets. The growing ubiquity and versatility of television technology and the appearance of international broadcasting networks have given the pub-

---

Small Wars Waged by U.S. Forces: Panama 1989

Panamanian dictator Manuel Noriega enjoyed a complicated relationship with the United States throughout the 1980s. On the one hand, he assisted the Reagan administration in the covert war against the Sandinista regime in Nicaragua and was a source of intelligence for the CIA. But Noriega also sold weapons and provided intelligence to various communist and Middle Eastern enemies of the United States. Worse, from Washington's viewpoint, beginning in 1985, he was seen as a threat to Panamanian democracy after having pressured the elected president to step down because the military could no longer work with his presidency. At the same time, General Noriega was clearly identified as a major actor in drug and money-laundering activities. From late 1986 until late 1989, the objective of the United States' Panama policy was deceptively simple: Noriega must go. The question was how to accomplish this end.

The U.S. was not ready to use force to remove Noriega. Unlike Marcos, Somosa, and Duvalier, Noriega was the general in charge of the armed forces, and he was not ready to retire. A crisis developed between 1987 and 1989 during which Noriega was indicted in Miami on twelve counts of racketeering and cocaine trafficking; the Panamanian president was ousted by the military; and the United States applied various alternatives to force—diplomatic, economic, and legal measures—to remove the general, without success. At the same time, the U.S. government ruled out U.S. military intervention except to protect the Panama Canal from attack and to protect U.S. lives. However, beginning in the spring of 1988, the Reagan administration did begin to reinforce U.S. forces in Panama, and contingency planning began in earnest.

In May 1989, Noriega allowed national elections, convinced that his puppet candidates would win. The Panamanian people disagreed. Although Noriega's candidates were proclaimed the winners, international observers announced that the Noriega regime had stolen the election by fraud. President Bush recalled the U.S. ambassador to Panama and persuaded every Latin American government—save those of Cuba and Nicaragua—to condemn the Noriega regime. While a war of nerves between the United States and Panama intensified during the summer of 1989, the Organization of American States tried unsuccessfully to negotiate with Noriega, attempting to persuade him to relinquish power. In September, President Bush announced that the United States no longer recognized the Panamanian government as legitimate, while at the same time reinforcing the U.S. presence in Panama.

A final Panamanian move to unseat Noriega, a coup attempt against the dictator by disaffected members of the Panamanian Defense Forces (PDF), failed in early October 1989. After this pivotal event, the Bush admin-

---

STRATEGIC ASSESSMENT 1996

LIMITED MILITARY INTERVENTION

lic the ability to observe the results of bombardments carried out by their forces. Precision strikes greatly lessen the chances that television viewers will be presented with disturbing images of civilian dead, wrecked hospitals, or burning houses of worship caused by U.S. bombs. The reduction of such damage by bombardment, compared with that inflicted by U.S. forces in World War II or even the Vietnam War, also lessens the chances that outraged international opinion can be mobilized against the U.S. government.

However, the rapid improvement over the past several decades in the accuracy, range, and power of bombardment by non-nuclear munitions has created unrealistic attitudes in the minds of some about the capabilities of such weapons. From the time when rapid-fire, long-range, high explosive artillery was developed in the late

nineteenth century, through the creation of strategic aerial bombing forces in the 1930s, to the contemporary use of cruise missiles, expectations have arisen about the ability of such weapons to make wars both short and free from high casualties. Strategic bombing theorists such as Giulio Douhet argued that no modern state could long withstand massive attacks on its urban centers. Aerial warfare prophets predicted that bombardment of enemy cities would rapidly lead to panic, the collapse of morale, and the crumbling of all resistance in a matter of days.

In fact, as the results of aerial bombing campaigns from the Second World War to the Gulf War have demonstrated, such operations can be an effective form of attrition warfare, slowly wearing down enemy will and destroying his means to resist. But human beings, whether military or civilian,

istration looked at its military options in a different light. On December 15, Noriega ordered his National Assembly of Representatives to declare Panama in "a state of war" with the United States. The next day, PDF forces opened fire on a car carrying four American servicemen, seriously wounding one. Late on December 17, President Bush ordered Operation Just Cause to be launched early on December 20, 1989.

Just Cause was carried out by a joint all-service task force based on two Army divisions, an independent Army brigade, a Marine Expeditionary Brigade, and smaller elite Special Forces and Army Ranger units. The task force was overwhelmingly superior in size, capability, and training to the PDF. By the end of daylight on the second day of the operation, SOUTHCOM forces had effectively crushed all resistance. By December 25, military operations were over—with the exception of efforts to capture Noriega. On December 24, he had taken refuge in the quarters of the papal nuncio.

Noriega was subjected to an intense psychological operations effort to break his morale and induce his surrender. Finally, on the evening of January 3, 1990, Noriega walked out of the nunciature and delivered himself to the Special Forces unit that had surrounded his hiding place. The Panamanian government that had been elected but prevented from taking office in May 1989 already had been installed by the American forces and recognized by Washington two weeks earlier. Operation Just Cause cost the U.S. military 23 dead and 324 wounded. The PDF lost over 300 men and had about 125 wounded. At least 200 Panamanian civilians were killed in the fighting and over 1500 were wounded.

Just Cause represents an excellent example of a small war. U.S. casualties were relatively light, operations were concluded in a very short time, all objectives were met, and the war received the overwhelming support not only of the American people but of Panamanians as well. However, Panamanian civilian losses were high. Although U.S. firepower was carefully planned and skillfully executed in an effort to keep casualties to a minimum, suppressive fires were heavy. In the densely urbanized areas where much of Just Cause was conducted, this inevitably led to the death or injury of many noncombatants.

Given the increasing urbanization of the world population and the growth of slum cities throughout Africa, Asia, and Latin America, Just Cause may indicate some sobering trends in the evolution of warfare. The application of heavy firepower in huge slums constructed from cardboard, plywood, and sheet metal may produce horrific civilian casualties. For psychological and political reasons, U.S. armed forces may need to rethink their doctrine for urban warfare.

INSTITUTE FOR NATIONAL STRATEGIC STUDIES **165**

have shown themselves to be far tougher psychologically under bombardment than had been supposed. Eventually, people may crumble under the weight of heavy sustained bombardment. But such resistance can last for years. In the interim, anger at the losses inflicted by the bombardment can actually increase determination to hold on and fight back.

Furthermore, lengthy bombardment operations by manned aircraft inevitably result in the destruction of aircraft and the death, injury, or capture of aircrews. For this reason alone, the use of unmanned means of bombardment has become increasingly attractive to the U.S. government. But even in bombardment operations in which U.S. forces risk little or no chance of casualties, such campaigns can still evolve into a test of wills between the U.S. and enemy public. The enemy may employ psychological warfare to induce doubts about the justice of the U.S. cause or guilt over the suffering being inflicted and thus persuade U.S. public opinion to end the bombardment. Even cruise missiles can go astray or be misguided due to faulty intelligence.

Given continuing improvement in guidance and explosives technology and the unwillingness of the U.S. public to suffer heavy casualties in limited war, bombardment will be an even more attractive option than in the past. Such operations may prove highly effective under appropriate circumstances. But they will not solve every military problem, nor will they be carried out without loss of innocent life.

Bombardment can be a useful instrument when applied with appropriate ex-pectations of its utility. When used in concert with other instruments, it can be a key factor in bringing an adversary to the negotiating table or causing him to cease hostile behavior. The bombing of the Bosnian Serb facilities in the late summer and early fall of 1995 did not stop the hostilities, but, coupled with the economic embargo on Serbia and with diplomatic pressure, did play a key role in bringing Serbia and its Bosnian Serb allies into serious peace negotiations.

Support for Allies in Small Wars and Insurgencies

Post-World War II, Soviet expansion and the resulting U.S. strategy of containment led to numerous violent conflicts along the East-West divide and throughout the so-called Third World. In only a few cases, notably in Korea, was there a classic military confrontation of invasion and defense. Insurgency, an organized movement aimed at the overthrow of a constituted government through the use of subversion and armed conflict, was the principal means by which the Cold War struggle was fought on the peripheries of its major theaters. In these small wars between U.S. and Soviet allies, the U.S. role took such forms as small-scale training and advisory roles, sometimes coupled with large aid flows (from the Greek civil war of the 1940s to El Salvador in the 1980s), or large-scale semi-covert operations with little if any involvement by the U.S. military (as in Afghanistan and Nicaragua).

After the national U.S. debate of 1946–49 was resolved in favor of containing Soviet expansion, public support for military assistance to embattled anti-communist governments became virtually pro forma for twenty years. In general, the deployments of small numbers of U.S. troops to various anti-communist conflicts were not weighed on a case-by-case basis. Instead, they were regarded as part of the overall anti-Soviet effort that the country had resolved to wage indefinitely.

But the trauma of Vietnam destroyed this consensus. As in other conflicts, the commitment of U.S. troops to the defense of the Republic of Vietnam began as an advisory and training effort. The U.S. resources invested in the struggle grew to enormous levels, with nearly 60,000 battle deaths, ex-

**Missile launching from
USS Arleigh Burke.**

ceeding those suffered by U.S. forces in any other war save the Civil War and World War II. Following the fall of South Vietnam in 1975, no U.S. administration could continue to count on automatic public acceptance of military support for U.S. clients in small anti-communist conflicts.

The possibility of the establishment of communist regimes in Central America in the 1980s did persuade a majority of the U.S. public to support a small-scale and temporary military presence in Honduras and El Salvador. But with the memory of Vietnam still fresh, such support was given reluctantly and was carefully circumscribed. After the collapse of the Soviet threat in 1989–1991, the rationale for such use of U.S. armed forces disappeared altogether. Unless and until the United States finds itself engaged in a protracted struggle with another world power, it seems certain that the American people will accept the deployment of military advisory and train-

ing missions to countries at war only after careful consideration of the particular circumstances and the U.S. interests involved.

Insurgencies remain capable of adversely affecting U. S. interests. When they do, Washington can provide the party it is supporting with advice, financial and material support, training, and, as a last resort, advisors or other U.S. military personnel operating with indigenous forces. In the past, based on theories of conflict and development espoused by social scientists and economists, U.S. counterinsurgency efforts placed great emphasis on addressing the insurgency's supposed socioeconomic causes. Experience and further reflection have indicated that such theories were inadequate. The grievances expressed by those involved—typically political—are also important causes of the insurgencies.

In addition to addressing grievances, techniques that the United States can use for countering insurgency include penetra-

Civilian Resistance

Civilian resistance by means of mass nonviolent direction, sometimes called "people power," has often been regarded by national security analysts with skepticism. They have seen it as perhaps playing a role in peripheral situations but not as an important factor when vital interests are at stake. In fact, mass demonstrations, strikes, and boycotts have played a major role in shaping the post-Cold-War international system. Civilian resistance was a prominent feature of the East European revolutions that ended communist rule in 1989–1991 and in reversing the 1991 Russian coup, which were events as important as any in recent decades. Since the late 1980s, civilian resistance has been relatively successful against authoritarian rule from the Philippines to South Africa. However, as of late 1995, it has been unsuccessful in Burma, Tibet, and China. Whether for good or ill, direct action by civilians has become part of the strategic mix.

Civilian resistance has rarely been discussed as something that can be encouraged and planned, either by governments or even by the participants. Nonviolent struggle is often assumed to be determined by structural factors and by the interaction of the opponents' will to repress and the civilians' capacity to suffer. But these assumptions mislead. Closely studied cases of the last fifteen years show that civilian resistance, like any other form of political behavior, depends on the quality of the strategic choices made by participants, and therefore on the advice and support they receive. The "people power" defense of Cory Aquino's 1986 election in the Philippines was successful in part because of the years of deliberate organization and training by social activists and in part because the U.S. government showed that it had stopped supporting Ferdinand Marcos. Student insurrectionists in Beijing's Tiananmen Square were not aided by their mistakes in tactics (not dispersing when faced with overwhelming odds) and strategy (failing to guarantee strong reaction in China to a massacre). The U.S. government cannot create civilian resistance, nor is it likely to directly sponsor groups to wage popular struggles abroad. But it can make use of civilian resistance by considering how to provide such movements with strategic support. More skillful assistance to the Civilian Crusade in Panama in 1987 might have obviated the need for the subsequent Operation Just Cause or rendered that operation less costly to all concerned. In some circumstances, encouragement and material support for civilian resistance can be an alternative to military deployment in a peace operation, accomplishing the same goals at lower cost and with less violence.

tion of the insurgent organization and aggressive patrolling, if the insurgents are operating in small units. If the insurgents are operating in an urban area, the emphasis should fall on penetrating their networks. Although shanty towns may appear to provide insurgents with the same advantage that mountains and dense forests do in a rural setting, an urban setting allows the government to concentrate its resources, while the insurgent must operate in a limited area. Although some U.S. technical support may help the government in these situations, what is most needed in the urban setting is old-fashioned police intelligence work. That is within the capabilities of even a poor government, as long as it is committed to supporting such police work. If the government is not, the United States is unlikely to have sufficient leverage to make the government change its mind.

If the promises held out by exponents of information warfare prove correct, it may be possible in coming years for small teams of American advisors to use enormous information resources in the defense of an embattled ally. Enemy forces might be located and subjected to devastating fire with few or no Americans exposed to risk. In such cases, U.S. military technology might make the direct involvement of U.S. forces larger than advisory teams in small wars unnecessary—unless, of course, U.S. opponents were to acquire similar capabilities.

Waging Small Wars with U.S. Forces

The United States engaged directly in numerous small wars before 1941, but very few thereafter. After the establishment of the Central Intelligence Agency in 1947 and the creation of a system of peacetime alliances in the late 1940s and early 1950s, Washington had new alternatives. When the U.S. government decided to solve a problem with a small measure of military intervention, covert action or the use of surrogates generally replaced the customary landing of Marines. Furthermore, during the struggle with the nuclear-armed Soviet Union, the direct engagement of U.S. forces carried risks that did not exist in pre-Cold War years. As a result, Washington tended to avoid such interventions for fear of provoking a Soviet response, which would in turn create the possibility of a high-stakes American-Soviet confrontation.

Occasionally, the U.S. government decided that it had no choice but to directly involve U.S. forces in a small war. This occurred in Lebanon in 1958, the Do-

The War Powers Resolution

Under the U.S. Constitution, Congress is empowered to declare war and to raise and support armies (Article I, Section 8) whereas the President is their Commander-in-Chief (Article II, Section 2). The framers of the Constitution understood that there would be emergencies when the President would have to take military actions without the consent of Congress, but they did not spell out what these might be, or whether these should be limited in duration. This uncertainty, and the reluctance of the courts to adjudicate, has resulted in a continuous tug-of-war between Congress and the President over his authority to deploy U.S. forces abroad and send them in harm's way. This dispute culminated in the enactment of the War Powers Resolution in November 1973, over President Richard Nixon's veto.

In the absence of a declaration of war or specific statutory authorization for the action taken, the Resolution establishes three basic procedures:

• Consultations. Over the 22 years since the Resolution came into effect, the requirement that the President consult with Congress, "in every possible instance" prior to introducing U.S. forces to hostilities or imminent hostilities abroad, has not been a burden. This is in part because the President is allowed discretion to determine whether prior consultations are possible, and in part because he has often limited consultations to informing Congressional leaders of the action he was about to take.

• Reporting. The Resolution requires reporting to Congress within 48 hours of introducing U.S. forces to hostilities or imminent hostilities [Section 4(a)(1)] and of other deployments of U.S. combat forces abroad [Sections 4(a)(2) and 4(a)(3)]. A report under Section 4(a)(1), but not under the other sections, starts a 60-day clock

Marines landing in Vietnam.

minican Republic in 1965, Grenada in 1983, Lebanon in 1983–84, Libya in 1986, the Iran-Iraq War in 1987–89, and Panama in 1989. Since fighting alongside even token allied forces tended to reduce outcries at home and abroad over "American imperialism," Washington sought and frequently obtained the assistance of allies in these wars. But if a situation were deemed critical enough to warrant the use of U.S. forces in combat, Washington could and did act unilaterally. As the cases above illustrate, this tendency increased substantially after the Reagan administration's buildup of armed forces, and after the decay of Soviet power became evident.

A number of factors—the end of containment, heightened American isolationism, the realignment of the balance of power between the President and Congress, and the increased American sensitivity to suffering or inflicting casualties—

suggest that there will be a great reluctance to engage in small wars in the immediate future. That is especially true in regard to the commitment of U.S. ground forces. One of the arguments in favor of engagement in a small war is the avoidance of fighting a major war by not allowing a problem to grow out of hand. But the U.S. withdrawals from Lebanon in 1984 and from Somalia in 1994—even if aberrations—tend to undermine this argument. Public outcry over U.S. casualties in wars with little popular support led to these withdrawals. And the lack of disastrous consequences following these U.S. retreats prompted questions about the rationale for the commitment of U.S. troops in the first place.

These questions were raised anew by the tortured debate over U.S. policy toward the war among the former Yugoslav republics. The outcome of the U.S. military's involvement in peacekeeping in Bosnia is likely to influence U.S. thinking about engagement in small wars for some time to come.

A second influential consideration is financial cost. Naval and air interventions in small wars have the advantage of being less likely to result in heavy casualties than ground intervention. This is particularly true given the superiority in both size and

that will result in mandating withdrawal of the U.S. forces upon expiration of that period, unless Congress has declared war, or specifically authorized the action, prior to that deadline. Out of some 40 reports submitted in 1973–1995, only the 1975 report on the Mayaguez incident specifically cited Section 4(a)(1).

● **Termination.** As just mentioned, the Resolution provides for mandatory withdrawal of U.S. forces 60 days after submission of the report (90 days, if the President certifies it is necessary), if Congress does not declare war or approve the engagement of the U.S. forces within that deadline. This provision has been criticized as encouraging a foreign power to wait out the deadline, hoping that Congress will fail to act. It is also alleged to be unconstitutional, because the President would be deprived of the opportunity to veto the withdrawal. A similar criticism is made of the provision in the War Powers Resolution which authorizes the Congress to mandate withdrawal of the U.S. forces at any time by Concurrent Resolution, because a Concurrent Resolution does not require the President's approval.

Concerns with the constitutionality of the War Powers Resolution have been voiced by every President since 1973, as well as by many members of Congress. In February 1995, the House passed a bill repealing much of the War Powers Resolution while placing strict limitations on U.S. participation in U.N. peacekeeping; a similar bill was sponsored by Senate Majority Leader Bob Dole (R-Kansas).

Congress is well aware that by controlling appropriations, it can preclude continuation of a military operation over a substantial period. However, Congress has been reluctant to use the power of the purse to stop operations such as the deployment of 20,000 troops to Bosnia in late 1995. The FY 1996 Defense Appropriations Act did contain a provision prohibiting any transfer of funds to finance this deployment unless expressly approved by Congress, but the the provision was not legally binding because it was only a "sense of Congress."

capabilities that the U.S. Navy and Air Force enjoy over their foreign counterparts. However, ships and aircraft seem increasingly vulnerable to mines, precision-guided munitions, and missiles. The damage suffered by the USS *Stark*, and the casualties among its crew, during American intervention in the Iran-Iraq war may be a portent. As the size and budgets of U.S. sea and air forces continue to decline and the cost of naval and air weapons rises, their use in small wars may become increasingly problematic. The loss of a single B–2 bomber would cost the Air Force well over $1 billion, when all costs are considered. Furthermore, such an aircraft would literally be irreplaceable. For the Navy to lose a single aircraft carrier would not only mean the loss of billions of dollars and possibly scores of high-performance aircraft; it could put at risk the lives of thousands of embarked personnel. Nearly a decade would pass before a functioning replacement for such a ship could be deployed. Along with the public concern about casualties, the services' concern about losing extremely valuable weapons platforms and their highly trained crews is likely to influence the involvement of the United States in future small wars.

Conclusions

The future of limited military intervention is difficult to predict. On the one hand, there is no longer a fear of Soviet intervention or gain that may lead the U.S. to intervene in the event of turmoil in far-off countries with which the U.S. has no security alliance. On the other hand, such turmoil seems to be more common (though now mostly for ethnic or religious reasons, rather as an ideological battle between the Free World and communism).

As a form of diplomatic leverage, the threat (or promise) to use U.S. ground forces becomes more credible if there is substantial U.S. public support for the operation in question. That support depends upon the perception that U.S. interests are at stake. Another major factor is the number of casualties that may be sustained; it

would appear that the U.S. public is becoming less willing to see casualties.

Since state failure and internal turmoil seem likely to become more common in the post-Cold War world, the U.S. military is likely to be tasked more often to perform evacuation and rescue missions. The ability to conduct such missions will be the by-product of maintaining a worldwide sea- and airlift capability necessary to project power.

Because sanctions, embargoes, and exclusion zones will be used more often in the post-Cold War world, the military will be tasked to enforce these measures. More aggressive interdiction can make sanctions more successful. Nevertheless, sanctions work most effectively when they are accompanied by other, forceful military initiatives.

While limited air strikes (or naval bombardments) are unlikely to cause the target country to abandon long-held objectives or to act against vital national interests, they can be effective at inducing a more limited change in policy.

Noncombat support for allies in small wars and especially waging small wars with U.S. forces are likely to be instruments used less often. Small wars during the Cold War were more likely to be ideological confrontations in which the U.S. took one side (at first, usually, the government side, but then late in the Cold War, more often the side of insurgents against communist governments). Post-Cold War, the small wars are more often ethnic conflicts, in which the U.S., if it intervenes, promotes a peaceful settlement; the U.S. is not likely to take the side of one ethnic group against another.

Military intervention will continue to be an instrument of national policy in the international system. With American history as a guide, even a thoroughly isolationist United States would continue to employ its armed forces abroad to defend its national interests. But under what circumstances armed forces will be used remains at present very unclear.

CHAPTER FOURTEEN

CHAPTER FOURTEEN

Classical Military Instruments

Introduction

Throughout history, the power of a nation has been cast in terms of the size and competence of its armed forces. Although a powerful military could not be sustained over the long haul without a prosperous economic base, it has been unusual to describe a country's power in terms of its economic output or its dominance of key industrial or trade sectors. More typical is Machiavelli's observation, "Good soldiers will always procure gold." That is no longer the case. A number of instruments of national power described in preceding chapters depend far more on economic size and vitality than on brute force of arms.

Nevertheless, military forces remain the most visible instrument of national power, and the effectiveness of many other instruments depends implicitly on their being backed by strong military forces. Thus, a great deal of truth remains in Frederick the Great's observation, "Diplomacy without military force is like music without instruments."

During the Cold War, the focus of U.S. force planning was on the global competition with the Soviet Union and its allies. The United States planned for high-intensity warfare against the large and relatively modern forces of the USSR. The geographic focus was on the defense of Central Europe, with a secondary focus on other regions, such as the Persian Gulf and Korea, where the United States had strong economic or diplomatic ties. The Clinton administration is the first since 1945 to shift the primary focus of its defense policies and budgetary decisions away from the threat posed by a large peer competitor. In 1993, Secretary of Defense Les Aspin's *Bottom-Up Review* changed the rationale for sizing and equipping U.S. armed forces, charging them with maintaining the capability to execute two nearly simultaneous major regional contingencies against competent, well-equipped regional powers.

Since it takes decades to conceive, develop, procure, and integrate a major new weapons system into the operational forces, the bulk of the equipment in the U.S. armed forces—and, indeed, most of the major procurement programs in progress or under consideration in the mid-1990s—were conceived during the Cold War, and are therefore geared toward high-intensity warfare against a major peer adversary. For the foreseeable future, consequently, the U.S. military will be adapting forces configured for high-intensity global warfare to other types of missions that it may be called upon to undertake. Meanwhile, each service is struggling to change its focus from warfare against a peer superpower to preparation for a wide variety of missions.

Instruments

Land Forces

The land forces of the U.S. military are composed of the U.S. Army and the land elements of the U.S. Marine Corps, both of which have attack helicopters integrated into their forces to provide mobile fire support. The Marine Corps also operates fixed-wing aircraft to support its ground forces.

Cold War Land Forces. Traditionally, land forces are the largest component of the armed forces in terms of manpower. Throughout the Cold War era, the massive ground forces provided by the United States and its allies were at the heart of the strategy to contain the expansion of the Soviet Union in Europe—and, to a lesser extent, to contain the expansion of communism in Korea and Southeast Asia. This defensive strategy required large forward-stationed forces that could be augmented by U.S.-based forces and were prepared to defend territory defined by specific treaty commitments.

The resultant force structure was configured for high-intensity warfare against the massive, heavily armored forces of the Soviet Union and its allies. U.S. military leaders acknowledged the possibility of a relatively long mobilization time and believed that massed firepower was the key to a successful defense against Soviet aggression. As a result, the U.S. Army maintained a large active-force structure backed by almost as many reserve forces, which would be available within several months of the decision to activate them. There was considerable concern that the amount of dedicated airlift and sealift available to transport this force to an overseas theater on a timely basis was inadequate. The solution was to work toward pre-positioning equipment for six divisions in Europe to augment the almost five division equivalents already in place.

The biggest land forces procurement programs of the 1970s and 1980s strengthened the capabilities to fight a high-intensity war against a large, heavily armored adversary. These procurements were the Abrams main battle tank, Bradley armored fighting vehicle, and Apache attack helicopter. Other major programs included a high procurement rate of TOW anti-armor missiles and armored self-propelled artillery. These programs upgraded key weapons systems to yield better protection (more capable armor and a smaller signature), more accurate and lethal firepower against armored targets, and greater maneuverability on the battlefield.

Shifting Emphases. With the dissolution of the Soviet Union, the requirement to fight two nearly simultaneous major regional contingencies has become the planning standard that determines the requirements for ground forces. The result has been a shift to mobility and rapid response capabilities.

The Army has responded with a number of initiatives. These are explained in *Force XXI*, the Army's statement on how to shape the context for the future. Broadly stated, the Army aims to exploit information technologies in order to fight more ef-

U.S. Active Force Structure Trends

- 1990 Total
- Base Force
- Bottom-up Review
- Desert Storm

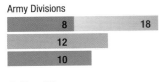

Army Divisions

8 | 18
12
10

Air Force Wings

10 | 22
15
13

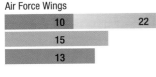

Navy Carrier Battle Groups

6 | 13
12
11

Marine Divisions

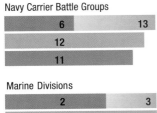

2 | 3
3
3

SOURCE: Secretary of Defense, Report on the Bottom-up Review, October 1993.

Defense Budget Authority by Department
(billion FY 96 $)

- Department of the Navy
- Department of the Air Force
- Department of the Army

SOURCE: FY 1996 Budget
NOTE: Total national defense budget authority includes elements other than the three items shown here.

DOD's National Defense Budget Authority
(in billions FY 1996 Dollars)

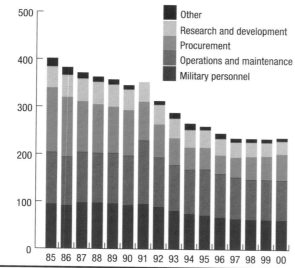

Legend:
- Other
- Research and development
- Procurement
- Operations and maintenance
- Military personnel

SOURCE: DOD

ficiently and maintain higher performance levels in both good conditions and bad. Within this context, the Army has a number of initiatives already well underway to respond to the new strategic environment.

The old assumption that the U.S., as part of NATO, would have to counter a massive land invasion of Western Europe has disappeared. In 1995, thinking holds that U.S. armed forces are most likely to fight a classical ground war remote from the places where U.S. land forces are routinely deployed (Korea remains an exception). The Army has begun to respond by transforming itself from a largely forward-positioned force ready to fight high-intensity armored warfare in Europe to a power-projection force based largely in the United States. This is most evident in the drawdown of the Army forces in Europe.

The Army's *Force XXI*

The Army has produced a report, *Force XXI*, to serve as a concept for full divisional operations for the Army of the early twenty-first century. It focuses on two key issues:

Power Projection. The Army notes that in 1989 it set in motion a withdrawal of large portions of its forces stationed overseas. It plans to go from 200,000 troops to 65,000 in Europe, withdraw its 10,000 troops from Panama, and thin out its forces in Korea. As an alternative, the Army is rounding out plans to be capable of deploying forces from the United States to respond to regional conflicts. It is closing in on a goal to project the following forces rapidly anywhere in the world when called upon:

■ A light brigade in four days.

■ A light division in twelve days.

■ A heavy brigade afloat in fifteen days.

■ Two heavy divisions from the United States in thirty days.

■ A five division corps in seventy-five days.

The capability to achieve this goal depends on both sealift and airlift. The United States Transportation Command (USTRANSCOM) has the responsibility to ensure that its components—the Army's Military Traffic Management Command (MTMC), the Navy's Military Sealift Command (MSC), and the Air Force's Air Mobility Command (AMC)—can transport the required forces.

Advances in Technology. The battlefield is being transformed as advances in technology are yielding new combat capabilities. The Army notes five key areas of rapid change that provide insights into the emerging battlefield:

■ The increasing lethality of weaponry is forcing units to disperse on the battlefield, complicating command and control of the forces.

■ A greater volume and precision of fire from greater ranges in all weather conditions is increasingly possible.

■ Integrative technologies such as digital communications and global positioning will provide the commander the opportunity to better organize and control his forces.

■ Smaller forces will be more capable of concentrating increased firepower with greater accuracy on their targets.

■ There will be a great advantage to the commander who can make the battlefield more transparent to himself and more opaque to the enemy.

These insights, the change in the strategic environment, and the influence technology is having on the battlefield are guiding the Army's planning as it develops doctrine, modernizes its equipment, and trains its forces.

Reserve Components

The Reserve components consist of seven organizational elements: the Reserves from each of the four services, the Coast Guard Reserve, and the Army and Air National Guard.

A Reserve component "vision," developed in the mid-1990s, calls for an integrated total force in which the Reserves are active participants in the full spectrum of prospective operations, from humanitarian assistance to regional conflict. In addition, the Army and Air National Guard have a constitutionally mandated role as an organized militia for use in missions assigned them by the states.

In the post-Cold War era, the Reserve components have become a larger fraction of the total force. But like the active forces, the Reserves are being reduced in size and restructured. This has not proven to be an easy task, particularly in the case of the Army National Guard and Army Reserve. Although the Army reached an agreement governing personnel levels and other matters with its two Reserve components in late 1993 (the so-called Off-Site Agreement), key issues remain.

The central unresolved issue pertains to the types of units operated by the Army National Guard. The Guard's eight combat divisions, which collectively account for some 110,000 personnel, have little applicability to the existing national security strategy. They cannot be adequately trained in time to meet the time-lines of the two MRC scenario DOD uses for sizing conventional forces. At the same time, the Army overall is considerably short of support forces (such as MPs, engineers, transportation units, etc.) to prosecute two MRCs. Estimates of the aggregate support deficiency range between 60,000 and 110,000 personnel. Pursuant to a recommendation of the Roles and Missions Commission, DOD is studying ways of restructuring the National Guard divisions to meet some or all of the support shortage. Political considerations and the need to maintain adequate Guard capabilities to perform the wide range of missions for the states will also affect the outcome of this effort, perhaps significantly.

Other initiatives being pursued across all services to enhance the effectiveness of the Reserve components include improving the equipment and increasing the training of the Army National Guard's fifteen enhanced readiness brigades (which do have a potential role in the two MRC scenario); investigating new methods of increasing Reserve availability for a wide spectrum of peacetime uses; and improving the overall integration of the Reserves with their active counterparts (e.g., by increasing the size of active cadres assigned to work with Reserve units).

Overall, the Army's active component was 40 percent smaller in the mid-1990s than it was a decade earlier, as the result of budget pressures and the changing strategic environment. The reserve component was reduced by a smaller amount. Savings from cuts to reserve units are smaller, and there is considerable political resistance in Congress and from state governments to cutting National Guard forces. Consequently, the reserve component accounts for proportionately more of the combat force structure than was the case during the Cold War. To take better advantage of this pool of combat potential, the Army has selected fifteen brigades from the National Guard whose readiness and equipment will be enhanced so that they will be ready within ninety days of mobilization to join active-duty forces in fighting a major regional contingency.

Although the absolute size of the Marine Corps has not declined as much as that of the Army, the Marines were a relatively small force to begin with. They never focused primarily on the defense of the central region of Europe against Soviet aggression. They have retained their traditional role as an expeditionary force, and the active structure of three divisions and three Marine aircraft air wings is being maintained with this point in mind.

Together, the land forces alongside aerospace and naval forces prepare to respond to two near simultaneous major regional contingencies in four phases:

- *Deterring or Halting Aggression.* Land forces, in conjunction with air and maritime forces, close the area of crisis to help allied forces establish a defensive posture to deter or halt the invasion of friendly territory. The Marine

M–1A1 Abrams tank breeches a berm during maneuvers, Operation Vigilant Warrior in Kuwait.

Corps can mount a forcible entry operation from offshore, if necessary. Light ground forces flown in by air would normally be the first to deploy, although heavy land forces could be part of the early arriving force if their equipment is pre-positioned in the theater or on ships nearby.

■ *Force Buildup.* Heavy ground forces arrive by air (personnel) and sea (heavy equipment) as reinforcements, typically over a period of one or two months. During that time, preparations can begin for a counteroffensive, since by this point the aggressor has most likely lost the initiative on the ground.

■ *Counteroffensive.* In a large-scale air and land counterattack, heavy land-force units go on the offensive to outmaneuver, envelop, and destroy enemy forces.

■ *Ensuring Postwar Stability.* Some land forces will often remain to secure borders or occupy territory and deter another attack by the aggressor.

The degree of confidence the U.S. can have in winning two nearly simultaneous major regional conflicts, should they occur, depends heavily on the conditions under which the U.S. would fight. The size of enemy forces and proximity to U.S. centers of power, amount of warning time, degree of participation by U.S. allies, and length of time separating the outbreak of the two conflicts would have a marked effect on the U.S.'s ability to quickly bring the conflict to a close under favorable conditions.

U.S. land forces in the mid-1990s are capable of executing the missions outlined above against any plausible adversary. Though smaller than at the close of Desert Storm, they are still larger than those of most other nations, and are far better trained and equipped than potential adversaries. If anything, the United States has increased its lead in conventional-force capabilities over potential foes such as North Korea or Iraq. While Saddam Hussein managed to keep many of his best forces intact, the effects of Iraq's defeat in 1991 and the subsequent economic embargo have prevented him from modernizing and upgrading his forces. North Korea is facing severe economic problems, and a fall-off of aid from Moscow and Beijing has limited its ability to modernize, maintain, and train on their equipment. In short, if faced again with a major regional contingency, U.S. land forces can be expected to outperform the enemy decisively.

A critical element in the U.S. ability to use land forces overseas is airlift, and, to a somewhat lesser degree, specialized sealift. Heavy ground forces bring considerable offensive firepower to the field, but at a price. For the bulk and mass of their equipment and their requirements for munitions, fuel, and other logistical support, considerable inter-theater lift is required to deploy them and to keep them operational. To ease this problem, the Army has taken steps to pre-position equipment closer to possible trouble spots. Equipment for two heavy brigades is being pre-positioned ashore in the Persian Gulf region, and a third heavy brigade set is positioned afloat on ships in the Indian Ocean.

Still, this is only the rough equivalent of one Army division; the Department of Defense estimates that four or five divisions would be needed to fight a major regional conflict. Deployment and support of follow-on divisions is dependent on sealift, which it takes a minimum of several weeks under the most favorable circumstances for a full division to be transported to the theater. It took about two months before the first heavy divisions were in place in the Persian Gulf in 1990. While the United States in 1996 could bring an equivalent amount of firepower to the battlefield with a smaller deployment, the disadvantage of fighting an aggressor in its own backyard with U.S. forces deployed over a long distance in unfamiliar surroundings will continue to present a formidable challenge to land forces.

Aerospace Forces

U.S. fixed-wing combat-aviation forces consist of three major components: the Air Force, Navy aircraft, and Marine Corps aircraft. The latter two typically operate from aircraft carriers and land bases, respectively, although both can operate either at sea or ashore if the operational situation requires it.

Cold War Aviation Forces. During the Cold War, U.S. aviation-force planning was largely focused on the Soviet Union, which possessed a large, capable tactical- and nuclear-strike air force. The Air Force and Navy responded by developing a series of air-superiority fighters that incorporated the latest technologies to maintain qualitative superiority over Soviet aircraft.

The Air Force tailored its force to fight in the center region of Europe against numerically superior Warsaw Pact forces. Its missions were:

- Establishing air superiority by shooting down enemy air-to-air combat aircraft, as well as intercepting and downing enemy bombers and strike aircraft.

- Suppressing enemy air defenses by destroying or neutralizing land-based surface-to-air missiles and anti-aircraft batteries.

- Attacking key installations that supported the Warsaw Pact's war effort, such as enemy airfields, bridges, ammunition depots, and rail marshalling yards.

- Attacking opposing ground forces, as well as providing close air support and battlefield interdiction (attack on targets not immediately engaged on the front lines).

The air-superiority mission was regarded as key. The Soviets and their allies had a large force of fighter aircraft, both interceptor and attack. Without allied air superiority, it would be very difficult to defend or counterattack on the ground, and damage suffered from Soviet air strikes on NATO's rear area could be crippling. This situation led to a force structure that balanced specialized air-superiority and ground-attack aircraft with large numbers of aircraft that could be adapted to either mission.

In the 1970s and 1980s, considerable investment went into ensuring U.S. air superiority: Large numbers of F–15 aircraft were procured, as were the F–16 multi-mission aircraft. The Airborne Warning and Control System (AWACS) was developed and deployed, and additional funding went into development of air-to-air missiles that incorporated the latest advances in technology.

U.S. Air Force F–16 Fighter.

U.S. Air Force's *Global Presence*

The U.S. Air Force has developed a white paper, *Global Presence*, to outline its strategy for the coming years. It is summarized here with key quotes from the document.

During the Cold War, the focus of U.S. Air Force planning was the threat presented by the Soviet Union which had large, relatively modern, and technologically advanced forces. The bulk of these forces were concentrated opposite the center region of Europe. Forward defense, deterring or engaging enemy forces close to their border, was a central component of the strategy to counter and contain the Soviet threat.

In the words of *Global Presence*, two factors have conspired to change that strategy:

■ As the 1980s ended, America moved from the Cold War's bipolar arrangement toward what was perceived to be a new, less-threatening political environment.

■ In the face of increasing demands on U.S. military forces, smaller forces, and shrinking defense budgets, we can no longer afford to physically deploy forces in every region of concern.

The Air Force active-force structure has dropped from twenty-five wings in FY 1986 to thirteen in 1995. In the same period, the number of wings forward deployed has decreased from nine to five. At the same time, U.S. military forces are involved in more operations of greater duration than at any time in the past twenty years.

In light of these factors, the Air Force has expanded the concept of presence beyond the physical stationing of aircraft in a region. *Global Presence* emphasizes that several advances in key areas of technology enhance the Air Force's ability to make its presence felt even from a distance:

■ Situational Awareness: advances in information-based technologies allow military forces to monitor and assess most global conditions rapidly and efficiently.

■ Strategic Agility: improvements in transport technologies enable rapid responses with a variety of military forces to distant locations.

■ Lethality: enhancements in weapons system technologies make it possible to achieve desired effects more quickly and at less cost.

Together, these advances make it possible, unlike during the Cold War, to station forces in the United States while maintaining the capability to project military power worldwide on a real-time basis. A theater commander can call on available airpower based in the United States or in another theater, confident that it will arrive on a timely basis. At the same time, a would-be aggressor would be made aware that although U.S. forces may not be stationed in the theater, they are not far away, and any violation of U.S. interests could be met promptly with U.S. military power.

Naval forces faced similar concerns about establishing air superiority in proximity to battle groups and in the skies over an amphibious landing area. The biggest aviation investment program in the 1970s and 1980s was the F–14 air-superiority aircraft, armed with the long-range Phoenix air-to-air missile. The second-largest aviation investment program was the F/A–18, a multi-mission aircraft capable of supplementing the F–14 and A–6 bomber in the air-superiority and ground-attack roles, respectively. This, together with ship-to-air missile defenses, meant the Navy could maintain a relatively high degree of survivability on the open ocean. However, as naval formations approached shore and came within range of Soviet land-based aircraft and cruise missiles, they would have had their hands full coping with large waves of attack aircraft and—by the 1980s—large numbers of anti-ship cruise missiles. The ability to operate in such a high-threat environment came at a price to other combat capabilities. The need for a heavy emphasis on self-protection left room on the carrier deck and in the surface ships' missile magazines for only a modest number of ground-attack aircraft and land attack cruise missiles.

Shifting Aviation Emphases. No opposing air force currently possesses a capability in terms of absolute numbers or technological sophistication in any way comparable to U.S. air power. The need for large numbers of combat aircraft dedicated primarily to shooting down enemy aircraft is therefore less critical than it was during the Cold War. As a result, U.S. aviation forces are able to focus more of their effort on bringing firepower to bear on the ground quickly and accurately enough to have a significant operational effect on the advance of enemy forces. The trend in future aircraft acquisition programs is to take advantage of advances in smart, precision munitions and multi-mission aviation platforms to focus more heavily on the ground-attack mission while maintaining capability for air superiority.

The Air Force is working to develop capabilities that will have a greater impact on the ground battle in a major regional contingency by developing, with the Navy in most cases, more lethal air-to-ground munitions. In addition, aircraft that during the Cold War had different primary missions are being configured to carry these munitions.

Long-range strategic bombers—including the B–1B, B–2, and B–52H—that can fly directly from the United States are being upgraded to carry advanced precision-guided munitions. This capability will enable operational commanders to call in air-delivered firepower without having to first deploy sea-or-land-based aircraft into the theater. Moreover, it provides a capability to strike targets deep in enemy territory. While these long-range bombers are not intended to match the sustained firepower of tactical aircraft operating in the theater, the flexibility to launch a strike at any place and any time is a meaningful military capability.

Suppression of enemy air defenses can be a slow process. The Air Force is modifying some F–16s to perform the role of neutralizing enemy surface-to-air missile defenses and thus clear the way for ground-attack sorties. To complement this program, the Air Force (together with the Navy, in most cases) is developing a new class of air-to-ground weapons with increased stand-off range and better accuracy. These improvements will allow tactical aircraft to attack heavily defended targets at the outset of hostilities while the campaign to suppress enemy air defenses is ongoing. The new munitions will also extend the combat radius of air-based weapons far beyond the flight radius of the delivery platform.

The largest recapitalization program pursued by the Air Force is the F–22 fighter, which will replace the F–15 air-superiority fighter. The F–22's stealth capability, supersonic cruise speed, high maneuverability, and advanced avionics are intended to ensure the continued superiority of U.S. air power against future advances in the air-to-air capabilities of potential adversaries. The F–22 will have a limited precision air-to-ground capability, carrying two joint direct air munitions (JDAMs) internally or—with some loss of stealth—extra JDAMs externally.

If a host nation is reluctant to let U.S. forces in, or if air bases have to be secured first, the delay in deploying land-based aircraft to a theater could be considerable. Carrier-based naval aviation provides, in addition to long-range strategic bombers, a way to launch air strikes without the need for on-shore facilities or support. Another method under consideration is the construction of a mobile offshore base—a modular assembly of floating platforms that can be positioned to provide a staging platform for aircraft as well as land forces.

The Navy is strengthening its capability to bring effective firepower to bear on land targets. With a greatly diminished threat to its operations on the open ocean, the Navy has turned its full attention to ways to affect battle in the littoral regions. For example, it is reconfiguring the carrier air wing to give it more offensive land-attack power. Other programs include the introduction of Tomahawk land-attack cruise missiles throughout the surface combatant and submarine forces, and an upgrade of the F/A–18 aircraft to give it the ground-attack capabilities (including night operations) with precision-guided munitions that it lacked in Desert Storm. An advanced version of the F/A–18 that is to be procured beginning in 1997 will have an extended combat range and carry a larger munitions load, thereby providing a greater power-projection capacity. A portion of the fleet of F–14 air-superiority aircraft is being modified to carry precision-guided munitions for attacking ground targets.

Due primarily to budget constraints and the collapse of the Soviet Union, the missions of U.S. aviation forces have to be done with a smaller force structure. In 1995, the Air Force was about half the size it was in the mid-1980s. Naval air forces have been reduced less and the Marine Corps air forces hardly at all.

U.S. aviation forces should be able to achieve air supremacy over any conceivable adversary for the coming decade and, with the planned modernization programs, to maintain its advantage well into the next century. Once enemy air defenses are suppressed, tactical aircraft and bombers can contribute to the ground battle by direct attack on enemy ground forces. A key priority at DOD is the development and procurement of more effective precision-guided munitions that can kill several armored targets with one launch. This capability will allow U.S. combat aircraft to attack enemy ground forces with improved effectiveness at the outset and enable a response to threatened aggression even before the United States can get ground forces in place.

Still, in the mid-1990s, the amount and type of payload that aircraft can bring to the battlefield, and therefore the number of targets they can strike, is limited. Deployments of aviation forces must be accompanied by land forces if an enemy force is to be driven out of territory it occupies. Aviation forces do not replace land forces, although the impact they can have on the ground campaign is growing.

Space Forces. U.S. space forces exist to perform three major missions: enhancing the capabilities of U.S. or coalition terrestrial forces by supporting their operations from space, ensuring U.S. ability to use space while denying it to enemies, and, finally, providing a supporting infrastructure for U.S. space activities. Space forces supplement and support the terrestrial force structure—allowing more effective and effi-

cient application of such force as their overall numbers decrease. In the future, space forces could evolve into an independent means of applying force, while maintaining the ability to support terrestrial forces—similar to airpower's evolution.

Given rapidly advancing technology, space forces will increase their ability to operate effectively and efficiently. As air, land, and sea force structures decrease, spacepower becomes even more important as a force multiplier. For example, as terrestrial assets become more limited, and more operations are conducted in remote regions around the world, space assets provide vital capabilities such as communication, intelligence gathering, monitoring, surveillance, and targeting. Spacepower offers a readily available global presence infrastructure—a consistent and unobtrusive forward presence.

Joint Requirements Oversight Council (JROC)

Much military planning is still done by the individual services with the challenges of forging them into an efficient, joint fighting force still left to be solved when the forces are fielded. The Joint Requirements Oversight Council (JROC) of the Joint Staff working with the Office of the Secretary of Defense and the military services has introduced a process to plan forces jointly from the ground up. This process begins with key capabilities that are needed in the forces and a multi-service, multi-agency team is formed to analyze which programs best provide the capability. The teams are called Joint Warfare Capability Analysis (JWCA) teams. During the planning cycle for FY 1996, nine teams were formed to analyze the requirements for:

- Deterrance and Counterproliferation of Weapons of Mass Destruction

- Regional Engagement and Presence

- Intelligence, Surveillance, and Reconnaissance

- Command and Control and Information Warfare

- Strike

- Land and Littoral Warfare

- Joint Readiness

- Sea, Air, and Space Superiority

- Strategic Mobility and its Protection

The results of this process were reviewed by the JROC, the Chairman and the Vice Chairman of JCS, then reported in the Chairman's Program Assessment. During the planning process to formulate the FY97 program and budget, this document served as a guide to the Secretary of Defense and his staff on requirements as seen by the senior military leaders from a joint perspective. The Vice Chairman of the Joint Chiefs of Staff views the JWCA process as a key mechanism to ensure that "the capabilities of the various key services are integrated to provide more joint, synergistic solutions to military problems." The JWCA process provides a means for the Chairman of the JCS to fulfill the important resource allocation responsibilities given him under the Goldwater-Nichols Act (recently reinforced by the Commission on Roles and Mission).

The focus of space forces has changed with the demise of the USSR, the rise of regional concerns, and the importance of space-based support to information-based warfare. The lack of communications and other infrastructure in regions where U.S. military forces are expected to deploy (as opposed to the NATO region) has increased demand for the readily available infrastructure of space-based communications, navigation, surveillance, and reconnaissance. Missile warning systems are being redesigned to improve detection of tactical ballistic missile launches, and such information is now being provided directly to the tactical user. Full integration of navigation aids such as the Global Positioning System (GPS) also increases tactical use of support from space.

Military space systems offer useful capabilities to the civil sector—navigation, weather monitoring, and communications. Civil space capabilities, on the other hand, offer military space consumers additional communications surge capabilities, weather monitoring, and multi-spectral remote sensing. The military also uses data from civilian radars for space surveillance. In addition, military, civil, and commercial collaboration may soon result in more effective and efficient spacelift capabilities. In the future, the military could benefit also from civil developments of reusable single-stage-to-orbit delivery vehicles.

The U.S. will enjoy a large advantage in the use of space forces in the foreseeable future. However, other nations have noted the U.S.'s, and its coalition partners', dependency on such forces. They are also realizing the benefits of receiving integral support from space. Maintaining the U.S.'s inherent "high ground" advantage will be important to ensure its, and its allies', future military superiority and ability to achieve national objectives.

Major Maritime Forces

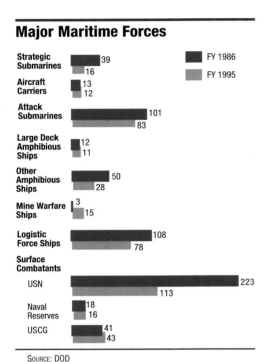

SOURCE: DOD

Maritime Forces

The United States's maritime forces are provided by the Navy in conjunction with the Marine Corps and the Coast Guard. Maritime forces ensure open access to the world's oceans and project firepower ashore. The ability to operate on the high seas in international waters gives maritime forces the advantage of being free of diplomatic constraints, such as national sovereignty and overflight rights. Their mobility and self-sufficiency mean they can be introduced to or withdrawn from an area with no reliance on host-nation support.

Cold War Maritime Forces. During the Cold War, the Navy focused on control of the high seas to safeguard the U.S.'s ability to reinforce NATO and Pacific allies by sea. The threat on the high seas was defined in terms of the numbers and capabilities of Soviet attack submarines and, in close proximity to the Soviet Union, surface combatants and attack aircraft, including medium-range bombers armed with anti-ship cruise missiles. Against these forces, the United States required considerable defensive capability to protect shipping lanes and its own combatant fleet.

The Marines and Coast Guard also contributed to maritime operations against the Soviet Union, although they maintained a strong planning focus on operations short of high-intensity war. The need to keep the sea lanes open in the face of the Soviet threat led to substantial investments in systems that could detect and destroy submarines in the open ocean and engage attacking aircraft at a considerable distance from the battle group. The force structure included a network of fixed acoustic arrays anchored on the ocean floor to listen for submarines; attack submarines; a large fleet of maritime patrol aircraft that could scan large areas of the ocean for submarines; surface ships with both active and passive ASW sensors as well as point defense against attacking aircraft and cruise missiles; and advanced aircraft that could engage enemy aircraft well away from the battle group, before weapons could be launched.

Department of the Navy's *Forward . . . From the Sea—Presence, Prevention, and Partnership for the Future*

The vision that guides the U.S. Naval Service—the Navy and Marine Corps—into the twenty-first century is *Forward . . . From the Sea*. It accounts for both the reorientation of the Department of Defense to a regional focus and the absence of a large peer competitor on the near horizon. Forward operations in peacetime and crisis periods are linked with those envisioned for the earliest phases of regional conflict. Recognition is given to the fact that naval forces are primarily designed to fight and win wars, while their day-to-day role is to be engaged forward for the purpose of preventing conflict.

The strategic imperative. Geography mandates the need for naval forces adequate to defend the lines of strategic approach that link the United States to other nations through the free flow of people, natural resources, manufactured goods, and services. Operating close to or in areas of special interest, naval forces can respond to rapidly evolving situations that portend a crisis. If a diplomatic or military crisis occurs, such forces can provide initial and timely means to defuse the situation or control escalation. If fighting breaks out, they provide the means for forcible entry and protective cover essential to the flow of follow-on land-based forces that will be deployed, supported, and sustained from the continental United States.

Peacetime operations and crisis response. Naval forces operate overseas in peacetime to prevent regional conflict. They are visible and tangible proof of U.S. political commitments and military strength. Their presence alone can serve to deter aggressors and maintain stability. They also remind potential belligerents that the entire military force of the United States may be brought to bear. The inherent mobility, flexibility, and self-sufficiency of sovereign naval forces allow unencumbered movement and access between theaters in response to emergent tasking across the entire spectrum of military operations.

Conflict operations. If deterrence fails and conflict ensues, naval forces are prepared to blunt initial attacks and prepare for the transition to high-intensity operations ashore. Inherent in this "enabling" mission are:

■ Focused intelligence collection and surveillance.

■ Precision strikes against key targets.

■ Insertion and support of special operations forces.

■ Seizure of ports, airfields, and beachheads ashore.

■ Actions to interdict lines of communication.

■ Measures to disrupt command and control.

The wide spectrum of operational capabilities of naval expeditionary forces—particularly the power-projection and forcible-entry capabilities embodied in carrier battle groups and amphibious-ready groups—allows seizing and holding of lodgments ashore, and thereby permits the delivery, protection, and support of ground forces and land-based air forces needed to prosecute the subsequent campaign. These versatile naval forces also provide a wide range of additional tactical and strategic options to the joint theater commander during every phase of regional conflict. And through securing the sea lines of communication, naval forces ensure the sustainment necessary for all of the forces involved to complete their mission.

Continued U.S. dominance of the seas and successful naval expeditionary efforts will depend upon application of modern technology and tactical innovation.

An aircraft carrier or amphibious ready group ideally would be escorted by six to eight surface combatants and one or two attack submarines. Surface combatants and attack submarines were also available to protect convoys carrying reinforcements from the United States to Europe or other overseas combat theaters.

By the late 1970s, the Navy concluded that dealing with the Soviet threat required a strong offensive strategy. Newer classes of Soviet submarines had extended the reach and lethality of the USSR's undersea fleet, and the expansion of the Soviet long-range Backfire bomber force (equipped with anti-ship cruise missiles) expanded greatly the area of the ocean in which U.S. and allied shipping was at risk.

Since maritime forces could not be everywhere at once, the Navy developed the Maritime Strategy to carry the battle to the source of the Soviets' combat power. This strategy called for an expanded offensive role for the Navy and Marine Corps. Primary tasks included keeping the sea lanes open for U.S. and allied shipping in wartime. But rather than wait for the Soviets to attack, the battle would be brought to them. The strategy called for a series of operations, including:

■ Holding Soviet ballistic missile submarines at risk.

■ Destroying the Soviet attack-submarine force with a massive, sustained anti-submarine warfare campaign.

■ Sinking Soviet surface ships both at sea and in port.

■ Using carrier battle groups and amphibious landing forces to seize or destroy bastions of Soviet naval power, such as Murmansk.

■ Threatening the Soviet homeland by striking targets with carrier-based aircraft and long-range cruise missiles or conducting amphibious landings where the Soviet forces were vulnerable in order to divert them away from the battle in the central region of Europe, where the Soviets and their allies were strongest.

This highly aggressive strategy led to an emphasis on offensive systems that could strike first and seize the initiative against Soviet forces. The strategy included attack of heavily defended targets, so considerable attention to self-defense was required to ensure survivability of the battle group as it closed to within attack range.

Shifting Emphases. In the mid-1990s, no nation can mount a sizable naval threat to U.S. forces far from its own shores, thereby easing the task of self-protection and defending merchant shipping on the high seas. This has allowed U.S. maritime forces to work on bringing a greater amount and more precise firepower to bear on the battle ashore.

The Navy and Marine Corps have adopted a strategic vision called *Forward . . . From the Sea* in which the focus is on the littoral, or coastal areas, of the globe in joint operations ashore, the contribution of naval forces will come "from the sea." The Navy and Marine Corps are prepared to provide the initial enabling capability for a joint operation and to continue participation in a sustained effort if necessary. A key element of the vision is the Navy's plan to improve its sealift capability to deliver heavy equipment and resupply major ground and air combat units in the theater of battle.

Operations on the littoral present different challenges than operations in the open ocean, and U.S. maritime forces are in the process of adapting. As maritime forces approach the shore, they come into range of attack from land. An increasing number of states can deploy land-based cruise missiles, whose short flight time poses a tough problem for defensive systems. Mines seeded in the shallow waters of the littoral present a threat to maritime forces operating in geographically restricted waters or approaching the shore to execute an amphibious landing. Mine sweeping is both difficult and time consuming. Lastly, diesel-electric submarines are increasingly making their way into the navies of potential adversaries. These craft are difficult to detect and prosecute, particularly in shallow water, and therefore would complicate maritime operations near shore and in proximity to geographic choke points like the Straits of Hormuz.

It will take a long time to fully adjust the force structure of maritime forces to the demands of the post-Cold War world. Aircraft carriers have a useful life of up to fifty years; major surface combatants and submarines, some thirty-plus years. The Navy faces the challenge of transforming a force optimized to defeat a peer superpower on the open ocean into one that can support regional littoral operations typical of the post-Cold War environment.

U.S. maritime forces are much smaller in the mid-1990s than in 1986. The biggest reduction has come in the number of attack submarines and convoy-escort surface combatants. This reduction reflects the diminished threat to battle groups and merchant shipping in the open ocean.

Joint Operations*

Future military operations will call on the capabilities of all the Services along with support from the defense agencies, other government agencies, and non-government organizations. Pulling these capabilities together for complex, dangerous joint military operations is the responsibility of the [Chairman of Joint Chiefs of Staff] and the Commanders in Chief (CINCS). They can fulfill this responsibility only if the Services and other supporting organizations provide the capabilities needed.

Operation Desert Storm demonstrated that the military capabilities developed separately by each of the Services are individually superb. But they do not work well enough *together.* Each Service develops capabilities and trains its forces according to its own vision of how its forces should contribute to joint warfighting. Not surprisingly, the Services' ideas about how to integrate all forces reflect their own perspectives, typically giving the other Services a role supporting the "main effort."

Each Service [has its own warfighting philosophy and force structure priorities] that guide internal decisions on systems acquisitions, doctrine, training, organization, management of forces, and the conduct of operations. *Forward . . . From the Sea; Force XXI;* and *Global Reach, Global Power* [are thoughtful statements of how each Service views its role in national defense]. These Service documents help form a joint vision, but collectively they [do not represent one]. Competing elements exist in these documents that must be reconciled [for a viable joint vision to be realized].

Basically, competition among the Services is a strength. The variety of Service perspectives adds breadth, flexibility, and synergy to military operations. Nevertheless integrating their warfighting concepts must receive more emphasis. Otherwise, the Services [will] only work to develop the capabilities they need to fulfill their own particular views.

We find a pressing need for a central vision to harmonize the Services' own views. This vision should drive joint requirements and serve as a basis for elevating the importance of joint operations as an essential "core competency" of all joint commanders and agencies.

In addition to the general aim of providing an overarching guide for developing joint warfighting requirements, a unified vision will give the Services guidance regarding the capabilities they should supply to unified military operations. With a common base of understanding, the CINCs and Services can have congruent expectations of the capabilities of forces assigned to CINCs by the Military Departments. The unified vision will provide a framework for the development of the common operational and organizational concepts needed for "baseline" joint force headquarters, and a common base for assessments of current and future joint capabilities.

* Excerpts from *Directions for Defense*, Report of the Commission on Roles and Missions of the Armed Forces, May 24, 1995, Chapter 2. Text in [ ] has been added by authors.

Guided missile destroyer.

The number of carriers and large-deck amphibious ships that can bring aircraft and forces to a conflict theater has decreased only marginally. Mine-warfare capabilities are increasing. New U.S. surface combatants carry a larger complement of Tomahawk cruise missiles, which can strike targets deeper in enemy territory, than the ships taken out of commission. Overall, the number of Tomahawk land-attack missiles carried by the fleet will actually increase. The principal operational challenge posed by the smaller fleet to military commanders is not so much warfighting, but that a peacetime overseas presence must be maintained at previous or greater levels with fewer ships.

In 1995, almost one-third of all U.S. maritime forces were continuously deployed overseas, even though the U.S. was at peace. A carrier battle group with supporting ships and a Marine expeditionary unit, the core of the Seventh Fleet, are permanently stationed in Japan. The newly es-

tablished Fifth Fleet is in the Persian Gulf region. The Sixth Fleet, with its home port in Italy, provides a full time presence in the Mediterranean Sea. Increasingly, maritime forces are used to provide a continuous peacetime U.S. military presence in important regions of the world.

Maritime forces have a key role in the U.S. strategy to fight two nearly simultaneous major regional conflicts. Forward-deployed maritime forces would be among the first to arrive in the vicinity of a crisis. Once there, they would establish maritime superiority, initiate mine countermeasures and would be available to immediately strike targets on land with tactical aircraft and cruise missiles. Ships equipped with the Aegis weapons system would provide local air and, in the future, theater ballistic-missile defense. Amphibious assault forces could conduct amphibious operations to establish a secure lodgment ashore in preparation for arriving land forces, or they could threaten amphibious assault to divert enemy attention and tie down enemy forces.

Conclusions

Classical military forces represent a powerful instrument of U.S. national power. With the end of the Soviet Union came the end of the only peer military competitor to the United States. For the immediate future, U.S. forces are far more capable, better equipped, and better trained than any conceivable adversary. In a classical high-intensity military conflict (such as Desert Storm), the nation can have high confidence in the superiority of U.S. forces.

However, in the event of two nearly simultaneous major regional contingencies, U.S. lift capacity would be stretched to the limit to bring heavy Army and Air Force units into the theater and support them. Depending upon the demands of the specific contingencies, other types of capabilities might be seriously stressed. Forces committed to other operations could also retard deployment of needed forces to regional contingencies. With the overseas presence of U.S. ground and air forces reduced by roughly 50 percent since 1986,

Major Recapitalization Programs
(procurement funding in billions of dollars)

System	Cumulative FY 1996–FY 2000
C–17 aircraft/NDAA	20.6
DDG–51 destroyer	17.1
F/A–18 E/F aircraft	16.9
F–22 aircraft	7.5
New attack submarine	7.4
V–22 tiltrotor aircraft	4.2
M1A2 tank upgrade	3.4

SOURCE: DOD

there is less margin for error in deciding where to deploy the remaining forces, and greater operational demands on those forces still remaining overseas.

Given that major equipment typically lasts decades (and major procurement programs, from conception to deployment, take a decade or more), the major equipment items in the U.S. armed forces will continue for some time to be items conceived and designed for use against the Soviet Union. With only modest amounts of newly designed military equipment being procured, there will be a relatively small turnover of major equipment items in the forces (and U.S. forces will be operating with an increasingly aging capital stock). Further, the major items in the fiscal year 1996–2000 procurement program were originally intended for high-intensity conflict against the Soviet Union and Warsaw Pact. For example, the primary mission for which the F–22 was designed is air superiority; likewise, the DDG–51 was designed to defend the fleet against massive manned air attacks and cruise missiles, as well as nuclear attack submarines. Fortunately, a weapons system that is useful against one type of threat usually has utility against others. But U.S. military services are inevitably finding themselves in the position of adapting equipment designed to deal with the Soviet Union for use in new types of warfare that were just emerging when the specifications and characteristics of the systems were laid down.

The relatively strong position of U.S. forces in the mid-1990s is not reason for complacency. While U.S. classical military forces should continue to be the world's best well into the foreseeable future, U.S. armed forces may find that they are con-

fronted with innovative warfare techniques and employment strategies for which they are not well prepared or equipped. For example, a nation could well choose to avoid challenging the United States in classical conventional battle by using or threatening to use weapons of mass destruction, sabotaging key automated information networks, or resorting to terrorism and guerrilla warfare tactics.

With smaller forces, the U.S. margin for error in procurement decisions, inefficiency, and duplication has narrowed. Increasingly, therefore, U.S. forces are striving to operate together in a complementary (rather than redundant) and mutually reinforcing fashion. In addition, greater attention is being devoted to planning that examines the capabilities U.S. forces will need to bring to the battlefield across service lines. These efforts are focused on the implementation of key recommendations by the Commission on Roles and Missions with respect to developing improved joint (all-service) visions to harmonize existing service doctrines; strengthening the Joint Warfare Capabilities Assessment (JWCA) process; and increasing the level of joint training.

Looking ahead to the twenty-first century, the U.S. military is scrutinizing the revolution in military affairs, which is discussed in the chapter on emerging military instruments. The willingness of the U.S. military leadership to pursue new opportunities offered by the rapid advances in technology and to embrace new organizational, and operation techniques will go a long way to determining success on the battlefield of the future.

CHAPTER FIFTEEN

Emerging Military Instruments

Introduction

With its victory in the Gulf War, the United States demonstrated an unprecedented mastery of conventional warfare—especially in the area of information technologies. Yet, the resources available to maintain such excellence are increasingly limited.

The Department of Defense is thus at a crossroads. On the one hand, it can incorporate the information revolution into its existing structures and doctrine, replicating present platforms in ever more sophisticated forms and creating a force designed to master today's challenges, notably the deterrence and suppression of major regional conflicts. On the other hand, the Defense Department may recognize that opponents in the mid-1990s pale in comparison with their potential successors and that sometime beyond the next decade, more sophisticated competitors will present far greater challenges. A strategy to prepare for the latter eventuality would emphasize technology, education, and doctrine rather than replicating today's platforms, albeit in more capable versions.

An important factor in deciding which approach to pursue is the extent to which current and future technologies can enable new instruments of national power—instruments whose utility would greatly transcend the goal of winning simultaneous major regional conflicts. This chapter explores three such new instruments.

The first, dubbed the "system of systems" by Vice Chairman of the Joint Chiefs Admiral William Owens, creates operational synergies by combining three systems normally considered separately—those that provide battlespace awareness, those that enhance command and control, and those that create precision force. Successful integration of such capabilities may permit entirely new instruments of military force that are far more precise and can be wielded from far greater distances than could anything in the arsenal of the mid-1990s.

The second instrument, extended information dominance, takes U.S. capabilities to acquire information dominance on the battlefield, and gives the results not only to U.S. forces but to allies. Providing bitstreams helps the United States influence the outcome of distant conflicts while avoiding many of the risks and costs of conducting warfare overseas. Such an instrument is particularly valuable when the United States's freedom of action is curtailed or when leaving fingerprints is undesirable.

The third instrument, hacker warfare, would permit the United States to corrupt or override information systems of potential foes and even put the latter's information infrastructures at risk without the direct application of force.

Instruments

The System of Systems

Major improvements in U.S. military capabilities should arise from simultaneous developments in battlespace awareness; advanced command, control, communications, computing, and intelligence (C^4I); and precision force. Some of the developments in these areas are the harvest of investments made in the 1980s; others were spurred by the Gulf War.

Individually, these new systems portend sharply increased effectiveness. Collectively, they promise to widen the lead of the U.S. military over its competitors, even in the face of declining defense budgets. Their integration would permit U.S. armed forces to see and respond to every militarily relevant object within a notional theater of operations—a cube of 200 nautical miles on a side. By contrast, systems of the mid-1990s can see fixed objects and groups of moving objects within a notional battlefield but not individual moving targets, and rarely in real time or with requisite precision for a direct unaided hit.

With the sytem of systems, the U.S. military will be able to engage in parallel warfare, that is, simultaneous strikes carried out with high precision against targets in widely separated locations.

See It. The first element of the system of systems, advanced battlespace awareness, couples digital sensor technologies with enough computer power to extract useful information from digital signals in near-real time. In the mid-1990s, battlespace awareness depends, in large part, on space-based systems for collection and distribution. Over the next decade, these systems will be supplemented by sensors on unmanned aerial vehicles (UAVs) and by cellular grids for robust multipoint to multipoint wide-area communications.

Advanced technologies will shift the role of battlespace intelligence. Traditionally, intelligence informed command decisions by providing information on such matters as whether a tank unit lay over the hill and what its strength might be. By contrast, tomorrow's intelligence will inform operational decisions by sending back the latitude and longitude of each individual tank in real time to precision-guided munitions (PGMs). In the same shift, platforms will move from the primary foci of engagement to units that service targets determined and located externally.

As the system of systems evolves, it may be increasingly understood as an autonomous entity that ladles information to a variety of users. But a robust entity capable of generating such streams of data bits to whomever needs them would take further work. Information from space satellites already comes in bitstreams. Similar capabilities from other long-range sensors (such as AWACS and JSTARS aircraft and Aegis cruisers) may have to migrate to networked swarms of less individually powerful forms to ensure survivability in an increasingly hostile environment where other nations perceive the United States's system of sys-

---

Where Should the System of Systems Put Its Smarts?

Tomorrow's system of systems can distribute its smarts in one of two ways. One method is to use intelligence, surveillance, and reconnaissance (ISR) and C^4I systems to find and locate targets with such precision that *externally guided* PGMs need little further smarts to land on a particular point (they need only know where they are and where the target is in real time). The alternative is to use ISR and C^4I systems to locate targets roughly and put enough intelligence in each *internally guided* PGM to hit the target on its own (examples include sensor-fused weapons and brilliant antitank munitions).

Internally guided PGMs have the advantage of working despite disrupted communications or degraded targeting systems. Yet, internal guidance requires more complex sensors; higher costs lead to smaller inventories (and higher costs in turn). Each sensor package must also be specifically tailored to a given target. Externally guided PGMs (such as glide bombs with GPS kits) are more sensitive to system disruptions but can use cheaper guidance and control units; they may be used in larger numbers, getting through on the basis of swarming.

If the trend in the U.S. military is toward internally guided PGMs, budgetary logic will discourage the development of very sophisticated ISR and C^4I systems; conversely, dependence on externally guided PGMs requires the acceleration of sophisticated ISR and C^4I systems. In the former case, the bitstreams that Washington can offer allies will have scant usefulness unless the United States supplies expensive internally guided PGMs to go with them. Yet, as the U.S. experience with Stingers for Afghan rebels suggests, such PGMs may end up in the wrong hands. Conversely, supplying externally guided PGMs and bitstreams may permit the United States to control the usefulness and thus effective proliferation of the latter under adverse conditions.

Potential Coverage by Unmanned Aerial Vehicles

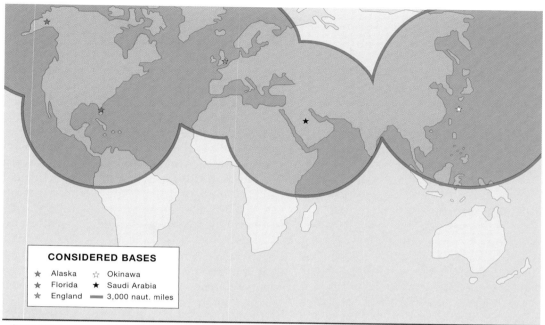

CONSIDERED BASES

★ Alaska	☆ Okinawa
★ Florida	★ Saudi Arabia
★ England	▬ 3,000 naut. miles

SOURCE: INSS drawing upon *Aviation Week and Space Technology*

tems as the U.S. center of gravity. New families of in-close sensors being developed for counterproliferation, as well as other types of sensors, would have to be adapted for tactical roles, such as listening for sounds that characterize weapons' discharges or sniffing the air for evidence of fuel expenditures. As human operators are taken away from sensor nets, new communications structures would become necessary to link sensor and shooter, and data links would have to become more cellular. Meanwhile, the fusion of data from various sensors, which is required to make a target determination, and the defenses against attacks on the dense communications required among disparate sensors all would have to be enhanced.

State It. The second element, C⁴I communications and data links, is growing apace with the advances in battlespace awareness. These enhanced capabilities allow the U.S. military to send information where it is most needed, whether to the front lines or the top of the chain of command. Key efforts include the Global Command and Control System (which can link the various command centers of the U.S. military in real time and near-real time) and C⁴I for the Warrior (whose goal is to deploy interoperable data terminals to give each

echelon access in a convenient format to the data streams it needs). Improvements in interoperability should lead to increased efficiency in the conduct of multiservice, that is, joint, operations. For instance, in 1995, Patriot missiles are typically slaved to a Patriot radar, a bulky and hard-to-deploy unit. If Patriot missiles could be guided by Aegis radars, then the United States could deploy more rapidly under some conditions. Only the missiles would have to be moved; the Aegis radar ship could get there on its own, if not there already.

If tomorrow's defense is to be conducted by multinational, that is, combined, forces, then the systems for U.S. information generation would need to be capable of being integrated with foreign command and fire-control systems. External systems integration would have to occur at several levels simultaneously: between U.S. data systems and those of allies; between the data flows that matter in U.S. doctrine and those required by the doctrines of allies; and between U.S. sensors and allied weapons platforms. Good standards can help here, but many problems still would have to be worked out on a country-by-country basis.

Vigilant Warrior

Vigilant Warrior illustrates the promise—and limitations—of stand-off warfare. In October 1994, the number of Iraqi tanks facing Kuwait rose sharply. To forestall a repeat of the August 1990 invasion, the United States dispatched aircraft, naval assets, and ground forces to Kuwait. This operation, ostensibly a joint military exercise, served as a reminder that the United States could and would intervene rapidly and decisively in the region. Iraqi forces pulled back, ending the crisis. A disengagement zone in southern Iraq was subsequently established.

Geostrategically, the operation worked; operationally, there was room for improvement. Although 165 aircraft were deployed, more than half of these were needed simply to achieve air superiority, leaving far fewer for ground attack. The 36,000 ground troops still took two weeks to deploy, and there was not enough weaponry to wage precision stand-off warfare. The total cost of the exercise exceeded half a billion dollars.

Stop It. The third and final element of the system of systems is precision force, made up for the most part of PGMs. Such weapons can put any locatable target at a high risk of destruction. Most targets can be dispatched with one shot; few can withstand a volley. Even though most of the PGM revolution has already occurred, PGMs continue to advance along three lines: human-guided weapons (such as fiber-optic-guided missiles and laser-guided bombs); signature-guided weapons (such as those guided by infrared, radar reflection, or acoustic homing); and location-directed weapons (those that aim for a given point by knowing where the target is and where it, itself, is). The U.S. military is developing new generations of fire-and-forget cluster munitions (such as sensor-fused weapons and brilliant antitank munitions), but the larger trend here and especially overseas is to develop weapons that can be guided to exact locations.

Long-range strike capability lets U.S. military forces target and destroy enemy platforms while operating beyond the reach of enemy weapons and sensors. This capability arises not only from accurate, long-range missiles but also from platforms that can operate far from their bases (such as refueled aircraft) or remain on extended station (such as nuclear submarines). Because technologies of range—jet and rocket engines, cruise-missile motors, nuclear reactors—tend to be expensive and improve rather slowly, the U.S. advantage in this area is relatively secure (in contrast to much of the U.S. lead in high-tech weaponry, which is based on information technologies' advancing everywhere at the same rate).

Another aspect of precision force is the tactical use of nonlethal technologies. (For a discussion of these technologies, see the chapter on Unconventional Instruments.) Carbon-fiber warheads on cruise missiles, for instance, were used in the Gulf War to short out Baghdad's power grid without causing permanent damage. Future warheads may include microwave bursts, which harm electronics more than they do people.

Finally, information technologies, notably distributed interactive simulation, also permit precision training. Simulation promises increasingly accurate emulations of friendly and opposing forces (both hardware and tactics) without the otherwise expensive cost of live exercises. It also permits tomorrow's forces to what-if a wide variety of future capabilities in an equally wide variety of potential but hitherto unseen environments. A software tool which combines topographic data and imagery has been used to create fly-through terrains to train U.S. pilots (e.g., going into Port-au-Prince, and Sarajevo). The same system was also used to help determine cease-fire lines in the Bosnian negotiations.

Applications. Apart from a greater assurance of prevailing in major regional contingencies, a system of systems presents two other major advantages: the U.S. military can, under more circumstances, conduct stand-off warfare (that is, operate beyond the reach of most hostile weapons);

Clementine satellite launch.

As an example of the new economies of sensors, $80 million sent five cameras and other rangefinding sensors to the moon, mapping the surface for less than a tenth of what NASA estimated it would cost.

and force can be used in a far more discriminating manner.

Stand-off warfare allows forces to engage an enemy with minimal exposure and without the need for constant sentinels, which in turn permits faster engagement and wider latitude in evaluating intervention. Consider the following scenario. With little warning, a hostile state launches a full-scale attack on a neighbor. It seeks to capture a target that will provide a hard position for subsequent thrusts, claims, negotiations, or defenses. The United States intervenes to thwart the capture of this target. Space-based assets deliver detailed imagery of the enemy order of battle; this imagery is supplemented by data from naval sensors in international waters. Baseline intelligence data on the attacking country are quickly converted into an inventory of strategic targets. Within hours, UAVs are dispatched from local air bases and surface ships to collect more data; some drop ground-based sensors along potential attack corridors. As the data arrive from space, sea, and air, they are fused at a command center, converted into target assignments, and apportioned to various attackers: cruise missiles in offshore ships and

submarines, nearby aircraft, strategic bombers from North America and regional bases, and offshore ground-strike forces readied for deployment. The resulting counterattack by U.S. and local forces destroys enough of the attacking force that the aggressor retreats.

Many features of this scenario are attractive: a large share of the attacking force is quickly located and defeated; the enemy's near-term objectives are frustrated; and U.S. forces present few targets, thus suffering few casualties. This last feature could be of growing importance if more and more adversaries acquire the means and will to use weapons of mass destruction. Under such conditions, it may be inadvisable to mass U.S. forces within the range of such weapons—and range is what differentiates the possession of such warheads (which is relatively easy) from the ability to deliver them and threaten U.S. forces (which is harder). Thus, stand-off capabilities permit U.S. operations to proceed with less risk, making such warfare an important component of U.S. power-projection capabilities.

Benefits also accrue in peacetime from the potential to carry out such an operation. The ability to project power at a distance, responding quickly to aggression, gives the United States considerable influence even where political or economic considerations inhibit the stationing of troops. The faster the United States can respond, the more easily U.S. forces can wait until the other side makes unambiguous moves to attack. U.S. forces do not have to rush to the ramparts with every twitch, and opponents cannot weary them with endless feints. Accidents that occur when two nervous forces face each other in close proximity can be avoided.

Logistics benefits from precision-warfare techniques in two ways: from the transition from dumb to smart rounds and from the use of information technologies. Without major requirements to move dumb rounds and the attending ground-support infrastructure, forces can be deployed more quickly and at less cost; the need for lift capacity can be minimized. That, in turn, eases scheduling pressures (for example, ships can be moved when

New Military Information Technologies and Deterrence

The destructive power of a battleship or a nuclear bomb is apparent to all. The power of information warfare is far less obvious. Thus, replacing tanks and warships with buried missiles that are linked to information systems may increase warfighting power, and yet prove too inconspicuous to deter.

Yet, if potential aggressors know that anything visible can be hit, then proving that their assets can be seen in sufficient detail may suffice to deter aggressive acts. Consider, first, a plausible U.S. strategy for conflict characterized by heightened sensitivity to casualties on either side. The United States locates a first set of targets, broadcasts their locations, hits them, and broadcasts their destruction. After this demonstration, each finding of a new target is broadcast, and U.S. forces allow enough time for its occupants to disable their platform and escape.

For peacetime deterrence, the United States might demonstrate to potential foes that their platforms are under continual, reliable, and precise surveillance. Such a policy carries risks; an opponent with such information may use it to gauge its own hiding techniques. Thus, the United States would need to hint that it knows more than it tells—clearly, some fine tradeoffs need be made. Nevertheless, a certain degree of openness could add deterrence value to efficient but subtle warfighting technologies.

It is also possible, at least in theory, that the deterrence aspect of some intelligence-based warfare technologies can be further demonstrated by putting together a simulation and making it available to potential aggressors. Doing so credibly is unfortunately problematic.

opposing forces are least prepared) and enables logistics dumps, because they are smaller (if not necessarily less valuable), to be more easily hidden and protected. With just-in-time delivery technologies, the amount of material that has to be stored in theater can be further reduced. During the Gulf War, thousands of containers were never opened and their contents remained unknown. Since then, the

Airtraffic control center on *USS Abraham Lincoln.*

The operational face of Dominant Battlefield Awareness.

DoD has used information technology to develop logistics systems which have containers, in effect, identify their contents and location in response to remote electronic polling. Supplies need only a theater of operations only when they are needed and not before. Both permit local bases to be replaced by offshore supply, either afloat or at mobile offshore bases constructed for that purpose. This reduces the logistics footprint and removes valuable targets from the battlespace.

Some applications of a system of systems also promise to limit unnecessary destruction. For instance, improvements in intelligence may permit U.S. forces to locate the command tank within a battalion; destroying it first could reduce the effectiveness of the remaining vehicles. Similarly, disruption of an enemy's com-

mand system or the networks that connect it to the field might cripple that enemy's ability to fight. The plight of Iraq's army in the Gulf War was a powerful reminder that forces cut off from their leadership typically become grossly ineffective. Indeed, one of the attractions of information warfare is that nonviolent means—for example, electronically disrupting C^4I systems—can precede or even replace violent conflict. The loss of much of its command system might well deter an enemy before it has embarked on an irreversible course. Nevertheless, casualty-free command-and-control warfare is not yet a realistic prospect.

Minimizing civilian casualties and collateral damage makes it easier for the United States to take the moral high ground, reduces domestic opposition to military operations, eases rebuilding efforts (which could save the United States money in postwar aid), and lends credibility to U.S. claims that it is targeting a state's political and military leadership rather than its people.

Limitations. Systems integration will remain both the biggest opportunity and greatest liability of tomorrow's system of systems. The information revolution is driven by commercial technology that becomes available to everyone simultaneously. The U.S. military's advantage in applying information technology to warfare does not derive from special access to this technology but from competence at systems integration. This reflects superiority in software, experience at solving military-integration problems, and the adaptability and high level of training of the U.S. armed forces. Yet, future systems integration cannot be taken for granted. Despite the lip service paid to the ideal of a joint interoperable information system, interoperability is often considered a cost add-on in service-acquisition decisions. Similarly, whereas the instruments of the system of systems are being inserted into the budget, an agreed-upon structure for such an integrated system is only starting to be developed—even as the need to connect computers and not just people makes it all the more necessary.

What is a Bitstream?

One of the glories of the digital era is that, in time, any piece of information, regardless of its original format, can be reduced to a series of bits, that is, 1's and 0's. Thus, facsimiles, maps, photographs, audio and video tapes, sheet music, radar reflections, game software, training manuals, and personnel records can all be expressed in the same way. Furthermore, they can all be conveyed in any media capable of transmitting a stream of bits, that is, a bitstream.

Ultimately, the only useful distinction between bitstreams would be between those that represent events as they happen (e.g., live video feed) and those that convey everything else. To be truly useful, for instance, UAV imagery of a battlefield ought to be in real time so that all information on various movements is current. By contrast, an instruction manual that contains video sequences need not be delivered as it happens.

Tying precision-strike warfare to intelligence-based warfare has a long way to go. In certain environments, U.S. forces might not be able to acquire dominant battlespace knowledge. Dense or thickly foliated terrain is harder to read than desert. Cloud cover inhibits collection of optical imagery. The farther from open ocean or U.S. bases that a battlespace lies, the harder it is to observe or target. Although known, fixed targets (as well as ships and some aircraft) can be engaged from a distance, attacking mobile ground targets is more difficult.

Stand-off warfare can be frustrated by foes who disperse their forces (making them easier to camouflage, conceal, and decoy) and limit their dependence on fixed sites and easily identifiable platforms. By so doing, they might ride out a U.S. stand-off attack and emerge with most of their punch left. Dispersed, inexpensive targets are cheaper to make than to destroy using stand-off weapons. A cruise missile, for instance, costs $1–2 million. The few stealth aircraft operations (which are equivalent to stand-off in terms of putting air crews at risk) in the U.S. inventory are expensive to replace, difficult to maintain, and carry light bomb loads. Using nonstealth aircraft against robust air-defense systems greatly increases the risk of losses and prisoners. Standing-off from not so far away may permit cheaper short-range weapons to be used but increases the exposure of U.S. forces accordingly. Because other countries are also honing their own battlespace acuity, U.S. assets, over time, will themselves become more visible at all ranges, particularly close ones. Most nations understand that Iraq blundered in letting the United States take six months to deploy; tomorrow's foes are unlikely to repeat this error and will be inclined to attack U.S. deployment from the outset.

Funding will limit the growth of the PGM stockpile. As long as other conventional munitions persist, units designed to use (or at least manage) them will also be limited. Pressure for their deployment and thus use will remain. Further, adverse environments, both meteorological and electromagnetic, reduce the accuracy of precision weapons. An enemy playing upon the sensitivity of the American public to collateral damage might try to frustrate the casualty-reducing potential of precision weapons by locating strategic targets in or near sensitive sites, such as schools or hospitals—a technique reportedly used in both Bosnia and Iraq.

Disabling enemy systems by targeting key nodes or by using less destructive soft-kill techniques might also be frustrated by the difficulty of knowing exactly what is connected to what. There is considerable difference between taking down an individual target and taking down a target system. Suppressing Iraqi air defenses was easier because they were based on the well-studied Soviet model; key nodes were therefore understood by the U.S. military. As the Soviet influence wanes, so wanes U.S. understanding of opposing defenses.

The success of precision attacks is heavily dependent on good intelligence (for example, identifying military command centers and leaders). Although the U.S. capacity for collecting electronic intelligence is keeping pace with the information-technology revolution, advances in encryption may reduce the U.S. ability to read the content of intercepted messages (although deriving intelligence based on message traffic patterns may remain valid). Gauging the intention of forces often requires human intelligence, and there is no reason to expect dramatic improvements in the efficiency of collection. Techniques to divine the structure of hostile information systems are not as yet well validated.

Lastly, even in the best of conditions, targets cannot always easily be found. With U.S. forces in control of Panama, General Manuel Noriega was hard to find. Despite overwhelming U.S. technological superiority in Iraq and Somalia, Saddam Hussein and Mohamed Farah Aideed could not be found at all.

Providing Bitstreams Versus Providing Arms

In some ways, providing bitstreams to an ally is similar to providing arms. Both help the ally with minimal risk to U.S. forces and are only as effective as an ally's ability to use them. Sometimes the two forms of aid are inseparable. A system to supply targeting data for use by PGMs has little value to a nation lacking such munitions.

Yet, these forms of assistance differ in several important ways:

- *Multiplication.* Arms add force; information multiplies it. Information can often have more leverage than can more arms—particularly as military contests take on a hide-and-seek, rather than force-on-force, character.

- *Delivery.* Once war starts, arms transfers become hazardous. Lines of communication, ports and transfer facilities, and warehouses become targets. Even smuggling small arms to insurgent groups (Afghan rebels, Nicaraguan *contras*) can be difficult, and larger transfers are more problematic still. Wartime delivery of bitstreams may also be interfered with, but there are more ways around the various obstacles, and their protection is generally less risky and labor-intensive.

- *Control.* Arms shipments can precede war. Yet, once the United States hands weapons over, it starts losing control over their use. Sometimes the ally has other plans for the weapons. At other times, an ally ceases to be: an enemy of our enemy (e.g., Iraq in its war against Iran) may later become an enemy of our friend; regimes tumble (e.g., the Shah's Iran); and nations fall (South Vietnam). Sophisticated arms that fall into the hands of enemies may deteriorate if U.S. maintenance is withdrawn, but they are still useful for a while. A bitstream can be turned off instantly if conditions warrant it—even if valuable archived data, as well as information on sources, methods, and capabilities, are left behind. Both arms and bitstreams can fall into enemy hands in the chaos of war; security regimes that can minimize the cost and likelihood of bitstream diversion appear more feasible.

- *Cost.* Tanks for allies are tanks that the United States no longer has. With bitstreams, once the data has been collected, software developed, and distribution established, the marginal cost of providing services to allies is generally cheap. How cheap depends on what adapting bitstreams for particular clients and exigencies, who pays for training, how much new infrastructure is needed, and how many new local sensors are required.

- *Fingerprints.* Arms are hard to supply in secret. Physical movements leave tracks, and captured material often can be traced back to the supplier. Bitstreams leave fewer tracks, are easier to disguise, and are harder to intercept. A captured M–1 tank makes a great visual on CNN; a captured bitstream, less of one.

- *Perspective.* The careful choice of what information to provide and how to provide it reflects and conveys the U.S. perspective on the meaning and purpose of conflict (in other words, what is important and what is worth doing). Our donated imagery, so to speak, is our vision. The ability to provide a similar perspective by selective weaponry supplies is more limited.

Extended Information Dominance

Warfare in the information age is becoming a high-technology game of hide-and-seek, with the seeking done by U.S. intelligence-based warfare systems—normally coupled with U.S. precision-strike forces.

Yet, there is no inherent reason that the United States cannot take these same capabilities, create a bitstream of information from the results, and feed this bitstream to other forces. By so doing, the United States can enhance its allies' effectiveness by making available to them the output from cutting-edge U.S. information systems—a vertical coalition, as it were.

Already, U.S. preeminence in long-range mobility and information systems is being recognized through the assignment of roles and missions within alliances and coalitions in which the U.S. military participates. Tomorrow's model is likely to be a mix of the United States using its own information dominance for its own forces and sharing some of it with allies. At one end, however, it is conceivable that U.S. military involvement in a conflict may be limited to whatever liaison is necessary to ensure the correct and efficient transfer of information to allies. Coalitions may arise in which the United States provides sensor data, analysis, and command data as bitstreams, while local allies supply human observation, command, and weapons delivery. While stand-off warfare promises to reduce U.S. casualties, limiting U.S. involvement in a campaign to the provision of information might reduce U.S. casualties to nearly zero and, in many cases, leave few fingerprints. Extended information dominance, as such, is an ideal type, but, as such, is an instrument of national power worthy of its own examination.

Precedents exist for helping allies by providing bitstreams. The United States shared intelligence with the Afghan rebels fighting the Soviets, who, themselves, shared information with the Argentines fighting British forces. In a sense, such an operation resembles arms sales.

Applications. The ability of U.S. forces to influence distant conflicts without being there may become a powerful new instrument of national power, filling in the current void between engagement and nonengagement. Six examples may be illustrative: fulfilling alliance obligations, substituting for stand-off warfare, exercising covert leverage, protecting borders, encouraging regional stability, and contributing to peace operations.

EMERGING MILITARY INSTRUMENTS

Emerging Concepts for Using Systems

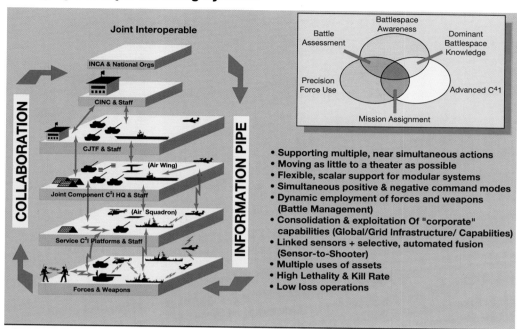

Joint Interoperable

- INCA & National Orgs
- CINC & Staff
- CJTF & Staff
- (Air Wing)
- Joint Component C²I HQ & Staff
- (Air Squadron)
- Service C²I Platforms & Staff
- Forces & Weapons

COLLABORATION

INFORMATION PIPE

Battlespace Awareness

Battle Assessment

Dominant Battlespace Knowledge

Precision Force Use

Advanced C⁴1

Mission Assignment

- Supporting multiple, near simultaneous actions
- Moving as little to a theater as possible
- Flexible, scalar support for modular systems
- Simultaneous positive & negative command modes
- Dynamic employment of forces and weapons (Battle Management)
- Consolidation & exploitation Of "corporate" capabilities (Global/Grid Infrastructure/ Capabilities)
- Linked sensors + selective, automated fusion (Sensor-to-Shooter)
- Multiple uses of assets
- High Lethality & Kill Rate
- Low loss operations

SOURCE: Joint Staff

● Bitstreams may let the United States fulfill its alliance commitments with far fewer deployments, and could ease the integration of new countries into its alliances. Indeed, the United States is already emphasizing the provision of C⁴I systems to Partnership for Peace countries as a step toward full integration. Unlike alliance membership, such assistance can be finely graded and thus doled out in degrees to specific countries.

● Bitstream supply may reduce pressure on U.S. forces to undertake stand-off warfare. For example, a country such as Kuwait could defend itself by installing a system of medium-range PGMs that are guided to specific locations using a combination of inertial navigation and global positioning; the locations are in turn, fed from U.S. bitstreams. Each missile could then be assigned to a moving armored vehicle with fairly high precision. The cost of such munitions may compare favorably with the one-time cost of the exercise Vigilant Warrior.

● If the United States chose to support one side in a murky conflict—say, Muslims in Bosnia—without risking U.S.

troops or compelling other great powers to intervene, surreptitiously providing that party access to U.S. bitstreams could be an effective option. Though major powers friendly to the other side of the conflict may suspect the United States is providing such assistance, its covert nature would elicit less of a reaction than would overt assistance.

● Bitstreams may help allies protect their borders against hostile infiltration without the need for cross-border incursions, such as Turkey's 1995 pursuit of Kurdish rebels into Iraq. Data collected remotely can substitute for costly and risky border patrols—and, unlike manned patrols, the cost-effectiveness of such surveillance rises sharply every year parallel with similar improvements in digital systems.

● Bitstreams may bolster regional security. Nations distrustful of their neighbors often turn to stocking armaments; this feeds arms races. If each nation could see the effect of its existing stockpiles multiplied as a result of access to U.S.-supplied bitstreams—and if nations understood that such access depended on defensive orientations and good behavior—the incentive for arms races might be reduced. For example, in Asia, where countries formally aligned with the United States nonetheless suspect each other, extending information dominance (in part to substitute for arms acquisition) might assuage old fears without generating new ones.

● Peacekeeping may be the most promising application of extended information dominance. The Sinai agreement between Israel and Egypt, for example, was reinforced by U.S. sensor systems that let each side monitor potential precursors of attack. Information systems that may be deployed in the Golan Heights can generate not only indications of impending attack but targeting information as well, thereby putting hostile encroachers at immediate risk.

Information Warfare Chart

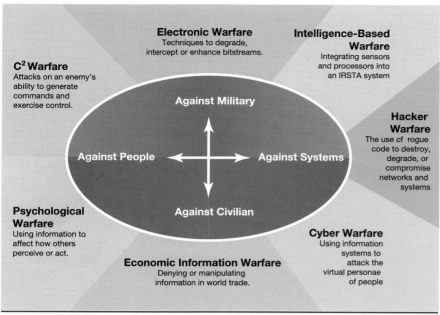

Electronic Warfare
Techniques to degrade, intercept or enhance bitstreams.

Intelligence-Based Warfare
Integrating sensors and processors into an IRSTA system

C² Warfare
Attacks on an enemy's ability to generate commands and exercise control.

Against Military

Hacker Warfare
The use of rogue code to destroy, degrade, or compromise networks and systems

Against People ←→ **Against Systems**

Psychological Warfare
Using information to affect how others perceive or act.

Against Civilian

Cyber Warfare
Using information systems to attack the virtual personae of people

Economic Information Warfare
Denying or manipulating information in world trade.

SOURCE: INSS

It might be worthwhile to open certain information sources to all. Open access would ease operations with unexpected allies and promote confidence-building, but capabilities so opened may be unavailable as discretionary instruments of U.S. national power.

Limitations. The amount of information needed to support stand-off warfare (to locate structures and major platforms) is large, but the data needed to support close-range warfare (to discover troops and their machines, and localize reports of activity) is much larger. Space and airborne sensors may suffice for the former, but the latter calls for far more intrusive sensors, as well as closer integration with friendly troops, platforms, and data. The placement and management of such sensors require either U.S. manpower or highly trained allies. Bitstreams may be subject to electronic attack; their receivers may be subject to broader information-warfare attacks. Sensors must come in much cheaper packages before they can be considered a cost-effective supplement to what ground forces (for example, reconnaissance units) can supply. Favoring the development of signature-guided PGMs might also reduce the richness of potential bitstreams the United States has to offer. If

not worked through in advance, systems integration between U.S. bitstreams and allied systems may not function smoothly. Further, if an ally is small, weak, or technologically incapable of assimilating digital information, U.S. assistance will be of limited help. Just providing information and nothing else would not work where there are no or very small local allied forces, as would be the case, for example, in the Caribbean.

Relying on information rather than more committed efforts may also deprive the United States of sufficient influence over the ends and means of conflict. For the most part, nations under attack may have little choice but to take what help they can get. At other times, a nation may have the choice between standing up to a bully or deflecting its wrath to a neighbor. U.S. commitment may make the difference in collective regional security.

Further, in a horizontal coalition, each side is responsible for what happens in its sector. In a vertical coalition, there is no such neat division of responsibility. U.S. data flows might enable recipients to engage in activities of which the United States does not approve, such as attacking nonmilitary targets. Short of pulling the plug, Washington's options for controlling such an ally may be limited.

Lastly, if bitstreams are easy and effective, the United States might tend to intervene too readily. Secret assistance provided through intelligence agencies can escalate into a deeper entanglement, and the United States could find itself involved in a conflict that, upon further reflection, it would have preferred to avoid.

Hacker Warfare

When farming was the essence of national economies, taking land was the essence of war. As agriculture yielded to industry, war too was industrialized; nations defeated foes by destroying their productive capacity. If this pattern holds for the information age, might war follow commerce into cyberspace, pitting foes for control of this undefinable but critical ground?

Information warfare can cover a great deal of ground, some of which is discussed in other chapters. The first two instruments covered in this chapter concerned the application of intelligence capabilities

B–2 Stealth Bomber.

to war. This third instrument covers attacks on critical national information systems themselves.

Applications. Motives for attacking the networks of an enemy include theft of services or data, corruption of information, denial of the network's service to its users, and control of the systems to which networks are attached. Networks can be attacked via inside paths or outside paths. The former mode of attack includes inserting bad hardware or software components at the source and also gaining the cooperation of insiders. Both of these methods, like intelligence recruitment, run a high risk of detection, and success is often fortuitous. Outside paths refer to unauthorized access over external routes, such as phone or Internet lines, and may yield two levels of access. User access—the ability to see and manipulate an individual's files and tap into common resources—is of some value to saboteurs. Even more valuable is super-user access—the ability to see and manipulate the files that make a system run. Outside paths are less risky and easier to repeat, but they are also easier to defend against.

If the United States could override an enemy's military computers, it might achieve an advantage comparable to neutralizing the enemy's command apparatus. Such attacks can be expected in future con-

flicts. However, since potential foes of the United States range from network-illiterate to network-dependent, the value of targeting military information systems will vary greatly in different situations.

Military systems designed for field use tend to be difficult to penetrate. Not meant for public access, they are often entirely independent systems. Instead, the hot-button issue of information warfare is an attack on a nation's commercial computer systems—telecommunications, power, banking, and safety systems. Making potential aggressors know that the United States could abjure brute force but still wreak havoc on their societies would be a powerful new instrument of power. Such influence could be exercised in a gradual way; a tap here and there (in other words, evidence that the United States can affect a nation's systems at will) might suffice to remind a nation's leaders of their vulnerability. If provocations persist, a harder stroke (such as corrupting the integrity of highly visible services but not necessarily damaging them) may cause the populace to feel that their leaders cannot protect them. If such deterrence failed, wholesale attacks on opponents' computers could undermine the advanced sections of these opponents' economies, hinder the mobilization of military power, and put heavy pressure upon hostile leadership.

Information technology can also permit the United States to push information past barriers and directly address citizens of other countries. The Internet is one such tool for disseminating information. Proposed satellite systems, such as Motorola's Iridium, promise relatively low-cost global access to anyone past the reach of national censors. Perhaps the most ubiquitous means of reaching others may be direct broadcast satellite. In the mid-1990s, technology lets a system operator cover most of Asia offering up to one hundred separate channels for less than a billion dollars. For most foreign-policy purposes, simply letting others access global news streams (e.g., CNN, BBC) is good enough. However, it is not inconceivable that the technologies that created the dinosaurs of *Jurassic Park* or the morphed Presidents of *Forrest Gump* could be employed in creating entirely synthetic imagery as well.

Defensive information warfare, employed as a tool to preserve the integrity of U.S. and other friendly nations' information systems, may be understood to be an instrument of national power in the same way as home guard forces have been. It is clear that the vulnerability of the U.S. information infrastructure is growing more acute. Not only are more activities becoming dependent on information systems, but these information systems are becoming more open to outsiders and, in the process, adopting technologies that make them less secure (for example, open operating systems, Web browsers, and distributed objects). Security technologies are themselves advancing, but hacker tools are becoming more sophisticated and easier to get and use.

Doctrine on how to defend the nation's information infrastructure is in flux. Some would designate a central government guardian; others hold that the responsibility for protecting various systems must rest with their owners. Protection is likely to be a matter of operator and user diligence coupled with third-party software tools and expertise. With minor exceptions (e.g., intelligence data on likely threats), everything one needs is likely to be commercially (and internationally) available. Whatever additional help the U.S. government can offer its friends (above and beyond what they can buy on their own) is likely to be modest.

An Open Global Defense Information Network

Access to a potential stream of bits is akin to an electrical outlet. Friendly nations plug their command systems, operators, and sensors into it and vitalize their defenses. The United States can cut off the power as it wishes. That said, there may be some advantages in making some information flows (with appropriate limits on coverage, acuity, and revelation) generally and globally accessible even during periods of tension.

What advantages may accrue from providing open connections? First, open (that is, widely known and frequently used) connection standards make vertical coalitions easier to establish by reducing obstacles to interoperability. Secondly, because a system's architecture reflects the interests and priorities of its owners, an open network based on U.S. capabilities will be geared toward looking for what concerns the United States most (such as armaments of a major regional contingency) rather than objects of little military concern (such as internal dissidents) or assets that only the United States has in abundance (satellites, long-range mobility assets, or blue-water submarines). Buying into the network would mean buying into these priorities. Thirdly, the United States would profit from other nations' contributions of their own bitstreams and software. Some offerings would be voluntary; others would be a *quid pro quo* for access to the system. Fourthly, letting nations benefit from a global network may make them more amenable to intrusive sensors in their spaces.

Even great powers might be willing to buy into the network for the purposes of confidence-building, easing interoperation in peace operations and ad hoc coalitions, and gaining tools that facilitate national management in such areas as the environment, disaster relief, national resources, transportation, and law enforcement. If the United States does not allow minor disagreements to prejudice open access, the system will be increasingly trusted as a global utility. The provision of more information about the United States and its allies might assure others. Nations that know they are being scrutinized by everyone may shy away from provocative measures. Despite most nations' desire to avoid dependence on systems that they do not own, access to the network, if reliable, might prove seductive. Then, if some nation should buck the system, it would find itself denied access precisely when it is most threatening—and for that reason, threatened. A gap in coverage may not last forever, but the time required for another nation to duplicate formerly available bitstreams may suffice to buy the time required to turn potential adversaries around.

Yet, openness has its costs: loss of discretion, technological leakage, exposure to malevolent intelligence. If access is always available, Washington cannot manipulate its provision to affect lesser conflicts or exercise influence over potential allies. Systems integration is a key U.S. core capability, but system standards (which make systems integration work) and other software capabilities, once viewed in their open form, may be copied by other nations. Open systems are also, for that reason, more vulnerable: sensitive data must be tightly secured, useful data must be authenticated and protected, valuable software must be controlled, and information should be culled so that its presence does not reveal too much about U.S. doctrine or intelligence methods.

The Global Positioning System (GPS) is a good illustration of the pros and cons of openness. Originally, GPS was supposed to be more accurate for U.S. forces than for others; but technology (notably, differential GPS—being installed all over Europe and East Asia) has levelled the playing field. The United States has gone far to assure nervous users elsewhere that it will not degrade the system for trivial cause (although local jamming in conflict zones is not so hard); even so, Russia's Glonass is used as a back-up and European systems are being contemplated.

Increasing Precision/Effectiveness of Weapons

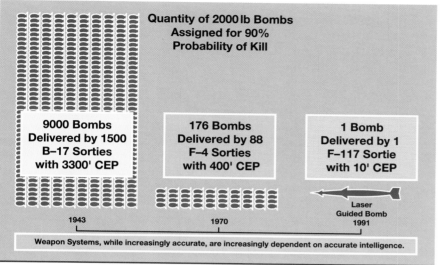

SOURCE: DIA

NOTE: CEP is circular error probability, that is, the circle within which there is a 50% probability the bomb will land.

combatants but the risk of collateral damage may be unknowable; the networks we trash may be our own.

At present, most computer systems are vulnerable to information attacks even if most intrusions are more annoying than dangerous. Yet, the frequency intrusions is rising, and the possibility of a digital Pearl Harbor cannot be dismissed out of hand. That being so, a nation's critical systems can be engineered to limit access sharply. Although neither quick nor free, the cost of such security measures would be small in comparison with a nation's overall defense costs. Indeed, defense of the nation's information infrastructure is more likely to become an instrument of U.S. national power than offensive information war. Such defensive measures would permit other avenues of U.S. power to be exercised with less fear of counterattack against its information infrastructure.

Conclusions

There is considerable debate over whether the injection of information technologies into defense systems can provide a basis for undertaking a revolution in military affairs (RMA). One good test is whether a new instrument of power is indeed revolutionary—whether it can alter relationships among states. Ancient innovations, for instance, shifted the balance of power back and forth between dismounted and mounted forces, and, consequently, between civilized and barbaric cultures. The advent of gunpowder doomed the isolated city-state. Napoleon's *levée en masse* redrew the map of Europe, setting off nationalistic reverberations that echoed for the next century. The Third Reich's *blitzkrieg* ushered in new forms of international coercion. And nuclear weapons, originally conceived as a force multiplier for conventional operations may have had the reverse effect; they made conventional conflict among nuclear powers a potential first step to mutual suicide and hence of sharply decreased utility. Whether or not the new military applications of information technologies constitute a true RMA will therefore depend on the new uses to which a military so equipped can be put.

Limitations. The issue of information warfare as an instrument of U.S. national power raises two fundamental questions: Are the technological means available? And, if so, would Washington use them?

Even if the United States has programs to wage information war, as has been frequently hinted, these are and will likely remain highly classified. Herein lies a drawback: unannounced weapons make poor deterrents. Yet, the tools of information war, once announced, may depreciate quickly. Networks are vulnerable because they are poorly secured; poor security persists because the probability and cost of intrusions are judged to be low. Once the U.S. information-warfare threat is unsheathed, there is likely to be an increased emphasis on security. By then, some systems may already have been compromised, but countermeasures are available to restore service and files while limiting further intrusions.

Further, the special vulnerability of the United States's own networks has been widely trumpeted, thus raising the question of whether residents of glass houses should threaten to throw stones. More generally, attacks on civilian targets are always difficult for the U.S. national command authority to authorize. Not only would the victims of information war include non-

The emerging military instruments of this section are in various stages of development. The United States is on the verge of having a system of systems that is capable of conducting stand-off and precision warfare, at least in favorable situations. A 1993 study argued that a fleet of stealth bombers armed with brilliant antitank munitions could stop an armored attack all by itself. The optimism may be premature, but clearly, the U.S. armed forces are moving in that direction.

The U.S. ability to extend information dominance is far less developed. The potential of such capabilities can be glimpsed, however, in the emerging role-sharing debates within NATO and in the United States's ability to supply certain intelligence data to selected allies under crisis conditions.

Many of the means for hacker warfare were becoming available in 1995. However, the well-wired United States remains more vulnerable to such attacks than most potential opponents.

With luck, these instruments will allow the United States to exercise a high degree of control over the emerging global security structure through its unique ability to intervene all over the world quickly, effectively, and at little cost. Even more impressive would be the ability to make a large difference in potential conflicts just through the supply of information and related software without leaving fingerprints, much less footprints. As with any new military instrument, particular attention may be necessary to turn new means of conducting war into effective means of deterring it.

As the U.S. military stands at a crossroads in deciding what it wants to be, it is by no means certain which way it will choose. Institutions, particularly triumphant ones—such as the U.S. military in the wake of its victories in the Cold War and Desert Storm—tend to avoid fundamental change. Technology will be sought and absorbed, but largely in the context of pre-existing assumptions about the organization of military force. The instinct of the U.S. military services will remain to confront aggression by projecting forces into harm's way and engaging the enemy until victory is secured. Stand-off warfare permitted by the system of systems deviates from that model; the provision of bit-streams alone is even further removed. If these instincts prevail, then the resulting choice may be made by default—the United States will have the preeminent military of the twentieth century just as this century is coming to a close.

Yet, the U.S. military may not have much choice but to change if it wishes to have a role in shaping the international security structure. With the Cold War over, the American public is finding it increasingly difficult to identify interests that merit the expenditure of U.S. blood. Even as the military enjoys high public esteem, the will to use military power to support the United States's ability to lead the world seems to be fading. Rather, the U.S. public would maintain its military power primarily to ensure that other nations do not directly challenge the United States with impunity.

If a peer military competitor emerges in a decade or two, however, the situation will be quite different. *Strategic Assessment 1995* rates hedging against this possibility as the most important long-term U.S. national-security challenge. Such a competitor might not openly challenge the United States but could seek undue influence in its region, perhaps supporting belligerent proxies or otherwise attempting to bend neighbors to its will. U.S. policymakers may wish to use instruments of U.S. military power to deter or defer the emergence of such a peer competitor without asking the American public to bear great risk or suffer casualties for such an end. Therefore, Washington will have to find ways of exerting military influence that will minimize such costs. The emerging instruments discussed above, particularly the extension of information dominance, may be the best methods available for achieving this end.

Defining the Revolution

Military Technological Revolution (MTR): the incorporation of radically advanced capabilities into existing military forces as equipment turns over—a passive revolution.

Revolution in Military Affairs (RMA): the adoption of radically more effective operational procedures and organizations in response to the opportunities offered by the MTR—an active revolution.

Revolution in Security Affairs (RSA)— the RMA plus other interesting changes in the security environment, many brought about by technology (e.g., the CNN-ization of war)—a passive revolution.

CHAPTER SIXTEEN

Countering Weapons of Mass Destruction

Introduction

The proliferation of weapons of mass destruction (WMD) has, in the mid-1990s, posed a dramatically increasing threat to the United States. This threat is multi-dimensional, for WMD include nuclear, biological, and chemical (NBC) weapons. Moreover, the threat has been compounded by the proliferation of ballistic and cruise missiles, which make longer-range delivery systems available to nations possessing WMD. (For a fuller treatment, see *Strategic Assessment 1995*.) The United States is responding to this threat by pursuing policies and initiatives designed both to prevent proliferation or limit it, and to minimize the strategic and tactical consequences should prevention fail.

Nuclear weapons. In the mid-1990s, the number of countries that have nuclear weapons, have the capability to produce nuclear weapons, or are seeking the capacity to produce and deliver nuclear weapons is approaching two dozen. In addition to the five declared nuclear powers, some states are judged to have either fully developed nuclear weapons (e.g., Israel) or the ability to assemble and deliver such weapons rapidly (e.g., India and Pakistan).

A number of states are attempting to obtain, or have the facilities to produce, weapons-grade fissile material (e.g., Iraq, Iran, and North Korea). A growing number of states possess the requisite scientific and industrial infrastructure to initiate a weapons program, while others appear to be in the early stages of acquiring the expertise and infrastructure needed for a nuclear-weapons program, often through the acquisition of nuclear reactors for ostensibly peaceful purposes (e.g., Algeria and Syria). Lastly, there is growing concern that terrorist groups and organized-crime syndicates could come into the possession of nuclear weapons—including crude radiological devices. These fears are fueled in part by concerns about a possible loss of control over stocks of weapons-grade nuclear material in the former Soviet Union.

Chemical and Biological Weapons. The number of countries with chemical and biological weapons is rising, and experience has shown that once states have made the decision to acquire a WMD capability, biological weapons (BW) and chemical weapons (CW) are generally pursued simultaneously.

Many experts believe that Iran, Iraq, Libya, Syria, Cuba, China, and North Korea, among others, have active biological-weapons programs. In the early 1990s, Russia admitted it had a BW program in the past, and concerns linger that this program still exists in some form and that Russia may be maintaining illegal capability to produce biological warfare agents. Other countries that may be pursuing BW include Argentina, Brazil, South Africa, India, Pakistan, and Laos. Thus, the problem, though global, is concentrated in regions of instability—some of which, such as the Middle East and Northeast Asia, are of key importance to the West.

The cost of acquiring a stockpile of chemical or biological weapons is small when compared with the cost of achieving nuclear capability. Biological and chemical weapons are relatively easy to acquire because almost all the technologies associated with them are widely available and used for legitimate commercial activities. In addition, defensive biological and chemical programs can provide cover for covert offensive BW and CW programs. For all these reasons, the production of BW and CW weapons is difficult to detect, and offenders can often plausibly deny that they are producing such weapons.

Alarmingly, states are acquiring BW capability and CW not just for deterrence but because they are perceived as operationally useful. Iraq used CW effectively against Iran throughout their nearly decade-long war, and Iraq also used chemical weapons against its own people. In addition, CW and/or BW are believed to have been used in conflicts in Afghanistan, Vietnam, Laos, and Cambodia. And the 1995 sarin gas attacks in Tokyo's subway demonstrated the feasibility of terrorist attacks using CW.

Missiles. Many NBC proliferators see missiles, and especially ballistic missiles, as the delivery system of choice. As of 1995, more than a dozen countries have operational ballistic missiles, and many more have missile-development programs or agreements to obtain ballistic-missile technology from others. Although most systems available to states seeking WMD capability (sometimes referred to as "proliferant states") are limited to a range of about 600 km, these ranges are increasing steadily. North Korea has flight-tested the 1,000-plus km-range No–Dong 1 and has under development a missile with a range of 3,500-plus km, the Taepo–Dong 2 (TD–2). A number of states are pursuing space-launch capabilities, which can also provide long-range military capability. Cruise missiles are also of growing importance to emerging powers. They are inexpensive compared with ballistic missiles and have increasing capabilities in terms of range, accuracy, and payload.

Instruments

Nonproliferation (Prevention)

The global proliferation of NBC weapons, their concentration in unstable regions vital to U.S. interests, the perception of their increasing military and political utility, and the greater likelihood of their use—in war, as a tool for political blackmail, or by terrorists—all serve to increase the threat to U.S. and allied forces. Instruments that aim at preventing or limiting the spread of such weapons are known as instruments of nonproliferation.

North Korea Theater Ballistic Missile Threats

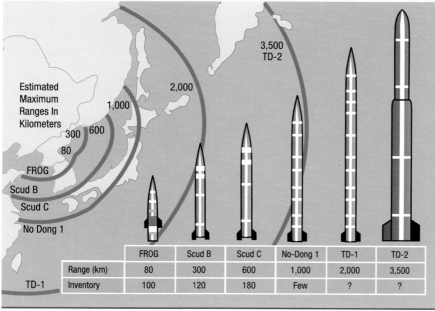

	FROG	Scud B	Scud C	No-Dong 1	TD-1	TD-2
Range (km)	80	300	600	1,000	2,000	3,500
Inventory	100	120	180	Few	?	?

SOURCE: BMDO

A Distinction in Terms: WMD and NBC

The term "weapons of mass destruction" (WMD) refers to nuclear, biological, and chemical weapons employed for the purpose of inflicting massive damage, including the killing of large numbers of civilians. The term consolidates nuclear, biological, and chemical weapons into one category because, despite differences in their effects and use, they share enormous lethality and symbolism. Thus, the concept of WMD is significant in a political rather than a military sense. By using the term "WMD," policymakers convey the message that the proliferation of these types of weapons is unacceptable and that their use would be considered an extremely grave matter.

However, for military operational purposes, a distinction must be made when considering the threats posed by nuclear, biological, and chemical weapons. The acronym NBC recognizes these differences. Also, "WMD" is an open-ended concept, potentially allowing for the development of other technologies of mass destruction. "NBC" is necessarily confined to the three named technologies. Nuclear weapons are the most lethal and the least easily defended against of these weapons of mass destruction. The use of biological weapons carries with it a potential for loss of life that approaches that of nuclear weapons; however, biological arsenals can be combatted to some degree with vaccines, masks, and proper warning. Chemical weapons are the least lethal of the weapons of mass destruction but can still have a profound effect on the battlefield or on civilian populations if used in sufficient quantities. Troops can defend themselves against chemical weapons with chemical detectors and protective clothing, but such equipment undermines operational effectiveness.

The proliferation process begins when a state first considers acquiring WMD and seeks to develop or obtain the technical and manufacturing expertise to do so. Prevention measures are most effective at these early stages and fall within a number of categories.

● *Dissuasion:* convincing non-WMD states that their security interests are best served by not acquiring WMD.

● *Denial:* attempting to limit a state's ability to obtain WMD technologies or devices.

● *Arms control:* seeking to set limits on or eliminate WMD through bilateral or multilateral agreements and the creation of international norms against proliferation, as discussed in the chapter on arms control.

● *International pressure:* punishing states who pursue acquisition of WMD with trade or economic sanctions, publicizing companies and countries that assist in the acquisition of WMD, and sharing intelligence.

While prevention efforts often are largely diplomatic in nature, defense-related agencies play an important supporting role. Their involvement may include providing inspection, verification, and enforcement support for nonproliferation treaties and control regimes; helping to identify states that might acquire, or are acquiring, NBC capabilities; and conducting interdiction missions.

The central tool of prevention traditionally has been arms control, which continues to be the focus of the world community's efforts to create norms against proliferation and to limit the spread of WMD. The primary international mechanism for controlling nuclear proliferation is the Treaty on the Non-Proliferation of Nuclear Weapons (NPT) and its associated monitoring arm, the International Atomic Energy Agency (IAEA). The Chemical Weapons Convention (CWC) , not yet in force as of late 1995, bans the production, use, possession, and transportation of chemical weapons. The Biological Weapons Convention (BWC), which has been in force since 1972, bans the development, production, stockpiling, or acquisition of biological or toxin agents and weapons. In addition to formal treaties, a number of multilateral regimes exist to prevent potential proliferators from gaining access to critical technologies and materials. For more information on these treaties and regimes, see the chapter on arms control.

Arms control and other prevention tools have had some important successes. In 1989–1990, South Africa reversed its policy on nuclear weapons, and Argentina abandoned the Condor missile program.

Middle East Proliferation Profile

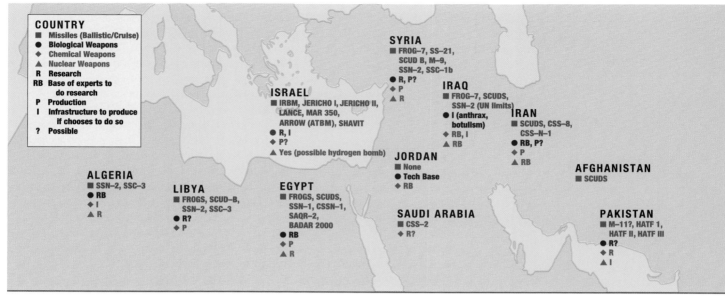

COUNTRY
- ■ Missiles (Ballistic/Cruise)
- ● Biological Weapons
- ◆ Chemical Weapons
- ▲ Nuclear Weapons
- R Research
- RB Base of experts to do research
- P Production
- I Infrastructure to produce if chooses to do so
- ? Possible

SYRIA
- ■ FROG–7, SS–21, SCUD B, M–9, SSN–2, SSC–1b
- ● R, P?
- ◆ P
- ▲ R

ISRAEL
- ■ IRBM, JERICHO I, JERICHO II, LANCE, MAR 350, ARROW (ATBM), SHAVIT
- ● R, I
- ◆ P?
- ▲ Yes (possible hydrogen bomb)

IRAQ
- ■ FROG–7, SCUDS, SSN–2 (UN limits)
- ● I (anthrax, botulism)
- ◆ RB, I
- ▲ RB

IRAN
- ■ SCUDS, CSS–8, CSS–N–1
- ● RB, P?
- ◆ P
- ▲ RB

JORDAN
- ■ None
- ● Tech Base
- ◆ RB

AFGHANISTAN
- ■ SCUDS

ALGERIA
- ■ SSN–2, SSC–3
- ● RB
- ◆ I
- ▲ R

LIBYA
- ■ FROGS, SCUD–B, SSN–2, SSC–3
- ● R?
- ◆ P

EGYPT
- ■ FROGS, SCUDS, SSN–1, CSSN–1, SAQR–2, BADAR 2000
- ● RB
- ◆ P
- ▲ R

SAUDI ARABIA
- ■ CSS–2
- ◆ R?

PAKISTAN
- ■ M–11?, HATF 1, HATF II, HATF III
- ● R?
- ◆ R
- ▲ I

SOURCE: INSS from various sources, including Congresional Research Service, Carnegie Endowment for International Peace Non-Proliferation Project; International Institute for Strategic Studies; Anthony Cordesman, *After the Storm.*

But despite arms-control efforts, the diffusion of WMD technologies has proven exceptionally difficult to control. In this regard, the Iraqi experience is revealing. While export controls did succeed in delaying and increasing the cost of Iraq's nuclear program, post-Gulf War discoveries revealed it to be much more advanced than most analysts had suspected. Thus, while arms-control and export-control regimes can be helpful in retarding and raising the cost of obtaining NBC weapons, states that are sufficiently motivated and possess adequate resources will probably succeed if they persist.

If increasing numbers of states do acquire WMD, other tools to enhance security must be employed, in particular, tools that afford some protection against these weapons. The remaining four instruments examined here are military instruments used to counter the threat of NBC weapons after an enemy has acquired them. Such instruments are generally known as instruments of counterproliferation. Deterrence remains the first line of defense, and counterproliferation instruments can strengthen deterrence. Should deterrence fail, however, the instruments of counterproliferation provide a measure of protection.

Nuclear Deterrence

During the Cold War, when strategic nuclear war was the central threat to U.S. national security, nuclear deterrence was the chief instrument of response. However, the last years of the Cold War saw a dramatic drawdown—partly negotiated, partly by unilateral choice—in the size and variety of the United States's theater nuclear arsenal. And the Cold War's end has brought a change in the entire nuclear environment, as well as questions about the utility of both strategic and theater nuclear weapons. Two issues stand out: (1) what role nuclear weapons have in the post-Cold War age; and (2) how effective nuclear deterrence will prove in regional conflicts where an adversary has NBC weapons.

In its 1994 Nuclear Posture Review (NPR) and subsequent affirmations, the Clinton administration reaffirmed the United States's need for a nuclear deterrent. Concretely, the administration identified a requirement to, among other things: maintain 3,500 strategic warheads; keep ICBMs and modernize the Minuteman III; complete the D–5 Trident missile purchase and maintain fourteen Trident boats armed with D–5s; adopt a stockpile stewardship program to assure a reliable, safe, and secure stockpile without nuclear testing; and commit the resources needed to verify START compliance and monitor Russia's strategic offensive modernization program. Strategically, the document seeks to hedge against the possibility of a reversal of democratization in Russia; to allow for the possibility of armed confrontation with a regional power that has acquired WMD; to continue to extend the U.S. nuclear deterrent to major allies; and to discourage or even reverse nuclear proliferation.

A key element in the rejection of nuclear disarmament is the realization that nuclear weapons cannot be disinvented; that is, the knowledge of how to make them is widespread and the most demanding part of the process (acquiring fissile material) is extraordinarily difficult to prevent. Even if the world's political processes sustain arms-control efforts and achieve related measures, such as a comprehensive nuclear test ban and cessation of the production of plutonium for weapons purposes, the problem of so-called virtual nuclear arsenals—the technical and industrial capability to create a nuclear arsenal quickly—remains.

Moreover, despite whatever arms pacts may be signed, reliable and effective verification measures do not yet exist. Thus, without the ability to verify universal nuclear disarmament, the United States would run a tremendous risk in eliminating its own nuclear deterrent. Many wary policymakers emphasize that, though diplomatic relations between Washington and Moscow have thawed considerably since 1989, Russia has continued to produce nuclear weapons while the United States has ceased its production. Other great powers, too, may someday construct large nuclear arsenals. Furthermore, many policymakers argue that the elimination of the U.S. arsenal would inspire other nuclear states to build up their arsenals in order to challenge U.S. power and deter U.S. conventional military forces. Further, some observers have pointed out that if the United States were to do away with its nuclear capability, many non-nuclear states that rely upon U.S. security assurances for their protection

Chemical Weapons in the Gulf War: Did Nuclear Deterrence Work?

Prior to the Gulf War, military assessments credited Iraq with a formidable arsenal of chemical weapons, including mustard gas, tabun, and sarin. Over the course of Iraq's nearly decade-long war with Iran, the Iraqi military gained extensive combat experience with chemical weapons, and CW use was by the end of the war an integral part of Iraqi warfighting doctrine. However, in spite of threats to turn the Gulf War into "the mother of all wars" and to "burn half of Israel to the ground," Iraq did not use chemical weapons when it faced the United States and its coalition. This came as a surprise to allied commanders, who anticipated that Iraq would attack with WMD early in the fighting in an effort to undermine U.S. public support for the war.

In the aftermath of the Gulf War, many factors were cited to explain why Iraq restrained itself from employing CW. Some analysts asserted that the Iraqi leadership feared the use of CW would cause the coalition to change the military objectives of Desert Storm to include the elimination of Saddam Hussein's regime. Others posited that Baghdad believed the use of CW would not have a significant impact on coalition forces due to their use of protective suits and chemical detectors. Still others claimed that atmospheric conditions unfavorable to effective CW use persisted throughout the ground campaign.

Perhaps the most prevalent argument attributed the decision to Iraqi fears of a U.S. or Israeli response with nuclear weapons. After the onset of hostilities in the Gulf War, it became apparent that the United States held an overwhelming conventional-force advantage over Iraq. However, in the months leading up to the Gulf War, U.S. political and military leaders, unsure whether the conventional superiority of their forces would deter WMD use by Iraq, indicated privately and publicly that the United States might retaliate with nuclear weapons if Iraq were to use chemical weapons. According to an Iraqi transcript of a meeting between U.S. Secretary of State James Baker and Iraqi Foreign Minister Tariq `Aziz, Baker told `Aziz, "God forbid . . . chemical weapons are used against our forces—the American people would demand revenge, and we have the means to implement this."

In late 1995 the Iraqi leadership told U.N. officials that they had interpreted Baker's warning to mean that the United States would use nuclear weapons against Iraq if Iraq used NBC against coalition forces. The Iraqis claim they took this warning seriously, and that while they had armed nearly two hundred SCUD warheads and bombs with chemical and biological agents for use against coalition forces and Israeli and Saudi cities, they did not use them because they feared U.S. nuclear retaliation.

Strategic Nuclear Launchers

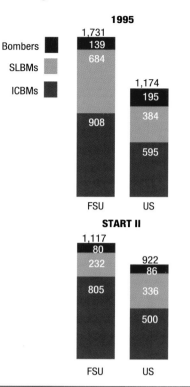

1995

Bombers
SLBMs
ICBMs

1,731
139
684
908
FSU

1,174
195
384
595
US

START II

1,117
80
232
805
FSU

922
86
336
500
US

SOURCE: International Institute for Strategic Studies. The Military Balance 1995/96 and Secretary of Defense, Annual Report to the President and Congress 1995.

would have an incentive to seek their own nuclear deterrent capabilities. Thus, the supposition one must take into account when developing a long-term vision of nuclear forces is that future challenges may again require a response of significant proportions. Whether the laws, rules, and institutions of the international system will be adequate to contain those challenges without the backing of proportionate force is doubtful. Whether nuclear weapons might be needed to provide such force is at least an open question

Below the level of great-power challenges lies the question of nuclear deterrence against a regional power possessing NBC weapons. The concern is that U.S. conventional capabilities may not serve as an effective deterrent against BW and CW use in limited or regional military engagements. Should Washington relinquish the option of retaliating in kind to CW (as it already has done with BW), nuclear weapons will then provide the only nonconventional military deterrent to the use of WMD against U.S. or allied forces.

In late 1995, Iraqi officials gave U.N. envoys the first authoritative, if perhaps incomplete, account of why they did not use biological and chemical arms against coalition forces. Even though Iraq had embarked on a much accelerated nuclear-weapons program after the invasion of Kuwait, and had reportedly loaded roughly two hundred bombs and missile warheads with biological agents, Iraqi officials claim that they did not use them because they interpreted a strong warning delivered by Secretary of State James Baker as implying that the United States would use nuclear weapons if Iraq used CW or BW against the coalition.

Such revelations bolster the need for continued credible nuclear capabilities as well as the need to resist attempts to delegitimize U.S. possession of nuclear weapons. Nonetheless, while apparently successful in deterring NBC use against U.S. and allied forces in the Gulf, the effectiveness of nuclear deterrence cannot be re-

lied on exclusively. A number of factors might lessen the credibility of a U.S. nuclear response in certain situations that are not difficult to imagine. First, asymmetrical interests are present in many, if not all, regional conflicts. A regional regime might be convinced that its survival is at stake while the U.S. interest in the conflict might well fall far short of that. A regime making such an assumption might gamble that Washington's stakes in the conflict would not be high enough to warrant a U.S. nuclear response to the regime's NBC use (especially if limited), with all the inevitable international political repercussions. Secondly, a desperate regime might reason that a limited U.S. nuclear response would cause no more damage to its military capabilities than a continued, unrelenting conventional attack. Thirdly, an enemy's use of NBC—perhaps even at the outset of hostilities, and not as an act of desperation— might be carefully measured to cause enough casualties to make the U.S. leadership reconsider the price of its intervention, yet not be of sufficient magnitude that it would be likely to provoke a nuclear response. Scenarios such as these—and others can easily be envisioned—suggest that while the United States must maintain a credible nuclear deterrent against NBC use, the efficacy of that deterrent cannot be relied on absolutely.

That said, deterring NBC armed regional aggressors will remain the United States's preferred and first line of defense. An essential element of such deterrence will be maintaining a credible capability across the spectrum of forces, from conventional superiority—including the ability to operate in an NBC environment supported by active and passive defenses and adequate counterforce capabilities—to a reliable and effective nuclear deterrent. However, it is also necessary to go beyond capabilities and reexamine how to think about and plan for deterrence in a regional conflict. For example, some of the assumptions on which U.S.-Soviet deterrence was founded (such as a basic and shared rationality) may not hold in regional conflicts. Articulating a regional deterrence and defense strategy (or strategies) will be a difficult but important challenge. Understanding deterrence and defense in a regional context will require a better appreciation of the military/cultural/political dynamics, as will a better understanding of possible employment doctrines of regional states with NBC weapons.

Another issue is the continued role for so-called tactical nuclear weapons, that is, weapons to be used on or near the battlefield against enemy military forces as contrasted with weapons that hold at risk deeper, "strategic" targets. By the end of the Cold War, the technical distinctions between tactical and strategic systems had become blurred. Continuing the trend in the last years of the Cold War of reducing dramatically the U.S. tactical nuclear arsenal, the Nuclear Posture Review endorsed a nonstrategic nuclear force structure consisting solely of Air Force dual-capable aircraft and Navy Tomahawk missiles, which could in an emergency be deployed on submarines.

Counterforce Capabilities

Counterforce—the ability to strike an enemy's forces before they can be used—has always been a central objective of military operations. In a WMD scenario, counterforce capabilities include the ability to

target, deny, interdict, or destroy hostile NBC forces and supporting infrastructure. Counterforce principles operate at all levels of military conflict and engagement. At the tactical level, for example, destruction of an enemy's artillery and supply capabilities is a prime method of suppressing that enemy's ability to deliver chemical or nuclear weapons in the field.

Even under the doctrine of mutual assured destruction, the ability to destroy an enemy's residual nuclear forces after an initial strike was seen as the most effective way of limiting damage should deterrence fail. In the post-Cold War world, strong counterforce capabilities serve not only to mitigate or eliminate existing NBC threats but to deter their creation in the first place.

The acquisition of offensive counterforce capabilities was partly a consequence of improved technological capabilities. Nonetheless, despite the push from technology, the progress of strategic counterforce capabilities was moderated during the Cold War, largely because counterforce capabilities sufficient to achieve a first-strike capability were considered destabilizing.

In a regional setting there would be a number of special political and operational aspects associated with attempting to destroy NBC-associated weapons and facilities. Such missions would impose unique considerations on all involved in the planning, decision, and execution, from the National Command authorities to the local commander. The character and symbolism of weapons of mass destruction would make striking NBC-related targets as much a political act as a military one. Political authorities would undoubtedly scrutinize closely any recommendation to destroy NBC-related targets. The requirements for success would also tend to be more stringent than for non-NBC counterforce strikes. Because collateral damage from the destroyed weapons can be so great, the effects of such damage would have to be known in advance and held to a minimum. These requirements would have to be taken into account during planning and might require unique technical capabilities. Taken together, these considerations would impose special burdens on the intelligence units and military forces if

Patriot Missile system.

Comparing Effects of Nuclear and Biological Release

Casualties from a Nuclear Release
(Either a small (10 kiloton) bomb or destruction of a nuclear reactor)

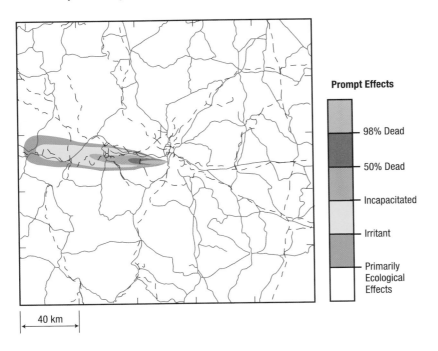

Prompt Effects

98% Dead

50% Dead

Incapacitated

Irritant

Primarily
Ecological
Effects

40 km

Casualties from Biological Weapons Release
(10 kg viable ANTHRAX)

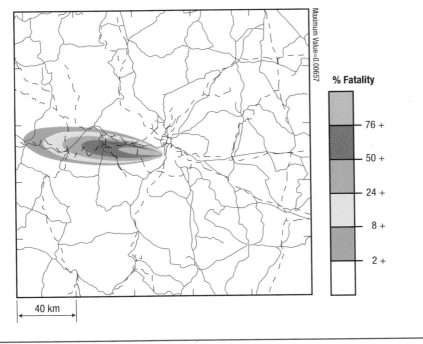

Maximum Value=0.00657

% Fatality

76 +

50 +

24 +

8 +

2 +

40 km

SOURCE: Robert M. Cox, NDU and Richard FRY, DGI

they were to undertake counterforce missions against NBC targets.

One lesson that potential adversaries learned from the Gulf War is that in order to survive in the face of U.S. conventional superiority, an enemy must go underground. In 1994, a Senate Armed Services Committee report acknowledged, "While Operation Desert Storm revealed the accuracy of U.S. precision guided missiles, it also revealed serious shortcomings in their lethality against buried, deep underground, or otherwise hardened facilities." Increasingly, regional powers are taking this lesson to heart, hiding their WMD facilities and stockpiles in underground bunkers in an effort to reduce the possibility of detection and the effectiveness of conventional weapons directed against them if they are detected. Such action places greater demands on both intelligence and counterforce resources, as capabilities must be improved to identify underground NBC targets and develop technologies to destroy them.

Active Defense

Active defenses—the ability to prevent weapons from reaching their intended targets—can enhance deterrence by denying an enemy the ability effectively to employ NBC-armed missiles and aircraft. Such defenses may become essential to ensure that the United States or its allies are not deterred by an NBC threat or do not have to suffer massive casualties unnecessarily.

The pursuit of active defenses against the greatest Cold War WMD threat—nuclear-armed Soviet ballistic missiles—was carefully circumscribed and formally limited by the Anti-Ballistic Missile (ABM) Treaty. In 1972, at a time when the number of offensive missiles and nuclear warheads numbered in the tens of thousands, the ABM Treaty was adopted on the assumption that in light of these great numbers, active defenses were simply not capable of defending against the full magnitude of the threat; mutual assured destruction was believed to be the more stable policy. Further, policymakers hoped that a limit on active defenses would encourage greater restraint in the production of offensive weapons and, conversely,

Chemical protection mask.

nuclear, biological, or chemical weapons would be an important consideration in future regional conflicts, for both military and political reasons.

Longer-range active-defense missiles, such as the Theater High-Altitude Area Defense (THAAD), will enable warheads to be intercepted at ever greater ranges. This is particularly important for defense against NBC warheads, because destroying them close to the intended target may not significantly reduce exposure to the agents they carry. The farther from the target that active missile defense systems can intercept an incoming warhead, the less the chance that the agent will affect friendly troops or territory. A near-miss with an NBC warhead might still do considerable damage to U.S. or coalition forces, or to civilian populations.

As proliferant states acquire longer-range missiles and NBC weapons, they could also acquire the ability to threaten U.S. territory. If the United States is seen to lack the means to defend its territory against proliferant states, it could undermine Washington's freedom to act in future crises. A debate continues in the United States about how much and what kind of active defenses to pursue. The Gulf War experience convinced the U.S. defense community of the military and political utility of having an effective theater ballistic-missile defense (TMD); a consensus to develop TMD clearly exists. However, no such consensus exists with regard to the merits of a national missile defense (NMD) system to protect the United States itself.

The NMD debate centers on two key points: first, the character and timing of the threat (that is, how long it will be before any NBC-armed adversary has the ability to launch such weapons by ballistic missile against the United States); and, secondly, the effect an NMD would have on the ABM Treaty and, in turn, U.S. relations with Russia. As of late 1995, the Clinton administration continued to affirm U.S. support for the ABM Treaty and maintain that technological development programs provided a sufficient hedge against future long-range missile threats to U.S. territory.

feared that the pursuit of active defenses would spur even greater offensive efforts. They also hoped that the ABM Treaty might provide a political basis for reductions in the offensive nuclear stockpiles of the United States and Soviet Union.

If the end of the Cold War was accompanied by a diminished perception of the Russian threat, it also resulted in an increased perception of the threat posed by regional powers. Indeed, as ballistic and cruise missiles become more available to emerging powers, the need for active defenses to protect U.S. forces in regions where NBC proliferation is taking place becomes clearer. Additionally, the evolution of missiles that are both longer range and mobile decreases the likelihood that counterforce options will be totally successful. The difficulties in locating and destroying mobile missiles were vividly demonstrated during the Gulf War. While not designed primarily to intercept SCUD-type missiles, the Patriot missile deployed to the Gulf did provide important psychological and political benefits in the prosecution of the war. From that experience, it became more apparent that effective active defenses against

However, Republican congressional leaders were increasingly questioning the ABM Treaty's continued relevance in a post-Cold War environment of widespread proliferation, and many urged the development for deployment of a national missile defense.

Passive Defense

Passive defense seeks to provide protection for U.S. and allied forces against an NBC attack. It can take many forms, from protective uniforms and masks to equipment incorporated into larger systems (such as entire naval vessels or air-base command centers) that enable them to operate in chemical, biological, and, in limited aspects, some nuclear environments. Passive defense includes detection and identification of NBC agents, medical response to NBC effects, and decontamination of equipment and facilities. Many analysts believe that a strong passive-defense capability serves as a deterrent, discouraging use of WMD by an adversary who knows that U.S. forces are able to operate in chemical and biological environments.

During the Cold War, passive-defense measures against chemical attack were taken seriously, especially by NATO forces in Europe. The massive Soviet threat to Europe included a threat of biological and chemical attack, and NATO forces were required to train to operate in such an environment. NATO's strategy included the option of a response in kind—that is, the use of chemical weapons against an attacker who had already employed them. A credible response in kind was contingent upon the ability of NATO's own forces to operate in a chemical environment. As with many Cold War situations, preparing for a massive Soviet attack against Europe provided the necessary training and equipment to fight in lesser contingencies where passive defense against chemical attack might be required. However, the U.S. Army prefers to avoid undertaking prolonged operations in protective chemical gear, owing to the severe limits such equipment places on effectiveness.

Following the Cold War, a number of circumstances have arisen that underscore the need for effective passive-defense equipment, including protective masks and suits. First, the spread of biological and chemical capabilities means that U.S. forces must be prepared to operate in a WMD environment worldwide. Secondly, since the threat is no longer localized in the relatively benign operating climate of Europe, the possibility of having to operate in chemical gear under harsher climatological conditions has increased. Thirdly, the CWC's requirement that all chemical stockpiles be destroyed within ten years of the treaty's ratification will, if ratified by the United States, preclude any possibility of Washington's threatening an in-kind response to the use of chemical weapons against U.S. forces. In the face of a proliferator armed with chemical or biological weapons, this inability to threaten response in kind may weaken deterrence and, in so doing, increase the chances that an adversary will use chemical weapons.

Robust passive-defense capabilities are key to operating without a significant loss in effectiveness in a BW or CW environment. Actions by the Department of Defense to improve chemical- and biological-defense capabilities include the integration

---

Missile Defense Systems

PAC 3 (Patriot Advanced Capability): Point or limited-area defense system. PAC 3 improvements include upgrades to radar and an improved hit-to-kill missile known as ERINT. Operational prototype in late 1990s.

THAAD (Theater High-Altitude Area Defense): Ground-based theater missile defense (TMD) system that will provide a wide-area defense capability by intercepting longer-range theater-ballistic missiles at higher altitudes and at greater distances. Provides upper-tier defense to complement point defense, such as Patriot. Operational in early 2000s.

Navy Lower Tier (AEGIS/SM–2 Block IVA): Could provide tactical ballistic-missile defense capability similar to PAC 3 from the sea. Operational in late 1990s.

Navy Upper Tier: Could provide extensive theater-wide protection, intercepting theater ballistic missiles outside the atmosphere as well as in the ascent and descent phases. If selected, available in 2002.

Corps SAM/MEADS (Medium Extended Air Defense System): Mobile lower-tier missile-defense system designed to protect moving combat forces against theater ballistic and cruise missiles. To be developed in cooperation with France, Germany, and Italy. Available in 2005.

Boost Phase Interceptor: An interceptor fired from an aircraft to shoot down a ballistic missile during the missile's booster phase when it is most vulnerable. In concept exploration as of 1995; available at the earliest in 2005.

Threat Ranges from Middle East Missiles

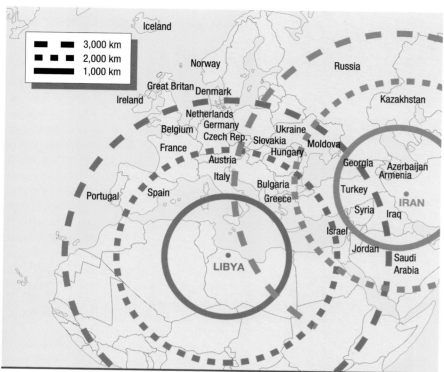

NOTE: Illustrating the threat were Libya or Iran to acquire the No-Dong 1 (1,000 km), TD–1 (2,000 km) or TD–2 (3,000 km) missiles.

of separate service programs into a consolidated DOD Chemical/Biological Defense Program. The goal of this program is to enhance the ability of U.S. forces to defend against BW and CW agents by developing and procuring the capabilities to avoid contamination (through adequate detection and warning/reconnaissance), protect forces (through individual and collective protective gear and adequate medical support), and improve decontamination measures.

In the future, U.S. forces must be prepared to operate in the presence of chemical and biological agents in an ever widening variety of contingencies. The ease with which chemical and biological agents can be manufactured and delivered means that these threats may be present even in peacekeeping operations. Despite advances, operating in chemical gear continues to place great physical and psychological stress on individual soldiers and units. The possibility that U.S. forces will be called upon to operate in the presence of an NBC threat means that continued improvements in individual protection equipment are necessary.

The likelihood that U.S. forces will often operate as part of a coalition raises questions about the possible political and military impact of NBC weapons on coalition cohesion. In the event of an NBC threat, it will not be sufficient for U.S. forces alone to have adequate protective equipment. An adversary might exploit gaps in the passive-defense capabilities of coalition partners, thereby undermining coalition cohesion and posing acute problems for political leaders and military commanders alike. Furthermore, in some situations, the issue of protection for civilians could become important—not just politically but also operationally. In many instances, for example, a largely civilian work force will be needed to maintain capabilities at ports and airfields. The absence of adequate personal protection for civilian workers will result in a degradation of operational capabilities, and may lead to deterioration in the political climate.

Conclusions

An ideal tool for national-security strategy combines two attributes. First, it should contribute to the deterrence of war. Deterrence remains the first line of defense against the use of nuclear, biological, and chemical weapons. Secondly, should deterrence fail, a useful military instrument must contribute to the successful prosecution of war by denying the enemy the ability to achieve its objectives—even if that enemy does resort to the use of NBC weapons.

The counterproliferation tools described above hold the promise of fulfilling these two requirements. To the extent that an enemy realizes the United States maintains the abilities to neutralize (or at least minimize the damage inflicted by) NBC weapons and to respond effectively to their use, counterproliferation tools may deter an enemy from aggression. This is termed "deterrence by denial." If an adversary knows that possession or even use of NBC weapons will not intimidate or defeat U.S. forces, the chances of that adversary's employing NBC weapons—or, indeed, engaging U.S. forces in the first place—will be reduced. However, if deterrence fails, the ability of U.S. forces to operate in an NBC

A THAAD test launch.

environment and respond decisively to NBC use will be crucial to success. Thus, maintaining adequate capabilities across the full range of counterproliferation tools—passive defense, counterforce capabilities, active defense, and nuclear deterrence—is simultaneously the best deterrent and the best way to minimize damage should deterrence fail.

Prevention tools are necessary but limited in what they can achieve. Despite some important successes, prevention tools have limited power to dissuade or deny those intent on achieving WMD capability. Chemical and biological weapons are relatively cheap and easy to acquire. A state determined to acquire them—or even nuclear weapons—can do so, given sufficient resources, time, and effort. Barriers to NBC possession and use are eroding. A number of nations seem intent on acquiring NBC weapons, despite efforts to codify international norms against posses-

sion of such weapons. The reasons are complex, but a growing number of states evidently see concrete warfighting utility in such weapons. For example, even though chemical weapons were used in the Iran-Iraq War, international condemnation was subdued.

The United States must strive to make deterrence as credible as possible. Achieving credible deterrence of NBC use in regional conflicts is a complex and uncertain task; nuclear weapons are necessary but not sufficient. Establishing and maintaining a credible deterrent against NBC use in regional conflicts will also require the ability to operate and prevail with conventional forces in an NBC environment. Achieving deterrence by denial will require continued attention to gaps in operational capabilities. The armed services will increasingly need to pay close attention to the consequences of WMD use against U.S. and coalition forces in regional conflicts and to the imperatives of operating in an NBC environment. The use, or threat of use, of such weapons will have far-reaching consequences on both the tactical and strategic character of the conflict.

Coalition warfare may be particularly affected by the use or threatened use of NBC weapons. A coalition will not be politically sustainable if some members are significantly more vulnerable to NBC attack than others. In addition, a coalition might not be sustainable if it cannot protect the citizens of a coalition country from NBC attack.

Proliferation will place additional strains on intelligence requirements. The potentially severe effects of NBC use against U.S. forces will require that increased intelligence resources be devoted to identifying and analyzing the NBC capabilities of potential adversaries on a real time basis. The consequences of failing to completely identify NBC targets could impose a heavy penalty on U.S. forces operating in the region. The demand for timely and accurate intelligence on enemy NBC capabilities and readiness will only increase in the years ahead.

CHAPTER SEVENTEEN

Summary: Using U.S. Power More Effectively

In the post-Cold War world, there has been a considerable alteration of the instruments of U.S. power, that is, the means available to the U.S. government to influence the behavior of other governments. In part because of stricter resource constraints and in part because the threats have changed, some of the mainstays of the policy of containment during the Cold War—such as the strategic nuclear forces and foreign aid—are becoming less central. At the same time, the U.S. government is developing a more diverse set of tools, taking advantage of profound changes in the world setting.

We begin our analysis of the post-Cold War instruments of U.S. power by analyzing how the world is changing from the perspective of U.S. security interests. Then we discuss the instruments of U.S. power, starting with those that use persuasion rather than force and proceeding to those that require progressively greater use of force. Using this principle, we arrange the instruments of U.S. power into three groups: non-military instruments, political-military instruments, and warfighting instruments. This arrangement emphasizes the traditional national security issues, not because we wish to slight environmental security or economic security but because,

as analysts of the National Defense University, we have decided to concentrate on the areas we know best.

The Post-Cold War World

The present world situation is characterized by its rapid pace of change. The world is undergoing three changes so sweeping that they may deserve to be called revolutions. A common characteristic of all three revolutions is that they make the world a more diverse place. Although this expanding diversity requires a more eclectic foreign policy approach, it also makes possible a wider variety of ways for the United States to work its will.

Geostrategic Revolution. Most apparent to analysts of international affairs are the geostrategic changes, which have several dimensions. With regard to relations among the major powers—which have historically been the main element in world politics—the long superpower confrontation during the Cold War is being replaced by a world of asymmetrical poles in which one (the U.S.) is much the strongest. The others powers, nevertheless, are important actors: the world has not become unipolar, as some imagined in the first moments after the Cold War. In the first blush of enthusiasm at the end of the Cold War, the great powers were all cooperating. Now, relations among some are cooler, and differences of perspective have become more pronounced. The hopes for a new strategic relationship between the U.S. and Russia are fading; Russia is feeling isolated and bitter about what is sees as others taking advantage of its temporary difficulties. China is feeling more powerful because of its spectacular economic growth; sometimes it acts like a normal player in international affairs, and sometimes it acts like the stereotype of the Middle Kingdom—not well informed about other states and assuming that it has a natural right to what it wants.

Another aspect of the global geostrategic scene has been the triumph of the idea of market democracy. While not always practiced, it is nearly universally regarded as the best way to run society. From this perspective, the world can be divided into three categories of states: those successful at implementing the goal of market democracy, those in transition from authoritarianism towards that goal (but at risk of becoming frozen with politicized economies and partially free political systems), and those troubled states that are falling further behind the rest of the world while in many cases struggling with ethnic and religious extremism. Some rogue states from among the troubled or transitional nations may be tempted to divert attention from domestic problems with external aggression aimed at establishing regional hegemony. The proliferation of weapons of mass destruction, particularly nuclear weapons, could make particularly dangerous a major regional conflict with such a rogue state. At the same time, conflicts within troubled states are likely to be as frequent, and in some cases, those states will fail—their governments will cease to function effectively, and civil society will degenerate into near chaos. The U.S. will have neither the means nor the will to intervene in every such case, but it will conduct humanitarian and peace operations in areas of its historic and strategic interest as well as in situations of horrendous suffering that offend U.S. sensibilities.

Perhaps the most novel feature of the geostrategic scene has been the explosion of transnational problems, that is, problems that cross borders but do not stem from the action of governments. International crime, terrorism, sudden mass migrations, and environmental threats are not susceptible to the traditional tools of statecraft designed for relations among sovereign governments.

International Affairs Budget Authority
(Billion FY 96 $)

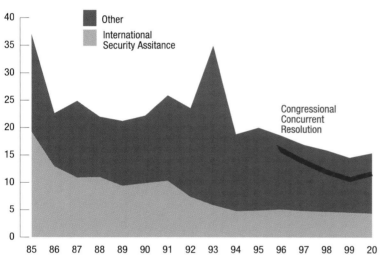

National Defense Budget Authority
(Billion FY 96 $)

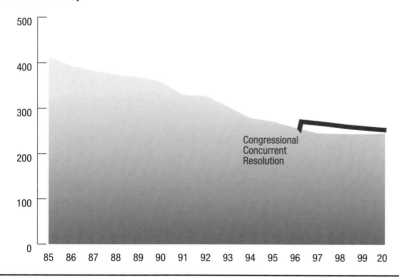

SOURCE: FY 1996 Budget and Concurrent Resolution on the Budget for Fiscal Year 1996. All data refer to fiscal years.
NOTE: The FY 93 spike in international affairs funding was due to an IMF quota increase.

Reductions in Defense and International Affairs Funding From 1985 through 1996

In FY 1985–95, there was a sharp decline in national defense funding, that is, in the 050 account in the federal budget, which includes nearly all the DOD budget as well as defense-related expenditures by other agencies, mostly the Department of Energy. In FY 1996 dollars, the 050 account budget authority declined from $412 billion in 1985 to $271 billion in 1995, a 34 percent reduction.

The largest reduction ($90 billion out of the total reduction of $141 billion) was in procurement, which fell by 64 percent. In FY 1995, the Army bought no new tanks and the Navy bought four ships; the services are operating with the large equipment stock bought during the 1980s buildup. Obviously, this is not a sustainable long-term procurement level, and so five-year plans include an eventual upturn in procurement, which will place further pressure on the budget.

Despite the widespread impression that the FY 1996 national defense budget grew, in fact, despite the $7 billion added by Congress to the Clinton administration budget request, budget authority in real terms shrank by 2 percent between FY 1995 and FY 1996.

The international affairs budget also dropped sharply in 1985–95. In constant 1996 dollars, the international affairs budget (the 150 account) fell 46 percent, from $37 billion to $20 billion, over that time.

However, the reduction was heavily concentrated in international security assistance (account 151), which went from $19 billion to $5 billion at 1996 prices, a 74 percent reduction. Between 1985 and 1995, the budget for all other international affairs items went from $18 billion to $15 billion (at 1996 prices). The budget for the conduct of foreign affairs and for foreign information and exchange programs actually increased in real terms. But the increase was modest, and the burden of work grew as the number of countries rose and as the world became a more complex place.

Information Revolution. Information technology has been improving roughly tenfold every five years, an unprecedented rate of change. Computers, faxes, fiber optic cables, and satellites speed the flow of information across frontiers, reinforcing the political trend towards increasingly open societies. No one can foretell all the ways in which information technologies will change traditional venues of national power, but certain useful themes are beginning to emerge. One is that access to information technology has become a prerequisite for economic growth, at least in developed countries. Another is that the ubiquity of global communication is creating new avenues for the interests, cultures, and values of the United States to radiate overseas, and vice versa. Yet another is that the extension of rapid communication and computer technological advances to the battlefield may make information-based warfare possible within a decade or two.

Revolution in Government. After decades of increasing state involvement in many areas of society in most countries, central governments have been on the retreat recently. Power is devolving: whether in Russia, the United States, the European Union or China, central governments are ceding more authority to regional and local governments. Central governments are also shedding functions, partly to reduce expenditures and contain budget deficits. Governments are also privatizing state enterprises, in line with the general mood that reliance on free markets is the way to boost growth. The power of international business has increased relative to that of governments. However, this shift may not diminish the ability of governments to mobilize resources to support perceived vital national interests, for instance, during wartime.

A phenomenon related to the decline of central governments has been less concern about the projection of national power abroad and more concern about domestic issues, especially the economy. In many countries, the argument is heard that only a strong economic base can provide the foundation for an active international role.

In the United States, the new focus on domestic issues has caused a decline in the resources available for foreign policy instruments. Between fiscal years 1985 and 1995, in real terms, funding for national defense fell 34 percent, and funding for international affairs fell 46 percent (referring respectively to the 050 and 150 accounts in the federal budget). The drop in international affairs funding was primarily in military aid; other international affairs funding fell 17 percent in real terms over the decade.

Both the Clinton and Congressional projections for defense and international affairs spending show continued reductions in real terms between 1996 and 2000. For national defense, the two agree on a 7 percent reduction. For international affairs, the Clinton budget projects a 23 percent reduction, while the Congressional concurrent resolution projects a 43 percent cut. Furthermore, the pressure for balancing the budget while protecting many domestic programs may push reductions for national security above the levels projected by either the administration or Congress. The lower resource levels will pose a serious challenge for exerting U.S. influence at the level of leadership, and over the full range of issues, that U.S. interests require and that the American public has come to expect.

Implications for the U.S. If the essential characteristics of the present strategic environment are uncertainty and change, historical experience suggests that the new world system may be more malleable now than it will be in a few years. International systems typically have had a life cycle in which the relations among the major powers start out flexible then become more rigid. The way in which the system is shaped tends to determine whether the major powers remain at peace. If past experience is replicated, then there is some urgency to focusing on international affairs now—to resolving the domestic debates about what the U.S. wants from the new world order and to maximizing the instruments of national power available to U.S. policymakers.

Three implications can be drawn from the new world situation for the instruments of U.S. power:

● A broader array of tools is needed to respond to the more diverse problems in the new geostrategic setting. The tools needed to strengthen market democracy are not necessarily the same as those required to deter rogues. Other tools are needed to deal with failed states, and yet others again to respond to transnational problems.

● Washington needs to stay on top of the information revolution as it changes established institutions and procedures. For instance, the world communications web brings an instant and increasing flow of news. Should Washington react passively, its agenda will be set by what is on the tele-

---

The Prospects for National Defense and International Affairs Funding in FY 1997–2000

The congressional concurrent resolution on the FY 1966 budget and the FY 1996 Clinton administration budget both present forecast for spending through at least FY 2000 plan, showing the overall government total and the amounts for each budget category, including nationla defense (account 050) and international affairs (account 150).

Both plans call for national defense budget authority to be reduced by 7 percent in real terms by FY 2000 from the FY 1996 level. The Clinton administration budget provided detailed breakdown of its spending plans by category. Under those plans, further reductions in personnel are programmed in order to pay for increased procurement. Despite the increase, procurement will remain significantly below the steady-state replacement rate, that is, the average age of major systems will continue to increase. In other words, it may be difficult to sustain the planned force levels with the resources programmed for defense.

For international affairs, the FY 1996 Clinton administration budget plan programmed a five-year reduction of 23 percent in real terms, while the congressional concurrent resolution on the FY 1996 budget called for a cut of 43 percent at constant prices. That would bring the international affairs budget (at 1996 prices) in 2000 to either 58 percent or 69 percent below that of 1985, depending on whether the administration or congressional plan is adapted. In late 1995, a compromise funding level between the two plans was agreed to by the administration and Senator Helms (R-North Carolina).

Any of these plans for reduction will be a great challenge to absorb. It will be difficult to maintain much of a foreign aid program, especially if contributions to multilateral institutions and aid to Israel and Egypt are sustained at anything like current levels. At the same time, the reduced international affairs spending will not have much effect on the overall deficit. All spending on international affairs is less than 2 percent of the overall government budget. The reduction—the allocation in 2000 would be $4.6 billion less than in 1995 under the Clinton plan and $8.7 billion less under the Congressional plan—will be small relative to the size of the $190 billion FY 1996 federal deficit. While much of the reduction may come from the foreign aid budget, there is also strong congressional pressure to cut the budgets of State, USAID, ACDA, and USIA as well as to combine some or all of those agencies. Under both congressional and administration budget plans, the U.S. will remain in arrears to the U.N. throughout the rest of the decade.

Both the Clinton and congressional plans would mean tight resource constraints for national security. And the situation could get worse, because of the pressure for balancing the budget. Both political parties want the budget balanced. The Republicans want a large tax cut. The Democrats want to protect spending on programs like health, education, and the environment. It will be difficult to achieve that combination of goals, unless the economic situation is particularly favorable, with low interest rates to cut the cost of servicing the national debt and rapid economic growth to raise revenue and keep down the cost of programs like unemployment insurance and welfare.

If the budget is to be balanced while taxes are cut and spending on health, education, and the environment is protected, and if the economy performs at the historic average rather than exceptionally well, then it will be necessary to make further cuts in other spending categories. The great unknown is what will happen to health care costs and to other entitlement programs. Perhaps savings will be made, through more efficient programs and changes in the way benefits are increased as the consumer price index rises. Besides those programs, defense spending is one of the few large items available to cut. Therefore, it could well be reduced below the current agreed level. A prudent national security planner will include in his scenarios one in which budgets are reduced appreciably more than presently planned. The fact that the President and Congress agreed in the FY 1996 budget on a forecast level of defense spending for 2000 does not by any means assure that those resources will actually be made available when 2000 arrives.

---

vision screen, but if Washington changes with the times, it can use its direct access to world publics to influence events more quickly and surely than ever. Similarly, if the revolution in military technology from the information explosion is integrated into a new way of conducting warfare—a revolution in military affairs—then the U.S. can increase its domination of the battlefield. If the U.S. remains passive, however, then it could become vulnerable to a mid-sized power that uses information warfare to disrupt the information networks on which the U.S. depends.

● There are greater opportunities and more necessity for Washington to leverage its power. In the past, such leverage came primarily through allied governments. Now, other institutions are increasingly important. Private voluntary organizations (PVOs) provide humanitarian relief more effectively than do governments. Sometimes an eminent private individual can explore what a rogue government is prepared to do to cut a deal, without Washington having to provide the rogue the legitimacy that would come from direct contact. Private business, acting for its own interests without direction from Washington, can often be used to advance U.S. goals, as when investors stimulate economic growth that reinforces market democracy or that cements a fragile peace.

Adapting the Instruments of U.S. Power to the New Situation

While the changes in the instruments in U.S. power have generally been motivated by the evolution of the world setting—the revolutions in geostrategy, information technology, and the character of government—much has occurred because of conscious decisions by the U.S. government to reinvent the ways it does business. As the goals of U.S. foreign policy have become more varied since the end of the Cold War, the U.S. government has relied on a wider array of non-military instruments, including more vigorous use of some instruments that had been at most of

secondary utility during the Cold War. At the same time, Washington has implemented innovations designed to reduce costs, taking advantage of changing circumstances to shed functions or institutions no longer needed while making more use of new opportunities.

Non-military instruments

Diplomacy. In the more fluid situation of the mid-and-late 1990s, the emphasis in diplomatic techniques is shifting from formal procedures, such as large semi-permanent negotiating delegations, to more ad hoc arrangements, such as contact groups, special envoys, shuttle diplomacy and liaison offices. The U.S. is also learning how to use to its advantage private and quasi-private diplomacy, such as former President Carter's 1994 missions to North Korea and Haiti. Instruments like recognition policy are being redefined, as in the case of using recognition as an inducement to encourage progress by Vietnam and North Korea (on POW/MIAs and nuclear non-proliferation, respectively). At the same time, much is being done to stretch dollars further.

There is new stress in the State Department: resources are declining; ambassadorial appointees sit idle for months owing to disputes between the administration and Congress; and the work load is growing as the number of countries and international crises increases. In this context, consideration is being given to organizational changes to a diplomatic structure that was created to serve the needs of a different time. One example of a change under way is the greater presence abroad of a wide array of U.S. government agencies: embassies have become less exclusively State Department preserves and more the locations for interagency functions under the looser leadership of the ambassador.

Public Diplomacy. The ideology upheld by the U.S. during the Cold War—that of freedom, democracy, and the market—has triumphed worldwide in the realm of ideas, though it has not fully translated into practice in many transitional or troubled states. The role of public diplomacy is therefore evolving from the battle to win minds for the Free World to persuading foreign gov-

A U.S. Marine CH–46 Sea Knight helicopter prepares to insert troops at Hat Yao, Thailand during exercise Cobra Gold '95.

ernments and publics to support more specific U.S. policies. In this task, the principal U.S. organization is the U.S. Information Agency (USIA), although there is increasing foreign attention to statements designed primarily for domestic audiences issued by spokesmen throughout the government. In a world saturated with information, the challenge for public diplomacy is how to communicate more effectively by enhancing and supplementing the increasing commercial information flow. USIA is becoming less a direct supplier of information and more of an organizer of the information. While the information revolution has made American television shows, movies, music, and brand names more pervasive, that does not necessarily translate into support for U.S. government policies. The direct government programs so important in the past, from radio broadcasts to cultural exchanges, are being refocused on those areas that private sector activity does not reach adequately. Meanwhile, Washington has stepped up its efforts to promote democracy, both through existing institutions like USAID and by relatively new quasi-governmental organizations like the National Endowment for Democracy.

International Organizations. Despite new concerns about multilateralism, the U.S. government is using international organizations and private voluntary organizations more often and in more varied ways to accomplish tasks that during the Cold War it might have done directly itself. The U.S. military has been working more directly with these organizations in places like Somalia, Rwanda, Haiti, and Bosnia. That has required both sides to adapt, given the considerable differences in organizational culture and approach (e.g., a command structure compared to a web of independent actors reliant on consensus-building). Contrast the close coordination between the U.S. military and PVOs in Bosnia with the distant and at times hostile relations in Vietnam a generation earlier.

Washington not only uses international organizations to address humanitarian concerns in disasters and genocidal ethnic strife, but also to mitigate the military threat to vital U.S. national interests from rogue states. In both of the most likely candidates for a major regional contingency, North Korea and Iraq, U.N. agencies were indispensable for verifying agreements about weapons of mass destruction, whereas during the Cold War, arms control agreements were generally verified by the U.S. directly. International Atomic Energy Agency on-the-ground inspections and, in Iraq, U.N. Special Commision-supervised destruction of nuclear, biological, and chemical (NBC) facilities show how important multilateral organizations can be for U.S. national security. At the same time, U.S. support for international organizations has been weakened since the immediate post-Cold War enthusiasm by continuing problems of bureaucratic inertia, wasteful spending, limited capabilities, and unmet (albeit exaggerated) expectations.

Economics. As in other fields, the trend is away from use of U.S. budget resources. So foreign aid is moving from direct bilateral budget assistance to new ways to mobilize resources for vital national purposes: consortia of concerned states, as for North Korea; international financial institutions, as for Eastern Europe and the former Soviet Union; and tapping largely dormant U.S. government resources, as with the use of the Exchange Stabilization Fund to lend $20 billion to Mexico. But the larger story is that as security threats have declined, Washington has used existing economic instruments (like trade retaliation) more vigorously against allies, which may endanger alliances in the long term. All too often, however, economic instruments have little effect, in part because the U.S. is not committing sufficient resources to make an instrument like foreign aid more effective. In other cases, economic instruments have too much effect collaterally, that is, they have such broad effects that they inflict unacceptable political damage, as when the prospect of withdrawing most-favored nation status from China over human rights problems resulted in deterioration of relations across the board. When the U.S. is prepared to inflict heavy collateral damage, then a coercive economic instrument like sanctions can have noticeable effects over time. Witness how sanctions have weakened Iraq's ability to threaten its neighbors and encouraged Serbia to reduce support for ethnic Serb forces in Croatia and Bosnia.

Intelligence. With the end of the pressing need to focus on the activities of the former Soviet Union, the targets of intelligence activities have become more diffuse. Debate continues about what intelligence is most needed and which activities are most appropriate for secret government analysis. For instance, a host of ethical and methodological questions have arisen over the possibility of the intelligence community sharing information with U.S. business. To collect data on issues like regional conflicts and transnational problems, intelligence satellites are being given a broader range of capabilities and are being used publicly, for example to demonstrate war crimes in Bosnia. In many areas where policymakers want information, the information explosion has brought forth a vast amount of open-source data. By some estimates, 80 percent of the information used by the intelligence community comes from open sources. Policymakers are likely to get their first news on fast-breaking developments from CNN. The intelligence community is therefore devoting more atten-

tion to what its consumers want and how best to package and deliver it. Higher priority is given to analysis of the vast flow of information available, and less to the collection of data. Also, more attention is being given to meeting the needs of military commanders for timely intelligence attuned to the battlefield situations facing operational commanders.

Political-military instruments

Productive and Technological Base. Little attention is being devoted to the Cold War concerns about industrial mobilization and maintaining an engineering lead (e.g., in aircraft engines or tank armor). Partly that is because of the changed political environment, but perhaps more important is the swelling "third wave" that is making information technology the center of economic growth. Contrary to concerns that U.S. productive and technological power is on the decline, the U.S. is in fact the world leader in information technology, especially in the increasingly important software area. U.S. technological and productive might is as powerful an instrument for Washington as it has ever been. To be sure, the way that power will be applied to defense production is changing. More of the research at the cutting edge of technology is being done by the private sector and less by the government. Defense will increasingly piggyback on commercial developments rather than drive technology forward. As more funds go into electronics and as the production of major battle platforms (planes, ships, tanks) shrinks, more collaboration among firms, including with foreign firms, will be necessary to ensure the survival of the core capabilities, such as the ability to build aircraft carriers or nuclear submarines.

Arms control. Despite the end of the Cold War, Russia remains indispensable to successful arms control. The issues on which Russia's support is vital include working out new arrangements for European security to supplement the Treaty on Conventional Armed Forces in Europe (CFE); solidifying the still-forming system for control of dangerous arms and dual-use technologies; and dismantling the Cold War nuclear weapons legacy, including the cooperative threat reduction program for greater security of nuclear material so as to forestall proliferation dangers.

At the same time, the focus of arms control has shifted from the Cold War concentration on Soviet missiles. The new priority is on nonproliferation of NBC weapons and missiles, building on the 1995 success in securing the indefinite extension of the Treaty on the Non-Proliferation of Nuclear Weapons (NPT). Mutually reinforcing arms control measures such as nuclear-weapons-free zones, a comprehensive test ban treaty, and a fissile-material production-cutoff treaty hold promise for strengthening the international non-proliferation regime. Meanwhile, the model of conventional arms control and confidence-building measures implemented with the former Warsaw Pact in the last years of the Cold War hold promise for application in other strife-torn areas of the world, such as Bosnia, Northeast Asia or the Levant.

Defense Engagement in Peacetime. Cold War interaction with foreign militaries, other than alliance partners, often meant providing developing countries with equipment at favorable prices, so as to shore up their ability to meet potential Soviet-inspired subversion or outright aggression. By contrast, the 1990s have seen a drop in arms deliveries, especially those with an aid component but also sales on commercial terms; even the large post-Desert Storm agreements with Gulf Arab states have not translated into larger deliveries. The focus of defense engagement has changed to foreign military interaction, such as professional education and combined military exercises, and high-level defense diplomacy, such as quasi-diplomatic trips by the regional commanders-in-chief. Engagement by the Defense Department has broadened to cover nearly all armed forces in the world, including military-military contacts with governments leery of U.S. security policy objectives. At the same time that more efforts are being made and countries involved, there has been a drawdown in the number of soldiers with foreign-area expertise, as well as a reduction in the number of units most likely to participate in foreign military interaction programs (e.g., engineers, military police, and medical units). The challenge is to find ways to use the declining resource more effectively and innovatively than ever before.

Security Relationships and Overseas Presence. The core of U.S. security policy during the Cold War was its alliances, especially NATO, for collective defense against the pressing common external threat from the Soviet Union. Post-Cold War, the role of the alliances is shifting to becoming the cornerstone (politically and militarily) around which ad hoc coalitions can be formed. Such coalitions are, for the foreseeable future, the likely way in which the U.S. will fight in major conflicts. NATO's combined joint task force (CJTF) concept is the most telling example of the new role of alliances; the delays in implementing the CJTF illustrate the difficulty in re-directing Cold War institutions toward future requirements, even where there is a clear military utility (in this case, for crisis response beyond NATO's borders). While alliances like NATO provide the military nucleus for an ad hoc coalition, there may well be political utility in including a large number of states, even if many bring little value added to the military force. The coalitions may include uncertain partners, which can require a delicate balancing of the issues on which Washington agrees with that partner compared to differences on other matters, e.g., ensuring the Pak-

U.S. Forces take control of Haiti's international airport, 1994.

istani forces in Somalia are well equipped to replace U.S. forces there, but at the same time not weakening the military aid restrictions that pressure Pakistan to roll back its nuclear weapons program.

Meanwhile, as force structure declines and support (at home and in the host countries) for large overseas bases becomes more open to question, the importance of the growing dependence on pre-positioned equipment ashore and afloat will continue to rise. [and there may be a place for new approaches such as mobile offshore bases.] A major issue for sustaining the U.S. existing structure of alliances will be finding ways to strengthen their security components irrespective of differences on trade issues, which are likely to be an area of vigorous disagreement.

Peace Operations and Humanitarian Support. The typical Cold War peace operation was patrolling a ceasefire line. With the end of the superpower rivalry, peacekeeping operations have generally focused on resolving internal conflicts within states rather than cross-border aggression. The missions are thus more complicated and more controversial, since there is less control over armed elements and, in some cases, virtually no organized government with which to work. The most critical elements to the success of complex peace operations can be getting right the mix of responsibilities between the U.S. military and civilian agencies and PVOs, as well as coordinating actions in the field. In the more complicated settings, U.S. military involvement can make the difference between success and failure, because of the special skills the U.S. military brings, from C3I to special operations (including civil affairs and psychological operations), and because of its overall leadership and managerial capabilities. While recognizing its vital role, Washington resists the assumption that it will automatically assume a dominant role in every such situation, preferring instead to concentrate on how to enhance prospects for success with limited U.S. participation. The record of success is mixed at best in operations in the absence of a peace accord where the peace force is seen as either ambivalent or an antagonist, that is, in expanded peacekeeping and peace enforcement. The problem is to contain or end the fighting without becoming a party to the conflict and without assuming responsibility for nation-building afterwards.

The prognosis for expanded peacekeeping and peace enforcement is uncertain. By its own account, the United Nations lacks the capacity to manage these ambitious missions, which means that they are only likely to occur where Washington opts to lead a coalition to undertake the action.

War-fighting instruments

Unconventional Military Instruments. Unconventional threats to national security challenge U.S. interests through indirect means such as terrorism, subversion, narcotics trafficking, and massive sudden refugee flows. Some of these threats are a useful way for the weak to attack the strong. Lately, they have become more salient, both because of the demise of the Soviet Union and the trend towards a more open world economy and freer movement of people. Ultimately, regional powers intent on systematically challenging U.S. interests may sponsor or organize the most serious unconventional threats. The responses to meet these threats will include an enhanced role abroad for U.S. law enforcement agencies, e.g., the FBI in counterterrorism, the DEA in counternarcotics, and the INS in enforcing restrictions on massive immigration flows. In some cases, the military may be called upon to assist with these law enforcement functions abroad, e.g., in drug interdiction. Unconventional military responses, such as Special Operations Forces (SOF) can broaden the range of options open to decision makers reluctant to resort to higher cost military measures, and they can minimize the collateral damage associated with more destructive measures. Nevertheless, the unconventional instruments are politically sensitive and hard to manage.

Limited Military Interventions. In some ways, the new environment is seeing a return to the pre-Cold War experience. For instance, the use of limited air strikes to

F-22 Fighter

force a government to change its behavior, such as the 1995 strikes against Serbian forces in Bosnia, is the modern equivalent of gunboat diplomacy, and the enforcement of sanctions bears considerable similarity to the old practice of laying siege. During the Cold War, insurgencies were generally ideological, and the U.S. usually openly supported one side. Now, insurgencies and civil wars are more often between ethnic groups, and the U.S. goal is peace between the two sides, one of which controls the internationally recognized government. While interethnic conflicts are becoming more frequent, the U.S. public may not support involvement in many such cases, since those conflicts often occur in areas where narrowly conceived U.S. geostrategic interests are slight, though the challenge to U.S. values (such as revulsion against genocide) may be high. Where the U.S. does become involved, its goals will usually be limited, e.g., to stopping genocide. In light of the experiences with the U.N., especially in Somalia and Bosnia, a decision to intervene will depend crucially upon clear military objectives, acceptable arrangements for command and control, the willingness of like-minded nations to contribute, and judgments about the necessary duration and costs of the operation.

Classical Military Instruments. While U.S. forces are far more capable than any conceivable adversary, parts of the U.S. military (specifically, U.S. lift capacity) would be strained in the event of two nearly simultaneous major regional contingencies. Also, with the overseas presence of U.S. ground and air forces reduced by about 50 percent between 1986 and 1995, there is less margin for error in deciding where to deploy the remaining forces. And given that major equipment typically lasts decades and that relatively little is being procured, the U.S. equipment will for the foreseeable future be items designed for use against the Soviet Union, which will have to be adapted for use in new types of warfare for which they may or may not be most appropriate. But perhaps more important than new equipment is new doctrine, that is, knowing how best to fight. Substantial progress has been made in refining doctrine since the end of the Cold War. The service departments have published their analyses of how best to reorient their activities for the new strategic environment, in their respective reports: the Army's *Force XXI*, the Navy's *Forward . . . From the Sea*, and the Air Force's *Global Presence*. The military as a whole is placing more emphasis on multi-service (joint) operations.

A challenge for the U.S. armed forces—one that requires particular consideration—is that they may be confronted with innovative warfare techniques and employment strategies specifically tailored to exploit U.S. weaknesses and geographic constraints. A nation, for example, could choose to avoid challenging the U.S. in classical conventional battle by using or threatening to use weapons of mass destruction, sabotaging key automated information networks, or resorting to terrorism and guerrilla warfare tactics.

Emerging Military Instruments. Information technology provides the best opportunity for the U.S. armed forces to develop new instruments of military power over the medium term. But to take full advantage of the incorporation of advanced capabilities in new equipment (a military technological revolution), new operational procedures and organizations are needed (a revolution in military affairs). The U.S. is on the verge of integrating the various systems—forming what has been called a "system of systems". This super-system would be capable of seeing all relevant enemy assets on the battlefield ("dominant battlefied knowledge," in the jargon of the trade), communicating this information almost instantly to combat units, and striking at these targets with unprecedented accuracy. With insightful leadership and hard work, these instruments will allow the U.S. to exercise a high degree of control over the emerging global security structure through a unique ability to intervene anywhere in the world quickly, effectively, and at relatively low cost, as well as to strike simultaneously at targets far distant from one another. In some cases, that intervention will be done directly by U.S. forces, whereas in other cases, the U.S. may be able to achieve the same results by providing its allies with real-time intelligence, systems expertise, and other software.

One caution is that the ability to use effectively the emerging military instruments will require serious attention to the protection of military information systems and critical civilian systems, to avoid retaliation in cyberspace. There is considerable interest in how the U.S. might conduct information war, for instance, against an opponents' communication system. But it is not apparent how vulnerable to such war are prospective U.S. opponents; a country like North Korea seems unlikely to be heavily dependent on modern computer technology.

Countering Weapons of Mass Destruction. The end of the Cold War was accompanied not only by a diminished perception of the Russian threat but also by an increased perception of the threat posed by regional powers. Regional rogues in possession of NBC weapons is a danger that has to be considered despite the vigorous U.S. program to prevent proliferation. Therefore, more attention is being devoted to how to counter weapons of mass destruction. The first choice is deterrence, but achieving deterrence in a regional context is more difficult than the Cold War task. A rogue with a few NBC

weapons may decide to use them as weapons of choice, whereas during the Cold War, the Soviets may well have considered NBC weapons to be a last resort. Furthermore, with the biological warfare and chemcial warfare conventions and the de-emphasis of tactical nuclear weapons, it may be difficult to threaten response in kind against a rogue with a few NBC weapons. Because of the problems for deterring regional rogues, more emphasis is being given to defensive measures. Some of these defenses are passive, including intelligence to identify the NBC capability of potential adversaries. The need for active defenses, like the Theater High-Altitude Area Defense (THAAD), to protect U.S. forces becomes clearer as ballistic and cruise missiles become more available to emerging powers.

General Conclusions about the Instruments of U.S. Power Post-Cold War

The end of the Cold War produced within the United States an understandable tendency to place greater emphasis on domestic concerns, resulting in calls for cuts in the budgets for most of the instruments of U.S. power, as well as for reorganization or fundamental reform of many foreign policy institutions. Five general conclusions can be drawn about applying U.S. power in the new environment:

New Ways of Applying U.S. Power. Enhancing the capability of the U.S. government to exercise influence abroad does not need to mean buying more of the same old product. The present foreign-policy and national-security establishment was created largely during the Cold War and reflects the priorities of that era. Different ways of doing business are being developed to draw upon the untapped strengths of the present organizations even while shifting resources away from areas that are no longer so relevant or practical. An important example is the reorientation of NATO away from defending against an

Tomohawk Cruise Missile Launch.

imminent Soviet attack towards being a vehicle for enhancing stability and security beyond NATO's present borders. In pursuit of this new purpose, the Partnership for Peace (PFP) program provides a means to draw upon NATO's unparalleled expertise at security and military cooperation. PFP also can improve the prospects for NATO expansion by building confidence among NATO's existing members in the capabilities of the new members and confidence in Russia about NATO's intentions.

In the changed strategic environment, vastly expanded use will be made of some instruments applied more sparingly in the past. One example is the use of international consortia to mobilize the resources and the political will needed to respond to regional threats. While the U.S. was the only country able and willing to take the lead in resolving the dispute about North Korea's nuclear intentions, the issue was of vital concern to Japan and South Korea, so it was only natural that the U.S. should ask them to play the major role in the Korean Peninsula Energy Development Organiza-

tion (KEDO) set up to provide North Korea with a less threatening means of meeting its energy needs.

The new ways of applying U.S. power are particularly important for issues such as transnational threats, which are becoming more important relative to the long-standing concerns about aggressive and destabilizing states. One development has been greater use in international relations of certain U.S. agencies which in the past had a lower profile, e.g., the FBI helping prevent nuclear smuggling, the DEA active in drug source and drug trafficking countries, the INS involved in sensitive decisions about refugee status. Issues like global warming and ozone depletion would similarly bring the EPA into negotiations over international treaties.

As part of the diversification from the traditional Cold War pattern of conducting national security affairs, the Department of Defense and the military services are being assigned a much wider array of tasks and are developing new ways of doing business. Some of these tasks, like foreign military interaction and humanitarian operations, were secondary functions during the Cold War that have now become more important and for which new techniques are being developed. Other tasks are new, like promoting respect abroad for democratic civilian control over the military. As for new ways of doing business, many come primarily from the ongoing information revolution. The technological base for the change is driven primarily by commercial capital rather than by governments. Militaries will not control the direction and pace of the advancing computer and telecommunication industries. The payoff for the military will come in adapting for its purposes what is developed in the commercial world.

Phasing Down Use of Some Instruments. At the same time that the U.S. is diversifying by more often bringing into play a wide range of instruments (some new, some used only sparingly in the past), the U.S. is reducing its reliance on some instruments that were central during the Cold War period. In particular, the U.S. is placing less importance on its weapons of mass destruction. The U.S. is giving up its ability to retaliate in kind against those who use chemical or biological weapons; it has dramatically reduced reliance on tactical nuclear weapons; and it is dismantling much of its Cold War inventory of strategic nuclear weapons. In addition, the U.S. has effectively ended military aid except to Israel and Egypt, other than minuscule amounts for military education and training.

In the past, the U.S. government carried out directly many functions that it no longer has the resources to do, or at least to do on a scale that can make as substantial an impact on a broad front. Examples include radio broadcasting and financing economic development. While Washington continues to fund radio broadcasting (especially Voice of America) and some foreign aid expenditures, the U.S. government plays a much smaller role in these areas than it did in past decades.

Working With the Private Sector. As the private sector grows in previously state-dominated societies and as U.S. firms operate more on a world scale, the U.S. government has increasing opportunities to make its influence felt through the private sector. The challenge for the U.S. government is reinventing institutions designed for the old way of doing business, so that the government can take advantage of new opportunities rather than staying stuck in the old rut. So, for instance, Washington's role will be making sure that the CNN reporters who provide the first news about a crisis have ready access to in-depth background briefings. Similarly, the Defense Department will be increasingly incorporating into military uses the information technologies developed by business.

The power of the private sector is an important element in accomplishing U.S. goals abroad. But the private sector cannot be expected to carry the burden of defending U.S. interests. The pervasiveness of American popular culture (such as music, movies, and brand names) and the strength of American high-technology industries (such as computer software and aerospace) add to U.S. power, but they cannot be the basis for U.S. global leadership on many vital security issues. Sports figures and rock musicians cannot stop the proliferation of nuclear weapons. No matter how much the economy and popular culture become glob-

alized, there remains an important role for the traditional government activities in foreign affairs and national security.

Applying Instruments for Limited Ends. During the Cold War, the ever-present competition with the Soviet Union meant that on each issue of international affairs, the most vital interests of the U.S. might come into play, as that issue became part of the global chess game. In a multipolar world of uncertainty and ambiguity, the U.S. government will often engage to promote limited U.S. interests. Given the limited character of what is at stake, it may not be credible for the U.S. to threaten to use, if need be, the full panoply of instruments it commands. For instance, nuclear deterrence against the Soviet Union was relatively straightforward compared with the problem of deterring a rogue actor like Mohammed Farah Adeed from disrupting a peacekeeping operation like that in Somalia.

There will be more situations in which Washington makes a small commitment but is not prepared to commit more. An obvious example is economic aid; compare the billions that followed the Camp David treaty between Israel and Egypt with the modest sums committed after Israel's accords with Jordan and the PLO.

Peace and humanitarian operations represent particularly difficult challenges for the military. As in Somalia, the commitment may start out as strictly limited but, through mission creep, evolve into a broad mandate that requires more forces and resources than the U.S. or the international community had expected. If the alternative to mission creep is withdrawal—which may be tempting if the initial effort results in an appreciable number of casualties—the perception of weakness can have a high cost for U.S. influence in other situations. The image of failure in Somalia has not been fully offset by success in Haiti. Even sticking with the original limited mission may cause problems, since the U.S. public may be dissatisfied if the U.S., once engaged, withdraws without addressing the underlying structural problems that caused the crisis. Despite such problems with large expanded peacekeeping missions, the U.S. is certain to continue to play an active role in humanitarian and peace operations: the relatively small resources required will often justify the potentially high benefits.

Coordinating Among Instruments. While coordinating the agencies of the U.S. government has always been a problem, the challenge is growing for several reasons. During the Cold War, coordination among U.S. agencies and policy instruments was simplified by the overwhelming priority given to containing Soviet communism. In the post-Cold War era, there is less clarity about which goals are central and which are peripheral. For instance, considerable effort has been needed to develop and implement a government-wide approach towards strengthening security cooperation with Japan at the same time the U.S. was vigorously pushing Japan to be forthcoming on trade issues. And because a wider array of policy instruments is being used, there are more agencies among which policy has to be coordinated.

As foreign policy goals become more complex and a greater variety of instruments are brought to bear on any one problem, interagency coordination and clear policy direction become all the more important. Close coordination among agencies and consultation between the administration and Congress are potent force multipliers. To this end, attention is being given to drawing lessons from earlier complex crisis management efforts.

In complex contingency operations which combine military and relief missions, coordination among agencies is com-plicated by the different time horizons on which each works. For instance, the military is often well positioned to respond quickly in a crisis, while USAID specializes in building indigenous capacities over the longer term in the partner country. The two time horizons do not necessarily meet easily, which can place unexpected additional strains upon military resources or jeopardize the success of the mission. For example, the military was able to quickly restore electricity for Haiti's capital city of Port-au-Prince but was not in a position to keep providing the electricity until USAID could help the local utility become strong enough to run all the aspects of a modern electrical supply system, from power generation to customer billing.

In sum, despite growing resource constraints, the U.S. government still has an impressive array of instruments to use to influence other governments. It is actively adapting those instruments to changing circumstances. While there are certainly shortcomings in the ways in which post-Cold War Washington applies the instruments at its disposal, Washington has had good success at achieving its goals, and the efficiency with which resources are used is improving steadily.

ISBN 0-16-048463-4

9 780160 484636